Globalization, Wages, and the Quality of Jobs

FIVE COUNTRY STUDIES

Globalization, Wages, and the Quality of Jobs

FIVE COUNTRY STUDIES

*Raymond Robertson, Drusilla Brown, Gaëlle Pierre,
and María Laura Sanchez-Puerta
Editors*

THE WORLD BANK
Washington, D.C.

ISBN: 978-0-8213-7934-9
eISBN: 978-0-8213-7955-4
DOI: 10.1596/978-0-8213-7934-9

Library of Congress Cataloging-in-Publication Data

Globalization, wages, and the quality of jobs : five country studies / edited by Raymond Robertson ... [et al.].
    p. cm.
  Includes bibliographical references and index.
  ISBN 978-0-8213-7934-9 (alk. paper) — ISBN 978-0-8213-7955-4
    1. Labor market—Developing countries. 2. Labor—Social aspects—Developing countries. 3. International trade—Social aspects. 4. Developing countries—Commerce. I. Robertson, Raymond, 1969- II. World Bank.
  HD5852.G58 2009
  331.1209172'4—dc22

                                                   2009008336

Contents

Tables

Preface

Since the early 1990s, most developing economies have become more integrated with the world's economy. Barriers to trade and foreign investment have been lifted, and international trade agreements have been signed. These reforms have led to important changes in the structures of these economies. The labor markets had to adjust to these major changes, and workers have been required to adapt.

An important research program was launched within the Social Protection Unit of the World Bank to understand the impact that these profound structural changes have had on workers in developing countries. In popular culture, especially in developed countries, globalization is often associated with unfair competition from sweatshops with lower ethical and safety standards. High-profile news coverage of poor working conditions in overseas operations of multinational enterprises has tended to confirm these views. While exposing these poor working conditions is necessary, it is also important to assess whether they represent isolated cases or a broader pattern in developing countries.

The empirical literature that exists, although vast, does not lead to a consensus view on the eventual impact of globalization on labor markets. While a significant number of studies found rising wage inequality following trade liberalization, recent examples (for example, Brazil and Mexico) complement early work that documented falling wage inequality in East Asian countries. Further research on this important issue is therefore needed to disentangle the conflicting results. In addition, one weakness of this literature is the little attention devoted to working conditions.

Understanding the effects of globalization is critical for policy makers concerned about employment and working conditions. Governments have and do play a role in designing social policies that help workers through these changes. However, given the current conflicting state of the literature, designing effective social policies is challenging.

To tackle these issues, the research program took a three-pronged approach:

- Undertaking a critical survey of the literature on the impact of changes in trade policy, foreign direct investment (FDI) exposure, and increasing competition from multinational firms on job creation and the conditions of employment
- Building a new analytical framework to carry out country studies
- Applying the framework to lower-middle-income countries.

This book presents the findings and insights of this research program. In particular, it shows how similar the experiences of low-income countries have been with globalization. It suggests that low-income countries' working conditions have improved in the sectors exposed to globalization. However, it also shows that the sustainability of these improvements and their positive effects on the rest of the economy are unclear.

Acknowledgments

This book is the fruit of the work of a team of economists from academia and the World Bank. Drusilla Brown conducted an extensive survey of the literature that guided the ensuing research and provided suggestions on the general storyline of the book and various chapters. Raymond Robertson designed the analytical framework and coauthored most of the case studies. Gaëlle Pierre and María Laura Sanchez-Puerta provided comments and guidance at all stages of the production of the book, participated in the writing of the overview chapter, and coordinated the efforts of all involved.

This research was supported by Robert Holzmann, Sector Director, Social Protection and Labor Department, Human Development Network at the World Bank, and financed through the Trust Fund for Environmentally and Socially Sustainable Development (TFESSD). The study benefited from useful comments and suggestions provided at various stages by Tim Conway, Amy Damon, Eric V. Edmonds, Tim Gindling, Paul Glewwe, Ruwan Jayasuriya, J. Humberto Lopez, Amy Luinstra, Daniel J. B. Mitchell, Richard Newfarmer, Pierella Paci, Carmen Pagés, Cristobal Ridao-Cano, Stefano Scarpetta, and Hach Sok.

Contributors

Drusilla Brown, PhD, Tufts University

Jean-Pierre Cling, PhD, Institut de Recherche pour le Développement, DIAL, Hanoi

Ardyanto Fitrady, MSc, Universitas Gadjah Mada, Yogyakarta

Poppy Ismalina, MEcDev, Faculty of Economics and Business, Universitas Gadjah Mada, Yogyakarta

Douglas Marcouiller, PhD, Saint Louis University, St. Louis, Missouri

Samsen Neak, MA, World Bank

Gaëlle Pierre, PhD, World Bank

Mireille Razafindrakoto, PhD, Institut de Recherche pour le Développement

Raymond Robertson, PhD, Macalester College, St. Paul, Minnesota

François Roubaud, PhD, Institut de Recherche pour le Développement

María Laura Sanchez-Puerta, PhD, World Bank

Sari Sitalaksmi, MMgt, Universitas Gadjah Mada, Yogyakarta

Alvaro Trigueros-Argüello, PhD, Salvadoran Foundation of Economic and Social Development

Abbreviations

ASEAN	Association of Southeast Asian Nations
ATC	Agreement on Textiles and Clothing
CAFTA	Central America Free Trade Agreement
EIC	Economic Institute of Cambodia
EPZ	export processing zone
FDI	foreign direct investment
FIRE	finance, insurance, and real estate
GDP	gross domestic product
GMIES	Grupo de Monitoreo Independiente de El Salvador
GNP	gross national product
GSP	Generalized System of Preferences
HS	Harmonized Commodity Description and Coding System
IIWD	interindustry wage differential
ILO	International Labour Organization
ISIC	International Standard Industrial Classification
LFS	labor force survey
MFA	Multifibre Arrangement
MFN	Most Favored Nation
NAFTA	North American Free Trade Agreement
NGO	nongovernmental organization
SAI	Social Accountability International
UNCTAD	United Nations Conference on Trade and Development
UNIDO	United Nations Industrial Development Organization

CHAPTER 1

Overview: The Promises and Perils of Globalization

Raymond Robertson, Drusilla Brown, Gaëlle Pierre, and María Laura Sanchez-Puerta

The increases in trade, migration, and investment across borders that are associated with the fall of regulatory barriers (hereafter "globalization") directly affect workers in both developed and developing countries. While most international trade and investment takes place between developed countries, globalization has increased dramatically in a number of developing countries. According to the World Development Indicators database (2008), the ratio of merchandise trade to gross domestic product (GDP) in the low- and middle-income countries increased from 31 percent to 57 percent between 1990 and 2007. In some countries these changes have been especially large. In Cambodia, this ratio rose to 112 percent from 22 percent over that time period. Changes in foreign direct investment (FDI) have also been significant. For South and East Asia, the ratio of inward FDI to GDP increased from 9.3 percent to 26.8 percent between 1990 and 2003. As with trade, changes in FDI varied a great deal across countries. In Indonesia, the ratio rose from 7.7 percent in 1990 to 32.7 percent in 1998, but fell back to 5.0 percent by 2003.[1]

These dramatic changes hold both promise and peril for workers in developing countries. Increases in foreign investment and export opportunity create the potential for rising wages and more employment. At the same time, however, globalization changes the structure of an economy. Even neoclassical trade theory predicts that opening up to trade will result in winners and losers. In addition to the issue of redistributing the gains are the costs involved with increased risk of job loss, movement between jobs and industries, and exposure to global economic shocks.

Understanding the effects of globalization is crucial for governments concerned about employment, working conditions, and ultimately, poverty reduction. Beyond job creation, improving the quality of those jobs is an essential condition for achieving poverty reduction. Moreover, there is now broad agreement that the core labor standards[2] as defined by the International Labour Organization (ILO) should be considered basic workers' rights. In addition to these rights, working conditions (wages, but also health and safety, hours, security, and benefits) characterize the quality of jobs.[3]

Although the literature on the effects of globalization on the labor market is large, there is no consensus on whether the effects are positive or negative. Brown's literature review (chapter 2 in this volume) shows that this body of work paints a somewhat inconclusive picture for at least three reasons.

First, studies that ask similar questions often generate conflicting results, suggesting more research is needed. This is the case, for example, for the impact of FDI on wages.

FDI has been linked to higher wages at the firm level and to rising wage inequality in both developed and developing countries. These results, mostly based on cross-section data, have been challenged by recent studies that use longitudinal firm-level data and suggest that after liberalization, FDI-linked firms may actually lower wages.

Second, the relatively few case studies that do exist provide interesting insights but are difficult to compare across countries. The case studies that have been carried out suggest that monitoring plays a significant role in firm-level working conditions, and that code compliance can improve factory performance. Overall, however, these case studies are often difficult to compare across countries because the interactions between local policies and globalization factors are difficult to separate when looking at a subset of firms within particular countries.

Third, and possibly the most important conclusion, is that very few (if any) systematic cross-country comparisons have been made of the relationship between globalization and working conditions. Few studies systematically evaluate the effects of globalization on working conditions either within or across countries. Two important exceptions are Hasan and Mitra (2003) and Flannigan (2006). The former is an eclectic collection of either theoretical or broad studies combined with four case studies. It does not provide or follow a unified, reproducible framework. Flannigan applies a consistent framework for aggregate cross-country analysis, but it does not account for demographic characteristics or within-country variations.

This volume adds to this literature in two ways. First, it provides a comprehensive literature review of the current wisdom on the topic and presents a micro-based framework for analyzing globalization and working conditions in developing countries. Second, it applies this framework to five developing countries.

The Links between Globalization and Working Conditions: Concepts and Analytical Framework

The goal of the framework is to provide a systematic way to analyze the link between globalization and working conditions that can be reproduced in any developing country. It proposes a three-step approach: The first step is to define "globalization." This term tends to have various meanings depending on the background of the person using it. Defining the concept shapes the understanding of globalization's effects on working conditions and, therefore, influences the appropriate way to study the link between them. Along the same lines, the second step is to define working conditions and place them in context within a particular country. This step is best done qualitatively by analyzing the evolution of regulations and institutions affecting working conditions. As with globalization, the chosen definition of working conditions will affect the analytical approach. The third step is to complement the qualitative analysis with a quantitative analysis of wages and measures of nonwage working conditions.

GLOBALIZATION: FROM VAGUE CONCEPT TO MEASURABLE VARIABLES

The first step in understanding the way in which globalization affects working conditions in a given country is to review the aspects of globalization that have affected that country's economy the most. For example, exports potentially have substantially different effects than imports, and FDI that produces for the domestic market has different effects than FDI that produces for export.

The low-income countries reviewed in this book primarily experience globalization as an influx of FDI seeking to export. Low income levels in the country make producing for foreign markets relatively more attractive than selling in the domestic market because demand is higher in foreign markets and domestic wages are lower than elsewhere in the world. The influx of foreign investment seeking export opportunities increases the demand for workers in the industries in which FDI is concentrated. In developing countries, these workers typically come from the agricultural or the informal nonfarm sectors. In this sense, the changes that are brought about through the influx of FDI producing for export are similar to broad patterns of economic development.

The movement from agriculture to industry is a well-documented accompaniment to development. Figure 1.1, taken from Chenery and Taylor (1968), shows the development path of a number of industrial countries. The decline in agriculture with the growth in industry is also evident in the cross-section, as shown in figure 1.2. Whether these changes have an impact on working conditions depends on how working conditions are defined, and whether working conditions differ systematically across sectors.

WORKING CONDITIONS: SELECTING THE MOST RELEVANT DIMENSIONS OF JOB QUALITY

Defining working conditions is important but difficult because jobs have many different characteristics. The main way to measure the quality of jobs is through the wage rate. Alternatively, job characteristics can be taken into account. To help identify the job characteristics that are relevant to a particular country, the framework chapter (chapter 3) explores the various definitions of working conditions. Because wage data are much easier to find than measurements of nonwage working conditions, most country studies can have a reliable and internationally comparable wage component. The data for other aspects of working conditions (benefits, air quality, noise, unionization, among many others) are scarce and generally not comparable across countries.

From a theoretical perspective, the relationship between wages and nonwage working conditions could be positive or negative. Using wages as a measure of working conditions, however, poses potential problems if workers receive higher wages as compensation for working in poor conditions. This is certainly the case, even in developed countries, in dangerous industries, such as mining. Since Adam Smith, economists have theorized that workers who take jobs in less favorable conditions must be compensated with higher wages; this is commonly referred to as *compensating differentials*. This theory implies that workers in developing countries who accept jobs with less favorable working conditions would earn higher than average wages.

Empirical evidence on the compensating differentials hypothesis has been surprisingly mixed. Villanueva (2007), Viscusi and Moore (1991), and Cousineau, Lacroix, and Girard (1992) find a positive relationship between risk and wages, while Dorman and Hagstrom (1998) find little, if any, evidence for compensating differentials for risk. Hersch (1998) finds strong evidence of compensating differentials for risk for women, but a negative relationship between risk and wages for white males. Studies in developing countries, such as Moll (1993) for South Africa and Arbache (2001) in Brazil, reject the compensating differentials hypothesis. Daniel and Sofer (1998) find a negative relationship between wages and good working conditions in France, but a positive link for unionized workers there.

FIGURE 1.1 **The Development Path (Time Series)**

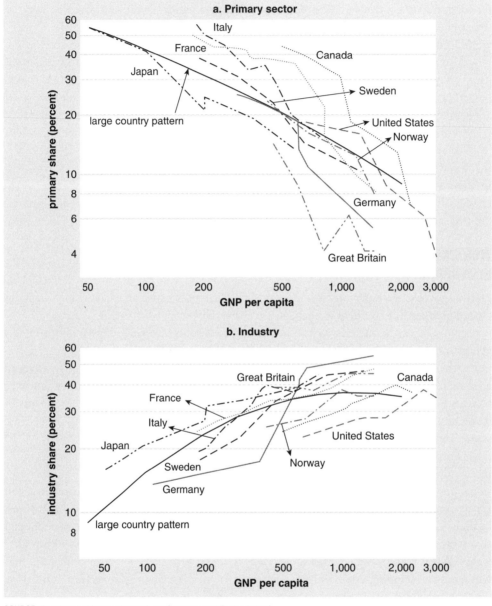

SOURCE: Reprinted with permission from Chenery and Taylor (1968).

These results suggest that in developing countries with questionable union strength, the relationship between wages and working conditions cannot be determined intuitively. The distinction may simply be between "good" jobs that have high wages and good conditions and "bad" jobs with low wages and poor working conditions.

If the direction of the relationship between wages and nonwage working conditions is not known, then wages may actually tell nothing about working conditions. Therefore, there are no clear expectations or consensus regarding the link between wages and nonwage working conditions; thus, the research in this volume contributes to the academic literature in a potentially important way.

There is little disagreement that working conditions are generally better in developed countries. Figure 1.3 illustrates this point; it shows that fatal injuries are negatively correlated with national per capita income. Working conditions may improve because developed countries specialize in industries with better conditions or because they raised standards through policy as income increased. In any case, movement from less-safe industries and increased workplace regulation and enforcement may both be linked to globalization. These regulations may become more stringent as wages increase, generating a positive relationship between wages and working conditions across countries. In developing countries, however, a positive relationship between wages and working conditions cannot be assumed. Therefore, finding nonwage measures of working conditions and comparing them to wage measures is important.

FIGURE 1.2 **The Development Path (Cross Section)**

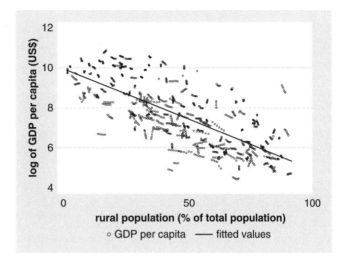

SOURCE: Authors' calculations from World Bank World Development Indicators (various years).

FIGURE 1.3 **National Income and Fatal Injuries**

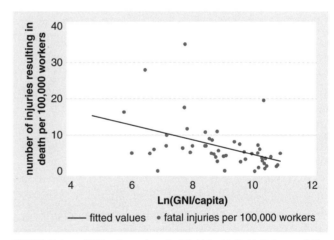

SOURCE: Data on GNI/capita are from the World Bank's Quick Reference Tables available online at http://go.worldbank.org/B5PYF93QF0.

NOTE: Fatal injuries data are the number of injuries resulting in death per 100,000 workers in 2004 (some are for 2003 or 2002). The correlation between fatal injuries and ln(GNI/cap) is -.4245**.

LINKING GLOBALIZATION TO WORKING CONDITIONS

When examining the link between working conditions and globalization within countries, the effects of workers moving between industries on average working conditions are based on the assumption that working conditions differ between industries and are relatively stable. This assumption has a very strong foundation in the empirical economics literature when wages are used to measure working conditions. Interindustry wage differentials (IIWDs) are among the most-documented and least-understood characteristics of wage structures. Higher- or lower-than-average wages paid to observationally identical workers in similar occupations have been observed in Europe (Edin and Zetterberg 1992; Wagner 1990; Haisken-DeNew and Schmidt 1998), Africa (Moll 1993), North America (Krueger and Summers 1988), and South America (Abuhadba and Romaguera 1993). Katz and Summers (1989b) and Papola and Bharadwaj (1970) find a high correlation across countries, suggesting that these differentials reflect industry characteristics and not national characteristics. Gittleman and Wolff (1993) show that the rank order of IIWDs is "remarkably stable" for 14 Organisation for Economic Co-operation and Development countries between 1970 and 1985, suggesting that these differentials generally do not respond to policy or changes in economic conditions.

The apparent stability and similarity of IIWDs make them interesting because it puts them at odds with the theory of perfectly competitive labor markets. In perfectly competitive labor markets, wages of nearly identical workers are equalized across industries. Helwege (1992) suggests that the stability of IIWDs and the lack of arbitraging in labor mobility may be a symptom of market failure. The three theoretical explanations with some empirical support in the existing literature are efficiency wages, rent-sharing, and unobserved workers' characteristics.[4] Krueger and Summers (1988) raise the possibility that these differentials may provide the basis for policy. Specifically, Katz and Summers (1989a) argue that if the rank-order of the differentials is stable over time, welfare could be improved by promoting the "high-wage" industries.

To investigate the effects of changes between industries implied by theory, the wage differentials between industries need to be estimated. Because worker characteristics also affect wages, individual-level data are necessary to estimate the differentials while controlling for other worker characteristics (such as gender, age, education, and other factors). Household and labor force surveys generally contain these data and are becoming increasingly available for this purpose.

IIWDs reveal much about the differences in conditions across countries. Differences in wages across industries can be compared to industry characteristics. Wage differences that are correlated with measures of globalization provide evidence supporting the hypothesis that globalization affects working conditions. For example, the correlation between FDI and changes in industry-specific wage differentials can inform the understanding of how labor markets work. To the extent that the correlation is positive, the effect of FDI on wages and working conditions remains specific to the affected industries, which implies that the gains are slow to spill over to the rest of the economy. This is consistent with the rest of the literature on spillovers.

Applying the Framework: Lessons from Five Country Studies

The country studies in this volume analyze the link between globalization and working conditions in Cambodia, El Salvador, Honduras, Indonesia, and Madagascar. These countries vary significantly in population, economic circumstances, region, history, and institutions. All have experienced liberalization and globalization in the last 20 years. The heterogeneity of these countries provides the basis for a useful comparison of the effects of globalization on working conditions.

As suggested in the framework, each country study has three main components: a description of the country's experience with globalization, a qualitative part that analyzes country-specific aspects of working conditions, and an analysis of changes in IIWDs that can be compared across countries. The findings of these studies are summarized in the remainder of this section.

In general, globalization has been characterized by export-driven FDI concentrated in relatively few sectors (generally textiles and apparel). Export-driven FDI in the apparel sector plays a prominent role in each country, although to varying degrees. In Cambodia, apparel made up 82 percent of all merchandise exports in 2003 (UNCTAD 2005). Nearly two-thirds of that total was destined for the U.S. market. Virtually all factories in the Cambodian garment sector are foreign owned. Honduras rose from being the 34th largest supplier of apparel to the U.S. market in 1990 to fourth place in 2003. In 2003, two-thirds of all Honduran exports to the United States were garments and more than 82 percent of all Honduran workers worked in foreign-owned factories (UNCTAD 2005, 41). A similar pattern emerges for El Salvador. For Madagascar, apparel exports from the Zone Franche[5] were the primary force behind the country's remarkable export growth and its transition from exporting primary products to exporting manufactured products between 1990 and 2005. By 2001, Madagascar had become the second most important clothing exporter in Sub-Saharan Africa as measured by total export value.

Indonesia, having a much larger population than the others, is more diversified. It underwent two distinct periods of liberalization. The first, roughly spanning the mid-1980s to the mid-1990s, mainly focused on the textiles and apparel sectors, while heavier industries were more important in the second wave that started in the mid-1990s and ran into the new century. Nevertheless, in 2003, Indonesia was the eighth largest apparel exporter in the world, ranking just below the United States. Indonesia later increasingly received FDI in the metal products and machinery and chemical industries. These industries experienced a corresponding increase in exports following the FDI inflows. Indonesia's more recent period, therefore, stands in contrast to the other countries in the study, for which FDI and exports still tend to concentrate in the textiles and apparel sectors.

The country studies show that these five countries went through very similar globalization experiences. Despite their many differences, it may be that a few commonalities—in particular, relatively less-developed industrial bases and low wage rates—were the main factors defining their globalization experiences. In fact, in the context of industrial development, it is not surprising that apparel would play a significant role in these countries. Many developed countries (including the United Kingdom, the United States, and Japan) had relatively large apparel sectors in the early stages of their development.

An investigation of the qualitative dimensions of working conditions, especially the roles of history, government regulations, and nongovernmental organizations (NGOs), reveals that exposure to foreign markets has brought international attention to working conditions in the export industry. This attention has taken the form of external pressure to improve working conditions from foreign governments, the ILO, and NGOs, and seems to have played a significant role in influencing government regulations, monitoring, and enforcement. Cambodia's experience is especially notable because it was the first country to have quota access for exporting firms specifically tied to working conditions. This suggests that participation in international markets has some positive externalities for working conditions.

Given the stability of IIWDs over time, changes in these differentials following episodes of increased integration into world markets would suggest a significant impact of globalization on workers. For the countries for which time-series data were available, the evidence suggested three connections between globalization and IIWDs: (i) FDI-intensive and export sectors paid wages significantly above the mean (Cambodia and Honduras), (ii) the wage premium in FDI-intensive and export industries increased over time, or (iii) the wage premium was positively correlated with exports and FDI.

Workers in the Cambodian textiles industry earned as much as 35 percent more than the country's mean wage. Honduran apparel workers also received a significant, though smaller, wage premium. In El Salvador, apparel workers were paid below-average wages (negative wage premiums) when FDI began to enter, but the apparel wage premium grew along with FDI and exports. Apparel workers in Madagascar's Zone Franche earned a significant wage premium that fell as the Multifibre Arrangement (MFA) was phased out in 2005.

The country studies also suggest that the positive impact of globalization may be short-lived. In industries in which FDI declines, employment shares and wage differentials fall. In the countries included in this study, the most prominent cases of falling FDI are Indonesia and Madagascar. The 1997 Asian crisis hit Indonesia especially hard and FDI flows were significantly negative for several years as capital left the country. The fall in FDI flows was detectable in the data on employment shares in agriculture; at the time of the Asian crisis, employment shares in agriculture increased, while wage premiums in manufacturing fell. Evidence from Madagascar and preliminary evidence from El Salvador suggest that the end of the MFA may have triggered a movement of capital out of these countries' apparel sectors toward lower-wage countries. As capital leaves, wage premiums in apparel fall.

Given statistically and economically significant differences in wages between industries, the movement of labor between industries also has important implications for average wage and nonwage working conditions. To the extent that agriculture is a primary alternative for many workers, the fact that agricultural wages and working conditions are significantly lower suggests that a move from that sector to the FDI-intensive exporting sectors represents an improvement in overall working conditions.

The findings suggest an interesting positive correlation between nonwage working conditions and wages. The country studies for the countries with data on nonwage working conditions (Cambodia, El Salvador, and Indonesia) provide a comparison of industry-specific measures of nonwage working conditions with wage differentials. In all cases, conditions in agriculture were found to be far below the economywide average. That is, working conditions in the default industry—agriculture—are very poor. In contrast, nonwage working conditions in the FDI-intensive export industries were found to be either at or above the economywide average.

Although the theory of compensating differentials holds that higher wages are necessary to offset adverse working conditions, the country studies suggest that working conditions are positively related to wages.[6] It appears that labor markets in export-oriented sectors that attract FDI are characterized by "good" jobs with high wages and better working conditions. In contrast, the agricultural sector (or more generally, the informal sector in Madagascar) offers "bad" jobs with low wages and poor working conditions. Thus, the positive correlation between wages and working conditions is more consistent with theories of efficiency wages and rent-sharing than with compensating differentials.

Overall, these country studies suggest that globalization has been associated with improvements in working conditions in the exposed sectors. The influx of export-focused FDI was positively correlated with wage premiums and working conditions, as employment in agriculture fell and apparel employment increased. This is not to say that the adjustment did not affect other important aspects of these countries' economies, in particular informality, which is not analyzed here, but the insights afforded by these studies suggest that they might serve as an important first step toward understanding the link between globalization and working conditions in developing countries.

Theoretical Considerations: The Apparel Sector

The evidence presented in this volume and elsewhere indicates that a simple textbook model of trade and wages is unlikely to provide much insight into how workers will fare in a globalizing economy. Since the early 1990s, in particular, sleek, streamlined, highly efficient supply chains have pulled up alongside labor markets characterized by imperfect competition, workers with low literacy and market experience, government failure, and poorly protected property rights. These supply chains may be bringing all kinds of benefits, such as knowledge capital and improved international allocation of production, but they may also be scouring the planet searching for vendors who are particularly adept at monopsonistic exploitation of labor.

Globalization and its implications for wages and working conditions in developing countries will ultimately depend on many factors. These factors include technology; worker preferences and bargaining power; the cross-sectoral integration of labor markets; the quality of governmental institutions; international trade policy; the transmission of knowledge through supply chains; the establishment and enforcement of international labor standards; the leverage exercised by consumers, stockholders, and reputation-sensitive international buyers; and the stability of labor markets.

A comprehensive theory of the impact of globalization on working conditions assumes, as a starting point, that principles and agents throughout global supply chains are acting to maximize some objective function given the available information and ethical and contractual constraints. Agents in the supply chain begin with stockholders and consumers; move through corporate sourcing and code compliance officers, factory managers, and engineers; and end with workers and their families. The central question is: how do globalization, in general, and trade policy, corporate policy, NGO interventions, and local government policy, in particular, affect the objective function, information set, and constraints that bind at the margin the actions of agents in the supply chain? From an empirical point of view, a more pointed question might be, what does a change in the globalization and policy environment reveal about the binding constraints and their consequences for working conditions?

The literature concerning the interactions between technology, goods markets, and labor relations is vast. Lazear and Oyer (2007) provide a detailed account of the theory and available empirical evidence about the determinants of working conditions.

Given the importance of the apparel sector in the globalization experiences of the countries studied in this volume, and the major changes in their globalization processes implied by the end of the MFA (see also box 1.1), this theoretical section uses the apparel sector as an illustration. Consider, therefore, five main constraints among those that exist in the apparel sector: technology, information imperfections, alignment of incentives, factor markets and prices, and quality.

TECHNOLOGY

The apparel sector is characterized by extremely fine divisions of labor. The production process for every single garment has been decomposed into a set of standardized seams of a particular type and length. In most apparel factories, each tailor sews only one seam on each garment. International standards for the time it should take a skilled tailor to complete a particular task have been determined within the industry by time and motion studies.

As a consequence, the effort by an apparel worker should be fully contractible. The following industrial characteristics would be expected:

- Piece-rate pay closely linked to individual production targets
- Comprehensive data collection on individual output
- High mobility of workers across employers
- Uniform pay by skill grade across apparel firms
- Multiple work shifts that optimize the use of capital and labor.

Given the studied efficiency of processes and technology in the apparel industry, why does the use of nonpecuniary motivational techniques, such as verbal and physical abuse, persist? Why do apparel firms renege on wage commitments that elicit work effort? Why do these firms break commitments that reward duration of employment, thereby losing investments in worker training? Why do they commonly choose a single shift with a shift length beyond the point of diminishing returns for labor productivity?

The personnel economics literature suggests a number of explanations for such market outcomes. For example, workers may be risk averse, to which factory managers respond by paying workers by the hour rather than by the piece. However, while such a compensation structure may address worker concerns about pay stability, incentives for effort are diminished. Factory supervisors may then resort to nonpecuniary motivational techniques.

Alternatively, international buyers may be concerned with product quality. While a factory manager can easily observe effort related to quantity of garments sewn, worker effort relating to product quality may be more difficult to quantify. In such a situation, the firm may employ multidimensional remuneration (that might include nonmonetary elements) designed to prevent a worker from focusing exclusively on quantity produced.

IMPERFECTIONS IN THE MARKET FOR INFORMATION

In fact, multiple explanations factor into managerial decisions that convert a common factory into a sweatshop, some of which relate to failures in the market for information.

> BOX 1.1 **Why Textiles and Apparel Matter: A Brief History of the MFA**
>
> In 1973, the United States, Canada, and Europe adopted the Multifibre Arrangement (also known as the Multifibre Agreement). Created in response to concerns about the loss of domestic textiles and apparel jobs to mainly low-income countries, the MFA established a system of quotas to limit the quantity of imported textiles and apparel products from specific countries. The quota system was both product- and country-specific. For example, Canada set up its own restrictions on the quantity of sweaters imported from each of a variety of low-income countries. Each low-income country had a different quota allocation.
>
> One of the main effects of this bilateral system was to create export opportunities in countries that would not have otherwise filled their quota allocations. A country that filled its quota would have an incentive to set up operations in countries with unused quota allocations. In this way, the MFA may have had a significant effect on the pattern of FDI flows across countries.
>
> The MFA was originally designed to be temporary, but continuous annual renewals made the agreement seem permanent. In response, the World Trade Organization modified the MFA into a new agreement called the Agreement on Textiles and Clothing (ATC) in January 1995. The goal of the ATC was to integrate the quota system into the WTO's General Agreement on Tariffs and Trade rules. The ATC also laid out a plan to phase out the quota system by December 31, 2004.[a] Since January 1, 2005, WTO rules have applied to products formerly affected by the quota system.
>
> Several studies have examined the potential effects of the end of the MFA. Evans and Harrigan (2004) find that filled MFA quotas generate significant wage premiums for the exporting countries. These premiums may have both increased the incentive to invest in these countries and increased the wages paid to workers. Wage patterns are consistent with industry-specific wage premiums like those that could be generated by quota access. UNCTAD (2005) suggests that the end of the MFA might change the location incentives of FDI and cause FDI to leave countries that previously enjoyed quota access and move to countries with lower wages or other production advantages.
>
> Several authors have suggested that the end of the MFA may mean a decrease in both exports and FDI in countries affected by the end of the MFA. If FDI and exports are both positively linked to working conditions, and the results of the country studies in this book seem to suggest that they are, the reduction of FDI and exports might lead to falling wages and deteriorating nonwage working conditions, both within industries and between industries as workers return to (or do not leave) agriculture. In the few examples for which capital outflows were observed, a decrease in wage premiums was detected.
>
> a. See http://olympicflame.org/publications/04-04-somo.htm for more details.

A factory manager may attempt to cheat workers out of their wages if the workers are young, female, illiterate, or have limited market experience. That is, the firm is exploiting deficiencies in the workers' information set.

Several factors can work to reduce exploitation over time. For example, reputation-sensitive international buyers can effectively pressure their suppliers to improve working conditions. Corporate, third-party, or legal codes regulating treatment of workers might remedy the information market failure affecting the ability of workers to bargain effectively on their own behalves. Or workers may become more market savvy after a period of factory employment.

Alternatively, factory supervisors may resort to traditional strategies for managing workers because they lack the knowledge to use more sophisticated human resource management techniques. Experimentation with management innovations is costly and risky, especially innovations in labor management, because human behavior is difficult to predict. Factory managers may find that the productivity implications of adopting new machinery and equipment are more predictable. Such calculations introduce a capital bias into the innovation process. Corporate codes of conduct that require factory managers to change their approaches to labor management might push factories to discover more humane labor management practices that, inadvertently, also improve productivity. Thus, it is possible that the main effect of corporate code enforcement is to transmit information to managers relating to humane labor management strategies that are also profit maximizing.

ALIGNED INCENTIVES

Humane labor management practices possibly maximize the total profit of an apparel enterprise. However, the switch from sweatshop-like labor management practices to higher-level systems may increase labor's cost share so much that the return to capital declines. The nature of pay incentives and pay levels necessary to induce labor performance that optimizes the total value of the enterprise could significantly alter the division of an enterprise's total surplus. As a consequence, factory managers may not introduce efficiency-enhancing innovations in the absence of pressure from competitors or consumers to do so.

In addition, corporate codes may force firms to pay wages actually promised or to honor long-term contracts. Imposing such accountability on factory managers could induce firms to move toward a more sophisticated labor management strategy. That is, constraining the firm's behavior along a couple of labor management dimensions might significantly alter the profit-maximizing strategy for managing workers. Factories forced to pay promised wages may choose to rely more heavily on the use of pay incentives that induce worker effort. Factories forced to grant severance pay may choose to invest in training and skills upgrading and to provide other incentives for workers to remain with the firm.

FACTOR MARKETS AND FACTOR PRICES

Wages in apparel relative to both the return to capital and wages in other sectors depend critically on the nature of the underlying factor markets. In a standard Heckscher-Ohlin–type model in which factors are freely mobile between sectors, the quantitative restriction on output by the apparel industry dictates relative factor prices.

The impact on factor prices of the removal of the MFA depends on whether a country is a winner or a loser in the termination of the system of bilateral quotas. Relatively high-cost producers will lose market share while low-cost producers will expand output. A country such as China that enjoys an expansion of exports as a consequence of the elimination of quantitative restrictions will see apparel output rise. This increase in apparel output is accompanied by a rise in the demand for unskilled labor, thereby raising wages relative to capital. By contrast, a country that loses a market for its apparel exports once the MFA has been eliminated will see apparel production decrease. Wages relative to the return to capital will also decline.

Evidence suggests, though, that the textbook view linking export quotas and wages is too simplistic to adequately understand the impact of the MFA on wages. As discussed previously in this chapter, workers in apparel appear to earn a wage premium relative to agricultural wages after controlling for worker characteristics. There are several possible—perhaps interrelated—explanations.

First, labor markets may be segmented. That is, workers are not able to move easily from one sector to another. This could particularly be the case for young, rural, female workers with low literacy and no market experience who, to get higher paying jobs, must migrate from the countryside to urban factory jobs. To do so, they might be confronted with leaving behind families or even, in many cases, their own children. In addition, it may be difficult for potential workers to enter manufacturing. Higher-than-market wages generate job queues that allow employers to be selective when hiring. The gains from being selective (for example, higher worker productivity) may outweigh the gains from paying apparel-sector market wages.

Second, apparel workers may have succeeded in capturing some of the quota rents generated by the MFA. Such an outcome could occur if quota licenses were not allocated to the highest bidders. Moreover, the apparel-to-agriculture wage premium may also be the result of reputation-sensitive international buyers. Anti-sweatshop agitation beginning in the early 1990s may have pushed vendors supplying the international market to upgrade working conditions, including wages.

Third, there may be unobservable worker heterogeneity. Workers employed in the apparel sector may have acquired skills earned with experience, abilities unrelated to educational attainment or personality characteristics, that are rewarded in a factory setting. The observed apparel-to-agricultural wage premium may simply be a return to these acquired skills.

QUALITY DOWNGRADING

One of the more curious features of quantitative restrictions is their impact on product quality. Quantitative restrictions tend to increase product quality. The price of a quota license is uniform across products within a quota category. For example, the cost of an import license may be $5 for a shirt regardless of the shirt's ultimate price. For a high-quality shirt that retails for $50, the quota license imposes a 10 percent additional cost. By contrast, for a basic shirt that retails for $20, the quota license imposes an additional 25 percent cost. As a consequence of the lower percentage cost of the quota license, firms selling higher quality, higher priced goods bid up the quota license price. Cheaper, lower quality products are squeezed from the market. Removal of quantitative restrictions should reverse the process. Indeed, Harrigan and Barrows (2006) documented a decline in average quality of apparel imports by the United States accompanying the end of the MFA.

The decline in the average quality of apparel imports is welfare-improving when viewed from the perspective of Western consumers because the quality upgrading that occurred during the tenure of the MFA was an artifact of its implementation.

However, the decline in quality affects both wages and the overall human resource management strategy for an apparel factory for several reasons. For example, producing quality garments requires skill and knowledge. Factories would optimally respond to the demand for quality by investing in training and skill development, introducing worker-friendly innovations that help the firm retain newly skilled workers, and compensating workers for the market value of their skills. As a consequence of the fall in the demand for skilled tailors that accompanied the end of the MFA, factory managers might have come to view individual apparel workers as disposable. The incentive to provide a worker-friendly environment could be greatly diminished.

Furthermore, quality can take several different forms. Conventionally, quality is related to materials and workmanship. However, some Western consumers also consider the underlying working conditions as a quality characteristic when purchasing apparel. Reputation-sensitive firms are more likely to enforce corporate codes of conduct relating to the treatment of workers than are firms that compete on price alone. Quality-sensitive international buyers have closer relationships with their vendor factories and visit frequently for the purpose of ensuring quality. These visits have been shown to improve working conditions (Locke, Qin, and Brause 2006). Thus, quantitative restrictions provided reputation-sensitive international buyers that sold premium-priced goods some protection from firms that competed on price alone. Quality downgrading following the end of the MFA may result in reduced sales by reputation-sensitive firms and diminished monitoring of working conditions.

Looking Ahead

This book aims to provide a better understanding of the effects of globalization on working conditions through systematic and comparable analyses of several developing countries. The positive correlations between FDI flows and interindustry wage premiums suggest a link between globalization, wages, and working conditions. This link has been beneficial for working conditions in the exposed sectors. Yet, questions remain about the durability of these effects, as well as about the broader impact on working conditions in other sectors. The studies presented in this book raise many questions that can guide future research, three important avenues for which are highlighted below.

GETTING AROUND DATA LIMITATIONS

This book hopes to provide an analytical framework that can be used in future cross-country research. Although the studies reveal that export-focused FDI has been positively correlated with wage differentials, both across industries and across time, evidence does not yet support a causal link between FDI and exports, on the one hand, and changes in wage differentials and working conditions, on the other. The Indonesia and El Salvador studies, however, do report regression analyses of the effects of FDI (or approved FDI) on wage differentials, and both find positive and statistically significant effects.

The main issue with uncovering this link is the lack of relevant data. A formal empirical analysis requires complete sector-specific FDI data, which are rare. Moreover, such analysis, if conducted, would have to rely on relatively few observations because there are few industries consistently identifiable in household surveys over time.

Reproducing these studies in other countries, and increasing the country set, could provide a check of the robustness of the current results. Expanding the number of countries would also permit researchers to take advantage of cross-country variation in FDI flows, exports, and industry differentials. Moreover, applying the approach presented in this book to countries that possess different characteristics would illuminate the generality of the results. Good candidates would include countries with export-processing zones, middle-income countries that had more developed industrial bases before trade liberalization, and larger developing countries (for example, China and India). Bangladesh, Sri Lanka, and Nicaragua are all low-income countries that also concentrate in apparel and therefore might make good candidates.

Another way to skirt the data issue would be to pool worker-level surveys to perform a cross-country comparison. Such an analysis could involve estimating IIWDs using worker-level data, controlling for individual characteristics from several countries, then pooling these data with information about sector-specific FDI, trade, and other measures of globalization. This approach would allow for both cross-sectional and time-series variation of globalization measures, and has proven effective in past studies examining globalization and nonwage measures of working conditions. (For example, see Mosley and Uno [2007]).

TAKING INITIAL CONDITIONS INTO ACCOUNT

The book suggests that the way the government reacts to globalization—through new regulations and institutions—influences the eventual impact that globalization has on working conditions. This role is not formally analyzed in the current country studies, but the analysis hints at possible important effects.

First, governments may impose specific regulations on firms that benefit from trade liberalization. In particular, given the commitment of Cambodia to ensuring good working conditions in firms that operated under the MFA, the fact that wage differentials in Cambodia's apparel sector are larger than those estimated in any of the other apparel-exporting countries in the studies suggests that monitoring is important.

Second, the action of national interest groups can influence the impact of globalization. For example, anti-sweatshop activists have played an important role in addressing some of the market malfunctions that produce poor outcomes for workers in a globalizing economy. Harrison and Scorse (2003), in their analysis of wage formation behavior in Indonesia during the 1990s, make a compelling case that a labor-management bargaining imbalance was particularly acute in the textiles, apparel, and footwear industries. Factories, forced to raise wages as a consequence of government action and anti-sweatshop agitation, were able to do so without cutting employment or production. Anti-sweatshop agitation has also been critical in transforming the state's role in worker-management conflict from taking the side of capital into that of honest broker. NGO- or government-sponsored programs targeted at providing general education and informing workers about their options can also help redress the bargaining imbalance (see, for example, Kim [2007] and Polaski [2006]).

Moreover, a set of labor market inefficiencies may be in place and be aggravated by increased globalization. Consider first, for example, the factors that undermine the bargaining power of workers in relation to factory managers. Both as a historical matter

(Brown 2002) and in factories around the world today, apparel workers are often very young, female, poorly educated or illiterate, and may not speak the language of their managers or supervisors (Kim 2007). Workers migrating to urban areas from the countryside may not even have market experience beyond a barter economy.[7] A second factor, often mentioned in passing but underappreciated, is the role that macroeconomic mismanagement plays in undermining the bargaining power of workers. The presence of a pool of unemployed workers out the back door of the factory greatly dampens the willingness of workers to voice their grievances. Frequent economic downturns often wipe out the gains that workers might have won during a preceding period of economic growth. Indonesia is the most dramatic example of this situation among the countries studied in this volume.[8]

TAKING A SECTOR-SPECIFIC APPROACH

The five country studies herein focus on the textiles and apparel sectors, because that is where FDI and exports have tended to concentrate. A concern about the studies' results is that the significant wage premiums and improved working conditions identified in the apparel sector may have been the result of the MFA or the subsequent ATC (see box 1.1 for a brief history). By having access to restricted U.S., Canadian, and European markets, these industries may have been capturing rents that they may have been sharing with workers through higher wages and better working conditions. As the end of the ATC approached, the evidence in several chapters of this volume suggests that FDI began to leave these countries. Preliminary evidence, notably for Madagascar, El Salvador, and Honduras, suggests that the decline in FDI and exports may be causally linked to falling wages and conditions in these sectors. This issue presents a significant opportunity for future research.

Thus, another research effort could focus on a particular sector rather than a particular country. For example, choosing the textiles and apparel sectors would enable an analysis to use the end of the MFA in 2005 as a natural breaking point for disentangling the conflicting effects of globalization on wages and working conditions. Three main empirical strategies could be pursued to better understand the links between international economic integration and working conditions.

First, the end of the MFA provides a natural experiment that can produce considerable evidence on the interaction between labor market outcomes and institutions. A number of inferences can be made about the impact of globalization on workers by observing changes in total apparel production, global market share, the apparel-to-agriculture wage premium, the wage-rent ratio, and labor's cost share. For example, an increase in the wage-rent ratio in countries acquiring market share and a decline in countries losing market share would be consistent with the standard textbook theory of trade and wage determination. By contrast, a decline in relative wages for all apparel workers worldwide is consistent with the view that apparel workers had managed to acquire some of the quota rents. Alternatively, market share and its relation to wages may depend on the activities of reputation-sensitive international buyers or NGO activity targeting working conditions. A decline in the apparel-to-agriculture wage premium might also indicate a decline in market share for reputation-sensitive international buyers or a fall in the reputation price premium.

If, conversely, the apparel-to-agriculture wage premium persists in the absence of the MFA, it could be posited that supply chains brought knowledge capital that permanently improved the management of labor in developing countries. In addition, inferences about the impact of corporate codes of conduct on labor outcomes may surface. An outcome in which countries with established reputations for humane treatment of labor are able to retain market share without reducing prices may also be observed. Such a price premium would be indicative of Western consumers' willingness to pay for "good" working conditions. Apparel producers in such countries may be able to remain price competitive without reducing wages. Such an outcome would indicate that humane labor management practices are also profit maximizing.

Second, framed field experiments have been used extensively in development economics generally, within the field of personnel economics, and in the study of human resource management practices in apparel and footwear factories. However, no field experiment in global supply chains to date has been sufficiently carefully designed to draw conclusions about the causal link between management of supply chains and outcomes for workers, their families, and communities.

Finally, the role of qualitative analysis is also potentially significant, especially in understanding the roles of safeguards and monitoring. Qualitative evidence from Cambodia suggests that safeguards and monitoring play an important role in improving working conditions (Polaski 2006). External pressure from the ILO also played a significant role in changing government regulation in Indonesia and El Salvador. These successes raise interesting hypotheses. For example, it is possible that FDI without monitoring may not have either increased wages or improved working conditions. If that is the case, the end of the MFA may not have significant implications for working conditions if monitoring mechanisms remain in place even if FDI leaves. Therefore, including qualitative assessments of the practice and efficacy of monitoring could improve the accuracy of any future study of globalization and working conditions.

Notes

1. The fall in FDI relative to GDP was mostly due to a fall in FDI rather than an increase in GDP.

2. The four core labor standards are elimination of all forms of forced or compulsory labor; effective abolition of child labor; equality of opportunity and treatment; and freedom of association and right to collective bargaining.

3. In addition to the Core Labor Standards, Elliott and Freeman (2003) also list dark, crowded, hot, noisy workplaces; no emergency exits or fire extinguishers; inadequate or no time to go to the toilet; no canteen or place to eat; abusive supervisors who strike young workers; below-minimum-wage payments; absence of written contracts; compulsory overtime; sexual or other harassment of workers; and late or short wage payments, among other concerns about working conditions in developing countries.

4. These ideas are developed in the "Theoretical Considerations" section of this chapter for the apparel sector.

5. Madagascar's export processing zone.

6. The positive correlation of wages and nonwage working conditions is particularly informative because wage data are often more complete than data on specific aspects of working conditions. A robust positive correlation between wages and nonwage working conditions suggests that changes in wages may foretell similar changes in nonwage working conditions.

7.　Several factors then conspire to preserve the bargaining imbalance. The use of the police power of the state to intervene in capital-labor strife on the side of capital has historically played a significant role in preventing workers and factory managers from negotiating a market-clearing equilibrium wage. As described in the country studies, concerns about government hesitation to actively support free association, particularly in export processing zones, have been raised in several countries, especially Honduras and El Salvador.

8.　This phenomenon was also evident during the anti-sweatshop movement of the early 20th century. For a detailed account of the relationship between macroeconomic volatility and working conditions in the U.S. apparel industry, see Brown (2002).

References and Other Resources

Abuhadba, M., and P. Romaguera. 1993. "Inter-Industry Wage Differentials: Evidence from Latin American Countries." *Journal of Development Studies* 30 (1): 190–205.

Arbache, Jorge S. 2001. "Wage Differentials in Brazil: Theory and Evidence." *Journal of Development Studies* 38 (2): 109–30.

Appelbaum, Richard P. 2004. "Assessing the Impact of the Phasing-Out of the Agreement on Textiles and Clothing on Apparel Exports on the Least Developed and Developing Countries." Report prepared for the ISBER Center for Global Studies, University of California, Santa Barbara.

Brown, Carrie. 2002. *Rosie's Mom. Forgotten Women Workers of the First World War*. Boston: Northeastern University Press.

Chenery, Hollis B., and Lance Taylor. 1968. "Development Patterns: Among Countries and Over Time." *The Review of Economics and Statistics* 50 (4): 391–416.

Cousineau, Jean-Michel, Robert Lacroix, and Anne-Marie Girard. 1992. "Occupational Hazard and Wage Compensating Differentials." *Review of Economics and Statistics* 74 (1): 166–9.

Daniel, Cristophe, and Catherine Sofer. 1998. "Bargaining, Compensating Wage Differentials, and Dualism of the Labor Market: Theory and Evidence for France." *Journal of Labor Economics* 16 (3): 546–75.

Dorman, Peter, and Paul Hagstrom. 1998. "Wage Compensation for Dangerous Work Revisited." *Industrial and Labor Relations Review* 52 (1): 116–35.

Edin, P., and J. Zetterberg. 1992. "Inter-industry Wage Differentials: Evidence from Sweden and a Comparison with the United States." *American Economic Review* 82 (5): 1341–9.

Elliott, Kimberly Ann, and Richard B. Freeman. 2003. "Vigilantes and Verifiers." In *Can Labor Standards Improve Under Globalization?* 49–72. Washington, DC: Institute for International Economics.

Evans, Carolyn, and James Harrigan. 2004. "Tight Clothing: How the MFA Affects Asian Apparel Exports." NBER Working Paper No. 10250, National Bureau of Economic Research, Cambridge, MA.

Flannigan, Robert J. 2006. *Globalization and Labor Conditions: Working Conditions and Worker Rights in a Global Economy*. Oxford, UK: Oxford University Press.

Gittleman, M., and E. Wolff. "International Comparisons of Inter-Industry Wage Differentials." *Review of Income and Wealth* 39 (3): 295–312.

Haisken-DeNew, J. P., and C. Schmidt. 1997. "Inter-Industry and Inter-Region Differentials: Mechanics and Interpretation." *The Review of Economics and Statistics* 79 (3): 516–21.

Harrigan, James, and Geoffrey Barrows. 2006. "Testing the Theory of Trade Policy: Evidence from the Abrupt End of the Multifibre Arrangement." NBER Working Paper No. 12579, National Bureau of Economic Research, Cambridge, MA.

Harrison, Ann E., and Jason Scorse. 2003. "Globalization's Impact on Compliance with Labor Standards." In *Brookings Trade Forum 2003*, ed. Susan M. Collins and Dani Rodrik, 45–82. Washington, DC: Brookings Institution Press.

Hasan, Rana, and Devashish Mitra, eds. 2003. *The Impact of Trade on Labor: Issues, Perspectives, and Experiences from Developing Asia*. Amsterdam: North Holland/Elsevier.

Helwege, J. 1992. "Sectoral Shifts and Inter-Industry Wage Differentials." *Journal of Labor Economics* 10 (1): 55–84.

Hersch, Joni. 1998. "Compensating Differentials for Gender-Specific Job Injury Risks." *American Economic Review* 88 (3): 598–627.

Katz, L. F., and L. H. Summers. 1989a. "Can Inter-Industry Wage Differentials Justify Strategic Trade Policy?" In *Trade Policies for International Competitiveness*, ed. Robert C. Feenstra, 85–116. National Bureau of Economic Research Conference Report Series. Chicago and London: University of Chicago Press.

———. 1989b. "Industry Rents: Evidence and Implications." *Brookings Papers On Economic Activity (Microeconomics)*: 209–75.

Kim, Jee Young. 2007. "Governance Beyond Borders: Anti-Sweatshop Regulation in Vietnam's Fashion and Footwear Industries." PhD dissertation, Department of Sociology, Harvard University.

Krueger, A. B., and L. H. Summers. 1987. "Reflections on the Inter-Industry Wage Structure." In *Unemployment and the Structure of Labor Markets*, ed. K. Lang and J. S. Leonard, 17–47. Oxford, UK: Blackwell Publishing.

———. 1988. "Efficiency Wages and the Inter-Industry Wage Structure." *Econometrica* 56 (2): 259–93.

Lazear, Edward P., and Paul Oyer. 2007. "Personnel Economics." NBER Working Paper No. 13480, National Bureau of Economic Research, Cambridge, MA.

Locke, Richard M., Fei Qin, and Alberto Brause. 2006. "Does Monitoring Improve Labor Standards? Lessons from Nike." Working Paper 24, Corporate Social Responsibility Initiative, John F. Kennedy School of Government, Harvard University, Cambridge, MA.

Moll, P. G. 1993. "Industry Wage Differentials and Efficiency Wages: A Dissenting View with South African Evidence." *Journal of Development Economics* 41 (2): 213–46.

Mosley, Layna, and Saika Uno. 2007. "Racing to the Bottom or Climbing to the Top?" *Comparative Political Studies* 40 (8): 923–48.

Papola, T., and W. Bharadwaj. 1970. "Dynamics of Industrial Wage Structure: An Inter-Country Analysis." *The Economic Journal* 80 (317): 72–90.

Polaski, Sandra. 2006. "Harnessing Global Forces to Create Decent Work: A Successful Experiment in the Cambodian Apparel Sector." Carnegie Endowment for International Peace, Washington, DC.

Sabel, Charles, Dara O'Rourke, and Archon Fung. 2000. "Ratcheting Labor Standards: Regulation for Continuous Improvement in the Global Workplace." KSG Working Paper No. 00-010, Kennedy School of Government, Harvard University.

UNCTAD. 2005. *TNCs and the Removal of Textiles and Clothing Quotas.* UNCTAD/ITE/ IIA/2005/1. New York and Geneva: United Nations.

United States International Trade Commission. 2004. "Textiles and Apparel: Assessment of the Competitiveness of Certain Foreign Suppliers to the U.S. Market." Investigation Number 332-448, Publication 3671, USITC, Washington, DC.

Villanueva, Ernesto. 2007. "Estimating Compensating Wage Differentials Using Voluntary Job Changes: Evidence from Germany." *Industrial and Labor Relations Review* 60 (4): 544–61.

Viscusi, W. Kip, and Michael J. Moore. 1991. "Worker Learning and Compensating Differentials." *Industrial and Labor Relations Review* 45 (1): 80–96.

Wagner, J. 1990. "An International Comparison of Sector Wage Differentials." *Economics Letters* 34: 93–7.

World Bank. various years. *World Development Indicators.* Washington, DC: World Bank.

CHAPTER 2

A Review of the Globalization Literature: Implications for Employment, Wages, and Labor Standards

Drusilla Brown

The dramatic expansion of international trade and investment over the last six decades has likely promoted economic efficiency, but the implications for workers have become the subject of intense debate. This chapter reports on the available empirical evidence about the relationship between a globalizing economy and employment, wages, working conditions, and core labor protections. It turns first to the impact of trade and foreign direct investment (FDI) on employment, wages, and working conditions. It then reviews two mechanisms used to address labor's concerns: (i) voluntary private monitoring initiatives through which consumers and investors have expressed their values relating to working conditions and (ii) labor protection clauses that have been introduced into international trade agreements.

Trade and Employment

The literature linking trade liberalization to employment is immense. As noted by Winters, McCulloch, and McKay (2004), most of these studies are partial equilibrium in nature and thus tend to overstate the impact of any exogenous changes. Even so, most studies find a relatively small impact of trade liberalization on employment.

Wacziarg and Wallack (2004) examine the intersectoral employment effects for 25 liberalization episodes in a set of developing and transition economies. Detailed manufacturing sector data for the period 1969–97 are obtained from UNIDO and data for nine broad sectors for the same period are obtained from the International Labour Organization (ILO). At the 1-digit level, trade liberalization is found to have either no effect or a negative (but insignificant) effect on sectoral employment shares. Considering a five-year window following an episode of trade liberalization, a typical liberalizing sector will sustain a 0.65 percentage point absolute change in employment share in the two years following the liberalizing episode. By contrast, a nonliberalizing sector will experience a 0.79 percentage point absolute change. That is, there is more labor movement in the nonliberalizing sector than in the liberalizing sector, though the difference is not statistically significant.

At the 3-digit level, the employment effects of trade liberalization are more pronounced. Wacziarg and Wallack (2004) report that a liberalization episode five years in the past will reduce the two-year growth in manufacturing employment in a country by 4.02 percentage points. They also find some, though mixed, evidence that labor market rigidities inhibit labor market responses. Labor market adjustments were larger for those trade liberalization episodes embedded in a broader set of market reforms in which governments removed domestic policies that might have counteracted the employment effects of trade liberalization.

Revenga (1997) also finds small employment effects for Mexico: tariff reductions had no statistically significant effect on employment, while removal of import quotas reduced employment minimally. However, labor had appropriated some of the rents created by import protection. As a consequence, the pro-competitive effects of trade not only reduced profit margins but also reduced wages in manufacturing. On average, wages in manufacturing declined by 3–4 percent, but decreases of as much as 10–14 percent were observed for other sectors. Similarly small employment effects are found in other studies as well (Pagés-Serra and Marquez 1998; Moreira and Najberg 2000; Rama 1994).

Larger employment and wage effects are found by Milner and Wright (1998) in their study of industry-level data in Mauritius. Wages and employment decline following trade liberalization. However, over the long run, wages and employment recover with employment even growing in the import-competing sector. Positive employment effects are particularly pronounced for women working in the apparel industry.

Currie and Harrison (1997) provide evidence as to why such employment (and wage) effects might be small. They analyze data from Morocco and find that the impact of trade on wages and employment depends on the degree of imperfections in the output market. For competitive markets in which profit margins are small, import penetration reduces employment. By contrast, for those markets with larger profit margins, virtually no change occurs in wages or employment. These results suggest that, at least for these cases, increased trade exposure was principally pro-competitive.

Observed changes might seem small if industry-level data mask interfirm labor movements. To illustrate this point, Levinsohn (1999) analyzes Chilean plant-level data for the period 1979–86. At the aggregate level, macroeconomic shocks and trade liberalization lowered manufacturing employment by 8 percent. However, nearly 25 percent of all workers changed jobs during the period, with larger firms increasing employment at the expense of smaller firms. Similarly, LaRochelle-Côté (2007) uses firm-level data to analyze the impact of tariff liberalization in Canada during the period 1988–94, when tariff rates declined from 6.9 percent to 1.8 percent on average.[1] Like others, he reports small—though not insignificant—effects of tariff reductions on employment. Job loss was more pronounced for less productive firms. Firms with average productivity subject to loss of tariff protection shed 11.3 percent of their workforce over a six-year period. By contrast, lower-productivity firms shed 20.8 percent of their workforce over the same period.

Analysis of French customs files for the period 1986–92 by Biscourp and Kramarz (2007) finds a stronger relationship between increased imports (particularly of finished goods) and destruction of production jobs. The impact of imports on employment depends critically on whether the domestic firm is competing in the market for final goods or intermediate inputs. Imports of finished goods destroy more jobs than imports of intermediate inputs.

More recently, several authors have emphasized the dynamic process through which globalization affects labor market adjustment (Utar 2007; Robertson and Dutkowsky

2002). Artuc, Chaudhuri, and McLaren (2007) estimate the mean intersectoral moving costs faced by a worker by using the U.S. Census Bureau's Current Population Surveys 1975–2000. In equilibrium, the moving cost is found to be about 13 times the average annual wage. A model simulation of the impact of trade liberalization on intersectoral labor movement indicates that a 40 percent reduction in manufacturing import tariffs reduces manufacturing share of employment from 25 percent at the beginning of the period to 16 percent over eight years. Manufacturing wages decline 22 percent immediately following liberalization, while steady-state manufacturing wages decline only 2.45 percent. Despite the decline in the manufacturing wage, all workers see an increase in their expected discounted lifetime utility as a consequence of the liberalization. While it is true that the manufacturing wage declines, wages in other sectors rise. All workers have a positive probability that they will move to one of those higher paying jobs.

Trade and Wages

Globalization may affect both absolute (or average) wage levels and relative wages between different groups. Globalization may affect absolute wages by inducing specialization that increases productivity, and relative wages by altering relative factor demands. For consumers, globalization (such as falling trade barriers) reduces prices, thus increasing real wages and purchasing power. Most studies, however, focus on the effects of globalization on relative wages because a vibrant debate still revolves around the topic.[2]

TRADE AND ABSOLUTE WAGES

Frankel and Romer (1999) and Noguer and Siscart (2005) find that countries that trade more have higher GDP per capita. Because their analyses are based on cross-section data, they assume that all countries follow similar development paths, and do not imply that trade liberalization (or changes in globalization over time) will necessarily produce higher wages. To address changes over time, Rama (2003) uses annual wage data from Freeman and Oostendorp (2000, 2001) to assess the net impact of trade openness on wages. Three different measures of openness are employed: (i) ratio of trade to GDP; (ii) openness policy as indicated by low tariffs, limited nontrade barriers, absence of marketing boards, no central planning, and low black-market foreign exchange premiums; and (iii) ratio of FDI to GDP. Other control variables in the regression model include wage rate, GDP per capita, country, year, occupation, and measures of political and economic liberty. The results indicate a negative and statistically significant effect of trade and trade policy on wages, while openness to FDI is found to be correlated with higher wages. A 20 percentage point increase in the ratio of trade to GDP leads to a 5–6 percent decline in wages. By contrast, a 1 percentage point increase in the ratio of FDI to GDP is correlated with a 1 percent increase in wages. FDI also appears to be an important determinant of the wage premium paid to skilled workers, with a 1 percentage point increase in the ratio of FDI to GDP correlated with a 5 percentage point increase in the return to a year of education.[3] Trade share of GDP, however, appears to have little impact on wage dispersion.

The short-run effects of liberalization may include adjustment costs and, therefore, differ from the long-run effects. To consider this possibility, Rama (2003) introduces long lags between changes in trade policy and wages. He finds that while the impact of trade on wages in the short run may be negative, the impact turns positive after about four years and is strongly positive after five years. It appears, then, that international trade is good for overall economic growth, which, in turn, has a positive impact on wages. The short-run negative impact appears to be the consequence of protracted periods of unemployment that accompany trade-associated economic dislocation.[4]

TRADE AND RELATIVE WAGES

The widening gap between wages paid to skilled and unskilled labor has received considerable attention since 1990. The debate began when labor economists noted that between 1979 and 1995, the real wages of U.S. workers who did not complete high school exhibited a 20.2 percent decline. Over the same period, high school graduates experienced a smaller 13.4 percent decline. In contrast, workers with 16 or more years of education had a 3.4 percent increase in wages. Globalization has been accompanied by significant changes in relative wages in developing countries as well, and studies of different countries and time periods often generate conflicting results.

The impact of trade on wages within the Heckscher-Ohlin model is traditionally articulated by the Stolper-Samuelson theorem: A rise in the price of a good will increase the return to the factor used intensively in the production of that good. Thus, for an unskilled labor–abundant developing country, opening to trade should raise the price of the unskilled labor–intensive good, thereby increasing the equilibrium wage paid to unskilled labor.

In light of the fact that U.S. imports appeared to be increasingly unskilled labor–intensive, the decline in the relative returns to unskilled labor in the United States is precisely what the Stolper-Samuelson theorem would lead us to expect from a globalizing economy. Trade economists, however, were skeptical of the trade-to-wages explanation, preferring instead to attribute the rise in the return to skilled labor to skilled labor–biased technological change. Trade economists based their conclusions on three arguments: (i) the volume of trade was not large enough and sufficiently unskilled labor–intensive to explain such a large swing in wages; (ii) prices of unskilled labor–intensive imports were not falling, as required for a Stolper-Samuelson explanation; and (iii) virtually all industries were shifting away from unskilled labor–intensive production techniques even as unskilled labor was becoming less expensive. All three of these arguments pointed to skilled labor–biased technological change rather than international trade as the major cause of the rise in the skill premium between 1980 and 1995.

The apparent lack of evidence for the Stolper-Samuelson explanation did not mean that globalization was not affecting wages. Williamson (2005), for example, argues that the failure to find a trade-wages link today is a consequence of focusing on data only since 1979. He believes that if analyses were to span the period 1940 to the present, trade would emerge as an important explanation for the growing wage gap between skilled and unskilled workers. Other links between globalization and the relative demand for skill are also possible. Acemoglu (2003) suggests that imports of technology-intensive intermediate inputs may be complementary with skilled labor. Feenstra and Hanson (1996, 2003) concur, albeit for a different reason. They argue that to accurately capture the impact of trade on wages today, the recently emergent phenomenon of outsourcing must be modeled. Western producers in many industries are increasingly taking the most unskilled labor–intensive parts of their production processes and relocating them in low-wage developing countries. Testing their outsourcing framework, Feenstra and Hanson (2003) find that international trade may well have been as important as computerization in moving the relative wages of skilled and unskilled workers.

A similar debate rages in studies of developing countries among those who argue that globalization has direct effects, indirect effects, and minimal (or no) effects on wage inequality. Trade liberalization may directly affect wage inequality if the trade-related skill premium is a function of the structure of protection in developing countries. Hanson and Harrison (1999) find that the structure of tariffs in Mexico disproportionately protected unskilled workers. A similar pattern of protection is found by Attanasio, Goldberg, and Pavcnik (2004) for Colombia; Currie and Harrison (1997) for Morocco; and Pavcnik et al. (2004) for Brazil. Thus, it is not surprising that the relative wages of unskilled workers declined following trade liberalization.

Given this structure of protection, trade liberalization should induce changes in prices, and thus lead to changes in relative wages consistent with the Stolper-Samuelson theorem. Robertson (2004) provides a clear example of the Stolper-Samuelson mechanism in his study of Mexican prices and wages for the period 1987–99. Mexican trade liberalization occurred in two steps. First, Mexico joined the General Agreement on Tariffs and Trade in 1986. Robertson finds that the relative price of skill-intensive goods rose in the immediate aftermath, accompanied by rising wage inequality. Subsequently, Mexico joined the North America Free Trade Agreement (NAFTA) in 1994. Increased trade with its more skill-abundant northern neighbors reduced the price of skill-intensive goods and also reduced wage dispersion. These comovements of factor and goods prices worked exactly as standard trade theory would predict, particularly in light of the fact that Mexico's tariff reductions in 1986 fell principally on unskilled labor–intensive goods, whereas the NAFTA tariff reductions focused more heavily on skilled labor–intensive goods.[5]

A similar relationship was identified by Bigsten and Durevall (2006) for Kenya; Lal (1986) for the Philippines; Winters (2000) for India; and Gonzaga, Filho, and Terra (2006) for Brazil. The Gonzaga, Filho, and Terra analysis is distinctive in that they first determine the degree to which tariff changes were passed through to domestic prices. Indeed, they find little correlation between tariff level and skill intensity. That is, Brazil was not offering greater nominal protection to the skilled labor–intensive, import-competing industry than to the unskilled labor–intensive, export sector. However, the pass-through to domestic prices of the tariff reductions was much greater in the import-competing sectors than in the export sectors. After controlling for pass-through, Gonzaga, Filho, and Terra (2006) find a decrease in earnings inequality and a 15.5 percent decline in the relative earnings of more-educated workers.[6]

Goldberg and Pavcnik (2005), however, challenge this Stolper-Samuelson–type explanation for the rise in the skill premium in developing countries following liberalization. For trade to alter relative wages through the Stolper-Samuelson channel, workers should be observed moving from contracting sectors to expanding sectors because it is the rise in demand by firms in the expanding sector for the factors these firms use intensively that bids up their relative return. The problem, though, is that most studies observe relatively little intersectoral factor reallocation. Attanasio, Goldberg, and Pavcnik (2004), for example, find no statistical link between tariff changes and employment shares by industry.

Goldberg and Pavcnik (2005) also note that the skilled-worker employment share has increased within most industries since 1985. The rise in employment of a factor that is also increasing in price is only consistent with cost minimization if that factor has also become relatively more productive. Therefore, they suggest that skill-biased technological change seems a likely explanation for the observed change in relative wages.

As in developed countries, however, skill-biased technological change is not necessarily independent of globalization. The increase in competition that follows trade liberalization may affect the relative demand for skill. Aghion et al. (2003) argue that trade liberalization exposes import-competing firms to competition. Firms close to the technology frontier may be able to survive by upgrading their technology, while those far from the technology frontier are unlikely to survive the intensified competition. The impact of trade then depends on which industries are most flexible and adaptable. The more efficient firms survive, increasing the overall productivity of the sector. To the extent that these higher quality firms also employ more skilled labor, the demand for skill will rise.

Just as import competition may eliminate less-productive firms, export opportunities may allow more-productive firms to expand. Harrison and Hanson (1999) in particular argue that exporting itself is a skill-intensive activity. Exporting may require additional machinery or technology. Wood (1995) argues that intensified competition from abroad will induce firms to adopt new technologies as a strategy to compete. Attanasio, Goldberg, and Pavcnik (2004) find support for this hypothesis for Colombia. Between 1984 and 1998, sectors experiencing the largest tariff reductions also increased their employment of skilled workers. Similarly, Acemoglu (2003) argues that when developing countries open to trade, they often increase their imports of technology-embodied capital, such as assembly machines and office equipment. This equipment will complement skilled labor and thus may bid up the skill premium.

Bustos (2005) finds supporting evidence for this argument in her analysis of the Argentinean manufacturing sector. Trade expansion drives the adoption of new technologies by increasing market size, improving technology transfer, and relaxing borrowing constraints. Large fixed costs of technology adoption pose significant barriers to success in exporting. Thus, only the most efficient firms enter this activity. Furthermore, foreign-owned firms have greater access to capital and thus are more able to overcome these technology barriers.

Foreign direct investment may also play a significant part in a globalization experience, contributing to a change in relative wages. Winters, McCulloch, and McKay (2004) note that the very low skill level of the least skilled workers in developing countries may be of little use to multinationals. Equivalently, skilled labor by developing country standards may be relatively unskilled by industrial country standards. Thus, when trade-oriented producers employ labor in developing countries, they may draw principally from the top end of the skill distribution. The Winters et al. argument is consistent with evidence that multinationals avoid locations with a high prevalence of child labor.

Feenstra and Hanson (1997) find an FDI bias toward skilled-labor demand in Mexico. In this case, U.S. multinationals outsource intermediate input production to *maquiladora* plants. This intermediate input production is unskilled labor–intensive from the U.S. perspective but skilled labor–intensive from Mexico's perspective. Thus, the return to relatively skilled labor is bid up in both locations. Similar results are found by Robbins and Grindling (1999) for Costa Rica and by Ho, Wei, and Wong (2005) in their analysis of trading between Hong Kong, China, and the Chinese mainland.

If foreign investment concentrates within a particular region within a country, globalization may have implications for regional inequality as well. In fact, Hanson (2007) finds that before the liberalization episode of the 1990s, the northern part of Mexico was already more trade-exposed than the south. This difference in relative exposure may, in part, explain the fact that incomes in the north were already higher than in the south during the preliberalization period. The 1990s' liberalization increased the trade-exposure gap between the northern and southern regions of Mexico. As a consequence, Hanson finds that the return to labor in the low-exposure states fell by 10 percent relative to high-exposure states following the 1990s' liberalization. By contrast, Topalova (2007) finds that the most trade-exposed rural poor in India gained less than other groups. Hanson's results for Mexico are echoed in anecdotal evidence from China. Most of the trade liberalization in China has focused on the coastal cities. The subsequent rise in income in these cities produced a widening gap between the urban coastal cities and the interior.

It is possible, of course, that globalization does not affect relative wages. Porto's (2006) analysis of the impact of Mercosur on the Argentine distribution of income finds a limited role for trade. Analyzing the National Household Expenditure Survey 1996–97, Porto finds that Mercosur benefited households throughout the income distribution and may have been pro-poor. Households at the bottom of the income distribution enjoyed a 6 percent increase in expenditures as a consequence of Mercosur. Based on this analysis, Porto argues that the rising inequality observed in Argentina during the 1990s was not a consequence of trade liberalization. Rather, Porto argues, financial reforms, privatization, deregulation, and the Brazilian currency devaluation are the more likely causes of income inequality in Argentina.

TRADE AND THE INDUSTRY WAGE PREMIUM

Although the rise in the skill premium is an important source of the increase in wage inequality that accompanies opening international trade, Goldberg and Pavcnik (2004) also document considerable cross-sectoral wage variation that is not explained by variations in gender, age, experience, or education. Though it is clear that these cross-sectoral wage differences exist, it is not clear that trade has much impact on them. Feliciano (2001) and Pavcnik et al. (2004) find no link between trade and industry wage premiums for Mexico and Brazil, respectively.

Nevertheless, trade liberalization may destroy sector-specific human capital in the import-competing sectors. Workers who lose their jobs as a result of a tariff reduction may not be able to transfer their skills to a new job. Goldberg and Pavcnik (2004) find that the industry wage premium declined for industries suffering the largest cut in tariff protection in Colombia. However, the trade-linked reduction in the sectoral wage premium was small. Townsend (2007) finds a much stronger link between tariff reductions and wage premiums for Canada accompanying the Canada-U.S. Free Trade Agreement. For each 1 percentage point reduction in the statutory tariff there was a 0.5 percent decline in the industry wage.

Firms engaged in export activity may pay a wage premium. The seminal work detecting a statistically significant link between export activity and wages is Bernard, Jensen, and Lawrence (1995). Analyzing U.S. plant-level data, they found that average wages plus benefits were statistically significantly higher for exporters as compared with non-exporters, even after controlling for capital per worker, size of plant, multiplant enterprises, industry, year, plant, age, and region.

Schank, Schnabel, and Wagner (2007) use the Bernard, Jensen, and Lawrence (1995) framework to analyze German plant-level data from the German Institute for Employment Research (IAB) Establishment Panel for the period 1995–97. Unlike Bernard, Jensen, and Lawrence (1995), Schank, Schnabel, and Wagner (2007) are able to control for observed and unobserved worker heterogeneity by linking plant-level data to employment statistics from the German Federal Labor Services. Each record includes an establishment identifier, thus allowing Schank, Schnabel, and Wagner (2007) to construct a linked employer-employee data set. They find that, after controlling for worker characteristics recorded in the labor data, the exporter wage premium is still positive but not as large as reported by Bernard, Jensen, and Lawrence (1995). The wage premium for an export firm was only about 1.8 percent for a blue-collar worker and 0.9 percent for a white-collar worker.

TRADE AND LABOR PRODUCTIVITY

Globalization may have an additional positive impact on labor if international integration boosts labor productivity. The link between trade and productivity gains is supported by several studies, including Harrison (1994) for Côte d'Ivoire, Aghion et al. (2003) and Topalova (2004) for India, Kim (2000) for the Republic of Korea, Pavcnik (2002) for Chile, Fernandes (2003) for Colombia, and Hay (2001) for Brazil. Less evidence, however, suggests that these productivity gains translate into higher wages. In fact, according to Rama (2003), Revenga (1997), and others, wages may have declined after trade liberalization.

A trade-productivity link could occur if more-productive firms select into export activity. Only the most productive firms may be able to compete in the international arena. Trade may also give rise to learning-by-doing effects. Firms entering the export market acquire knowledge and expertise that raise productivity. Aw, Chung, and Roberts (2000) for Korea and Van Biesebroeck (2005) for Côte d'Ivoire find that productivity rises following entry into the export market. De Loecker (2007) finds evidence of trade-linked learning-by-doing in his analysis of Slovenian manufacturing data for the period 1994–2000. The transition from a centrally planned economy to a trade-exposed, market-based economy provides a natural experiment in which to study the impact of export activity on firm productivity. After controlling for selection, De Loecker finds a strong impact of export activity on productivity, particularly for those firms exporting to Western Europe and North America. Exporting firms became 8.8 percent more productive than comparable non-exporting firms, though there was considerable cross-firm variation.

India provides a good example of the way in which export orientation changes labor management practices so that they raise productivity and product quality. Beginning in the mid-1980s, India's automobile industry grew rapidly and attracted significant FDI flows. As a consequence of domestic-content requirements, local components producers were required to significantly increase quality and productivity. Okada (2004) reports that firms responded by hiring more educated and qualified workers for production and managerial positions. Firms also emphasized cognitive skills and behavioral traits in recruitment and increased formal training in quality control and line management.

International Trade and Working Conditions

International trade may affect workers through nonwage working conditions, such as discrimination in employment, child labor, employment security, and informal employment. One widespread concern is that globalization has produced a "race to the bottom" in legal labor protections.

TRADE, FDI, AND GENDER DISCRIMINATION IN EMPLOYMENT AND WAGES

The pro-competitive effect of trade is thought to potentially reduce some discriminatory behavior, particularly in the employment of and wages paid to women. Indeed, the impact of globalization on the employment prospects of women is so pronounced in some developing countries that the workforce in export sectors is becoming feminized. Female workers may be disproportionately represented in the export sector in developing countries because these sectors are unskilled-labor intensive. Examples of this phenomenon are reported by Kabeer (2000) for young women in the Bangladesh apparel industry; Head (1998) with regard to the impact of changes in European Union trade policy related to canned fruit and its impact on female workers in Paarl, South Africa; and Milner and Wright (1998) for Mauritius. Başlevent and Onaran (2004) also find some evidence of an effect of export orientation on female labor force participation in Turkey. Analyzing labor force survey data for the period 1988–94, they find that employment of single women is positively correlated with trade openness. Married women also respond to export orientation in the traditionally female textiles and food sectors.

It is possible that the dominant role of female employment in the export sector is a consequence of the pro-competitive effect of trade. The pro-competitive effect may extend to wages too if cost-minimizing exporting firms eschew gender discrimination. Evidence on the pro-competitive effect of trade on gender wage differentials can be obtained by comparing male and female wages following an episode of trade liberalization. For example, García-Cuéllar (2002) analyzes data for Mexico, examining the gender gap in industries for which there has been an increase in import penetration or termination of import licensing requirements relative to other industries. The male-female wage gap is found to narrow disproportionately in these sectors. By comparison, Berik, Rodgers, and Zveglich (2004) find gender discrimination in wages rising with international trade in their analysis of Taiwan, China, and Korea over the period 1980–99. Black and Brainerd (2004) consider the evidence on trade and nondiscrimination for the United States. They note that the intensification of competition that comes about with globalization should pressure firms engaging in gender discrimination to end this suboptimal practice. Indeed, they find for U.S. industries between 1976 and 1993 that the residual gender gap narrowed more rapidly in concentrated industries than in competitive industries. Thus, the pressures of international trade appear to erode the ability of firms in concentrated industries to indulge a taste for discrimination.

These studies may miss some subtle variations across income groups and occupation groups that affect gender wage differentials. Oostendorp (2004) employs the ILO October

Inquiry—which reports wages by gender in 161 occupations for 80 countries—for 1983 through 1999. In the base data set, the average occupational gender gap, as measured by wages, is 13 percent in developed countries and 4 percent in developing countries.

After sorting countries by income, occupational gender discrimination is regressed on GDP per capita, trade openness, and FDI. Of interest is the result that gender discrimination is positively correlated with GDP per capita in low-income countries, but not in high-income countries. Thus, there appears to be some nonlinearity in the relationship between gender discrimination and income. Trade and the gender wage gap are negatively correlated for both low- and high-income countries. However, for FDI, nonlinearity is again observed: the gender gap falls with FDI in low-income countries but rises in high-income countries.

Some difference between high- and low-income countries is expected. Trade would normally be expected to raise the return to low-skilled workers in developing countries and raise the return to skilled workers in developed countries. Women may also have a different skill set than men, producing a differential impact for international trade. To the extent that women are differentially low skilled, trade would be expected to raise wages of women in developing countries. Women in developed countries would only gain if the pro-competitive effect of trade increased pressure on firms with a taste for discrimination.

Oostendorp (2004) then sorts occupations into high wage and low wage. Presumably, high-wage occupations are also high-skilled occupations. He finds the following:

- Trade and FDI reduce the gender wage gap for highly skilled workers in high-income countries and low-skilled workers in low-income countries. This is consistent with the hypothesis that as trade expands production in those goods in which a country has a comparative advantage, there is an increase in the relative demand for female workers and a rise in their relative wage.

- Trade and FDI reduce the gender wage gap for low-skilled workers in high-income countries. This is consistent with a pro-competitive effect on gender-discriminating employers in shrinking industries in high-income countries.

- FDI increases the gender wage gap for high-skilled occupations in poor countries. Thus, the pro-competitive effect of trade does not appear to be an important determinant of gender wage discrimination in developing countries. It is also possible that the technology embodied in FDI raises the demand for skill, limiting the pro-competitive effects of globalization.

TRADE AND CHILD LABOR

The interaction between globalization and child labor is complex. According to economic theory, trade may increase child labor if globalization provides new work opportunities for children and their families. Trade also has relative price and wage effects that may alter each family's child labor choices. Households endowed with the country's scarce factor will suffer a decline in wealth and may, as a consequence, increase child labor, while households endowed with the abundant factor will do the opposite. Overall, to the extent that trade increases national income and relaxes liquidity constraints, the national level of child labor in a globalizing economy should decline. Finally, child labor may decline with globalization because children typically lack the skills required to produce goods for export.

In their seminal analysis of Vietnam's integration into the global rice market, Edmonds and Pavcnik (2005) find that the incidence of child labor depends on each family's asset holdings. Between 1993 and 1998, the removal of rice export restrictions increased the domestic price of rice by 29 percent, which increased the return to arable land and the wages of adults employed in rice production. Edmonds and Pavcnik (2005) find that households with large and medium landholdings reduced the amount of time their children worked and increased leisure and schooling. The effect was particularly pronounced for older girls. However, children in families with small landholdings increased their supply of labor to the rice market. Furthermore, urban households suffered a decline in real income when the price of rice rose. These families also increased the time their children spent working. On balance, however, child labor declined in Vietnam following the liberalization of the rice market. A 30 percent increase in the price of rice resulted in a 9 percentage point decline in child labor.

Edmonds and Pavcnik (2006) report similar results for a cross-country analysis in which trade openness and child labor are negatively correlated. Each 1 percent increase in trade openness reduced child labor by 0.7 percent. Edmonds and Pavcnik (2006) find that the negative correlation between child labor and trade is primarily driven by trade-related income growth.

Neumayer and de Soysa (2005a) consider the impact of FDI on child labor. Not only do countries open to trade have a lower incidence of child labor, countries with a larger stock of foreign capital also have fewer working children. Indeed, little empirical evidence indicates that capital owners are attracted to markets in which child labor is common. In fact, the opposite appears to be the case.

TRADE AND JOB SECURITY

Exposure to international trade inevitably leads to short-term employment disruptions as workers move from one sector to another. Indeed, Edwards and Edwards (1996) find a positive correlation between duration of unemployment and degree of liberalization by sector. However, Matusz and Tarr (1999), surveying a large number of studies, find that these trade-related increases in unemployment are short. Harrison and Revenga (1998) conclude that the adjustments in Costa Rica, Peru, and Uruguay were nearly instantaneous.

TRADE AND THE INFORMAL SECTOR

The consequences of trade for labor interests in developing countries turn critically on the impact on the informal sector. Firms facing new competitive pressures from imports may seek to cut costs by shifting some of their employment to the informal sector. Such workers typically lack standard legal protections provided by minimum wage laws, hiring and firing regulations, and retirement benefits. Furthermore, considerable evidence suggests that workers in the informal sector earn lower wages even after controlling for observable worker characteristics.[7] Theoretical support for such employment practices is provided by Goldberg and Pavcnik (2003).

Three studies empirically analyze the probability of employment in the informal sector following trade liberalization. Currie and Harrison (1997) in their study of Morocco find that public-sector firms increase the proportion of temporary workers following trade liberalization. However, in a study of Brazil, Goldberg and Pavcnik (2003) find that cross-sectoral variation in tariff changes is not a significant determinant of the probability of employment in the informal sector after controlling for individual worker characteristics.

In contrast, Goldberg and Pavcnik (2005) find that trade liberalization was accompanied by an increase in informal employment in Colombia. However, this relationship disappeared following a labor market reform that provided firms with increased flexibility in terminating workers. Thus, it appears that trade liberalization does not increase the probability of informal employment, provided there is sufficient labor market flexibility. In Colombia, the culprit was high severance payments.

LABOR PROTECTIONS AND COMPARATIVE ADVANTAGE

Factors affecting labor standards can reasonably be divided into two classes: economically driven decisions at the firm level and government regulations. Governments may consider the effects on firms when setting regulations. In particular, governments may be motivated to reduce labor protections if they affect comparative advantage. The literature on the link between labor market institutions and economic performance is immense. This review is confined to those studies that directly relate to trade performance.

Busse (2002) addresses the link between labor protections and trade in the context of the Heckscher-Ohlin (factor proportions) model. The impact of labor practices on comparative advantage depends on the way in which each particular practice affects the supply of unskilled relative to skilled labor. Forced labor and child labor likely expand the relative supply of unskilled workers. By contrast, discrimination in employment, particularly if the practice prohibits women from working in particular industries, may reduce the supply of labor. The impact of unions on the supply of labor is ambiguous. If the union is trying to exercise monopoly control of the supply of labor, it will reduce the supply of labor and reduce comparative advantage in labor-intensive goods. However, it is possible that the union actually helps the labor market function, improving communication between workers and employers. Any subsequent productivity improvements may enhance productivity in labor-intensive goods.

Busse (2002) considers the marginal impact of various labor practices on comparative advantage. Labor force participation by females improves comparative advantage in unskilled labor–intensive goods. Weak protections against child labor and forced labor are also correlated with comparative advantage in unskilled labor–intensive goods. Countries with strong right-to-organize contexts export fewer labor-intensive goods than their labor endowment would suggest they should.

The increase in the minimum wage in Indonesia during the 1990s provides an interesting opportunity to specifically assess minimum wage legislation in a developing country context. During this period, the nominal minimum wage was quadrupled, doubling in real terms. Rama (1996) and Harrison and Scorse (2004) both find little to no effect of the Indonesian legislation on employment. Harrison and Scorse (2004), in particular, argue that monopsonistic employment practices were particularly challenging in the textiles, footwear, and apparel sectors. Furthermore, they argue that globalization in general and anti-sweatshop agitation in particular may have diminished monopsonistic exploitation practices by foreign-owned and export-oriented firms.

Harrison and Scorse (2004) find that by 1996, foreign-owned and export-oriented firms were more likely to be in compliance with minimum wage legislation than were domestically owned firms, even controlling for worker and plant characteristics. However, the authors attach an important caveat to their results. Export-oriented firms began the decade with poorer compliance performance than firms supplying the domestic market. Not until the middle of the 1990s did export-oriented firms produce a record of compliance that exceeded that of producers for the domestic market. Harrison and Scorse (2004) speculate that anti-sweatshop agitation early in the decade, along with U.S. threats to retract tariff preferences under the Generalized System of Preferences, may have raised wages in export-oriented firms. That is, they find some evidence that, before minimum wage legislation, Western buyers were typically sourcing from low-cost vendors paying below-market wages.

Foreign Direct Investment and the Labor Market

Internationally mobile physical capital has the opportunity to seek out low-cost, high-quality labor with which to work. The well-articulated fear of labor advocates is that internationally mobile capital will be attracted to labor markets with low wages and poorly protected labor rights. Furthermore, national governments may erode labor protections to attract capital.

FDI AND EMPLOYMENT

Several theoretical models of the determinants of FDI have been proffered. Markusen (1984) and Helpman (1984) identify two main drivers. Horizontal FDI substitutes for international trade and occurs when frictions inhibit trade in goods. Vertical FDI takes place when multinationals seek to access low-wage labor for some unskilled components of the production process. In both cases, FDI should be stimulated between headquarters and a host with different factor endowments.

Contrary to this theoretical reasoning, early statistical analysis using industry-level data suggested that a difference in factor endowments was not an important determinant of FDI location. For example, Brainard (1997) finds that U.S. affiliate sales back to the parent are not correlated with a difference in factor endowments between host and parent countries. Similarly, Blonigen, Davies, and Head (2003) find that sales by foreign affiliates of parent firms go up as skill differences between the home and host go down. Thus, they find little evidence that FDI is motivated by differences in factor endowments.

However, more recent analyses, such as Yeaple (2003); Hanson, Mataloni, and Slaughter (2003); and Feinberg and Keane (2006), uncover a role for relative factor endowments and prices. These studies find that FDI installed in those industries in which the host has a comparative advantage does increase affiliate sales back to the home country.

Hanson, Mataloni, and Slaughter (2003) provide an example of how the recent analysis of the determinants of FDI was undertaken. Their principle data source is the U.S. Bureau of Economic Analysis. The U.S. government requires U.S. multinationals to complete a confidential survey on the operations of the parent and any foreign affiliates in which the parent has at least a 10 percent equity stake. Data provided include industry identification, imported intermediate inputs, affiliate wages and employment for production and nonproduction workers, and return on capital. Hanson, Mataloni, and Slaughter (2003) also collected data on industrywide wages from the UNIDO Industry Database and on trade barriers from the United Nations Trade Analysis and Information System. Finally, the Heritage Foundation and the *Wall Street Journal* maintain scores on "economic freedom," such as respect for property rights, extent of government regulation, and prevalence of black-market activities.

Hanson, Mataloni, and Slaughter (2003) find that trade costs are strongly negatively correlated with imported intermediate inputs as a share of affiliate revenues. The own-price elasticity of demand for imported inputs is –3.28. That is, a 1 percent drop in input prices resulting from a reduction in trade costs leads to a 3.3 percent increase in the quantity of imported intermediate inputs demanded by the affiliate. More important for the purposes of this review, imported-input demand is negatively related to host-country wages for unskilled workers and positively related to skilled wages. For each 1 percent increase in unskilled wages, imported-input demand declines by 0.32 percent. However, for each 1 percent increase in skilled wages, imported-input demand rises by 0.36 percent. That is, U.S. firms appear to be seeking locations in which production wages are low but there are also sufficient numbers of high-skilled workers for nonproduction tasks. The results obtained by Hanson, Mataloni, and Slaughter (2003) using firm-level data are corroborated by Yeaple's (2003) analysis of U.S. industry-level data and by Braconier, Norbäck, and Urban's (2005) analysis of FDI flows from U.S. and Swedish multinationals.

Sourcing from foreign affiliates also appears to be sensitive to other factors, including trade costs, preferential market access, and trade incentives in export processing zones (EPZs). The benefits of EPZs include tax holidays, expedited transit through customs, and tariff breaks on imported equipment. Indicators of economic freedom are also positively correlated with affiliate activity.

DO MULTINATIONALS PAY HIGHER WAGES?

Some of the most severe criticisms of globalization concern pay and working conditions in global supply chains. However, until very recently, the evidence appeared to strongly support the conjecture that multinationals pay higher wages than domestically owned firms. Aitken, Harrison, and Lipsey (1996) find that foreign-owned firms paid wage premiums of 38 percent in Mexico, 18 percent in República Bolivariana de Venezuela, and 12 percent in the United States. Griffith and Simpson (2003) report a positive FDI premium for the United Kingdom; Lipsey and Sjoholm (2001) find a 12 percent premium for blue-collar workers in Indonesia and a 22 percent premium for white-collar workers. Te Velde and Morrissey (2003) find premiums between 8 and 23 percent for Cameroon, Ghana, Kenya, Zambia, and Zimbabwe. Görg, Strobl, and Walsh (2002) find confirming evidence for Ghana. These studies typically analyze manufacturing survey data and control for worker and plant characteristics that might account for differences in productivity and wages.

Several possible explanations for the foreign-ownership wage premium have been suggested. Aizenman and Spiegel (2002) argue that this phenomenon occurs in national markets in which property rights are poorly enforced. In such situations, ex post monitoring of compliance with a labor contract will be accomplished by paying an efficiency wage. Aizenman and Spiegel argue that foreign-owned firms have more difficulty monitoring such contracts and, therefore, have to pay a higher wage to achieve compliance. Alternatively, the entrance of multinationals into a labor market may bid up the equilibrium wage. However, if there is some segmentation in the labor market, wages of domestically owned firms may not rise in parallel. Fosfuri, Motta, and Rønde (2001) argue that workers in multinationals are exposed to proprietary technology requiring costly training. Multinationals may want to deter manpower turnover to retain training investments. Budd, Konings, and Slaughter (2005) argue that rent-sharing is taking place between the headquarters and subsidiaries. There is a positive correlation between profitability and wages. Finally, Conyon et al. (2002) argue that multinationals have more successful human resource management practices that involve higher wages.

Although these results appear robust, Martins (2004) challenges the underlying assumptions based on analysis of data from Portugal. He notes, for example, that foreign-owned firms have different observable characteristics than domestically owned firms. The Ministry of Employment surveys employers and employees in all firms with at least one employee. Firms report workforce characteristics (gender, qualifications, tenure, wages, and hours worked), geographical location, industry, sales, and foreign-ownership share.

After regressing hourly wages on human capital characteristics, firm characteristics, and foreign-ownership status, Martins (2004) finds that foreign-owned firms pay 8 to 13 percent more than domestically owned firms. However, Martins then uses propensity score matching to assemble a data set of closely matched foreign-owned and domestically owned firms. Foreign-owned firms matched on education, experience, tenure, gender, firm size, region, and industry pay no more than domestically owned firms. For some specifications, they even pay less. Furthermore, Martins' (2004) work is distinct because he is able to follow individual workers through the foreign acquisition process, enabling him to control for unobserved worker heterogeneity. In this phase of his analysis, he finds that wages decline by 3.3 percentage points following acquisition. He argues that the decline occurs because domestic firms pay above-market wages before acquisition. Domestic firms that will be acquired pay 11.7 percent more than domestic firms that will not be acquired. However, after acquisition, these newly acquired firms will pay only a 7.1 percent premium. Thus, more highly paid workers suffer a pay cut that averages 4.6 percent following acquisition.

Almeida (2007) also analyzes these Portuguese data and reaches essentially the same conclusion. The firms that will be acquired by a foreign entity are larger, employ a more-educated workforce, and pay a higher wage for both skilled and unskilled workers than do comparable firms that will remain domestically owned during the period under study. Foreign firms choose to purchase those Portuguese firms that have higher-than-average productivity and already have employment and business practices similar to those of the parent company.

This outcome is consistent with two theoretical models of corporate takeovers. Schleifer and Summers (1988) argue that a takeover allows a new owner to renege on an implicit contract between workers and the previous owner. Alternatively, Lichtenberg and Siegel (1990) argue that takeovers occur when a firm is poorly run. In this case, a poorly run firm would be one that is overpaying its workers.

Several researchers have used the difference-in-differences approach with varying results. Lipsey and Sjoholm (2003) reanalyze their Indonesian data from 2001, yet still find higher wage growth for newly purchased firms. By contrast, Conyon et al. (2002) analyze a panel of U.K. firms and find that newly acquired firms exhibit more rapid wage growth than domestically owned firms that are not acquired. However, this rapid wage growth precedes acquisition. Such an outcome is consistent with a "cherry-picking" hypothesis: foreign investors are selecting firms that are already more productive and, therefore, paying higher wages.

Girma and Görg (2007) also analyze U.K. data with a difference-in-differences propensity score-matching estimator. Data were drawn from the Annual Respondents Database provided by the Office of National Statistics. The authors selected 14,000–19,000 establishments for each year of the study period (1980–94) using a stratified sampling scheme. The estimated impact of foreign acquisition depends on the nationality of the headquarters of the multinational acquiring the firm and the skill level of the worker. For all firms, foreign acquisition raises wages for nonproduction workers by 2.6 percent in the first year; increases are not statistically significant in subsequent years. By contrast, foreign ownership appears to increase wages of production workers by 5.4 percent in the first year, rising to 7.5 percent after three years.

Girma and Görg (2007) then turn to an analysis of the impact of the nationality of the acquiring firm. They estimate that U.S. multinationals increase the wages of nonproduction workers by 13 percent and the wages of production workers by 13 percent within two years following acquisition. By contrast, it appears that acquisition by European Union multinationals has no statistically significant effect on wages in their U.K. subsidiaries. Finally, firms headquartered other than in the United States or the European Union appear to increase the wages of production workers by 4.4 percent in the first year and 6.8 percent in the second year following acquisition.

FOREIGN DIRECT INVESTMENT AND CORE LABOR PROTECTIONS

Given the theoretical argument and empirical evidence, though limited, that capital is attracted to a low-wage environment, it is reasonable to consider the possibility that competition to attract FDI has generated a race to the bottom in labor protections. Furthermore, Rodrik (1998) acknowledges that trade openness may lead domestic producers to seek relief from costly labor standards. However, capital owners are not the only factor of production competing in the political arena. Workers in a globalizing economy also face more wage, price, and employment volatility. Governments may be pressured to play a risk-reducing role for labor through either expenditures or regulations.

Historically, labor in the West has typically won this political contest. Huberman (2002) examines the evolution of labor protections during the first globalization century, a period characterized by profound convergence in factor prices. Convergence in labor market institutions might be expected to have occurred, as well. However, this was not the case until the eve of World War I. For the most part, countries typically developed idiosyncratic labor protections reflecting their own political and social institutions.

Moreover, to the extent that standards converged, they converged up. Huberman and Lewchuk (2002) discuss the emergence of the labor compact between 1850 and 1913. In their view, the increases in wage and employment instability that accompanied rising trade shares led workers to demand greater government protections against employment risk and uncertainty. Governments that adopted labor protections also found labor willing to support greater trade liberalization. Thus, trade begat labor protections and labor protections begat trade openness.

Rodrik (1999) comes to the same conclusion based on analysis of data from the second half of the 20th century. Those open economies with the largest terms-of-trade volatility also have larger governments.

Similar results are found by Busse (2004). He explores the determinants of some core labor practices in 70 developing countries for the period 1970–2000. Protections against forced labor, discrimination in employment, and child labor are positively related to national income, human capital formation, and trade openness. Indeed, the empirical evidence reported up to 2000 provides little evidence that a global downward spiral in labor protections had taken place. Examples of such studies include Rodrik (1996), Oman (2000), and OECD (1996, 2000). Kucera (2002) summarizes his results as follows:

- Higher labor costs negatively affect FDI, particularly when controlling for productivity.
- Inward FDI is positively correlated with the rights to free association and collective bargaining.
- Greater political and social stability and labor force quality promote economic growth, which, in turn, attracts FDI.

Several studies have emerged since 2000 that draw on improved labor protections and regulations for a large sample of countries. Kucera (2002) is the first of several to employ finer measurement of labor protections. Multiple measurements for each right are employed to test robustness. For example, measurements of free association and collective bargaining include the unionization rate; tabulation of violations from textual sources; labor violations in EPZs; and Freedom House indicators of civil liberties, political rights, and democracy.

The dependent variable in Kucera's (2002) FDI equations is each country's share of global FDI inflows. Control variables include wages in manufacturing, population, per capita GDP, trade share of GDP, exchange rate, urbanization rate, and literacy rate. With the exception of wages, FDI share is found to be strongly positively correlated with each of these variables. For each of the core labor protections Kucera (2002) finds the following:

- Civil liberties have two effects on FDI. Greater civil liberties are positively correlated with higher wages, which tends to deter FDI. However, after controlling for wages, greater civil liberties attract FDI.
- Child labor affects FDI through its relationship with both labor costs and quality of labor. Child labor is found to negatively affect labor quality and thus deters FDI. Child labor is not found to lower wages, although results are mixed with low statistical significance, suggesting that child labor has a limited (probably negative) impact on FDI.
- Gender inequality is found to negatively impact FDI. Representation of women in administrative and managerial occupations is positively correlated with FDI. However, significance is weakened when regional dummies are included.

Several authors find results similar to Kucera's (2002). For example, Neumayer and de Soysa (2004, 2005a, 2005b) study the relationship between globalization and various core labor protections. Countries with more-open trade have fewer violations of rights to free association and collective bargaining, more effectively protect women's rights, and have a lower incidence of forced labor and child labor. These results are true for both the global sample and a subsample of developing countries. FDI is uncorrelated with rights violations.

These conclusions are roundly challenged by conventional wisdom. Critics usually point to China as an example of a country that represses worker rights but enjoys enormous success in exporting and attracting FDI. According to the FLA (2005), China has the worst record on wage and hours violations as regulated by national law and codes of conduct when compared with nearly all other Asian countries. Berik, Rodgers, and Zveglich (2004) observe, though, that:

- China falls in the middle of the regional distribution of wages in the textiles and clothing sectors.
- China does not only compete on low wages. They are also the fastest at clearing goods through customs and otherwise moving shipments.

Ghose (2003) concurs that there is little evidence of a competitive dilution of labor standards, with one exception. He argues that a group of developing countries has not participated in the recent wave of globalization. These countries have experienced a decline in employment and labor standards. Given the difficulty of measuring labor standards, Ghose (2003) argues that the best indicator for an international comparison of labor standards is the nonwage component of workers' remuneration, which is highly correlated with wage income. By this measure, labor standards have improved in Asia since 1980 though with a dip during the 1997 financial crisis, while they have declined in Latin America. Indeed, according to Tokman (1997), 90 percent of new jobs in Latin America between 1985 and 1995 were in the informal sector.

However, Singh and Zammit (2004) argue that these variations are more likely associated with variations in the level of economic activity rather than its composition. In light of the fact that globalization typically increases economic activity while altering its industrial composition, Singh and Zammit (2004) argue that it is unlikely that globalization is the cause of declining working conditions in some regions.

Baldwin (2003) makes a similar argument with regard to labor standards in industrial countries. He notes the precipitous decline in the unionization rate since 1980, but does not believe that this turn of events is related to the pressures of globalization. Rather, he notes that deunionization has occurred in all sectors, trade-exposed or not, and posits that changes in popular attitudes and general disenchantment with unions are the more likely causes.

Indeed, little to no evidence indicates that legally mandated changes in labor protections are systematically related to FDI flows or globalization generally, with the possible exception of EPZs as discussed below. However, as with other aspects of globalization and labor, recent trends and empirical results are suggestive of a possible link and, thus, worthy of further exploration. Much of the informed view of the relationship between trade and employment conditions generally was the result of the emerging consensus among trade economists that globalization was not a significant factor in explaining trends in labor markets in the late 1990s. However, modeling innovations and empirical results reported by Feenstra and Hanson (2003) suggest that trade economists were underestimating the impact of outsourcing on wages in industrial and developing countries. Feenstra and Hanson argue that outsourcing accounts for half of the decline in wages of unskilled relative to skilled workers in the United States between 1979 and 1990. A similar analysis applied to employer-based access to health insurance and retirement benefits may also demonstrate a globalization link. Thus, analysts may need to reexamine the impact of globalization on labor practices, not through legally mandated protections, but rather through the types of jobs available, wages, employment benefits, and other important dimensions of working conditions.

FDI and Child Labor

The tentative conclusions put forward by Kucera (2002) on the negative link between child labor and FDI discussed in the preceding section are strengthened by several authors. For example, Busse and Braun (2003) find that multinationals prefer sites with less child labor. However, child labor is positively correlated with the export of labor-intensive goods. Busse and Braun (2003) adopt several definitions of child labor—child labor force participation rates, secondary school enrollment, and measures of enforcement. They then regress FDI per capita on GDP, growth, trade, an indicator of democracy, and measures of child labor for 132 countries. FDI is strongly negatively correlated with the child labor force participation rate and positively correlated with secondary school attendance. The analysis is then repeated including only countries with GDP per capita below $2,995 in 2000; the statistical results are essentially unchanged.

In a follow-up study, Braun (2002) explores why child labor deters FDI. Drawing on Hussain and Maskus (2003), Braun (2002) estimates a system of three equations that link child labor, economic growth, and FDI. Results are consistent with the hypothesis that child labor reduces human capital formation. Lower human capital formation then lowers the growth rate, making such a country less attractive to foreign investors. The author also finds little evidence that child labor attracts FDI by depressing labor's cost share.

Labor Standards Enforcement as a Signal for Property Rights Protection

Some argue that labor protections attract FDI not because capital owners value the protection of labor in and of itself, but because labor protections may signal a willingness to protect rights generally, or the presence of legal labor protections may be correlated with property rights protections. Investors may reasonably conclude that governments that do a poor job protecting labor rights will also fail to adequately protect the rights of capital owners and investors. The World Bank (2003) noted this sentiment in a survey of executives in 107 multinational enterprises in the extractive, agribusiness, and manufacturing sectors (2002–03). For example, investors believed that laws that are unevenly enforced increased investor risk and raised the possibility that selective enforcement could be used for strategic purposes to accomplish protectionist objectives.

Cross-country statistical analyses of the impact of institutions and corruption on FDI yield mixed results. Wei (2000a, 2000b) finds FDI and corruption are strongly negatively correlated, while Wheeler and Mody (1992) find no significant link. In part, the mixed results are the consequence of the poor quality of available measures of corruption. Corruption indexes are often composites of surveys of officials, business people, newspaper articles, and other assessments.

FDI and Economic Security

The decline in wages following a takeover by a foreign firm, discussed above, is one of the forces that may be eroding a sense of security among workers in a globalizing economy. Scheve and Slaughter (2004) note that capital mobility may make the demand for labor more elastic and may also increase uncertainty in employment or wage outcomes. Empirical analysis from the United Kingdom during the 1990s finds that increased FDI activity is positively correlated with worker perceptions of insecurity.

Similarly, three studies find job security with foreign-owned firms is lower than with domestically owned firms. In these studies, job insecurity arises because foreign-owned firms are more likely to shut down and relocate. See Bernard and Jensen (2007) in their study of the United States and Bernard and Sjoholm (2003) in their study of Indonesia. Harrison and Scorse (2004) also find an increased probability of shutdown by exporters in Indonesia, particularly in the textiles, footwear, and apparel industries.

Export Processing Zones

EPZs have grown rapidly over the last 30 years. According to the ILO (2003), 25 countries had EPZs in 1975; 116 countries had such zones in 2002, employing 13 million workers. EPZs particularly focus on the production of labor-intensive consumer goods such as clothing. EPZs are generally found to benefit the host economy through increased foreign exchange and total employment (Jayanthakumaran 2003). There may also be spillovers to the larger economy in the form of learning, human capital formation, and demonstration effects (Johansson and Nilsson 1997). Typically, wages are lower in EPZs than in the host economy in general. This effect, however, appears to simply reflect broader gender discrimination within the host economy (Madani 1999). The issue of challenging working conditions in EPZs arises from longer work hours, a more grueling pace of work, and the absence of a right to collective bargaining (ILO 2003).

Cling, Razafindrakoto, and Roubaud (2005) document the remarkable impact of the Zone Franche in Madagascar. They argue that this zone accounted for nearly three-fourths of Madagascar's goods exports for 1991–2001, making Madagascar the second largest exporter of clothing in Sub-Saharan Africa. The zone's export performance allowed Madagascar to reduce its heavy reliance on exports of agricultural products such as coffee, vanilla, cloves, and shrimp. Employment mirrored the export expansion. Between 1995 and 2001, employment in the zone rose from 3 percent to 10 percent of total employment. One-third of all private formal workers are now employed in the zone.

Cling, Razafindrakoto, and Roubaud (2007) reexamine wages and working conditions in the Zone Franche following the end of the Multifibre Arrangement (MFA; as reported in chapter 1 of this volume). Wages for zone workers declined relative to industrial wages in the formal, private sector, though they remain above wages in the informal sector. Furthermore, hours of work increased and benefits such as medical services and paid holidays were reduced. This turn of events provides some evidence that workers in the zone had captured some of the economic rents associated with the MFA.

Less rigorous analysis reaches similar conclusions to those of Cling, Razafindrakoto, and Roubaud (2005). Jayanthakumaran (2003) takes a cost-benefit approach to assessing the value of EPZs. According to his line of reasoning, an EPZ generates a social benefit only if the payment to local factors of production exceeds the opportunity cost of employment in the EPZ. With regard to labor, the question is whether there is a gap between the wage paid in the EPZ and the opportunity cost of EPZ labor. Based on estimates from Warr (1990) and Curry and Lucking (1991), Jayanthakumaran (2003) reports the following premium of EPZ wages relative to opportunity costs: Indonesia (25 percent), Korea (9 percent), Malaysia (17 percent), the Philippines (36 percent), and Sri Lanka (25 percent). That is, the wages paid in the EPZs in these five countries considerably exceed the opportunity cost of labor.

In a similar vein, Blanco de Armas and Sadni-Jallab (2002) consider the impact of EPZs in Mexico on employment patterns. They report that during the 1990s, employment in Mexico outside of the *maquiladoras* was virtually flat. In 1988, Mexican nonmaquiladora manufacturing employed 2.7 million workers. By 1990, this figure had only risen to 2.8 million and never exceeded 2.9 million in any year during the decade. By comparison, employment in the maquiladoras rose from 350,000 jobs in 1988 to 980,000 jobs in 1998. It is difficult to attribute all of this differential growth to Mexican EPZs. Investors intent on investing in Mexico may simply have been choosing maquiladoras because of their low cost as compared with other Mexican locations. Nevertheless, it appears that all of the increase in manufacturing employment in Mexico during the 1990s was for the purpose of exports and the existence of the maquiladoras may have enhanced Mexico as an export platform.

However, there is little evidence that the Mexican maquiladoras led to skill upgrading. Blanco de Armas and Sadni-Jallab (2002) report that the fraction of workers employed in the maquiladoras rated as "skilled" was only 6.6 percent in 1988 and rose only to 7.2 percent in 1998. By comparison, 27.2 percent of workers in nonmaquiladora manufacturing were rated as skilled in 1988.

By contrast, Aggarwal (2005) uses a survey approach to analyze the labor issues relevant to the success of EPZs in India, Sri Lanka, and Bangladesh. Investors were asked a range of questions relating to their reasons for selecting a particular location and were found to value physical infrastructure, tax benefits, and locations near cities and ports. For labor, investors viewed access to an educated and disciplined workforce as more important than low wages. However, investors also sought zones that were excluded from enforcement of labor laws. In fact, nearly 100 percent of respondents rated labor law exclusions as "most important."[8]

Perman et al. (2004), report that many EPZs attract responsible companies that offer attractive working conditions and competitive compensation. However, there are some important exceptions. Trade unions were not allowed in Bangladesh EPZs until November 2006; when they were permitted, restrictions on free association were imposed. Similar restrictions apply to unions in Togo. Unions were also prohibited in Kenya until 2003 and were only allowed following a series of violent confrontations between workers and anti-riot police. Even where workers' rights are legally mandated, poor enforcement may render them weak. Workers' rights organizations provide a long list of anecdotes involving violent repression of free association, gender discrimination, excess hours of work, and significant health and safety concerns. In some cases, poor working conditions in EPZs are similar to those in the economy proper and thus, are not directly attributable to EPZs. Furthermore, there are some cases in which working conditions are better and some worse than in the economy overall.

Private, Voluntary, and Intergovernmental Agreements and Working Conditions

Given the limitations of using international trade negotiations within the World Trade Organization (WTO) to manage humanitarian externalities arising from the labor practices of trading partners, the focus is now placed on other channels through which these concerns might be mediated. Freeman (1994) argues that labels can be used to identify products made under humane working conditions. Several such certification agencies are actively monitoring production facilities in Asia and Latin America. The efforts of these groups are detailed in Elliott and Freeman (2003).

Elliot and Freeman (2003) advance the case for product labeling, citing considerable evidence of the willingness of consumers to pay higher prices for humane working conditions. For example, a Marymount University survey implemented in 1995, 1996, and 1999 found that 85 percent of respondents said they would pay $1 more for a $20 item. Similarly, a University of Maryland survey undertaken in 2000 found that consumers would be willing to pay $3 more for a $20 garment. Finally, citing standard laboratory evidence from the "Dictator's Game," in which one player is instructed to split $100 with a second player, only 20 percent of players opted to keep the entire amount for themselves. The survey evidence is particularly strong where it pertains to child labor and safe working conditions. Similarly, Hiscox and Smyth (2006), in a field experiment, find a striking willingness to pay for labeled products.

Levi and Linton (2003) analyze the impact of fair trade on coffee producers, finding that coffee campaigns have improved the lives of small-scale coffee farmers and their families. The benefits accrue from increased wages, links to farming cooperatives, access to capital markets, and technological assistance. However, the coffee cooperatives are only able to sell about half of their crops at the fair price. The Fair Trade Federation (2009) estimates that global sales of fair trade products reached $2.6 billion in 2006.

CERTIFICATION

Many apparel vendors now regard acceptable working conditions as a selling point for their products and have looked to the various product-labeling agencies to certify compliance with a set of working-conditions codes. Although these certification efforts began with the intent of monitoring factory conduct, they have gradually emerged, at least in part, as a channel through which optimizing labor management practices have been transmitted from the certification industry to apparel vendors. For example, factories seeking Social Accountability International (SAI) certification may work for several years to achieve certification readiness. The process includes information sessions in labor management practices provided by SAI certified trainers. SAI, in particular, has not only sought to sell its labor standards certification as a product attribute attractive to consumers, but also to make the case to vendors that adherence to SAI-approved labor practices will increase efficiency and lower the cost of production. To this end, SAI has encouraged and supported cost-benefit analysis of achieving certification readiness.

The Kenan Institute Asia (2003) followed six Thai apparel factories between May 2000 and May 2003 as these factories worked their way toward SAI certification. Researchers weighed the cost incurred from initial and surveillance audits, training, and implementation of health and safety rules against the benefits of lower accident rates, manpower turnover, reject rates, and improved production efficiency. One of the significant challenges a factory faces in attempting to achieve certification is controlling excessive overtime hours without reducing total factory output or worker compensation. This can only be accomplished by increased capital investment unless, of course, the factory can find a strategy for increasing labor productivity. In one case, Kenan Institute Asia researchers identified a factory seeking SAI certification that learned to use pay incentives linked to individual or group performance to control excessive overtime. By contrast, a second factory in the study failed to make significant changes in its human resource management practices. Instead, they simply resorted to subcontracting work to an uncertified factory during periods of high demand. These two cases neatly demonstrate that the certification process can spur factories to search for and discover labor management practices that are both more humane and profitable—but it is possible to achieve certification without doing so.

The SAI protocol was also adopted by Chiquita Banana in Latin America. Werre (2003) documents significant benefits for workers, as a consequence. Findings include the following:

- Auditing indicated that many permanent workers were classified as temporary and, thus, did not receive full compensation and benefits. This was rectified as a consequence of the audit.
- A new Occupational Health and Environment Management system was installed in Costa Rica, resulting in a 40 percent reduction in the number of accidents.

Benefits of certification were also enjoyed by the intermediaries:

- The decline in the accident rate lowered the cost of insurance.
- Several European retailers chose Chiquita as their main supplier as a result of Chiquita's commitment to humane labor practices and sustainable agriculture.

FAIR TRADE

Although SAI is only engaged in certification, a second set of organizations engage in both monitoring and marketing. Shreck (2002) presents a case study analysis of a fair trade initiative overseen by the Fair Trade Labeling Organization (FLO) for bananas grown in the Dominican Republic. The study finds that the benefits to banana growers include the following:

- A premium of $1.75 per 40-pound box was financed by consumers.
- Some of the labeling premium paid by consumers was also used to finance road preparation and the purchase of irrigation equipment.
- Loans were available to help certified firms recover from Hurricane George in 1998 and to improve farm infrastructure and fruit quality.

Shreck (2002) also highlights some problems with this initiative:

- Many producers did not know what FLO certification implied or how to differentiate certification from other forms of development aid.

- Certified firms are more likely to devote all of their land to banana production, raising concerns about crop diversification and its benefits.

- The irrigation equipment purchased following Hurricane George created a significant debt burden that took years to repay.

- Some growers felt that the exporter was able to capture the premium. The payment structure was confusing and it was not always clear to the grower who was receiving the labeling premium.

Bacon (2005) surveyed 228 farmers in northern Nicaragua on their experience accessing organic and fair trade markets. Coffee prices between 2001 and 2003 were at their lowest levels in a century, following the disintegration of the international coffee agreement. Permanent employment in Central America's coffee market had declined by 50 percent and seasonal employment by 21 percent. As a consequence, Nicaragua had been experiencing a rural-urban migration to the urban poverty belts. Conversion of coffee agro-forestry systems in Costa Rica to treeless cattle pastures had accelerated hillside erosion (Bacon 2005, 498).

Bacon's survey results are as follows:

- Small-scale farmers did not have access to the certification procedure used to determine coffee quality and price. However, small coffee growers could gain access to the quality certification process through cooperatives and marketing associations.

- Cooperatives allocate some of the price premium paid by fair trade and organic markets to investment in infrastructure, debt retirement, housing, and education.

- Of farmers who had diversified into organic, fair trade, or roaster-direct market channels, 8 of 180 feared losing their farm to debt. By comparison, of those that did not diversify, 8 of 44 had similar fears. It should be noted, however, that this survey response procedure does not account for endogeneity—those growers with the financial wherewithal to make investments in diversification may be more financially sound than other growers.

The impact of fair trade on coffee producers in Tanzania is reported by Parrish, Luzadis, and Bentley (2005). Access to fair trade outlets increased financial capital at the farmer level by 42 percent. The study argues that fair trade organizations more closely link farmers to the global market, improve financial flows that reach the local level, and improve farmers' bargaining with the market. A similar positive outcome is reported by Doherty and Tranchell (2005) in their study of the Day Chocolate Company in Ghana. Day provides small-scale cocoa farmers in Ghana with direct access to global markets by making farmers equity owners in the company.

CORPORATE CODES OF CONDUCT

The certification and marketing of products meeting minimal labor standards has also been undertaken by some large, reputation-sensitive brands. Many Western corporations that source from factories in the south and east have developed corporate codes of conduct that establish minimum working conditions for their suppliers. Corporate codes are not without their critics. Such codes may displace government regulation or labor organizations and exist principally to limit the legal liability of the buyers. Furthermore, auditors internal to the multinational corporation may not have an interest in identifying code violations. A proliferation of codes, one for each customer, may also be confusing and inefficient for monitored factories. Complaints, in particular of monitoring fatigue, are common.

To determine the impact of corporate codes on working conditions, Locke, Qin, and Brause (2006) analyze a rich data set that includes compliance performance for 468 factories supplying Nike with footwear, apparel, and sporting equipment. Their findings are discussed below.

Factories in countries with a high rule of law index have better code compliance. Variation in the rule of law index explains 9 percent of the variation in code compliance in the absence of regional fixed effects. When regional fixed effects are introduced, rule of law loses some of its explanatory power but remains statistically significant.

Furthermore, larger factories have poorer code compliance performance than smaller factories. Locke, Qin, and Brause (2006) suggest that smaller factories may be easier to control and monitor than larger factories. However, there are two other possible explanations. First, factories presumably become large because they are more profitable. Thus, the finding that larger factories have poorer code compliance than smaller factories suggests that poor working conditions jointly produce more profitable factories and poorer compliance performance. That is, good working conditions may not be good for business. Second, very large factories may be engaged in mass production of relatively simple items whereas smaller factories are more likely to be producing higher quality, more complex products. To the extent that a more sophisticated workforce is necessary to produce higher quality products, these high-end, smaller factories may have found it profit-maximizing to employ more sophisticated labor management practices.

In addition, the frequency and nature of the contact between Nike and the factories also has a significant relationship with compliance performance. Frequent factory visits by Nike personnel, from both compliance and production units, are positively correlated with compliance performance; factories that have achieved the rank of strategic partner within the Nike supply chain have better compliance performance. Locke, Qin, and Brause (2006) suggest that Nike's sourcing and production teams encourage their main suppliers to use more sophisticated management practices such as Lean and Total Quality Management. These production systems emphasize product quality and communication within the factory. As a consequence, there may be some spillover from the management of the production process to the management of labor.

However, compliance performance is poorer for factories that have a longer relationship with Nike or that dedicate a large fraction of their production capacity to Nike. The longer relationship results are consistent with the possibility that the Nike sourcing unit has recently been developing new relationships with factories that have stronger compliance performance. Indeed, Locke, Qin, and Brause (2006) report that 43 percent of prospective factories fail Nike's initial prescreening approval process.

The result that Nike-dedicated factories have poorer compliance records is surprising, however. One would expect that the more dependent a factory is on a single buyer, the greater the leverage the buyer would have in the relationship. However, Locke, Qin, and Brause (2006) consider the possibility that multiple buyers demanding compliance performance increases the pressure a factory feels to comply with buyer demands relating to working conditions. There may also be greater learning and information-sharing across buyers, which promotes code compliance.

Locke, Qin, and Brause (2006) also ask whether the compliance auditing process improves working conditions. Of the factories in their data set, 117 were audited twice; there was a significant increase in the average audit score for the reaudited factories. It might be suspected that poorly performing factories were selected for a second audit, and the firms that survived were only those that improved their compliance performance. However, in fact, the average initial score for the reaudited factories was statistically equal to the score of the factories that were only audited once. Thus, it does not appear that the reaudited factories were drawn from the low end of the compliance performance distribution. Factories most likely to receive a second audit were strategic partners and factories that dedicated a large fraction of their production capacity to Nike. Factories in countries with weak legal labor protections were also more likely to be reaudited.

Weil (2005) finds supporting evidence that buyer-enforced code compliance can improve working conditions in his analysis of the U.S. apparel industry. The U.S. Department of Labor has put pressure on large manufacturers to monitor compliance with minimum wage laws by their subcontractors. The Labor Department conducts random inspections of these subcontracting factories. Analysis of a set of random inspection–based surveys of apparel contractors in Los Angeles for the period 1996–2000 finds that minimum wage compliance pressure is greatly increased when buyers collaborate with government agents to enforce wage laws. The prospect of lost business for a noncompliant factory poses a far greater pecuniary penalty than the fines imposed by the U.S. government. Furthermore, the probability of detection is far higher when buyers coordinate enforcement with government officials. Weil also finds that compliance performance is higher for factories producing goods requiring higher worker skills.

CODE COMPLIANCE AND THE TRANSMISSION OF LABOR-RELATED KNOWLEDGE CAPITAL

Two cases in which multinational corporations can have a mitigating effect on market failures that give rise to inefficiently poor working conditions are discussed above. First, multinationals can play a role in helping factories internalize the external effects that their working conditions have on Western consumers. Second, Harrison and Scorse (2004) identified the role that Western corporations play in weakening the monopsonistic employment practices exercised by apparel, textiles, and footwear firms in Indonesia. Corporate codes provide the third impetus to improving working conditions in developing countries. Historically, discovering profit-maximizing management practices has been a matter of some serendipity in uncovering failure in the market for information. U.S. apparel firms 80 years ago were led to experiment in labor management prices as a strategy to compete with armaments factories for labor. The working conditions exposés of the last 15 years have had a similar impact on Asian factories.

Ichniowski, Shaw, and Prennushi (1997) demonstrate for the U.S. steel industry that more sophisticated human resource management systems are positively correlated with plant-level productivity and product quality—enlightened labor management practices are good for business. However, notions of enlightened labor management are difficult to accept. Factory managers often do not change their labor management practices until external events force experimentation. Anti-sweatshop activity appears to have had a hand in precipitating precisely this type of experimentation in innovative labor practices in global apparel supply; these changes have turned out to be both more humane and more productive.

Sabel, O'Rourke, and Fung (2000) provide a critical assessment of the process and mechanisms through which multinationals may affect working conditions in global supply chains. They argue that corporations with far-flung global supply chains have "mastered the disciplines that foster excellence and innovation among their own … suppliers" (Sabel, O'Rourke, and Fung 2000, 1). The specific knowledge these firms have about continuous improvement in production efficiency and product quality can be turned toward social concerns, as well. Through setting their own corporate codes of conduct, educating factories on acceptable labor management practices, and partnering with NGOs that deliver services to workers and monitor working conditions, corporations with global supply chains can meaningfully improve the lives of workers and model exemplary corporate behavior for their competitors. Okada (2004) calls such supply chains learning chains. In streamlined global supply chains, "…modes of knowledge and skill diffusion are becoming increasingly explicit, standardized, and codified. Codification and standardization facilitate the process of accumulating and sharing common knowledge within the supply chain" (Okada 2004, 1281).

Riisgaard (2005) details the 2001 agreement between Chiquita and COLSIBA (the Coordination of Latin American Banana Workers Unions). Corporations that engage in a program of continuous improvement in labor practices may be rewarded by socially conscious consumers and stockholders. Price, quality, and productivity benefits may also accrue, to the extent that these more humane work practices are also more efficient.

Anecdotal evidence supports Sabel, O'Rourke, and Fung's (2000) theory. Compliance with corporate codes of conduct began as a policing operation during the early 1990s. Over time, however, some compliance officers became increasingly discontented with the check-list approach to compliance. One compliance officer described his practice of adopting a more holistic approach. Rather than simply noting a factory's compliance with a list of working conditions, the compliance office has begun to take each example of a failure to comply as an opportunity to teach factory management about strategies for improving its production process. In one example, the compliance officer noted that a recent change in the layout of the production floor had exposed workers to a new safety hazard. The compliance officer took the opportunity to point out to the factory that it did not have a strategy for "managing change." He then discussed with the factory the range of issues that must be addressed systematically each time a change in the production process is contemplated.[9]

Consider two further illustrations from apparel manufacturing. Compliance officers commonly focus attention on low average wages and long hours of work. Inevitably, policing wages and hours of work led some compliance officers to consider the core cause of low worker productivity.[10] During factory inspections, it was common to observe some idle workers and others with piles of garment components next to their workstations. Ultimately, compliance personnel were able to link the inefficient allocation of work on the floor to low factory productivity and, therefore, low wages and long hours of work.

The solution to this problem then lay not in policing factory conduct but, rather, providing factories with information on production technology that would balance the flow of work through the factory.

Factories have also been encouraged by their customers to introduce pay incentives linked to productivity. If a factory manager understands that a carefully designed and well-articulated payment scheme could increase productivity, the manager has an incentive to actually pay the wages promised. The hope is that code violations relating to nonpayment of wages may thus become less common in factories with incentive-based pay.[11] Thus, some of the strategies for achieving corporate code compliance could potentially raise factory profits, providing factories an incentive to voluntarily remain in compliance. Under such a scenario, the corporate code is no longer a binding constraint. Factories voluntarily adopt labor practices that exceed those required by their corporate customers. If these innovative practices relating to labor management are, in fact, profit maximizing, the challenge to corporate compliance officers is greatly diminished. In light of the fact that the corporate code is not a binding constraint for such innovating factories, compliance officers can simply observe the human resource system rather than monitor adherence to an array of complex codes. That is, innovative labor management practices provide an observable signal to the corporate compliance officer that the factory is in compliance with the corporate code.

Two empirical papers find some tentative results on the impact of corporate codes of conduct on the adoption of efficiency-enhancing labor management practices. Brown et al. (2006) examine a buyer-organized demonstration project on anemia and intestinal parasites undertaken in seven Bangalore apparel factories. The two buyers were U.S-headquartered multinationals that sourced from but did not own Indian apparel factories. A careful experimental design and identification strategy was especially important for evaluating the true impacts of treatment, because the "raw" pre-post comparison was confounded by other factors, misleadingly suggesting little benefit of the intervention. The study period for this intervention was coincident with factory organizational changes that were implemented in anticipation of the termination of the MFA on January 1, 2005.

The authors use evidence on gender, marital status, birth control practices, and anemia status to identify treated workers who should exhibit a differential impact of treatment as a result of the progression from helminthic infestation to anemia and/or treatment with a full, medically appropriate regimen of medications. The *difference-in-differences-in-differences* estimated impact of a full regimen of treatment with the deworming drug albendazole and iron supplements is 6.18, representing an 8 percent increase in productivity for anemic workers. For one ownership group that exhibited significant cross-worker externalities of treatment, productivity increased by 10 percent for the entire factory. The large productivity gains from treatment stand in sharp contrast to the very low cost ($0.08 per year per worker for the deworming drug).

Before treatment, anemic workers were found to be as productive as nonanemic workers, even controlling for age, education, and experience. The fact that treatment significantly raised the relative productivity of anemic workers implies that anemic workers have some innate ability that compensates for the adverse consequences of their poor health and, therefore, are latent high productivity workers. It is likely that anemic workers with average innate ability are terminated or self-select out of factory employment because of their poor health.

The treatment program also lowered manpower turnover, reducing the probability that an anemic worker would leave the factory during the eight-month duration of the study by as much as 38 percent. Results indicate that the retention rate improved because anemic workers valued the access to medical treatment for their poor health rather than the impact treatment had on their productivity.

The buyers directed the intervention and subsidized its cost. This role was critical for identifying this profit-increasing labor management innovation for all vendors in their supply chains for at least three reasons:

- The buyers had a stronger prior belief concerning the impact of worker health on productivity than the factory managers.

- Most vendor ownership groups were too small to experiment with more than one production system innovation at a time.

- Changes in market conditions confounded experiments in labor management practices.

The last two considerations, in particular, created substantial cross-supply-chain externalities of experimentation by a subset of vendors.

Indeed, health-related activities have become an important part of corporate social responsibility activity by multinationals. For example, Malick, Alilo, and McGuire (2004) report on the partnership between the Academy for Educational Development and ExxonMobil to produce and distribute insecticide-treated bed nets in Africa.

Intergovernmental Agreements on Trade and Labor Practices

The WTO charter provides little scope for protecting the interests of labor. Governments are limited to the use of Article XX(e), which allows the prohibition of imported goods made by prison labor. The link between labor practices and trade is more commonly found in regional trade agreements.

Charnovitz (2005) discusses the manner in which labor standards have been incorporated into regional trade agreements, detailing how labor standards can be brought into trade negotiations outside the WTO. Agreements involving the United States tend to emphasize transparency and access to courts. By comparison, the European Union is more likely to emphasize public participation and discourse. In both cases, labor provisions typically only require governments to enforce their own national laws.

NAFTA is the only agreement with an intergovernmental commission to facilitate coordination on labor issues. As of May 2005, 31 cases had been submitted to national administrative offices (Hufbauer and Schott 2005, 120.) These cases mostly involved the right to free association and trade sanctions have not been a factor in any of them. By comparison, provisions of the U.S. Generalized System of Preferences place considerable demands on recipients. Beneficiaries are expected to adopt internationally recognized labor protections—the rights to free association and collective bargaining; prohibition of forced labor and exploitative child labor; and acceptable working conditions, including minimum wages, maximum hours, and basic protections for health and safety.

Threats by the United States to withdraw preferences often trigger a dramatic response on the part of the threatened government, as documented by Compa and Vogt

(2001) and Frundt (1998). The deeper question, though, is whether this frenzied response actually improves working conditions and economic efficiency.

Schrank (2006) argues that pressure on the Dominican Republic to improve its working conditions succeeded by stimulating human resource upgrading. Skill upgrading then also facilitated the transition to more sophisticated production systems. The Dominican Republic responded to U.S. demands by (i) adopting a new labor code in 1992 that protected the rights to organize, strike, and receive a just wage; (ii) developing capacity to enforce new labor protections; and (iii) developing a fully professional set of inspectors trained to help employers comply with the law by engaging in human resource development and employing best practices relating to labor management. These training programs were paid for with a training tax imposed on firms in the EPZs. Based on interviews with industry managers, training for line workers and middle managers helped the apparel factories transition from linear to modular production systems. Industry developed more generally as newly trained workers and managers were subsequently able to enter more sophisticated product markets such as consumer electronics, information technology, and services.

Perhaps the most intriguing trade policy–related intervention concerning labor practices is the U.S.-Cambodia Textiles Agreement/ILO Better Factories Cambodia project. Polaski (2004) describes the Cambodian experiment in which the Cambodian government, the U.S. government, the ILO, NGOs, and apparel retailers partnered to expand markets for apparel factories with responsible labor management practices. Cambodia's apparel quota allocation under the MFA was linked to ILO reports on working conditions. Under the U.S.-Cambodia agreement, Cambodia received a basic quota allocation. The Cambodian government then required all textiles and apparel firms seeking an export license to participate in the ILO's Better Factories Cambodia project. Factories were inspected and received recommendations on improving workplace conditions, training in workplace management, and ongoing compliance monitoring. The U.S. government then augmented Cambodia's quotas by 9 percent in 2000 and again in 2001. In the subsequent three years (2002–04) Cambodia received quota bonuses of 9 percent, 12 percent, and 18 percent.

Polaski (2006) notes that this arrangement has three distinct features. First, the incentives were positive. Cambodia received its basic quota regardless of whether workplace conditions improved. Anti-sweatshop agitation has a downside risk for workers. Workplace conditions that appall Western consumers may be an efficient equilibrium outcome for a developing-country labor market. Anti-sweatshop agitation that ultimately forces workers into employment outcomes that are worse than sweatshop employment does not make workers better off. Thus, if Cambodia calculates that improving working conditions is not efficiency enhancing, it will not suffer a negative consequence in the form of a loss of trade.

Second, the system helped align national interests with individual factory interests. Factories with poor workplace conditions reflect badly on Cambodia as a source for reputation-sensitive buyers. Pressuring all Cambodian firms to improve working conditions simultaneously helps internalize this negative externality.

Third, factories identified by the ILO as having violations and that did not improve conditions were entered into the ILO reporting system, with the nature of the violations fully detailed. This step provided a level of transparency not available in any of the private monitoring systems.

Polaski (2006) analyzes the compliance reports from ILO inspections and finds that nearly 70 percent of factories that were inspected at least twice implemented at least one-third of the ILO-recommended changes in labor practices. The greatest progress was made on payment of wages and on health and safety, with 95 percent in compliance by the second inspection. Similarly, rights to free association are now protected in 76 percent of factories. Factories had more difficulty remedying violations concerning hours of work. Only 41 percent of factories were in full compliance with limits on overtime, and 33 percent had made no improvement.

It is difficult to assess the impact of this arrangement on productivity; however, evidence suggests that buyers were attracted to the overall package of price, quality, and working conditions offered by Cambodian factories. Polaski finds that exports of nonquota goods expanded more rapidly than quota-constrained exports. Between 1999 and 2002, quota-constrained exports from Cambodia to the United States rose by 44.8 percent. During the same period, exports of garments that were not quota controlled increased by 302 percent.

The employment and poverty impacts of the program were also striking. Employment in the Cambodian garment sector rose from 80,000 workers in 1998 to 325,000 in 2006. Employees are typically young females from rural households. Polaski (2006) reports that the typical apparel worker earns US$50 per month. By comparison, the average monthly income for an entire rural household is US$40 per month. The Asian Development Bank has documented that remittances from apparel workers to rural households has had a substantial impact on rural poverty.

Polaski (2006) also reports cost-benefit calculations. The cost of the initial three-year monitoring program was $1.4 million, which averages to about $2.33 per worker per year. The benefit to the Cambodian economy of the 9 percent increase in the 2002 quota bonus was estimated to be $56.4 million. Furthermore, 13,000 new jobs were created that year, paying wages of $9.5 million.

Despite the end of the MFA in 2005, the Better Factories Cambodia project continued. The ILO planned to continue monitoring through 2008 and to assist the Cambodian government in developing its own autonomous monitoring organization. This final step will test the ability of the ILO to develop monitoring and enforcement capacity within a national government.

Conclusions

Much of the economic analysis undertaken in the 1990s, particularly by trade specialists, was fairly optimistic: (i) the impact of trade on labor was small but largely positive; (ii) trade appeared to have little impact on wages and the distribution of income; (iii) foreign-owned and export-oriented firms paid higher wages; and (iv) there was little to no evidence of a race to the bottom in labor standards. However, the results of several empirical studies suggest that trade economists may have been underestimating the negative impact of globalization on wages and working conditions.

The literature relating globalization and working conditions is immense and yet still incomplete. In the chapters that follow, an analytical framework and country case studies provide a richer understanding of the impact that globalization has had on working conditions in several low-income countries.

Notes

1. LaRochelle-Côté (2007) regresses firm-level employment on industry-specific covariates, time-varying macroeconomic factors, applicable tariffs, the ratio of liabilities to assets, a measure of industry restructuring, and a measure of enterprise-level total factor productivity.

2. A second strand of this literature addresses the link between trade and poverty. That literature is not addressed here, but the reader is directed to three surveys: Winters, McCulloch, and McKay (2004); Goldberg and Pavcnik (2004); and Gunter and van der Hoeven (2004).

3. A similar result is found by Feenstra and Hanson (1997).

4. Ferreira and Litchfield (1999) find a similar result in their study of Chile.

5. Robertson collected data on prices and wages from Mexico's National Institute of Geography, Information, and Statistics; the Mexican Industrial Census and the National Urban Employment Survey; and the Mexican Monthly Industrial Survey.

6. Of course, there are examples with no apparent link between the tariff structure and changes in relative wages. Chamarbagwala (2006) analyzes Indian employment and unemployment data for the period 1983–2000 and finds that trade liberalization has had two distinct effects on the skill and gender distributions. Despite the fact that the highest levels of protection were provided to the import-competing industries that were most capital-, technology-, and skilled labor–intensive, India experienced a considerable widening of the skill wage gap. Trade in manufacturing benefited skilled men and trade in services benefited skilled women. Overall, the male-female wage gap narrowed for high school and college graduates.

7. Drawing mainly on evidence from Latin America, Maloney (2004), however, presents the view that informality in some countries may be preferable because it offers higher wages and more flexibility.

8. Other possible responses included "not important," "important," and "very important."

9. Confidential communication with the author, January 27, 2004.

10. Confidential communication with the author, February 13, 2004.

11. Confidential communication with the author, February 2, 2004.

References

Acemoglu, D. 2003. "Patterns of Skill Premia." *Review of Economic Studies* 70 (2): 199–230.

Aggarwal, Aradhna. 2005. "Performance of Export Processing Zones: A Comparative Analysis of India, Sri Lanka and Bangladesh." Working Paper No. 155, Indian Council for Research on International Economic Relations, New Delhi.

Aghion, P., R. Burgess, S. Redding, and F. Zilibotti. 2003. "The Unequal Effects of Liberalization: Theory and Evidence from India." Unpublished, London School of Economics.

Aitken, Brian, Ann Harrison, and Richard Lipsey. 1996. "Wages and Foreign Ownership. A Comparative Study of Mexico, Venezuela and the United States." *Journal of International Economics* 40 (3/4): 345–71.

Almeida, R. 2007. "Labor Market Effects of Foreign Owned Firms." *Journal of International Economics* 72 (1): 75–96.

Aizenman, Joshua, and Mark M. Spiegel. 2002. "Institutional Efficiency, Monitoring Costs, and the Investment Share of FDI." NBER Working Paper No. 9324, National Bureau of Economic Research, Cambridge, MA.

Artuc, Erhan, Shubham Chaudhuri, and John McLaren. 2007. "Trade Shocks and Labor Adjustment: A Structural Empirical Approach." NBER Working Paper No. 13465, National Bureau of Economic Research, Cambridge, MA. http://www.nber.org/papers/w13465.

Attanasio, I., P. Goldberg, and N. Pavcnik. 2004. "Trade Reforms and Wage Inequality in Colombia." *Journal of Development Economics* 74 (2): 331–6.

Aw, B. Y., S. Chung, and M. Roberts. 2000. "Productivity and Turnover in the Export Market: Micro Evidence from Taiwan and South Korea." *The World Bank Economic Review* 14 (1): 1–65.

Bacon, Christopher. 2005. "Confronting the Coffee Crisis: Can Fair Trade, Organic, and Specialty Coffees Reduce Small-Scale Farmer Vulnerability in Northern Nicaragua?" *World Development* 33 (3): 497–511.

Baldwin, R. E. 2003. *The Decline of the US Labor Unions and the Role of Trade.* Washington, DC: Institute for International Economics.

Başlevent, Cem, and Özlem Onaran. 2004. "The Effect of Export-Oriented Growth on Female Labor Market Outcomes in Turkey." *World Development* 32 (8): 1375–93.

Berik, G., Y. Rodgers, and J. Zveglich. 2004. "International Trade and Gender Wage Discrimination: Evidence from East Asia." *Review of Development Economics* 8 (2): 237–54.

Bernard, A., and B. Jensen. 2007. "Firm Structure, Multinationals, and Manufacturing Plant Deaths." *Review of Economics and Statistics* 89 (2): 193–204.

Bernard, A. B., J. B. Jensen, and R. Z. Lawrence. 1995. "Exporters, Jobs, and Wages in U.S. Manufacturing: 1976–1987." In *Brookings Papers on Economic Activity. Microeconomics*, 67–109. Washington, DC: The Brookings Institution.

Bernard, A., and F. Sjoholm. 2003. "Foreign Owners and Plant Survival." NBER Working Paper No. 10039, National Bureau of Economic Research, Cambridge, MA.

Bigsten, Arne, and Dick Durevall. 2006. "Openness and Wage Inequality in Kenya, 1964–2000." *World Development* 34 (3): 465–80.

Biscourp, Pierre, and Francis Kramarz. 2007. "Employment, Skill Structure and International Trade: Firm-Level Evidence for France." *Journal of International Economics* 72 (1): 22–51.

Black, S., and E. Brainerd. 2004. "Importing Equality? The Impact of Globalization on Gender Discrimination." *Industrial and Labor Relations Review* 57 (4): 540–59.

Blanco de Armas, Enrique, and Mustapha Sadni-Jallab. 2002. "A Review of the Role and Impact of Export Processing Zones in World Trade: The Case of Mexico." W.P. 02-07, Centre National de la Recherche Scientifique, Ecully, France.

Blonigen, Bruce A., Ronald B. Davies, and Keith Head. 2003. "Estimating the Knowledge-Capital Model of the Multinational Enterprise: Comment." *American Economic Review* 93 (3): 980–94.

Braconier, Henrik, Pehr-Johan Norbäck, and Dieter Urban. 2005. "Multinational Enterprises and Wage Costs: Vertical FDI Revisited." *Journal of International Economics* 67 (2): 446–70.

Brainard, S. Lael. 1997. "An Empirical Assessment of the Proximity-Concentration Trade-Off between Multinational Sales and Trade." *American Economic Review* 87 (4): 520–44.

Braun, Sebastian. 2002. "Core Labour Standards: Friends or Foe? The Case of Child Labour." *Weltwirtschaftliches Archiv* 127 (4): 765–91.

Brown, D., T. Downes, K. Eggleston, and R. Kumari. 2006. "Human Resource Management Technology Diffusion through Global Supply Chains: Productivity and Workplace Based

Health Care." Discussion Paper No. 0616, Department of Economics, Tufts University, Medford, MA.

Budd, J. W., J. Konings, and M. J. Slaughter. 2005. "Wages and International Rent Sharing in Multinational Firms." *Review of Economics and Statistics* 87 (1): 73–84.

Busse, Matthias. 2002. "Do Labor Standards Affect Comparative Advantage in Developing Countries?" *World Development* 33 (11): 1921–32.

————. 2004. "On the Determinants of Core Labour Standards: The Case of Developing Countries." *Economics Letters* 83 (2): 211–17.

Busse, Matthias, and Sebastian Braun. 2003. "Export Structure, FDI and Child Labour." Discussion Paper No. 216, Hamburg Institute of International Economics, Hamburg.

Bustos, Paula. 2005. "Rising Wage Inequality in the Argentinean Manufacturing Sector: The Impact of Trade and Foreign Investment on Technology and Skill Upgrading." Center for International Development, Harvard University, Cambridge, MA.

Chamarbagwala, Rubiana. 2006. "Economic Liberalization and Wage Inequality in India." *World Development* 34 (12): 1997–2015.

Charnovitz, Steve. 2005. "The Labor Dimension of the Emerging Free Trade Area of the Americas." In *Labor Rights as Human Rights*, ed. Philip Alston, 143–76. New York: Oxford University Press.

Cling, Jean-Pierre, Mireille Razafindrakoto, and François Roubaud. 2005. "Export Processing Zones in Madagascar: A Success Story under Threat?" *World Development* 33 (5): 785–803.

————. 2007. "Export Processing Zones in Madagascar: The Impact of the Dismantling of Clothing Quotas on Employment and Labour Standards." Working Paper No. DT/2007/06, Institut de Recherche pour le Développement, DIAL, Paris.

Compa, Lance, and Jeffrey Vogt. 2001. "Labor Rights in the Generalized System of Preferences: A 20 Year Review." *Comparative Labor Law and Policy Journal* 22 (2-3): 199–238.

Conyon, M., S. Girma, S. Thompson, and P. Wright. 2002. "The Productivity and Wage Effects of Foreign Acquisition in the United Kingdom." *Journal of Industrial Economics* 50 (1): 85–107.

Currie, Jane, and Ann E. Harrison. 1997. "Sharing the Costs: The Impact of Trade Reform on Capital and Labor in Morocco." *Journal of Labor Economics* 15 (3): S44–71.

Curry, S. R., and R. Lucking. 1991. "Report on Shadow Prices for Sri Lanka." A Report Prepared for National Planning Department, Ministry of Policy Planning and Implementation, Development and Project Planning Centre, University of Bradford, United Kingdom.

De Loecker, Jan. 2007. "Do Exports Generate Higher Productivity? Evidence from Slovenia." *Journal of International Economics* 73(1): 69–98.

Doherty, Bob, and Sophi Tranchell. 2005. "New Thinking in International Trade? A Case Study of The Day Chocolate Company." *Sustainable Development* 13 (3): 166–76.

Edmonds, Eric V., and Nina Pavcnik. 2005. "The Effect of Trade Liberalization on Child Labour." *Journal of International Economics* 65 (2): 401–41.

————. 2006. "International Trade and Child Labor: Cross-Country Evidence." *Journal of International Economics* 68 (1): 115–40.

Edwards, Sebastián, and Alejandra Cox Edwards. 1996. "Trade Liberalization and Unemployment: Policy Issues and Evidence from Chile." *Cuadernos de Economía* 33 (99): 227–50.

Elliott, Kimberly Ann, and Richard B. Freeman. 2003. "Vigilantes and Verifiers." In *Can Labor Standards Improve Under Globalization?* ed. K. A. Elliott and R. B. Freeman, 49–72 and 143–50. Washington, DC: Institute for International Economics.

FLA (Fair Labor Association). 2005. "Annual Public Report 2005." FLA, Washington, DC. http:// dev.fairlabor.org/2005.

Fair Trade Federation. 2009. "Fair Trade Facts." Washington, DC. http://www.fairtradefederation .org/ht/d/sp/i/197/pid/197.

Feenstra, Robert C., and Gordon Hanson. 1996. "Foreign Investment, Outsourcing, and Relative Wages." In *Economy of Trade Policy: Essays in Honor of Jagdish Bhagwati,* ed. R. C. Feenstra, G. Grossman, and D. Irwin, 89–128. Cambridge, MA, and London: MIT Press.

———. 1997. "Foreign Direct Investment and Relative Wages: Evidence from Mexico's Maquila-doras." *Journal of International Economics* 42 (3-4): 395–413.

———. 2003. "Global Production and Inequality: A Survey of Trade and Wages." In *Handbook of International Trade,* ed. E. Kwan Choi and James Harrigan, 146–85. Oxford: Blackwell Publishing Ltd.

Feinberg, Susan E., and Michael P. Keane. 2006. "Accounting for the Growth of MNC-Based Trade Using U.S. MNCs." *American Economic Review* 96 (5): 1515–58.

Feliciano, Z. 2001. "Workers and Trade Liberalization: The Impact of Trade Reforms in Mexico on Wages and Employment." *Industrial and Labor Relations Review* 55 (1): 95–115.

Fernandes, A. M. 2003. "Trade Policy, Trade Volumes and Plant-Level Productivity in Colombian Manufacturing Industries." Policy Research Working Paper No. 3064, World Bank, Washington, DC.

Ferreira, Francisco H. G., and Julie Litchfield. 1999. "Calm after the Storms: Income Distribution and Welfare in Chile 1987–1994." *World Bank Economic Review* 13 (3): 509–38.

Fosfuri, A., M. Motta, and T. Rønde. 2001. "Foreign Direct Investment and Spillovers through Workers' Mobility." *Journal of International Economics* 53 (1): 205–22.

Frankel, Jeffrey A., and David Romer. 1999. "Does Trade Cause Growth?" *American Economic Review* 89 (3): 379–99.

Freeman, Richard B. 1994. "A Hard-Headed Look at Labor Standards." In *International Labor Standards and Global Economic Integration: Proceedings of a Symposium,* ed. W. Sengenberger and D. Campbell. Washington, DC: U.S. Department of Labor.

Freeman, R., and R. Oostendorp. 2000. "Wages around the World." NBER Working Paper No. 8058, National Bureau of Economic Research, Cambridge, MA.

———. 2001. "Globalization and Wages." Development Research Group, World Bank, Washington, DC.

Frundt, Henry J. 1998. *Trade Conditions and Labor Rights: U.S. Initiatives, Dominican and Central American Responses.* Gainesville: University of Florida Press.

García-Cuéllar, R. 2002. "Is Trade Good for Women? Evidence for the Lower-Skilled in Pre- and Post-NAFTA Mexico." PhD dissertation, chapter 1, Economics Department, Harvard University, Cambridge, MA.

Ghose, A. K. 2003. *Jobs and Incomes in a Globalizing World.* Geneva: International Labour Office.

Girma, Sourafel, and Holger Görg. 2007. "Evaluating the Foreign Ownership Wage Premium Using a Difference-in-Differences Matching Approach." *Journal of International Economics* 72 (1): 97–112.

Goldberg, Pinelopi, and Nina Pavcnik. 2003. "The Response of the Informal Sector to Trade Liberalization." *Journal of Development Economics* 72 (2): 463–96.

———. 2004. "Trade, Inequality, and Poverty: What Do We Know? Evidence from Recent Trade Liberalization Episodes in Developing Countries." In *Brookings Trade Forum 2004*, ed. Susan Collins and Carol Graham, 223–69. Washington, DC: Brookings Institution Press.

———. 2005. "Trade Protection and Wages: Evidence from the Colombian Trade Reforms." *Journal of International Economics* 66 (1): 75–105.

Gonzaga, Gustavo, Naércio Menezes Filho, and Cristina Terra. 2006. "Trade Liberalization and the Evolution of Skill Earnings Differentials in Brazil." *Journal of International Economics* 68 (2): 345–67.

Görg, H, E. Strobl, and F. Walsh. 2002. "Why Do Foreign-Owned Firms Pay More? The Role of On-the-Job Training." IZA Discussion Paper No. 590, Institute for the Study of Labor, Bonn.

Griffith, R., and H. Simpson. 2003. "Characteristics of Foreign-Owned Firms in British Manufacturing." NBER Working Paper No. 9573, National Bureau of Economic Research, Cambridge, MA.

Gunter, Bernhard G., and Rolph van der Hoeven. 2004. "The Social Dimension of Globalization: A Review of the Literature." *International Labour Review* 143 (1-2): 7–37.

Hanson, Gordon H. 2007. "Globalization, Labor Income, and Poverty in Mexico." In *Globalization and Poverty*, ed. Ann E. Harrison, 417–56. Chicago: University of Chicago Press.

Hanson, G., and A. Harrison. 1999. "Trade Liberalization and Wage Inequality in Mexico." *Industrial and Labor Relations Review* 52 (2): 271–88.

Hanson, Gordon, Raymond J. Mataloni, and Matthew J. Slaughter. 2003. "Vertical Production Networks in Multinational Firms." NBER Working Paper No. 9723, National Bureau of Economic Research, Cambridge, MA.

Harrison, A. 1994. "Productivity, Imperfect Competition and Trade Reform: Theory and Evidence." *Journal of International Economics* 36 (1-2): 53–73.

Harrison, A., and G. Hanson. 1999. "Who Gains from Trade Reform? Some Remaining Puzzles." *Journal of Development Economics* 59 (1): 125–54.

Harrison, Ann, and Ana L. Revenga. 1998. "Labor Markets, Foreign Investment and Trade Policy Reform." In *Trade Policy Reform: Lessons and Implications*, ed. J. Nash and W. Takacs. Washington, DC: World Bank.

Harrison, Ann, and Jason Scorse. 2004. "Moving Up or Moving Out? Anti-Sweatshop Activists and Labor Market Outcomes." NBER Working Paper No. 10492, National Bureau of Economic Research, Cambridge, MA.

Hay, D. A. 2001. "The Post-1990 Brazilian Trade Liberalization and the Performance of Large Manufacturing Firms: Productivity, Market Share and Profits." *Economic Journal* 111 (473): 620–41.

Head, Judith. 1998. "Ek Het Niks-I Have Nothing: The Impact of European Union Policies on Women Canning Workers in South Africa." University of Capetown.

Helpman, Elhanan. 1984. "A Simple Theory of International Trade with Multinational Corporations." *Journal of Political Economy* 92 (3): 300–16.

Hiscox, Michael J., and Nicholas F. B. Smyth. 2006. "Is There Consumer Demand for Improved Labor Standards? Evidence from Field Experiments in Social Labeling." Department of Government, Harvard University.

Ho, Lok Sang, Xiangdong Wei, and Wai Chung Wong. 2005. "The Effect of Outward Processing Trade on Wage Inequality: The Hong Kong Case." *Journal of International Economics* 67 (1): 241–57.

Huberman, Michael. 2002. "International Labor Standards and Market Integration before 1913: A Race to the Top?" University of Montreal, Paper prepared for the conference "The Political Economy of Globalization: Can the Past Inform the Present?" Trinity College, Dublin, August 29–31.

Huberman, Michael, and Wayne Lewchuk. 2002. "European Economic Integration and the Labour Compact, 1850–1913." *European Review of Economic History* 7 (1): 3–4.

Hufbauer, Gary Clyde, and Jeffrey J. Schott. 2005. *NAFTA Revisited: Achievements and Challenges.* Washington, DC: Institute for International Economics.

Hussain, M., and K. Maskus. 2003. "Child Labour Use and Economic Growth: An Econometric Analysis." *The World Economy* 26 (7): 993–1017.

ILO (International Labour Office). 2003. "Employment and Social Policy in Respect of Export Processing Zones (EPZs)." GB.285/ESP/5, Committee on Employment and Social Policy, International Labour Office, Geneva.

Ichniowski, C., K. Shaw, and G. Prennushi. 1997. "The Effects of Human Resource Management Practices on Productivity: A Study of Steel Finishing Lines." *American Economic Review* 87 (3): 291–313.

Jayanthakumaran, K. 2003. "Benefit-Cost Appraisals of Export Processing Zones: A Survey of the Literature." *Development Policy Review* 21 (1): 51–65.

Johansson, H., and L. Nilsson. 1997. "Export Processing Zones as Catalysts." *World Development* 25 (12): 2115–28.

Kabeer, Naila. 2000. *The Power to Choose: Bangladeshi Women and Labour Market Decisions in London and Dhaka.* New York: Verso.

Kenan Institute Asia. 2003. "SA8000 Implementation: Cost-Benefit Analysis in Thailand." Unpublished, Bangkok, Thailand.

Kim, E. 2000. "Trade Liberalization and Productivity Growth in Korean Manufacturing Industries: Price Protection, Market Power and Scale Efficiency." *Journal of Development Economics* 62 (1): 55–83.

Kucera, David. 2002. "Core Labor Standards and Foreign Direct Investment." *International Labour Review* 141 (1-2): 31–69.

Lal, Deepak. 1986. "Stolper-Samuelson-Rybczynski in the Pacific: Real Wages and Real Exchange Rates in the Philippines, 1956–1978." *Journal of Development Economics* 21 (1): 181–204.

LaRochelle-Côté, Sébastien. 2007. "Tariff Reduction and Employment in Canadian Manufacturing." *Canadian Journal of Economics* 40 (3): 843–60.

Levi, Margaret, and April Linton. 2003. "Fair Trade: A Cup at a Time?" *Politics and Society* 31 (3): 407–32.

Levinsohn, James. 1999. "Employment Responses to International Liberalization in Chile." *Journal of International Economics* 47 (2): 321–44.

Lichtenberg, R., and D. Siegel. 1990. "The Effect of Ownership Change on the Employment and Wages of Central-Office and Other Personnel." *Journal of Law and Economics* 33: 383–408.

Lipsey, R., and F. Sjoholm. 2001. "Foreign Direct Investment and Wages in Indonesian Manufacturing." NBER Working Paper No. 8299, National Bureau of Economic Research, Cambridge, MA.

———. 2003. "Foreign Firms and Indonesia Wages: A Panel Study." NBER Working Paper No. 9417, National Bureau of Economic Research, Cambridge, MA.

Locke, Richard M., Fei Qin, and Alberto Brause. 2006. "Does Monitoring Improve Labor Standards?" Working Paper 24, Corporate Social Responsibility Initiative, Harvard University.

Madani, D. 1999. "A Review of the Role and Impact of Export Processing Zones." Working Paper No. 2238, World Bank, Washington, DC.

Malick, Diara, Martin Alilo, and David McGuire. 2004. "Corporate Social Responsibility and Public-Private Partnership: The Case of the Academy for Educational Development and ExxonMobil." *Development* 47 (3): 69–77.

Maloney, William F. 2004. "Informality Revisited." *World Development* 32 (7): 1159–78.

Markusen, James R. 1984. "Multinationals, Multi-Plant Economics, and the Gains from Trade." *Journal of International Economics* 16 (3-4): 205–26.

Martins, Pedro S. 2004. "Do Foreign Firms Really Pay Higher Wages? Evidence from Different Estimators." IZA Discussion Paper No. 1388, Institute for the Study of Labor, Bonn.

Matusz, Steven J., and David Tarr. 1999. "Adjusting to Trade Policy Reform." Policy Research Working Paper No. 2142, World Bank, Washington, DC.

Milner, Chris, and Peter Wright. 1998. "Modelling Labour Market Adjustment to Trade Liberalisation in an Industrialising Economy." *Economic Journal* 108 (447): 509–28.

Moreira, Maurìcio M., and Sheila Najberg. 2000. "Trade Liberalisation in Brazil: Creating or Exporting Jobs?" *Journal of Development Studies* 36 (3): 78–99.

Neumayer, Eric, and Indra de Soysa. 2004. "Trade Openness, Foreign Direct Investment and Child Labor." *World Development* 33 (1): 43–63.

———. 2005a. "Globalization and the Rights to Free Association and Collective Bargaining." *World Development* 34 (1): 31–49.

———. 2005b. "Globalization, Women's Economic Rights and Forced Labor." Labor and Demography Paper No. 0509011, EconWPA.

Noguer, Marta, and Marc Siscart. 2005. "Trade Raises Income: A Precise and Robust Result." *Journal of International Economics* 65 (2): 447–60.

OECD (Organisation for Economic Co-operation and Development). 1996. *Trade, Employment and Labour Standards: A Study of Core Workers' Rights and International Trade*. Paris.

———. 2000. *International Trade and Core Labour Standards*. Paris.

Okada, Aya. 2004. "Skills Development and Interfirm Learning Linkages under Globalization: Lessons from the Indian Automobile Industry." *World Development* 32 (7): 1265–88.

Oman, Charles. 2000. *Policy Competition for Foreign Direct Investment: A Study of Competition among Governments to Attract FDI.* Paris: OECD.

Oostendorp, Remco H. 2004. "Globalization and the Gender Wage Gap." Policy Research Working Paper No. 3256, World Bank, Washington, DC.

Pagés-Serra, Carmen, and Gustavo Marquez. 1998. "Trade and Employment: Evidence from Latin America and the Caribbean." RES Working Paper No. 4108, Inter-American Development Bank, Washington, DC.

Parrish, Bradley D., Valeria A. Luzadis, and William R. Bentley. 2005. "What Tanzania's Coffee Farmers Can Teach the World: A Performance-Based Look at the Fair Trade-Free Trade Debate." *Sustainable Development* 13: 177–89.

Pavcnik, N. 2002. "Trade Liberalization, Exit, and Productivity Improvements: Evidence from Chilean Plants." *Review of Economic Studies* 69 (1,238): 245–76.

Pavcnik, N., A. Blom, P. Goldberg, and N. Schady. 2004. "Trade Liberalization and Industry Wage Structure: Evidence from Brazil." *World Bank Economic Review* 18 (3): 319–44.

Perman, Sarah, Laurent Duvillier, Natacha David, John Eden, and Samuel Grumiau. 2004. "Behind the Brand Names: Working Conditions and Labour Rights in Export Processing Zones." International Confederation of Free Trade Unions, Brussels.

Polaski, Sandra. 2004. "Cambodia Blazes a New Path to Economic Growth and Job Creation." Carnegie Paper No. 51, Carnegie Endowment for International Peace, Washington, DC.

———. 2006. "Harnessing Global Forces to Create Decent Work: A Successful Experiment in the Cambodian Apparel Sector." Carnegie Endowment for International Peace, Washington, DC.

Porto, Guido G. 2006. "Using Survey Data to Assess the Distributional Effects of Trade Policy." *Journal of International Economics* 70 (1): 140–60.

Rama, Martín. 1994. "The Labor Market and Trade Reform in Manufacturing." In *The Effects of Protectionism on a Small Country: The Case of Uruguay*, ed. M. Connolly and J. de Melo. World Bank Regional and Sectoral Studies, 108–23. Washington, DC: World Bank.

———. 1996. "The Consequences of Doubling the Minimum Wage: The Case of Indonesia." Policy Research Working Paper No. 1643, World Bank, Washington, DC.

———. 2003. "Globalization and the Labor Market." *The World Bank Research Observer* 18 (2): 159–86.

Revenga, Ana. 1997. "Employment and Wage Effects of Trade Liberalization: The Case of Mexican Manufacturing." *Journal of Labor Economics* 15 (3): S20–S43.

Riisgaard, Lone. 2005. "International Framework Agreements: A New Model for Securing Working Rights?" *Industrial Relations* 44 (4): 707–37.

Robbins, Donald, and T. H. Grindling. 1999. "Trade Liberalization and the Relative Wages for More-Skilled Workers in Costa Rica." *Review of Development Economics* 3 (2): 140–54.

Robertson, R. 2004. "Relative Prices and Wage Inequality: Evidence from Mexico." *Journal of International Economics* 64 (2): 387–409.

Robertson, Raymond, and Donald H. Dutkowsky. 2002. "Labor Adjustment Costs in a Destination Country: The Case of Mexico." *Journal of Development Economics* 67 (1): 29–54.

Rodrik, Dani. 1996. "Labor Standards in International Trade: Do They Matter and What We Do
about Them." In *Emerging Agenda for Global Trade: High Stakes for Developing Countries*, ed.
R. Lawrence, D. Rodrik, and J. Whalley, 35–79. Washington, DC: Overseas Development
Council.

———. 1998. "Why Do More Open Economies Have Bigger Governments?" *Journal of Political
Economy* 106 (5): 997–1033.

———. 1999. "Democracies Pay Higher Wages." *The Quarterly Journal of Economics* 114 (3):
707–38.

Sabel, Charles, Dara O'Rourke, and Archon Fung. 2000. "Ratcheting Labor Standards: Regulation
for Continuous Improvement in the Global Workplace." The Center for Law and Economic
Studies, Columbia Law School.

Schank, Thorsten, Claus Schnabel, and Joachim Wagner. 2007. "Do Exporters Really Pay Higher
Wages? First Evidence from German Linked Employer-Employee Data." *Journal of International Economics* 72 (1): 52–74.

Scheve, Kenneth, and Matthew J. Slaughter. 2004. "Economic Insecurity and the Globalization of
Production." *American Journal of Political Science* 48 (4): 662–74.

Schleifer, A., and L. Summers. 1988. "Breach of Trust in Hostile Takeovers." In *Corporate Takeovers:
Causes and Consequences*, ed. A. Auerbach, 33–68. Chicago: University of Chicago Press.

Schrank, Andrew. 2006. "Labor Standards and Human Resources: A Natural Experiment in an
Unlikely Laboratory." Department of Sociology, University of New Mexico, Albuquerque.

Shreck, Aimee. 2002. "Just Bananas? Fair Trade Banana Production in the Dominican Republic."
International Journal of Sociology of Agriculture and Food 10 (2): 13–23.

Singh, Ajit, and Ann Zammit. 2004. "Labour Standards and the 'Race to the Bottom': Rethinking
Globalization and Workers' Rights From Developmental and Solidaristic Perspectives." *Oxford
Review of Economic Policy* 20 (1): 85–104.

Stolper, W. F., and P. A. Samuelson. 1941. "Protection and Real Wages." *Review of Economic Studies*
9: 58–73.

Te Velde, D., and O. Morrissey. 2003. "Do Workers in Africa Get a Wage Premium if Employed in
Firms Owned by Foreigners?" *Journal of African Economies* 12 (1): 41–73.

Tokman, V. 1997. "Jobs and Solidarity: Challenges for the Post-Adjustment in Latin America." In
Economic and Social Development into the XXI Century, ed. L. Emmerij, 449–71. Washington,
DC: Inter-American Development Bank.

Topalova, P. 2004. "Trade Liberalization and Firm Productivity: The Case of India." IMF Working
Paper 04/28, International Monetary Fund, Washington, DC.

———. 2007. "Trade Liberalization, Poverty, and Inequality: Evidence from Indian Districts."
In *Globalization and Poverty*, ed. Ann E. Harrison, 291–336. Chicago: University of Chicago
Press.

Townsend, James. 2007. "Do Tariff Reductions Affect the Wages of Workers in Protected Industries? Evidence from the Canada-U.S. Free Trade Agreement." *Canadian Journal of Economics*
40 (1): 69–92.

Utar, Hâle. 2007. "Import Competition and Employment Dynamics." Department of Economics, University of Colorado at Boulder.

Van Biesebroeck, J. 2005. "Exporting Raises Productivity in sub-Saharan African Manufacturing Firms." *Journal of International Economics* 67 (2): 373–91.

Wacziarg, Romain, and Jessica Seddon Wallack. 2004. "Trade Liberalization and Intersectoral Labor Movements." *Journal of International Economics* 64 (2): 411–39.

Warr, P. 1990. "Export Processing Zones." In *Export Promotion Strategies*, ed. C. Milner, 130–62. New York: Wheatsheaf.

Wei, Shang-Jin. 2000a. "How Taxing is Corruption on International Investors?" *Review of Economics and Statistics* 82 (1): 1–11.

———. 2000b. "Local Corruption and Global Capital Flows." *Brookings Papers on Economic Activity* 31 (2000-2): 303–46.

Weil, David. 2005. "Public Enforcement/Private Monitoring: Evaluating a New Approach to Regulating the Minimum Wage." *Industrial and Labor Relations Review* 58 (2): 238–57.

Werre, Marco. 2003. "Implementing Corporate Responsibility: The Chiquita Case." *Journal of Business Ethics* 44 (2-3): 247–60.

Wheeler, David, and Ashoka Mody. 1992. "International Investment Location Decisions: The Case of U.S. Firms." *Journal of International Economics* 33 (1-2): 57–86.

Williamson, Jeffrey G. 2005. "Winners and Losers over Two Centuries of Globalization." In *WIDER Perspectives on Global Development*, UNU-WIDER, 136–74. New York: Palgrave Macmillan.

Winters, L. Alan. 2000. "Trade Liberalization and Poverty." Discussion Paper 7, Poverty Research Unit, University of Sussex.

Winters, L. Alan, Neil McCulloch, and Andrew McKay. 2004. "Trade Liberalization and Poverty: The Evidence So Far." *Journal of Economic Literature* 42 (1): 72–115.

Wood, A. 1995. "How Trade Hurt Unskilled Workers." *Journal of Economic Perspectives* 9 (3): 57–80.

World Bank. 2003. "Race to the Top: Attracting and Enabling Global Sustainable Business, Business Survey Report." Corporate Social Responsibility Practice, World Bank, Washington, DC.

Yeaple, Stephen R. 2003. "The Role of Skill Endowments in the Structure of U.S. Outward Foreign Direct Investment." *Review of Economics and Statistics* 85 (3): 726–34.

CHAPTER 3

Globalization and Working Conditions: A Framework for Country Studies

Raymond Robertson

This chapter presents a framework for analyzing the link between globalization and working conditions in developing countries. The comprehensive literature review in chapter 2 of this volume reveals a wide range of possible approaches to studying this link, ranging from firm-level case studies to econometric analyses of aggregate data. Because there are many possible ways to analyze the effects of globalization on working conditions, it is important to establish the criteria that guide the framework presented in this chapter—relevance, comparability, and feasibility.

Each country's history, economic conditions, and institutions are unique; hence, identifying and incorporating each country's individual circumstances is necessary for a successful country study. A meaningful study will address dimensions of globalization that define the country's experience with globalization. For example, countries that experience globalization mainly through imports that compete with domestic production are different from countries that experience globalization through low-wage exports. Therefore, it is important first to characterize the country's experience with globalization.

Likewise, the dimensions of working conditions that are relevant for each country need to be identified. The way in which globalization is defined will shape the thinking about globalization's effects on working conditions and, therefore, the appropriate way to study the link. As with globalization, the definition of working conditions will affect the choice of an analytical approach. Therefore, the second section of this chapter provides a scheme for defining working conditions.

Cross-country comparisons require that differences in methodology be minimized across countries to ensure meaningful comparison of results. The third section, therefore, contains a general theoretical framework that links the various measures of globalization and the various measures of working conditions. This section also discusses how previous studies approached the issue and what these studies reveal about the effects of globalization on working conditions in developing countries.

The theoretical framework provides guidance about appropriate data and an empirical approach. The data and the empirical approach should be comparable across countries, which implies that relevance and comparability criteria are constrained somewhat by feasibility. For the framework to be feasible it must be based on data that are reasonably available; yet, these data must be comparable across countries. The available data need to be collected at the appropriate level of aggregation and cover comparable populations and variables. In the past, data availability has constrained the ability of researchers to conduct comparable cross-country studies.

The fourth section of this chapter contains a step-by-step approach to implementing a study of working conditions in developing countries using the proposed framework. This section includes a discussion of appropriate data, methodology, and critical estimation issues that should be incorporated into an effective study. The goal of the section is to facilitate the application of this approach to generate high-quality studies that will expand the understanding of how globalization affects workers in developing countries.

Defining Globalization

The first step in studying the effects of globalization is to carefully identify the mechanism of globalization and understand how policy and global trends affect it. The term "globalization" could encompass the transmission of ideas; the intermingling of cultures; the preservation or loss of national identity; exchanges of technology, capital, workers, and products across borders; and the role of international nongovernmental organizations. While these are all important concepts, most economic studies focus on migration, trade, or foreign investment, for three important reasons. The first is that flows of labor, goods, and capital are often either the primary mechanism or the motivation for most definitions of globalization. When pressed for a formal definition, many people who use the term "globalization" have some aspect of migration, trade, or investment in mind. A second reason is that migration, trade, and investment are generally more measurable than other aspects of globalization (such as culture or ideas). Third, barriers to two of these—trade and investment—have been significantly reduced since the late 1980s. It is possible that the wave of liberalization of trade and investment has been driving the current "era of globalization" in developing countries.

The framework and subsequent studies in this volume primarily focus on trade and investment. Although migration flows have been increasing and remittances are playing an increasingly important role in many migrant-sending countries, restrictions on migration have not significantly changed. Furthermore, in most countries, the link between globalization and working conditions seems more direct when globalization is defined as trade or investment.

The second step is to understand the nature of changes in globalization. Both the speed and dimensions of globalization are relevant to understanding how globalization affects workers. The remainder of this section, therefore, discusses facets of trade, foreign investment, and liberalization.

TRADE

Globalization, in its narrow economic definition, occurs through imports and exports of goods. Trade liberalization generally involves reducing tariffs, quotas, and other barriers designed to reduce imports. Exports may increase if trading partners lower barriers or as a result of a domestic export-promotion policy.

Services are playing an increasingly important role in international trade. Services fall into two categories: professional services (insurance, banking, and accounting) and less skill-intensive services (personal services). Professional services account for most of the rise in trade in services. Concerns about working conditions are less relevant for professional services than for manufacturing. In addition, governments are only now starting to collect data on trade in services. Therefore, while services are important, most studies focus on trade in goods and the remainder of this chapter will maintain that focus. Imports, exports, intraindustry trade, and total trade have different effects on workers, and each is considered in turn below.

Imports

Typically, the main concern with imports is that they increase competition for domestic firms. Facing increased competition, domestic firms may feel pressure to lower prices, and to lower prices they must lower costs. Lowering (or not improving) working conditions is one way to reduce costs. An increase in imports, however, does not necessarily lead to rising import competition. If imports complement domestic production, imports can lower costs and encourage domestic production. If, however, imports are perfect substitutes for domestic products, rising imports will, at best, hamper growth of domestic firms and, at worst, eliminate domestic production. Furthermore, while lowering trade barriers is generally followed by increased imports, the amount that imports increase may not be a direct function of the tariff reduction. Therefore, there is no single link between imports and working conditions, or between imports and competition faced by domestic firms.

The most accurate way to assess the competition posed by imports would be to compare the prices of imported goods with prices of identical domestic goods (box 3.1). The lack of appropriate data makes this a difficult task in practice. Another way to assess the degree of competition between domestic goods and imports is to estimate the elasticity of substitution between imported goods and domestic goods, which requires detailed consumption data (for consumer goods) and production data (for imported inputs used by domestic firms).

The most practical approach is to compare the quantity of imports to the size of domestic production (commonly known as the "import penetration ratio"). When using this approach, industries must be defined as specifically as possible to prevent invalid comparisons.

Exports

Changes in exports may be highly correlated with changes in imports. In fact, globalization is often thought of as a simultaneous increase in both, resulting in increased global "engagement" overall. Exports may increase with imports for several reasons. First, increasing foreign demand might coincide with domestic trade liberalization and the rise in

BOX 3.1 Quantities or Prices?

Richardson (1995) made an important contribution to the trade and wages debate by using trade theory to raise concerns about the use of imports as a measure of globalization. One of his main points was that growth, or business-cycle expansion, could (and usually does) induce an increase in import quantities as a result of rising demand. He suggested that it is important to include changes in output prices in analyses of globalization, because an increase in imports accompanied by an increase in import prices could have positive implications for workers. It is, therefore, important to have an appropriate theoretical foundation when choosing variables.

exports and imports might simply be coincidental. Second, exports may rise as a result of reciprocal liberalization. If a country has a trade agreement with a partner, they may both reduce tariffs, thus causing imports and exports to rise at the same time. Third, if a country imports parts for assembly, exports of final goods (often in the same industry) will increase.

Exports may also be independent of rising imports. Rising exports are also often the result of specific government policies designed to encourage exports. For example, the high-performing East Asian countries used government-directed export-promotion policies to increase exports. Exports may, therefore, increase in the same or different sectors than those affected by stronger import penetration. As a result, job destruction will take place in some sectors while job creation occurs in others, possibly in different locations.

The effect of exports on employment and working conditions may differ depending on the nature of the goods that are being produced.[1] In fact, empirical evidence is mixed (see box 3.2). One basic criterion that determines these effects is the technological complexity of the goods' production, which can range between two extremes. At one end is simple assembly of imported inputs. The goods can range from apparel to computers, but the production process is simply assembly. At the other extreme is original brand-name manufacturing in which the exports are products that are designed domestically and sold in foreign markets under a unique brand name (often associated with specific retailers in developed countries). These effects differ because working conditions generally improve with technological complexity, and technological complexity often rises with worker training and human capital. The result is that the correlation between exports and working conditions is not necessarily linear.

> BOX 3.2 **Export Studies Find Mixed Effects**
>
> Gruben and McLeod (2006) find that increased exports of textiles and apparel increased both female and male schooling and decreased the incidence of child labor in developing countries. They also note that a survey conducted in Bangladesh and Indonesia reported that exporting firms paid higher wages than did firms that produced solely for the domestic market, while Berik (2000) finds that export orientation was negatively related to wages in Taiwan, China.

Another issue that arises with a growing export orientation is the way in which contractual relationships affect working conditions and wages. Firms that produce for export under contract with foreign firms may be more likely to adopt different working conditions because of pressure exerted by the foreign firm. If higher working standards are important to the foreign firm, the contracting firms may increase working standards to comply with the preferences of the foreign firm. Elliott and Freeman (2003) describe several cases in which pressure from foreign affiliates led to changes in working conditions.

Intraindustry Trade and Total Trade

Intraindustry trade is defined as simultaneous imports and exports of similar products, and is extremely common today, accounting for more than 60 percent of world trade. Intraindustry trade is often linked to production fragmentation, such as outsourcing and assembly-based trade. The effects of such imports are different from the effects of imports of consumption goods; these imported inputs may actually enhance domestic production for firms that use imported inputs, while increasing competition for firms that produce inputs. These imports are strongly correlated with exports. Therefore, in cases where intraindustry trade is important, one common approach is to use total trade instead of disaggregating imports and exports.

Total trade flows often capture effects on working conditions that are not accurately captured when imports and exports are considered separately because imports and exports may have confounding effects. Because imports can be either complements or substitutes for domestic production, and exports of different levels of sophistication can have opposite effects, total trade can capture the net effect of these forces. Total trade also captures the net effects of interindustry and intraindustry trade and thus is the appropriate instrument for capturing aggregate effects of globalization.

FOREIGN DIRECT INVESTMENT

Foreign investment can be categorized as either portfolio or direct investment. Portfolio investment includes stocks, bonds, and other very mobile assets that may not have any direct impact at the firm level. In contrast, foreign direct investment (FDI) usually includes physical plants and assets, which are generally considered to be more relevant for an analysis of working conditions.

As with trade, there is no clear inherent link between FDI and working conditions (box 3.3). Two critical aspects of FDI have different implications for workers. The first is the orientation of the foreign firms' production, which can be directed at either its own domestic market or foreign markets. The second is ownership share. Each of these is discussed in detail below.

Production Orientation

The literature defines two ways that foreign firms could produce complementary products—through "forward" and through "backward" links. Foreign firms' products could be new varieties that are not direct substitutes for domestic products, and therefore just expand the product space, a forward link. Additionally, foreign firms can use inputs produced by domestic firms or produce inputs for domestic firms, either of which is a backward link. When

BOX 3.3 FDI Studies Generate Conflicting Results

Slaughter (2002) finds that inward FDI is positively and significantly related to skill upgrading (which should imply rising average wages) across several countries, while Berik (2000) finds that outward FDI is negatively (but not significantly) related to wages in Taiwan, China. Mehmet and Tavakoli (2003) find that FDI is positively related to GDP growth in the Philippines and Singapore, but is negatively related to GDP growth in Thailand and China. Their results also show that FDI is positively related to real wages in the Philippines, but negatively related to wages in China, Singapore, and Thailand. Coe, Helpman, and Hoffmaister (1997) find that the research and development capital stock of a country's trading partners (the countries from which they import machinery and equipment) produces substantial spillovers and is positively and significantly related to total factor productivity, though the effects are greater for East Asian countries than for other regions.

complementary with domestic firms, FDI can "crowd in" domestic investment; that is, foreign investment may encourage domestic investment, expand economic activity, and increase labor demand. Market structure and regulatory institutions also shape the role of FDI in the domestic economy, which is particularly relevant for investment in public goods, such as utilities.

Foreign firms may enter a market to avoid import tariffs and still serve the domestic market, thus circumventing domestic production protections. In that way, foreign firms increase competition for domestic firms. The degree of competition depends on the degree of substitutability between goods produced by foreign companies and domestic goods. In this situation, FDI has much the same effect as imports that compete with domestic producers: it puts pressure on firms to lower costs, which may adversely affect working conditions.

Alternatively, foreign firms may enter to produce goods intended for export. Goods produced for export may be simple assembly, or might incorporate more technology and concomitant opportunity for domestic advancement. Firms that produce for foreign markets are less likely to compete with domestic firms, and therefore may directly increase the demand for labor.

Ownership Share

Foreign firms can either build new plants or acquire existing plants. New plants may be 100 percent foreign-owned or be a joint venture, with a mix of foreign and domestic capital. Plants with 100 percent foreign ownership may have more foreign links and import more technology. Alvarez and Robertson (2002), for example, suggest that firms that are totally foreign-owned are less likely to engage in research and technological upgrading, but these firms may also be more likely to use state of the art technology. Firms with mixed ownership may be more likely to engage in technological upgrading and may also cause "spillovers," with effects that are more extensive than those with just foreign capital.

Foreign firms can directly affect employment and working conditions if they have different policies than those of the host country. Foreign firms may also affect other firms in the market. These spillover effects have received much attention in the economics literature, but there is little agreement about the extent to which foreign firms affect domestic firms. Foreign firms may increase labor demand and therefore cause wages in the entire labor market to increase. They may also set industry standards that competing firms are compelled to follow. The concept of spillovers often justifies studying the effects of FDI on industry-level employment and working conditions.

FACETS OF LIBERALIZATION

Countries can become increasingly exposed to foreign markets in three ways. First, global trends, such as falling transportation costs, may reduce what Lall (2002) calls a country's natural isolation. Second, a country's trading partner may liberalize trade or investment (for example, ending the Multifibre Arrangement). Third, a country may change its own barriers to trade and investment. Liberalization can be slow or rapid; industry-specific or broadly based; and unilateral, bilateral, or multilateral. These differences affect the methodology of the country study, the choice of measures, and the relevant time frame.

Speed

Liberalization can be slow or rapid. Examples of slow liberalization include a gradual phase out of tariffs and a gradual decline in transportation costs. An example of sudden liberalization would be joining the World Trade Organization and immediately adopting a conforming tariff code. How different rates of liberalization contribute to its success has engendered much debate. Liberalization speed is especially relevant when focusing on worker wages or displacement (discussed below). In particular, liberalization speed will affect the relevant time frame for the empirical study. Trade, migration, and FDI can all affect wages and working conditions. Box 3.4, below, describes a study that compares these forces directly following Mexico's liberalization.

BOX 3.4 An Example Comparing Trade, Migration, and FDI on Absolute Wages

This box provides an example that directly compares different measures of globalization on wages in Mexico. Mexico's liberalization was characterized by significant increases in trade, migration, and FDI, creating an excellent opportunity to compare these forces simultaneously.

Globalization. Trade volumes, foreign investment, and migration controls during liberalization era

Working conditions. Measured using absolute real wage levels (relative to U.S. wages)

Data. The data are derived from a time series of household surveys. The data are not panel, so this study allocates labor to different age-education categories, then takes the average wage of each cell divided by the average wage of U.S. workers in the same age-education group, and uses these averages as the dependent variable.

Theoretical framework. Robertson's (2005) theoretical framework assumes that workers are not mobile across cities and that the effects of the driving variables are not diffused beyond the individual city-cells. A simple supply and demand model motivates the comparison of the effects of trade, FDI, and border enforcement on absolute wage levels in Mexico. Absolute Mexican wages are normalized by U.S. wage levels to provide a basis for comparison.

Estimation equation. The estimation regression applied is

$$w_{ict} = \alpha_0 + \alpha_1 time + \beta_1 FDI_{ct} + \beta_2 Trade_t + \beta_3 Migration_{ct} + e_{it},$$

in which w represents wages for worker group i in city c at time t. The variable t represents a time trend, and *FDI*, *Trade*, and *Migration* represent variables that capture these aspects of globalization. Robertson (2005) earlier identifies FDI as being export oriented, and, because Mexico has a large share of intraindustry trade, total trade rather than imports and exports is used to capture the effects of trade. The analysis is a quantitative study in that it uses trade and FDI volumes and does not focus on a pre- and post-event analysis. This framework allows the study to directly compare the various effects of different measures of globalization on wage levels. The results suggest that total trade contributes to rising wages, but border enforcement (as a measure of migration costs) lowers wages. The results for FDI are mixed, which is supported by previous research that shows that firms in Mexico with 100 percent foreign ownership are less likely to invest in innovation at the firm level.

SOURCE: Robertson 2005.

Dimension

Trade liberalization can be horizontal or vertical. Horizontal liberalization reduces tariffs across the board or for a "large" number of industries. The degree of tariff reduction for various industries may affect relative prices, depending on whether all tariffs are reduced equally. Vertical liberalization reduces tariffs in one or a small number of industries. Vertical liberalization changes relative prices and will have a more localized effect than horizontal liberalization.

Defining Working Conditions

The first goal of this section is to decompose the general concepts of employment, wages, and working conditions to identify precisely the variables of interest for an empirical study. The second goal is to relate each variable to the theoretical framework, discussing caveats as appropriate.

The third goal is to discuss the current state of economic knowledge as it relates to each variable. However, the knowledge of the way in which globalization affects working conditions (employment, wages, and other facets) is limited, especially for developing countries. Furthermore, because of data limitations, studies of the effects of globalization on working conditions in developing countries often use rudimentary econometric techniques, such as trends over time or before and after comparisons around a globalization event. Studies generally examine FDI, export orientation, or total trade and their effects on such characteristics as total employment, wages, skill level, productivity, child labor rates, and education participation (Ghose 2000; Carr, Chen, and Tate 2000; Kabeer 2004; Kaplinsky 2001; Moss, Ramachandran, and Shah 2004).

EMPLOYMENT

Lall's (2002) theoretical overview of the possible effects of globalization on employment points out that, unless globalization is well defined, the link is unclear. Neoclassical trade theory offers little guidance in this area, generally speaking, because the most common Ricardian and Heckscher-Ohlin trade models assume full employment. This assumption is obviously questionable in most developing countries. The main concern for employment, however, is whether globalization results in a net gain in jobs. There are several ways to approach that question, some of which are discussed below.

Employment Levels

Employment levels are important for many developing countries, normally characterized by high rates of underemployment or surplus labor. In such countries, the net employment change resulting from globalization is the main focus. Evaluating the link between globalization and employment levels seems relatively straightforward. With aggregate employment data by sector, an analysis would first identify the change in the globalization variable (trade or FDI) by sector, and compare employment changes in the affected industries with a control group. This approach would allow the reallocating effects of increased trade, or the expansion effects of FDI, to be captured. The main difficulties arise from identifying an appropriate control group, controlling for macroeconomic factors, and controlling for endogeneity.

The empirical evidence on the link between globalization and employment levels is mixed. One reason is time frame. In the long run, employment depends on national economic growth. In the medium run, employment depends on whether trade is accompanied by other factors that are also conducive to growth, such as strong institutions, and the degree to which domestic production is a complement to or substitute for the relevant measure of globalization. In the short run, the issue of globalization and employment depends on adjustment, as described in the following discussion of unemployment rates.

Unemployment Rates

Unemployment rates have a cyclical component and a long-run component. The long-run component is generally driven by government policies such as unemployment insurance. Economies with more generous unemployment insurance packages generally have higher unemployment rates. Furthermore, unemployment may not be a relevant concept in many low- and middle-income countries that lack unemployment insurance and with large informal sectors. In these countries, unemployment is a luxury the poor cannot afford; the question is more the "quality" of employment. Therefore, few studies focus on globalization and long-run unemployment rates.

Short-run unemployment rates are generally driven by national business cycles. Despite years of research, the understanding of what drives business cycles is still limited. Unemployment rates are typically highly correlated across regions, suggesting that forces driving national business cycles also drive regional unemployment rates.

An economy's adjustment to a new liberalization policy may be rapid or slow but will affect workers in either event, because an economy in flux creates and destroys job market opportunities. The key issue when looking at the link between globalization and unemployment rates is worker adjustment. Liberalization often induces a change in the allocation of workers between and within sectors. To move between sectors, workers leave their jobs and, ideally, find jobs in other sectors. Job search can be slow and costly; therefore, unemployment rates will increase if the change in the economy was large and rapid and it takes time to find new jobs. Thus, the link between globalization and short-run unemployment rates is not considered permanent and may fade out as the economy adjusts.

Displacement Probabilities

An alternative criterion through which to gauge the effects of globalization on employment is the probability of displacement. The analysis of displacement probability consists of two components. First, workers may have an increased risk of losing jobs because globalization increases competition. This risk is not trivial. It can be measured through the correlation between the rate of job loss (turnover) and globalization events.

The second link between globalization and displacement probability relates to the overall volatility of the economy. Some studies have begun to look at the link between globalization and volatility, but this is still a young literature, focused more on the harmonization of business cycles across integrating countries.

Job-Search Duration

The time it takes to find a job is a measure of hardship for workers. Globalization may affect unemployment duration by inducing a reallocation of workers across sectors and changing the relative demand for skills. Workers with skills that are less in demand after globalization may have a more difficult time finding jobs following displacement (regardless of whether the displacement is directly related to globalization). The length of time it takes to find a job is, therefore, one measure of globalization's effects on workers.

Formal versus Informal Sector Employment

One of the main employment concerns in developing countries is employment in the informal sector. Several papers (Maloney 2004, for example) suggest that employment in the informal sector is linked to productivity in the formal sector and that workers often enter the informal sector to escape the cumbersome burdens imposed on the formal sector. These results, however, may be limited to Latin America. The informal sector is also commonly believed to be an alternative for workers who cannot find jobs in the formal sector (see Marcouiller, Ruiz de Castilla, and Woodruff 1997). The informal sector, although very heterogeneous, often coincides with very poor conditions and low wages. These poor conditions are especially prevalent in the informal sector in poorer countries.

Therefore, globalization could have two different effects on informal sector employment. In the short run, the adjustment that comes with trade liberalization could result in rising informal sector employment. In the medium run, the size of the informal sector would be linked to productivity and expanding opportunities in the formal sector that may come with globalization. Empirically, the results seem to be mixed. For example, Goldberg and Pacvnik (2003) look at the effects of trade liberalization on the informal sector in developing countries and find no link in Brazil but a positive relationship in Colombia that is linked to labor market institutions.

WAGES

The first variable to analyze in a determination of the effects of globalization on workers and working conditions is wages. Wages often account for a major portion of income for workers, and data on wages are easier to find and analyze than other aspects of working conditions.[2] Furthermore, wages are considered a good proxy for measuring the effects of globalization on workers—nearly all current empirical studies of the effects of globalization on workers focus on some aspect of wage income.

A large literature (indeed, entire fields of economics) analyzes factors that affect wages. A worker's wage is affected by the economywide average wage, the worker's personal characteristics (gender, age, education, ability, occupation), and the worker's industry. Globalization affects all three of these, but in different time frames. Average wages are affected in the long run. Wage changes resulting from different personal characteristics are affected in the medium run, and industry-specific wages are affected in the short run. Each of these is discussed in turn.[3]

Average Wages (Absolute Wage Levels)

Average wage levels can be decomposed into two components: short run and long run. Short-run wage levels are generally determined by business cycle effects. As the economy improves and unemployment falls, average wages rise. Long-run average wages, however, are determined by productivity. Comparing cross-country wages and productivity levels reveals a very strong positive relationship. Over time, rising productivity generally leads to higher wages.

Because absolute wage levels are tied to productivity in the long run, the key link between wage levels and trade is through productivity. Globalization can increase productivity in several ways. First, trade can increase competition, causing the least productive firms to contract or disappear, thus raising average productivity. Globalization also gives firms access to a wider array of inputs, which should boost productivity, and may induce innovation and training, also boosting productivity.

Average wages are also affected by other factors. Technological change, labor supply (such as births and migration), and local labor market conditions all influence wage levels; therefore, it is important to control for as many of these other factors as possible when trying to identify the link between globalization and wage levels.[4]

Personal Characteristics and Relative Wages

Personal characteristics such as age, education, gender, social capital, networks, and ability all combine to affect an individual's wage. For example, men are generally paid more than women. If women's wages rise on average, a female's wage is likely to be affected. Changes in the "returns" to different personal characteristics are often the result of economywide changes that occur in the medium run (that is, they require some movement of workers between industries). These changes are often referred to as changes in relative wages because they describe changes between workers in groups defined by these characteristics (for example, changes in the relative wages of females).

Perhaps the most common way to define relative wages is between skill groups, such as between workers with different levels of education or in different occupations (typically, production and nonproduction workers). Relative wages can also be defined for men and women, for people with different levels of experience, for workers in firms with different levels of foreign capital, and for workers in different industries. See box 3.5.

Nearly all of the several ways to evaluate the effects of globalization on relative wages are based on the concepts of supply and demand. Globalization is generally considered to affect labor demand. Rising exports increase the demand for workers involved in making the exported good, while rising imports that compete with domestic production reduce the demand for labor.

If the question were how tariffs affect relative wages, one could link the changes in tariffs to changes in relative prices, then map relative prices to changes in relative wages. This approach is called a "price study" and can be carried out in four basic steps. First, establish whether the change in tariffs across industries is correlated with skill intensity, that is, whether tariffs on industries that use relatively more-skilled workers fell more than tariffs on other

BOX 3.5 **Wage Inequality**

Although more than 100 papers analyze the relationship between globalization and wage inequality, the theoretical and empirical link between them remains contested. Studies of trade and wages in developing countries have also generated conflicting results. Wood (1997) summarizes several studies that indicate that, following trade liberalization, wage inequality rose in Latin American countries but tended to fall in East Asian countries. Goldberg and Pavcnik (2007) provide a comprehensive review of the literature on the distributional effects of globalization.

goods. Second, check the correlation between tariff changes and changes in relative prices—falling tariffs are generally linked to falling prices. Third, compute the correlation between changes in relative prices and changes in relative wages. Once these three basic steps are complete, the last step is to check for any other factors (such as changes in technology or supply) that might also be affecting relative wages.

Berik (2000) uses a combination of FDI and trade to compute globalization in Taiwan, China. She measures the ratio of outward FDI to GDP by industry. Because of data concerns she turns the variable into a dummy equal to 1 if the ratio is greater than 0.05. In addition, she computes export orientation as the value of exports as a share of sectoral gross output. She tests the effects of these measures of globalization on wages using two independent wage equations by gender, and a third equation measuring gender wage inequality. She includes the share of salaried workers in total employment to proxy for skill level by industry, the capital to labor ratio in each firm to proxy for labor productivity and technology, and the female share of employment for each industry. Dummies for firm size and year fixed effects are also included. Gruben and McLeod (2006) also note the importance of separating males and females in econometric models because different industries affect genders differently. In their study, they test for the effects of increased exports on schooling outcomes, on family factors such as age at marriage and childbirth, and on labor force participation of children. They use aggregate data from 48 countries that were part of the Multifibre Arrangement, and individual-level private survey information, and focus on the apparel and shoe industry to test for the effects on female outcomes.

Industry-Specific Wages

Workers with identical characteristics in identical occupations often earn different wages in different industries. These industry-specific wage differences have been incorporated into several studies (for example, Revenga [1997] and Cragg and Epelbaum [1996]). The idea is that in the short run, workers (and capital) cannot move between industries, and therefore the effects of an industry-specific change will affect wages in a particular industry before the effects can spread to the rest of the economy and affect the returns to other personal characteristics (such as the returns to education) or average wage levels. To the extent that these premiums are important in determining workers' wages, and that they can be directly linked to measures of globalization, they provide perhaps the most straightforward way to analyze the short-run effects of globalization on wages. The technical details of using this technique are described in the annex to this chapter.

LABOR STANDARDS

In 1998, the International Labour Organization (ILO) defined "core" labor standards. These four standards include freedom of association and the right to organize, freedom from forced labor, elimination of child labor that is harmful to the child or interferes with schooling, and nondiscrimination in employment (Center for Global Development 2004). These core standards are incorporated into ILO conventions that member countries have a chance to ratify. In doing so, countries adopt what could be termed international working condition standards. These conventions illustrate the fact that working conditions may be the result of globalization as manifested through exposure to organizations and nations that adopt common ideals (akin to international peer pressure), which could call into question whether working conditions are directly related to the economic and financial globalization measures discussed above. See box 3.6.

Unionization

Unions are important to the extent that they affect other aspects of working conditions that are difficult to measure, such as the resolution of grievances, protection from employer abuses, or productivity. On the one hand, unionization in the population as a whole may increase if industries with higher-than-average unionization rates expand relative to others as a result of globalization. Unionization may also increase if foreign firms welcome unions, if they increase productivity, reduce turnover, or create a positive public image. On the other hand, globalization may weaken unions. Firms may threaten to move abroad to discourage union activity. Foreign firms may also seek ways to discourage unions if the firms believe that unions reduce productivity, or increase wages beyond increases in productivity.

> ### BOX 3.6 Globalization and Nonwage Working Conditions
>
> Several studies analyze the link between globalization and nonwage working conditions. Kucera (2002) finds a zero-to-positive relationship between FDI and core labor standards. Daude, Mazza, and Morrison (2003) find that civil liberties are associated with more FDI. Mosley and Uno (2007) find that FDI is negatively associated with observed violations in workers' rights. Overall, this literature provides little, if any, support for the hypothesis that FDI worsens working conditions or that FDI seeks out countries with poor labor standards.

Firm- or industry-level data are generally the most appropriate to analyze the link between unionization and globalization. Unionization differs by firm, and differences across firms provide important information about how globalization affects unionization. Changes in unionization can then be categorized as those that occur across industries (if globalization's effects vary across industries) and those that occur within firms.

In the absence of firm-level data, industry-level data could be used as long as the data include information about rates of unionization. If industry-level data are used, the differences across firms are assumed to matter less than differences across industries. These data would allow estimation of the contribution of the movement of workers between industries on unionization rates. If the industry data are sufficiently disaggregated, the effects of outsourcing on unionization could possibly be identified. If unionization rates differ between subsectors, outsourcing may affect subsectors differently, thereby affecting aggregate unionization rates.

Hours

Hours worked are an important aspect of working conditions, and are generally determined by local labor law. Labor law, however, usually just sets a maximum, and firms are able to hire workers for contracts that stipulate fewer hours than the national full-time norm. Firms also alter hours as a result of short-term fluctuations in demand.

Hours would, however, be a relevant metric of working conditions that might be linked to globalization if firms specifically engaged in international trade were either exempted from national convention or were not subject to normal enforcement of labor laws. In this case, the movements between covered and uncovered sectors would contribute to the overall effect of globalization on hours.

Child Labor

The link between globalization and child labor has received much attention in the popular press and increasing attention in the academic literature.[5] Elliott and Freeman's (2003) four examples of links between globalization and labor standards are either primarily focused on (three of the four) or linked to child labor. Child labor is affected by business cycles or liberalization shocks in the short run and by growth in the long run. Therefore, determining an appropriate time frame is as relevant for child labor as for other measures of working conditions.

Benefits

In addition to wages, firms might provide benefits such as contributions to social security, training, vacation time, and insurance contributions to workers. Some benefits are mandated by the government and others are provided on the firm's own initiative. Shocks to particular industries in the short run, movement between industries in the medium run, and growth in the long run can all be linked to liberalization, but data that measure these benefits at the industry level are often difficult to find. As a result, there are very few, if any, specific studies of the link between globalization and worker benefits.

Theoretical Framework for Determining the Effects of Globalization on Working Conditions

The central purpose of economic theory is to formalize thinking in ways that help guide empirical analysis. This section presents a general theoretical framework for describing the relationship between globalization and working conditions. The theory presented here is general enough to help to identify the relationships of interest without being too technical. For the following discussion, "working conditions" include employment (employment levels, unemployment rates, displacement probabilities, job-search duration, formal vs. informal sector employment), wages (average wages, relative wages, industry-specific wages), or other aspects of working conditions (unionization, hours, child labor, benefits) previously defined in the chapter.

A useful starting point is the most general Heckscher-Ohlin framework of trade by comparative advantage. This model, however, makes many assumptions that render a strict application impractical. Relaxing some of these assumptions allows focus to be placed on the relevant questions while preserving enough theoretical discipline to provide specific predictions and guidance to get meaningful empirical results.

For example, the neoclassical Heckscher-Ohlin model assumes that factors are perfectly mobile between industries, which is only true in the long run. For working conditions, the framework in this chapter suggests that globalization measures, such as trade liberalization or capital inflows, will first have industry-specific effects before affecting the rest of the economy. In the short run, workers cannot move easily between industries, making a Ricardo-Viner (or "specific-factors") model more appropriate. If mobility between industries is costly, or if efficiency wages are allowed in the framework, short-run effects could take some time to spread throughout the economy. In the short run, workers may not be mobile between industries (Elliott and Lindley 2006) so globalization may affect firms within particular industries first. In the medium run, workers (and capital) begin to move between industries. New innovations are implemented and production techniques may change. Therefore, if medium-run effects are of interest, between-industry employment shifts must be evaluated.

Furthermore, the basic Heckscher-Ohlin model does not specifically incorporate nonwage working conditions, potentially complicating the theoretical link between globalization and overall working conditions. Different measures of globalization have different implications for working conditions. In addition, the basic Heckscher-Ohlin model does not usually include institutional factors (such as minimum wages, mandated benefits, or government enforcement of labor laws) operating at different levels in the economy (government, industry, and firm). Institutional factors generally emerge more clearly in the long run. In the long run, working conditions may be affected by international pressure and economic development.

While short-run, medium-run, and long-run effects are interrelated, it is useful for the purposes of framing an empirical study to identify and discuss each channel separately while keeping the basic model in mind. In an empirical study, focusing on the effects of globalization in the order in which they unfold in time is a pragmatic approach. These effects are individually discussed in the remainder of this section.

WITHIN-INDUSTRY CHANGES (SHORT RUN)

Firms are the basic decision-making units on the supply side of the economy. Interactions between firms and workers determine labor market outcomes. Globalization affects these interactions. For example, an increase in economic activity (from the opening of export markets or the arrival of noncompeting foreign firms) could increase the demand for workers. Or firms might change working conditions as a defensive maneuver in response to globalization effects such as rising import competition or the arrival of competing foreign firms. These changes may be limited to the affected industries and not spread through the rest of the economy if adjustment costs are high. In many developing countries, adjustment costs may be quite high in the short run (Heckman and Pagés 2000), meaning that workers (and capital) cannot shift between industries. The effects of globalization are therefore identifiable at the firm and industry levels. See box 3.7.

For example, an increase in demand for workers can tilt power toward workers, and workers can begin to demand incremental improvements in wages and working conditions. As long as productivity is increasing, firms may be inclined to acquiesce to these demands and to take steps to improve working conditions within the affected industries. Or perhaps firms feel pressured to cut costs and increase output because of increased competition. Working conditions, such as wages or safety expenditures, could be one way in which firms reduce costs. As affected firms take these steps, other firms in the same industry may be pressured to take similar steps either to attract workers (if demand is increasing) or to cut costs (if demand for workers is falling).

BOX 3.7 Example: Short-Run, Industry-Specific Wages

Picking the appropriate time frame for a study is important. Several studies, such as those described in this box, focus on the short run by looking at industry-specific wage premiums. As always, successful studies such as these carefully define both globalization and working conditions.

Globalization. Trade liberalization (tariff reduction)

Working conditions. Industry-specific wages

Data. Time series of household surveys for Mexico (Feliciano 2001) and Colombia (Goldberg and Pavcnik 2005).

Theoretical framework. The theoretical framework applies to the short run described above; it assumes that workers are not mobile across industries and, therefore, the effects of the driving variables are not diffused beyond individual industries.

Estimation equation. The estimation strategy consists of two parts. The first part is to estimate the individual industry-specific wages. The dependent variable is the log of individual wages (ln$w$) for individual i in industry j at time t. The independent variables are individual characteristics (X) and industry-specific dummy variables (I).

$$\ln w_{ijt} = X_{ijt}\beta_X + I_{ijt}D_{jt} + \varepsilon_{ijt}$$

The estimated industry-specific wage premiums are the D coefficients for each industry j at time t. These interindustry wage differentials (IIWDs) have several advantages for understanding working conditions and globalization. Krueger and Summers (1988) established this technique in the labor economics literature. They estimated IIWDs for a set of N industries and N-1 dummy variables. Because the estimated differentials were sensitive to the omitted industry,

(continued)

Therefore, one way to identify the effects of globalization on working conditions is to hold the distribution of workers between industries or firms constant and focus on the changes within industries or firms.

BETWEEN-INDUSTRY SHIFTS (MEDIUM-RUN, GENERAL EQUILIBRIUM)

Theory predicts that both foreign investment and trade will cause a shift of workers between industries. Imports of final goods that compete with domestic production and foreign investment outflows would cause workers to leave affected industries, while capital inflows and export opportunities would induce movements into the industries experiencing these situations.

The effects of foreign investment inflows are illustrated in figure 3.1. Figure 3.1 shows how foreign investment in the manufacturing sector affects the production possibilities frontier of a country with two goods: manufacturing and agriculture. Initially, the economy produces where the price line (P) touches the production possibility frontier. At this point, the country produces M manufacturing and A agriculture.

they suggested an approach that normalizes the differentials (and approximated the resulting standard errors) so that the differential estimates do not depend on the omitted industry. Haisken-DeNew and Schmidt (1997) describe a method that adjusts the differentials so that they measure the difference between each industry's wage and the overall mean, rather than the omitted industry, and also produces the correct standard errors. This method has been incorporated into popular statistics programs, such as LIMDEP and GAUSS (by Haisken-DeNew and Schmidt [1997]) and STATA (by Wiggins [1998]). Once obtained, the correct IIWD estimates can be formally compared with various measures of globalization and analyzed over time.

Feliciano (2001) and Goldberg and Pavcnik (2005) use the estimated differentials in a second-stage estimation equation that uses the estimated industry-specific wage premiums as the dependent variables and measures of globalization as the independent variables. These globalization measures could include tariffs, trade flows, or FDI, and are represented here as T:

$$D_{jt} = T_{jt}\,\delta_T + F_{jt}\gamma_F + u_{jt}.$$

The variable F includes time and industry fixed effects, which are possible to include because the estimated industry differentials form a panel (both time-series and cross-section data). The effects of globalization are then considered to be measured by the estimated γ coefficients.

With similar household surveys, common industry definitions, the same set of controls for personal characteristics, and similar earnings variables, the IIWDs and the results that follow from them can be compared across countries. The earnings equations must be as similar as possible if the estimates and subsequent results are to be compared.

SOURCES: Feliciano 2001; Goldberg and Pavcnik 2005.

Holding manufacture and agricultural output prices constant, the inflow of foreign capital causes the manufacturing industry to expand and, necessarily, the agriculture industry to contract.[6] Manufacturing increases from M to M′, and agricultural production falls from A to A′. This change causes workers to move from agriculture to manufacturing. If working conditions differ between agriculture and manufacturing, this movement changes average working conditions. If working conditions in manufacturing are better than in

FIGURE 3.1 **Effects of FDI in Low-Income Countries**

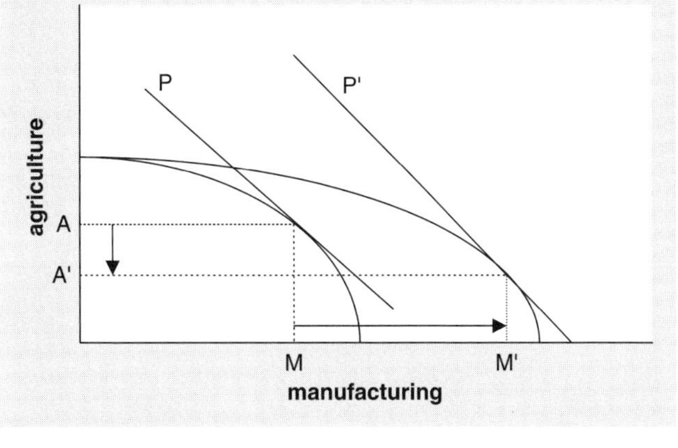

SOURCE: Author.

agriculture, foreign investment improves average working conditions because it caused workers to move from poor conditions to better conditions.

The effects of export opportunities are similar. While the change in figure 3.1 assumes that output prices do not change, export opportunities would cause prices in the export sector to increase. This change is shown by the production possibilities frontier graph in figure 3.2. Figure 3.2 shows that export opportunities in the manufacturing sector would cause resources to shift from agriculture to manufacturing. Initially, the economy is at A and M. The increase in the price of manufacturing causes agricultural production to fall from A to A' and manufacturing output to increase from M to M'. Again, if working conditions are better in manufacturing, export opportunities that cause a shift of employment between industries would improve average working conditions.

The effects of FDI and increased exports are similar in that they both induce a shift from agriculture to manufacturing. In many cases, foreign investment comes to a country with the intention of producing for export, which would cause both effects to occur. The effect of this shift in resources would be to increase the demand for workers in the expanding sector (manufacturing). (See box 3.8.) The effects of increased demand for workers in manufacturing would depend on whether workers are mobile between industries. If workers are perfectly mobile between industries, wages should equalize across industries. In fact, as illustrated below, this is generally not the case. Industry-specific factors can affect average industry wages. To the extent that worker mobility is limited between industries, the increase in labor demand in manufacturing would cause both its employment share and the wage differential between manufacturing and agriculture to increase (see figure 3.3).

FIGURE 3.2 **Effects of Rising Export Opportunities in Low-Income Countries**

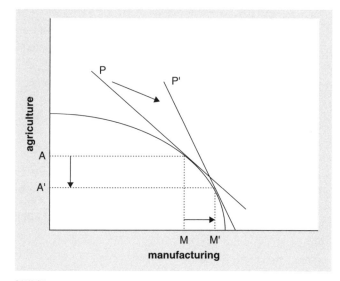

SOURCE: Author.

The increase in labor demand pulls workers from agriculture. This is, in effect, a decrease in supply of labor to agriculture, which causes the IIWD to increase and agriculture's employment share to fall.

The effects of movements between industries on average working conditions are based on the assumption that working conditions are different between industries and relatively stable. When measuring working conditions with wages, this assumption has a strong foundation in the empirical economics literature. A more complete discussion of the IIWD literature is found in the annex to this chapter.

BOX 3.8 **Example: Medium-Run Effects, Wage Inequality**

In the medium run, workers can move between industries and economywide effects start to emerge. In the context of wage inequality, these studies often rely on the Stolper-Samuelson theorem that links changes in relative wages to changes in output prices. To proceed, these studies first define globalization and working conditions.

Globalization. Trade volumes and industry prices during liberalization era

Working conditions. Relative wages (inequality resulting from personal characteristics)

Data. Beyer, Rojas, and Vergara (1999) use household survey data over time to esti-mate the skill premium (the wage of skilled workers relative to less-skilled workers) and then use data on prices, openness, and labor supply to explain the premium. Robertson (2004) uses average wages of nonproduction and production workers to estimate the skill premium and then compares movements in relative wages with changes in relative product prices.

Theoretical framework. Both studies are medium-run studies that allow the movement of workers between industries to diffuse the effects of globalization throughout the economy. Their theoretical foundations, in particular, rest in the Stolper-Samuelson theorem. Although it has several variations, the most formal Stolper-Samuelson theorem shows that an in-crease in the relative price of, say, skill-intensive goods (relative to the output price of less skill-intensive goods) will raise the wages of skilled workers and lower the wages of less-skilled workers.

Estimation equation. Beyer, Rojas, and Vergara (1999) use a first-stage estimation equa-tion like the equation in box 3.4. However, rather than focusing on industry-specific wages, Beyer, Rojas, and Vergara estimate the premium that comes from more education. They then use this premium in a second-stage equation. Robertson (2004) uses several different esti-mation approaches, which can all be summarized by the simple equation

$$relativewage_t = \lambda\, relativeprices_t + \varepsilon_t.$$

The main difference between this approach, used by both Beyer, Rojas, and Vergara (1999) and Robertson (2004), and the ones in boxes 3.4 and 3.7 is that it focuses on the time-series dimension, which allows both studies to identify the contribution of changes in prices to changes in wage inequality. Beyer, Rojas, and Vergara (1999) also include the relative supply of educated workers and trade volume (as a share of GDP). Both studies find that changes in relative prices play a significant role in explaining wage inequality, as suggested by the Stolper-Samuelson theorem.

SOURCES: Beyer, Rojas, and Vergara 1999; Robertson 2004.

FIGURE 3.3 **The Effects on Manufacturing of an Increase in Relative Labor Demand**

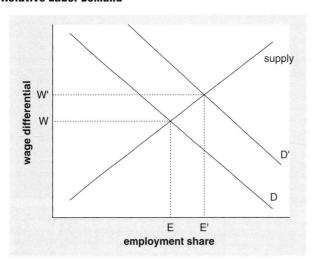

SOURCE: Author.

ECONOMIC DEVELOPMENT AND POLICY (LONG RUN, GROWTH)

Differences between developed and developing countries are generally considered to be long-run differences in the sense that development is a slow and gradual process. Whether globalization generally, or liberalization specifically, helps increase long-run living standards is a topic of much debate.

Development

Developed, high-income countries generally have better working conditions than do developing countries. Many components of working conditions follow this pattern; for example, the length of the standard work week in manufacturing, and the number of fatal accidents per 100,000 workers, both fall as gross national income (GNI or log GNI) per capita rises.[7]

Rising income is probably a necessary, but not sufficient, condition for development. Other factors such as rule of law, transparency, efficacy of services, and other institutional characteristics play a significant role in translating rising income into development. If globalization contributes to development, it would not be unreasonable to expect globalization to contribute to improving working conditions.

However, the link between globalization and development seems most valid in the very long run. The link between trade and per capita income has been confirmed in studies across countries at a particular point in time (cross-section studies). These studies, however, only suggest that liberalization would lead to higher growth if all countries follow the same path to development. That is, any policy prescription would require the assumption that developing countries are just farther behind the developed countries on the same development path. These studies do not imply that liberalizing countries will immediately experience rising living standards. In fact, the time-series link between trade liberalization and rising per capita income is uncertain and not well understood. This difference suggests that studies that look at the long-run link between globalization and working conditions should seek panel data that cover a long time frame. These panel data would allow one to understand the path countries take in improving working conditions as they develop.

Policy

As countries integrate through trade, they exchange ideas and negotiate common standards. Standards and conventions are more likely to be adopted as countries continue to integrate. Countries might then move toward harmonizing standards through government policy. There are many examples of such indirect effects of the globalization of trade, including the effect of being exposed to nongovernmental organizations and watchdog groups (for example, see Elliott and Freeman [2001]) and the effects of public opinion on firm behavior.

Few studies have focused on these aspects of globalization (Elliott and Freeman 2001, 2003; Brown, Deardorff, and Stern 2003; Harrison and Scorse 2004); the ones that do are often, by necessity, more qualitative in nature. Furthermore, the policy channel is idiosyncratic; it is strongly affected by political factors that economists find difficult to quantify and analyze empirically. Institutions matter, as does the focus of international attention. Therefore the policy environment must be considered and appropriately incorporated into the framework.

Application: Step-by-Step

A useful study of the effects of globalization on working conditions does not need to include all of the different measures of globalization and working conditions described above. The elements should be combined so that the most specifically defined, yet pressing, questions can be addressed. A thorough study, however, may contain several different measures of globalization and working conditions. Once these elements have been identified, the relevant empirical approaches are relatively straightforward.

One of the goals of this volume is to show the results of applying this methodology to various developing countries. To be comparable, the studies had to contain similar methodological characteristics; yet, to accurately represent each country, the studies had to contain some country-specific elements. As this section progresses, specific examples from the country studies are used to illustrate the main points.

DESCRIPTIVE ANALYSIS

The first part of each country study is a descriptive analysis of the nation's experience with globalization, which helps identify the key variables to be used in the empirical analysis (tariff changes, imports, exports, FDI). For example, FDI may play an important role in some countries, while import competition may be more relevant in others. The descriptive analysis helps frame the emphasis placed on particular variables in the empirical work.

The descriptive analyses also assess the degree of competition faced by domestic firms resulting from globalization. The degree of competitiveness can be relatively straightforward to assess, depending on the level of aggregation of the data. With appropriately disaggregated production data, competition can be assessed using simple correlation coefficients. Trivially, if the government reduced tariffs on a particular sector, the analysis would focus on that particular sector. For a broader liberalization, however, calculating the correlation between the change in tariffs or imports (if intraindustry trade is not the focus) and economywide employment or production share in the economy would be the starting point. A small correlation would suggest that the government lowered tariffs most on industries that were least important, as measured by production, in the economy. Of course, whether the imports are intermediate inputs or are for domestic consumption must first be discerned.

The sections of the country studies describing experiences with globalization led to the possibly surprising result that many of the most salient aspects of their globalization experiences were strikingly similar, even though the countries vary markedly in geography and history. Although such concurrence may not apply to every group of countries, it does help draw out some interesting lessons about the effects of globalization on working conditions.

WORKING CONDITIONS

Three criteria should be used to determine the relevant variables for working conditions: relevance, comparability, and feasibility (availability of data). Relevance depends on the intended audience of the study and the interests of those conducting the study. If the topic of interest is the effects of globalization on workplace safety, for example, then data on workplace safety need to be found or collected. Such data are typically hard to find and difficult to collect without the help of a legal mandate. It is then important to find the closest possible measures in available data.

In the country studies in this volume, data availability was a critical factor in determining which working conditions to examine. El Salvador's data, for example, contains very specific information about many nonwage working conditions. In contrast, data from Honduras contains very limited measures of nonwage working conditions. For comparability, all the studies contain a section focusing on industry-specific wages. One of the globalization experiences shared by all five countries (although to somewhat varying degrees) was a significant role for the textiles and apparel industries. This meant that wages in the apparel industry relative to country-specific mean wages could serve as a common thread.

TIME FRAME

The theoretical framework set forth in this chapter suggests that different measures of working conditions would be related to different measures of globalization in different time frames. Because the long run is generally best captured in cross-country studies, single-country studies will best be served by focusing on the short and medium runs. Which of these is appropriate will depend on the variables chosen for analysis. For the most part, however, medium-run studies (3–20 years) are the most effective at capturing the effects of globalization on working conditions. Therefore, the best data would be those that can span several years to facilitate comparisons across time. Fortunately, four of the five countries (all but Cambodia) in this volume had available data that allowed for comparisons across time.

DATA

Studies of the effects of globalization can be conducted at the industry level, the firm level, or the worker level. Studies at each of these levels have important, distinctive characteristics, and each study will answer slightly different questions. This section describes data that may be used in future studies.

Trade, Tariffs, and FDI

Although trade and tariff data are officially kept by each country, several agencies cooperate to collect and harmonize that data. Perhaps the best example of this is the World Integrated Trade Solution (WITS), produced by the World Bank in collaboration with the United Nations Conference on Trade and Development (UNCTAD). This free software (http://wits.worldbank.org/witsweb) provides access to the COMTRADE database (maintained by the United Nations Statistical Division), the TRAINS database (maintained by UNCTAD), and the World Trade Organization Integrated Database. While the WITS software is free, access to the databases themselves is not.

UNCTAD also compiles foreign investment data and maintains two products to make those data available. UNCTAD's FDI statistics database includes aggregate inflows, outflows, and stocks for 196 countries. Its World Investment Directory contains more detailed statistics on transnational companies in selected countries. Central banks and national government agencies also often collect more detailed foreign investment statistics, but availability of these data varies among countries.

Industries

Industry-level data often come from government surveys or mandatory reporting. They are most useful for identifying changes among industries and changes in aggregate variables (such as employment, average wages, or production shares). High-frequency, industry-level data are also very useful for capturing the time paths of different variables, such as relative wages, production shares, and employment, because it is easier to remove the business-cycle component from high-frequency data. An advantage of these data is that they are often easy to find. The main disadvantage is that they lack the level of detail to accurately capture many of the aspects relevant to analyzing the effects of globalization, such as workers' demographic characteristics.

Firms

Firm-level data are ideal for identifying the effects of globalization on working conditions across firms and thereby identifying composition effects. The key, of course, is to have some measure of working conditions at the firm level, which is rare. Firm-level data also allow for the identification of effects of globalization on plant survival (if firms or plants are followed over time). For example, Bernard, Jensen, and Schott (2006) show that competition from low-wage countries increases the probability of closure or contraction of low-productivity plants, but can be positively correlated with expansion of high-productivity plants. The net effect on employment, wages, and working conditions would be revealed, however, at the industry level. The main disadvantage of these data is that they are difficult to find, especially in developing countries. Notable exceptions include Chile (Pavcnik 2002; Alvarez and Robertson 2002), Mexico (Hanson and Harrison 1999; Verhoogen 2007), and Indonesia (Lipsey and Sjoholm 2004a, 2004b). Even when collected, these data may not be available consistently over time, or may be limited to specific sectors (particularly manufacturing).

Workers

Worker-level data are found in household surveys, labor force-surveys, and consumption surveys, and are becoming increasingly available for developing countries. Many studies analyze these kinds of data in developing countries. Several studies have used worker-level data to evaluate the effects of globalization on wages, job loss and unemployment duration, and wage inequality. Labor force or household surveys generally include demographic data that enable the researcher to control for education, age, and other worker characteristics that may mask the effects of globalization. Such data also help identify the effects on workers in different demographic groups. Data from household surveys may also include information about hours worked, benefits, and other aspects of working conditions that are not available from aggregated or firm-level data. Household surveys also often contain industry of employment and cover many sectors of the economy. The availability and coverage of labor-force (or household) surveys in each of the countries studied in this volume led the authors to focus on worker-level data.

METHODOLOGY

Globalization studies can be sorted into three groups according to methodology: event studies, price studies, and quantity studies. Event studies compare the variables of interest before and after a globalization event (for example, rapid trade liberalization). Price studies, mainly applied to studies of globalization and wage inequality, are based on the neoclassical trade theory (the Stolper-Samuelson theorem) that suggests that globalization affects relative wages through changes in relative prices. Quantity studies link quantity measures (such as imports, exports, or FDI) with labor market variables. Each approach has advantages and disadvantages, as discussed below.

Event Studies

An event study is an effective analysis tool for comparing working conditions before and after a liberalization event, such as a rapid change in tariffs, or any event for which a clear date delimits the "pre" and "post" periods. The benefits of event studies are that they are straightforward and easy to implement. The key to a successful event study is to control for all the other factors that may have changed at the same time. Mexican trade liberalization (specifically, joining NAFTA) is a perfect example of the perils of the event study. NAFTA went into effect January 1, 1994. In December 1994, the Mexican peso collapsed and sparked a deep recession in Mexico. NAFTA may have contributed to the collapse of the peso, but most scholars agree that macroeconomic factors largely unrelated to NAFTA were the main culprits. Regardless, wages dropped sharply in 1995. Event studies that tried to identify the effects of NAFTA in Mexico have found it difficult to identify the effects of NAFTA separately from the effects of the peso crisis.

Nevertheless, an event study is often an excellent tool with which to start an analysis because it will highlight what most analysts care about: the bottom line. For example, wages are either different after liberalization or they are not. If they are not, and there are no confounding events that may have also affected wages, then it is difficult to make the case that liberalization had a significant effect on wages. Prominent examples of event studies include Revenga (1997) and Feliciano (2001), which both focus on Mexico's decision to join the General Agreement on Tariffs and Trade.

Several of the studies in this volume rely on important events, either implicitly or explicitly. All of the countries experienced relatively rapid moves toward globalization. In many countries, the end of the Multifibre Arrangement in 2004 played a significant role and therefore emerges as an important event.

Price Studies

Aggregate variables, such as inflation, interest rates, unemployment, and changes in GDP, affect wages and employment. These aggregate variables also affect domestic demand, which affects imports, and domestic production capacity, which affects exports. The result is that changes in imports and exports can change for reasons not related to trade policy, liberalization, or changes in foreign competition.

Trade theory, therefore, relies more on changes in relative prices to capture the effects of trade liberalization. If the price of a good changes relative to other goods in the economy, the change will affect the working conditions (especially wages) within that industry. Therefore, when considering the link between liberalization and working conditions, one possibly important variable is the industry-level price relative to all other industries.

There are several examples of price studies in developed countries (Lawrence and Slaughter 1993; Leamer 1998; Slaughter 2000), but very few for developing countries.[8] Product-price data in developing countries are difficult to find and match with worker data. Nonetheless, the studies that have been done have revealed links between globalization and changes in wage inequality that are consistent with trade theory and suggest that changes in product prices (that can be linked to tariff changes) affect relative wages.

Quantity Studies

Quantity studies are those that relate imports and exports to working conditions. Data on imports and exports have several advantages. First, these data are generally easy to obtain, especially at aggregated levels. Second, imports and exports are key variables in analyzing globalization.

However, import and export data also have one major disadvantage. These variables are not necessarily compatible with a strong theoretical foundation—there are many reasons for which imports and exports might change, and these reasons may be correlated with other factors that are affecting labor market conditions. As a result, a correlation between imports or exports and working conditions could be spurious.

For example, one of the most important determinants of imports is domestic demand. Increasing domestic demand is generally a sign of an expanding economy. When the economy expands, however, wages rise and unemployment falls. Working conditions may improve as workers get more power in the labor market. As the economy expands, however, imports increase. Ignoring the role of domestic demand could generate a positive, but specious, correlation between imports and wages.

To address this problem, disaggregated industry-level imports and exports are useful. These data allow the focus to be put on the industry-specific effects of trade while controlling for other factors that may affect working conditions and globalization measures.

EMPIRICAL ANALYSIS
General Framework

The description above isolates many possible globalization and working condition variables, resulting in a very large number of possible combinations of a single globalization variable and a single working condition variable (which is why globalization studies tend to generate disparate results).

The task now is to develop a generalized estimation approach that can be easily adapted to the different combinations of globalization and working condition variables. In the most general sense, interest lies in estimating the following relationship:

$$y_{it} = \alpha + \beta X_{it} + e_{it}, \tag{3.1}$$

where y represents working conditions (employment, wages, or other facets of working conditions), X represents a vector of globalization variables (such as imports, exports, trade barriers, or FDI) for an individual identifier (worker, firm, or industry) i at time t. The error term is a composite term that may include specific effects for each group or time period.

There are two general concerns with the above specification: time frame and the presence of fixed effects. Because of possible fixed effects, equation (3.1) should be estimated in differences:

$$\Delta y_{it} = \alpha + \beta \Delta X_{it} + e_{it}. \tag{3.2}$$

Differencing removes the individual-specific fixed effects that are often correlated with unobserved characteristics.

The second issue is the time frame over which to difference the data. For short-run studies, the difference should be over the shortest period possible. For medium-run studies, a three-to-five-year difference is often appropriate.

At this point, there will be many particular estimation issues that relate to the specific combination of variables chosen. Once these are addressed, the results can be combined with the descriptive analysis on the nature of globalization to complete the analysis of how globalization affects working conditions in a given country.

Estimation Issues

While each country study faces different estimation issues depending on the data and approach used, several key issues affect all studies. The first is endogeneity, which is particularly relevant for studies of FDI and wages. Wages, either high (representing qualified workers) or low (representing potential labor cost savings) may attract FDI; therefore, attempts to assess the relationship between globalization and wages without accounting for endogeneity will generate inaccurate conclusions. This highlights the importance of including the time dimension in a study.

Other possible variables that could be driving a revealed relationship must be also controlled for. The example of NAFTA and the peso crisis above illustrates this point. Although studies often define globalization differently and test different outcomes, several factors are common among them. One is the inclusion of year dummies or time trends (or both); a second is the inclusion of either country or industry-level fixed effects. The studies mentioned throughout this chapter have some method to account for time and country or industry effects. Many also isolate effects by gender, industry, economic classification, or country.

Technical Annex: Empirical Methodology

This section briefly describes some of the empirical methods mentioned in this chapter or used in the country studies in the following chapters. The goal of this annex is to provide background and support for using the different empirical approaches.

INTERINDUSTRY WAGE DIFFERENTIALS

Given the frequent focus on interindustry wage differentials in the literature, this section provides references, context, and methodology to help researchers implement studies focusing on industry-specific wages.

Motivation

Interindustry wage differentials (IIWDs) are among the most-documented and least-understood characteristics of wage structures. Higher- or lower-than-average wages paid to observationally identical workers in similar occupations have been observed in Europe, Africa, North America, and South America.[9] Katz and Summers (1989b) and Papola and Bharadwaj (1970) find a high correlation across countries, suggesting that these differentials reflect industry characteristics, not national characteristics. Gittleman and Wolff (1993) show that the rank order of IIWDs is "remarkably stable" for 14 Organisation for Economic Co-operation and Development (OECD) countries between 1970 and 1985, suggesting that these differentials do not usually respond to policy or changes in economic conditions (in the OECD).

The apparent stability and similarity of IIWDs suggest that they are an appropriate measure of working conditions for several reasons. First, their apparent stability and similarity across countries put them at odds with the theory of perfectly competitive labor markets. In perfectly competitive labor markets, wages of nearly identical workers are equalized across industries. Helwege (1992) suggests that the stability of IIWDs may be a symptom of a market failure. Because labor market failures might be less surprising, if not expected, in developing countries, the one theoretically appropriate approach would be to focus on IIWDs. Second, the stability of the wage differentials suggests that movements from low-wage industries to high-wage industries are welfare-improving. Indeed, Katz and Summers (1989a) argue that if the rank-order of the differentials is stable over time, welfare could be improved by promoting the high-wage industries. Reflecting conventional wisdom, Katz and Summers (1989a) assume that IIWDs reflect a deep industry characteristic that is not affected by policy or by changes in economic conditions.

Although IIWDs are generally stable over time, it is possible that large changes in policies might affect IIWDs. If labor mobility across industries is imperfect (but not zero), a sector-specific shock would increase both employment shares in that industry and the industry-specific wage premium. In other words, if an industry experiences a positive shock, such as an increase in investment or export potential, the wage premium would be affected first, before any effects are experienced by the rest of the economy. This suggests that the effects of globalization might be appropriately measured by IIWDs. As a result, several studies have focused on IIWDs to study the link between trade liberalization and wages (Cragg and Epelbaum 1996; Pavcnik et al. 2003; Attanasio, Goldberg, and Pavcnik 2004).

Estimation Approach

Estimating IIWDs begins with a standard Mincerian log wage equation for individuals i at time t. This equation is generally estimated using ordinary least squares (OLS), as follows:

$$W_{it} = X_{it}B + Y_{it}C + e_{1it}, \tag{3.3}$$

where X_{it} is a vector of industry-of-employment dummy variables and Y_{it} is a vector of other individual-specific characteristics. The vector Y_{it} contains, at a minimum, variables that capture the effects of occupation, marital status, and gender. When the constant term is suppressed, the vector of coefficients B contains the average wages for each industry, conditional on elements of Y_{it}. The differential is the difference between each coefficient in B and the employment-weighted mean wage, net of the effects of variables contained in Y_{it}. Haisken-DeNew and Schmidt (1997) demonstrate how to appropriately calculate the differences and, more important, the standard errors for IIWDs.

If the k elements of the coefficient vector $B = (b_0, b_1, b_{k-1}, 0)$, then the adjusted coefficient vector is calculated using weights w as

$$\begin{aligned} b^* &= b - (-w, w, \ldots, w)'b \\ &= [I - (-w, w, \ldots, w)']\mathrm{b} \\ &= [I - W]b. \end{aligned} \qquad (3.4)$$

Equation (3.4) shows that the adjusted coefficients are presented as the difference from a weighted average of the OLS-estimated coefficients. When using the corrected coefficients, it is also important to correct the standard errors. Haisken-DeNew and Schmidt (1997) argue that the appropriate estimate of the standard errors is

$$\hat{S}(B) = \sqrt{w'\Phi((b^*))b^* - w'D(V(b^*))}, \qquad (3.5)$$

in which $\Phi(\bullet)$ is defined as an operator that changes a column vector into a diagonal matrix whose diagonal is made up of the elements of the vector, and $D(\cdot)$ transforms a diagonal matrix into a column vector whose elements are the elements of the diagonal. $V(\cdot)$ is the (relevant part of the) variance-covariance matrix of the estimated coefficients. Correcting the standard errors is important for accurate hypothesis testing.

ORDERED PROBIT

When the dependent variable in a regression has only two values, such as 0 and 1 (standing for "yes" or "no," or "employed" or "not employed"), special regression techniques are appropriate for proper estimation and interpretation. The most popular choices include the logit model, the linear probability model, and the probit model. When the dependent variable takes on a limited number of values, such as "red," "white," or "blue," the appropriate estimation approach is the multinomial logit or multinomial probit. If the limited number of values can be meaningfully sorted, the appropriate approach is usually the ordered probit or ordered logit. These approaches are similar to an ordinary regression framework except that the dependent variable has a limited number of responses and those responses can be ranked. The results are interpreted as the effect that a one-unit change in an independent variable has on moving from one choice to another. Details of these approaches can be found in econometric textbooks, such as Greene (1997) and Maddala (1983).

The basic idea behind this approach is that the probability of observing a certain outcome is a function of a number of underlying characteristics. To separately identify different potential outcomes (that, again, are arranged in a meaningful order), the approach uses a set of cut points that separate the options. Thus, the probability of observing a given outcome within the set is the probability that the estimated equation (including the random error) falls between the bordering cut points. If option i is bordered by cut points with c_{i-1} and c_i, and we were considering a linear explanatory equation with k variables and a random (normally distributed) error e, then we would observe outcome i if

$$\Pr(c_{i-1} < b_1 x_{1j} + b_2 x_{2j} + \ldots + b_k x_{kj} + e_j < c_i). \tag{3.6}$$

The coefficients b are then interpreted as the effect of each variable x on the probability of moving "up" the ordered dependent variable sequence.

THE HECKMAN SELECTION CORRECTION

In some empirical applications, some of the relevant data is not actually observed. For example, females might decide not to work if their market wage is too low. Because they do not work, however, their actual market wage is not observed. Wages are only observed if above a minimum threshold, often called a reservation wage. A selection model accounts for these missing data because the fact that they are not observed can introduce bias.

Estimating a selection model begins with a selection equation that states that the dependent variable in the wage equation will only be observed if

$$z_i \varphi + e_{2i} > 0, \tag{3.7}$$

in which z_i represents a vector of factors that affect the reservation wage, and e_{2i} is an error term, assumed to have a mean of zero and variance of 1. The problem arises because the error terms in equations (3.3) and (3.7) are potentially correlated, or

$$corr(e_1, e_2) = \rho, \tag{3.8}$$

which is problematic when ρ is not zero.

To correct for this problem, the Heckman approach uses variables that affect selection, but do not (directly) affect wages, to estimate the inverse hyperbolic tangent of ρ. Incorporating this estimate into the estimation of equation (3.3) corrects for the possible selection bias. Thus, the key to addressing this problem is finding variables that would affect the selection equation but do not belong in the wage equation. With such variables, the Heckman selection model generates corrected estimates.

Notes

1.   A country may want to know if expansion of its export sector is due to poor working conditions. This is a different notion than the effect of globalization on working conditions. In this case, the conditions that fostered exports were in place before the expansion of exports. Furthermore, working conditions might be "poor" relative to trading partners, rather than within the country itself. The question of whether globalization affects working conditions, therefore, changes within a country over time.

2.   One concern might be about the firm's ability to substitute poor working conditions for low wages (that is, inducing workers to accept poor working conditions in exchange for higher wages). While anecdotal evidence suggests that this occurs, the empirical evidence suggests that this trade-off may not be empirically relevant (see the discussion of compensating differentials in chapter 1). This means that wages and working conditions can be analyzed separately, although one should be mindful of the possibility of such a trade-off.

3. Another aspect of wages worth mentioning is income risk. Because people will exchange income for security, economists have argued that risk makes people worse off. Globalization may either increase or decrease income risk. In the short run, a globalization policy (such as a tariff reduction) induces movement between sectors and creates the possibility of job loss. It may also make income in the future less certain. If firms are subject to a more volatile economic climate, globalization may make wages more volatile. By the same token, increased trade liberalization with more stable countries may have the opposite effect. Krebs, Krishna, and Maloney (2005) find that trade liberalization in Mexico increased income risk. They show that this increase in risk can be expressed as a fall in welfare. Household surveys contain the most appropriate data with which to analyze the link between globalization and income risk. The correlation between a measure of income risk of workers in industries affected by globalization and a measure of globalization would indicate whether globalization increases income risk.

4. Mehmet and Tavakoli (2003) use the ratio of net FDI inflows to total investments (foreign and domestic) when testing the effect of FDI on wages. They also use simple ordinary least squares models using aggregate country-level data for four different countries. They estimate each country separately and include time trends for each country. In addition, they include dummy variables for each country to separate time periods when the trends were different.

5. In particular, see Edmonds and Pavcnik (2005).

6. This is simply an application of the Rybczynski theorem.

7. Data on work week and fatal injuries are available from LABORSTA (a database of the International Labour Office Bureau of Statistics) yearly data, tables 4b and 8b at http://laborsta.ilo.org. Work week is average work week in manufacturing. The correlation between work week and GNI per capita was –0.3264 in 2004. ,The correlation between fatal injuries (the number of injuries resulting in death per 100,000 workers) and the natural logarithm of GNI per capita was –0.4245 in 2004.

8. Exceptions include Beyer, Rojas, and Vergara (1999) and Robertson (2004).

9. For examples, see Edin and Zetterberg (1992); Abuhadba and Romaguera (1993); and Gatica, Mizala, and Romaguera (1995).

References

Abuhadba, M., and P. Romaguera. 1993. "Inter-Industry Wage Differentials: Evidence from Latin American Countries." *Journal of Development Studies* 30 (1): 190–205.

Alvarez, Roberto, and Raymond Robertson. 2002. "Exposure to Foreign Markets and Plant-Level Innovation: Evidence from Chile and Mexico." *Journal of International Trade and Economic Development* 13 (1): 57–87.

Attanasio, Orazio, Pinelopi K. Goldberg, and Nina Pavcnik. 2004. "Trade Reforms and Wage Inequality in Colombia." *Journal of Development Economics* 74 (2): 331–66.

Berik, Gunseli. 2000. "Mature Export-Led Growth and Gender Wage Inequality in Taiwan." *Feminist Economics* 6 (3): 1–26.

Bernard, Andrew, J. Bradford Jensen, and Peter K. Schott. 2006. "Survival of the Best Fit: Competition from Low Wage Countries and the (Uneven) Growth of US Manufacturing Plants." *Journal of International Economics* 68 (1): 219–37.

Beyer, Harald, Patricio Rojas, and Rodrigo Vergara. 1999. "Trade Liberalization and Wage Inequality." *Journal of Development Economics* 59 (1): 103–23.

Brown, Drusilla K., Alan V. Deardorff, and Robert M. Stern. 2003. "The Effects of Multinational Production on Wages and Working Conditions in Developing Countries." NBER Working Paper No. 9669, National Bureau of Economic Research, Cambridge, MA.

Carr, Marilyn, Martha Alter Chen, and Jane Tate. 2000. "Globalization and Home-Based Workers." *Feminist Economics* 6 (3): 123–42.

Center for Global Development. 2004. "Global Trade, Jobs, and Labor Standards." Center for Global Development, Washington, DC.

Coe, David T., Elhanan Helpman, and Alexander W. Hoffmaister. 1997. "North-South R & D Spillovers." *The Economic Journal* 107 (440): 134–49.

Cragg, M., and M. Epelbaum. 1996. "Why Has Wage Dispersion Grown in Mexico? Is it the Incidence of Reforms or the Growing Demand for Skills?" *Journal of Development Economics* 51 (1): 99–106.

Daude, Christian, Jacqueline Mazza, and Andres Morrison. 2003. "Core Labor Standards and Foreign Direct Investment in Latin American and the Caribbean: Does Lax Enforcement of Labor Standards Attract Investors?" Unpublished, Inter-American Development Bank, Washington, DC.

Edin, P., and J. Zetterberg. 1992. "Inter-Industry Wage Differentials: Evidence from Sweden and a Comparison with the United States." *American Economic Review* 82 (5): 1341–9.

Edmonds, Eric, and Nina Pavcnik. 2005. "Child Labor in the Global Economy." *Journal of Economic Perspectives* 18 (1): 199–220.

Elliott, Kimberly Ann, and Richard Freeman. 2001. "White Hats or Don Quixotes? Human Rights Vigilantes in the Global Economy." NBER Working Paper No. 8102, National Bureau of Economic Research, Cambridge, MA.

———. 2003. *Can Labor Standards Improve Under Globalization?* Washington, DC: Institute for International Economics.

Elliott, Robert J. R., and Joanne K. Lindley. 2006. "Trade, Skills and Adjustment Costs: A Study of Intra-Sectoral Labor Mobility." *Review of Development Economics* 10 (1): 20–41.

Feliciano, Zadia M. 2001. "Workers and Trade Liberalization: The Impact of Trade Reforms in Mexico on Wages and Employment." *Industrial and Labor Relations Review* 55 (1): 95–115.

Gatica, J., A. Mizala, and P. Romaguera. 1995. "Inter-Industry Wage Differentials in Brazil." *Economic Development and Cultural Change* 43 (2): 315–32.

Ghose, Ajit K. 2000. "Trade Liberalization, Employment and Global Inequality." *International Labour Review* 139 (3): 281–305.

Gittleman, M., and E. Wolff. 1993. "International Comparisons of Inter-Industry Wage Differentials." *Review of Income and Wealth* 39 (3): 295–312.

Goldberg, Pinelopi Koujianou, and Nina Pavcnik. 2003. "The Response of the Informal Sector to Trade Liberalization." *Journal of Development Economics* 72 (2): 463–96.

———. 2005. "Trade Protection and Wages: Evidence from the Colombian Trade Reforms." *Journal of International Economics* 66 (1): 75–105.

———. 2007. "Distributional Effects of Globalization in Developing Countries." *Journal of Economic Literature* 45 (1): 39–82.

Greene, William H. 1997. *Econometric Analysis.* Upper Saddle River, NJ: Prentice Hall.

Gruben, William C., and Darryl McLeod. 2006. "Apparel Exports and Education: How Developing Nations Encourage Women's Schooling." *Economic Letter—Insights from the Federal Reserve Bank of Dallas* 1 (3): 1–8.

Haisken-DeNew, J. P., and C. Schmidt. 1997. "Interindustry and Interregion Differentials: Mechanics and Interpretation." *The Review of Economics and Statistics* 79 (3): 516–21.

Hanson, Gordon, and Ann Harrison. 1999. "Trade, Technology, and Wage Inequality in Mexico." *Industrial and Labor Relations Review* 52 (2): 271–88.

Harrison, Ann, and Jason Scorse. 2004. "Moving Up or Moving Out? Anti-Sweatshop Activists and Labor Market Outcomes." NBER Working Paper No. 10492, National Bureau of Economic Research, Cambridge, MA.

Heckman, James, and Carmen Pagés. 2000 "The Cost of Job Security Regulation: Evidence from the Latin American Labor Market." NBER Working Paper No. 7773, National Bureau of Economic Research, Cambridge, MA.

Helwege, J. 1992. "Sectoral Shifts and Inter-Industry Wage Differentials." *Journal of Labor Economics* 10 (1): 55–84.

Kabeer, Naila. 2004. "Globalization, Labor Standards, and Women's Rights: Dilemmas of Collective (In)action in an Interdependent World." *Feminist Economics* 10 (1): 3–35.

Kaplinsky, Raphael. 2001. "Is Globalization All It Is Cracked Up to Be?" *Review of International Political Economy* 8 (1): 45–65.

Katz, L. F., and L. H. Summers. 1989a. "Can Inter-Industry Wage Differentials Justify Strategic Trade Policy?" In *Trade Policies for International Competitiveness*, ed. Robert C. Feenstra, 85–116. Chicago and London: University of Chicago Press.

———. 1989b. "Industry Rents: Evidence and Implications." *Brookings Papers on Economic Activity, Microeconomics*, 209–75.

Krebs, Tom, Pravin Krishna, and William Maloney. 2005. "Trade Policy, Income Risk, and Welfare." NBER Working Paper No. 11255, National Bureau of Economic Research, Cambridge, MA.

Krueger, Alan B., and Lawrence H. Summers. 1988. "Efficiency Wages and the Inter-Industry Wage Structure." *Econometrica* 56 (2): 259–93.

Kucera, David. 2002. "Core Labour Standards and Foreign Direct Investment." *International Labour Review* 141 (1-2): 31–69.

Lall, Sanjaya. 2002. "The Employment Impact of Globalisation in Developing Countries." Working Paper 93, Queen Elizabeth House, Oxford University. Prepared for the International Policy Group.

Lawrence, Robert, and Matthew Slaughter. 1993. "International Trade and American Wages in the 1980s: Giant Sucking Sound or Small Hiccup?" *Brookings Papers on Economic Activity 2: Microeconomics,* 161–226.

Leamer, Edward E. 1998. "In Search of Stolper-Samuelson Linkages between Trade and Lower Wages." In *Imports, Exports, and the American Worker*, ed. S. Collins, 141–202. Washington, DC: Brookings Institution Press.

Lipsey, R. E., and F. Sjoholm. 2004a. "FDI and Wage Spillovers in Indonesian Manufacturing." *Review of World Economics/Weltwirtschaftliches Archiv* 140 (2): 321–32.

———. 2004b. "Foreign Direct Investment, Education and Wages in Indonesian Manufacturing." *Journal of Development Economics* 73 (1): 415–22.

Maddala, G. S. 1983. *Limited-Dependent and Qualitative Variables in Econometrics*. Cambridge University Press.

Maloney, William F. 2004 "Informality Revisited." *World Development* 32 (7): 1159–78.

Marcouiller, Douglas, Veronica Ruiz de Castilla, and Christopher Woodruff. 1997. "Formal Measures of the Informal-Sector Wage Gap in Mexico, El Salvador, and Peru." *Economic Development and Cultural Change* 45 (2): 367–92.

Mehmet, Ozay, and Akbar Tavakoli. 2003. "Does Foreign Direct Investment Cause a Race to the Bottom? Evidence from Four Asian Countries." *Journal of the Asia Pacific Economy* 8 (2): 133–56.

Mosley, Layna, and Saika Uno. 2007. "Racing to the Bottom or Climbing to the Top?" *Comparative Political Studies* 40 (8): 923–48.

Moss, Todd J., Vijaya Ramachandran, and Manju Kedia Shah. 2004. "Is Africa's Skepticism of Foreign Capital Justified? Evidence from East Asian Firm Survey Data." Working Paper No. 41, Center for Global Development, Washington, DC.

Papola, T., and W. Bharadwaj. 1970. "Dynamics of Industrial Wage Structure: An Inter-Country Analysis." *The Economic Journal* 80: 72–90.

Pavcnik, Nina. 2002. "Trade Liberalization, Exit, and Productivity Improvements: Evidence from Chilean Plants." *Review of Economic Studies* 69 (1,238): 245–76.

Pavcnik, N., A. Blom, P. Goldberg, and N. Schady. 2003. "Trade Liberalization and Industry Wage Structure: Evidence from Brazil." Department of Economics, Dartmouth College, Hanover, NH.

Revenga, Ana. 1997. "Employment and Wage Effects of Trade Liberalization: The Case of Mexican Manufacturing." *Journal of Labor Economics* 15 (3(part 2)): S20–S43.

Richardson, J. David. 1995. "Income Inequality and Trade: How to Think, What to Conclude." *Journal of Economic Perspectives* 9 (3): 35–55.

Robertson, Raymond. 2004. "Relative Prices and Wage Inequality: Evidence from Mexico." *Journal of International Economics* 64 (2): 387–409.

———. 2005. "Has NAFTA Increased Labor Market Integration between the United States and Mexico?" *The World Bank Economic Review* 19 (3): 425–48.

Slaughter, M. 2000. "What Are the Results of Product-Price Studies and What Can We Learn from Their Differences?" In *The Impact of International Trade on Wages*, ed. R. C. Feenstra, 129–70. Chicago: University of Chicago Press.

———. 2002. "Does Inward Foreign Direct Investment Contribute to Skill Upgrading in Developing Countries?" SCEPA Working Paper 2002-08, Schwartz Center for Economic Policy Analysis, New School for Social Research, New York.

Verhoogen, Eric. 2007. "Trade Quality Upgrading, and Wage Inequality in the Mexican Manufacturing Sector." Discussion Paper 0607-08, Department of Economics, Columbia University, New York.

Wiggins, Vince. 1998. "Grand2: Stata Module to Compute an Estimate of the Grand Mean/Intercept Differences." Statistical Software Components No. S355201, Department of Economics, Boston College, Chestnut Hill, MA. http://fmwww.bc.edu/repec/bocode/g/grand2.ado.

Wood, Adrian. 1997. "Openness and Wage Inequality in Developing Countries: The Latin American Challenge to East Asian Conventional Wisdom." *The World Bank Economic Review* 11 (1): 33–57.

CHAPTER 4

Globalization and Working Conditions: Evidence from Cambodia

Samsen Neak and Raymond Robertson

Cambodia underwent a dramatic economic transformation from socialism to export-oriented capitalism beginning in the mid-1970s. Cambodia's socialist history differentiates it from the other countries in this volume but, like the other countries, globalization has played a significant role in Cambodia's adjustment. Cambodia's experience with globalization has primarily centered on the rise in both FDI and exports in the garment sector and, to a lesser extent, construction related to tourism. The rise of the garment sector was accompanied by an increase in international attention to working conditions. Foreign direct investment (FDI), access to export markets, and international attention are correlated with working conditions in the garment sector, which compare positively with working conditions in other sectors of the Cambodian economy. In particular, hourly wages in the garment sector are 29 percent higher than average monthly wage earnings, and this premium increases to nearly 44 percent when controlling for the fact that workers in the garment sector are predominantly young and female. Furthermore, other measures of working conditions seem to be higher in the garment sector than in other sectors. For example, the accident rate is lower in the garment sector than in any other sector.

Quantifying the effect of globalization on working conditions is difficult. One challenge is that a large proportion of workers—as high as 85 percent as estimated by the Economic Institute of Cambodia in 2005[1]—are employed in the informal sector. In the absence of formal legal protections, managers or owners may force employees to work longer hours and engage in exploitative child labor. Furthermore, workers have no representation, few days off, and low benefits.[2] Therefore, the second section of this chapter provides a more qualitative analysis and overview of globalization and working conditions. This qualitative analysis indicates that globalization in Cambodia seems to have brought international buyers, the government, factory owners, and trade unions together in a strong commitment to maintaining a reputation for compliance with corporate codes relating to working conditions in the country's clothing export niche market.

The first section of this chapter describes the globalization experience in Cambodia and provides descriptive statistics about its evolution. The second section provides a qualitative analysis of globalization and working conditions by focusing on the garment sector. The third part analyzes household surveys to assess the impact of globalization on wages and working conditions.

Globalization in Cambodia

Perhaps the most widely accepted definition of globalization in economic studies is openness to trade and FDI. As in the other countries in this volume, trade and FDI have played a significant role in Cambodia's globalization experience. This section, therefore, discusses the evolution of certain aspects of trade and FDI in Cambodia.

In Cambodia, globalization in general and economic integration or trade liberalization in particular have evolved significantly. This evolution tracks three main economic policy regimes: before 1989, 1990–92, and 1993–2004. Throughout this period of liberalization, trade rose from about 5 percent of GDP to well over 120 percent, as can be seen in figure 4.1.

TRADE AND TARIFF POLICY

During the 1980s, Cambodia's trade regime was typical of a socialist country, marked by cooperation with the socialist bloc of the former Soviet Union and isolated from the West. Trade was firmly controlled by the state.[3] In 1989, the government moved away from socialism by initiating a free market–oriented program, liberalizing trade, and encouraging FDI. These reforms, which included the removal of all quantitative restrictions, allowed state-owned enterprises greater autonomy and enabled privatization of state-owned firms and other state assets.

The government adopted free market mechanisms and allowed individuals private ownership of land and other physical assets. The state-owned, monopolized foreign trade company was abolished and a new foreign investment law that allowed private exporters and importers to engage in trading activities was promulgated. By 1989, the volume of international trade recorded at US$200 million and quasi-official, crossborder trade with Thailand and Vietnam had expanded significantly. Both formal and informal trade activities rose gradually afterward, with the trade to GDP ratio reaching 20 percent.[4]

In 1993, another wave of dramatic change took place in the transitional economy following the conduct of the first U.N.-backed general election. A coalition government

FIGURE 4.1 **Trade as Percentage of GDP**

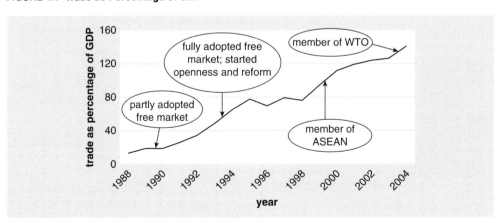

SOURCE: Authors' construction.

NOTE: ASEAN = Association of Southeast Asian Nations; WTO = World Trade Organization.

committed to democracy and a free-market economy was elected. This government launched a series of far-reaching structural reforms, along with the introduction and accelerated implementation of a program of deeper and wider economic integration and trade openness. According to the First Socio-Economic Development Plan 1996–2000, liberal trade and investment policy was the basis for developing the country's external trade. The government committed—through the strengthening of its external sector—to reintegrating the domestic economy into the regional and global economies. The main strategies included joining the Association of Southeast Asian Nations (ASEAN[5]), gaining full Most Favored Nation (MFN) and Generalized System of Preferences (GSP) status with its trading nations, participating in economic cooperation with the Great Mekong Subregion, and other such initiatives, and the wide promotion of foreign investment within the 1996–2006 time frame (Royal Government of Cambodia 1996).

These policy visions set forth by the national plan generated several results during the mid- and late 1990s. First, quantitative restrictions on exports and imports ended in 1994. Second, gaining MFN status facilitated access to the U.S. garment market in 1996, and obtaining GSP status provided access to clothing markets in the European Union in 1997. Cambodia was also granted preferential tariff rates by 28 countries in 1999.[6] Third, the government signed bilateral trade and investment protection agreements with various countries during the 1990s.[7] Fourth, membership in ASEAN was secured in 1999 and, as a result, Cambodia now offers and enjoys the lower ASEAN Free Trade Area tariff rates. Fifth, the government joined the Great Mekong Subregion, integrating its transportation infrastructure and facilitating trade with five other Mekong countries; and formed triangle development zones along the borders with neighboring countries Lao PDR, Thailand, and Vietnam. Finally, the country became a member of the World Trade Organization in 2003. Box 4.1 provides more detail about this evolution.

INVESTMENT REGIME

Cambodia's globalization experience was also characterized by the inflow of FDI. The enactment of the Law on Investment in 1994, which replaced the 1989 Investment Law, created an open and liberal investment regime (U.S Embassy, Cambodia 2004; UNCTAD/ICC 2003; UNESCAP 2004).

While the government was promoting economic integration and enacting structural reforms, the inflow of foreign investment fluctuated. These swings seemed not to be the result of globalization itself, but rather the result of regional economic instability, internal political uncertainty, and institutional weaknesses in Cambodia. The IMF (2004) identified weak governance, weak rule of law, high energy costs, political instability, and small domestic market size as the main factors behind FDI fluctuations.

Figure 4.2, which illustrates the changes in foreign investment in Cambodia relative to GDP, indicates that 1994 was a significant starting point for the inflow of foreign capital. Total inflow in 1994 was US$69 million and the FDI-to-GDP ratio was 2.5 percent. This flow sharply increased in 1995 (US$151 million) and in 1996 (US$294 million). FDI decreased sharply in 1997 (US$204 million) because of the Asian financial crisis and a domestic political crisis, which shook investor confidence. Private investment resumed in 1998 (US$243 million), then steeply declined until

BOX 4.1 **Evolution of Cambodian Trade Policy**

1980s

- Tightly controlled trading system: level and composition of trade determined through quantitative restrictions and state-owned trading bodies
- Embarked on liberalization in the late 1980s
  - abolished state monopoly of foreign trade
  - promulgated a foreign investment law, enabling private companies to engage in foreign trade

1990s

- Largely removed restrictions on the ability of firms and individuals to engage in international trade (1993)
- Eliminated all quantitative restrictions on trade (1994)
- Gained MFN status from the United States (1996); GSP status from the European Union (1997); MFN/GSP status from 28 countries (1999)
- Became a member of ASEAN in (1999)
- Committed to a gradual reduction in most tariff rates by 2010

2001

- Reduced maximum tariff rates from 120 percent to 35 percent and reduced the number of tariff bands from 12 to 4
- Lowered average unweighted tariff rates to 16.5 percent from 17.3 percent in 2000 and 18.4 percent in 1997
- Eliminated most nontariff trade barriers

2002

- Initiated a Triangle Economic Cooperation strategy between Cambodia, Vietnam, and Lao PDR, focusing on commerce, industry, public works and transportation, and tourism

2003

- Accession to WTO

SOURCE: Authors, based on UNDP (2004) and World Bank (2004).

2003 (US$84 million), and recovered in 2004 when the country absorbed US$131 million from foreign capital flows.

With greatly simplified and reduced trade tariffs and weak border controls, Cambodia is now regarded as a highly open economy. The U.S.-based Heritage Foundation's 2006 index of economic freedom (http://www.heritage.org/Index/Country/Cambodia) gives Cambodia a score of 2.68 (putting the country in the "Mostly Free" category) and ranks Cambodia 68 of 157 countries.[8]

FIGURE 4.2 **FDI in Cambodia as Percentage of GDP**

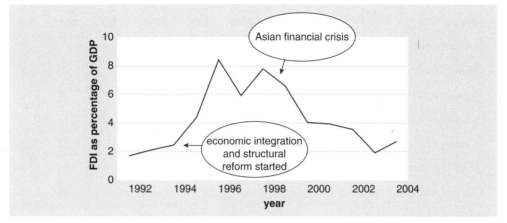

SOURCE: World Bank World Development Indicators 2006.

TRADE AND FOREIGN DIRECT INVESTMENT

Trade and FDI have concentrated primarily in the garment sector. As trading activity increased in general, exports of ready-made garments grew rapidly. While garment exports accounted for 20 percent of total exports in 1996, this share increased to 80 percent between 2002 and 2005. The share of agricultural products in total exports, including fish, has declined, although this sector's export volume increased. The share of agricultural products in total exports fell from about 36 percent in the late 1990s to approximately 14 percent in the early 2000s. Yet, in absolute value, agricultural exports increased from an annual average of US$250 million during 1996–99 to about US$300 million during 2000–05, according to data estimated by the National Bank of Cambodia. Principle agricultural exports include paddy rice, rubber, and fish.

Intermediate products accounted for as much as half of aggregate imports. The import of fabrics to supply garment industry production took the largest share, while petroleum imports was the runnerup. Other imports were mainly consumer products, ranging from rice and food products to construction materials to cosmetics. Table 4.1 shows the evolution of merchandise trade from 1996 through 2005. The growth of the textiles and garment sector, along with the relative decline in agriculture, is especially apparent.

The increase in trading activity was notably driven by FDI projects in garments and the construction of hotels and restaurants after the country opened its economy in the early 1990s. According to the IMF (2004), FDI was heavily concentrated in the tourism and construction sectors from 1994 to 1996, in logging activities from 1996 to 1998, and in the garment industry from 1998 to 2004. Long-term capital stock reached US$1.9 billion by 2005. As figure 4.3 shows, 25 percent was invested in garment factories and 14 percent in hotel construction. The industry and services sectors together absorbed more than 95 percent of foreign investment stock while agriculture—in which more than 70 percent of the country's labor force is employed—received only 4 percent.

TABLE 4.1 **Merchandise Trade in Cambodia, 1996–2005**

Indicator	1996	1998	2000	2002	2003	2004	2005
Total goods exports[a] (US$ million)	510	802	1,397	1,770	2,087	2,589	2,910
Share of textiles and garment (%)	20	47	73	79	78	80	78
Share of agriculture[b] (%)	36	36	17	13	15	13	14
Share of re-export[c] (%)	44	15	8	6	6	5	5
Total goods imports (US$ million)	1,054	1,166	1,936	2,361	2,668	3,269	3,928
Share of garment-related material (%)	—	17	27	30	30	31	28
Share of petroleum (%)	—	27	17	15	16	19	21
Share of import for re-export (%)	—	8	5	4	3	3	3

SOURCE: Compiled from data provided by National Bank of Cambodia.

NOTE: — = Not available.

a. Total goods exports include unrecorded export figures estimated by the National Bank of Cambodia. These unrecorded figures consist primarily of agricultural products such as logs, sawn timbers, rubber, paddy rice, furniture and wood products, fish, and second-hand clothes and gems.

b. Includes unrecorded agricultural exports.

c. Re-export mainly consists of cigarettes, beer, used motorcycles, and electronics.

LABOR FORCE AND EMPLOYMENT SHIFT

The employment structure within the three main sectors of Cambodia's economy has not changed significantly. Employment share in the agricultural sector (including fisheries and forestry) remained dominant at 71 percent in 2004, experiencing a decrease of 5 percentage points from 76 percent in 1993. The employment share of services remained

FIGURE 4.3 **FDI Stock by Sector through 2005**

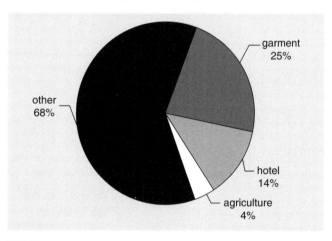

SOURCE: Authors' calculation based on data provided by the National Bank of Cambodia.

constant at 17 percent during the decade 1993 to 2004. As shown in figure 4.4, an increasing share of employment in the industrial sector replaced the decreasing share of the agriculture sector. The industrial sector share rose 5 percentage points, from 6 percent in 1993 to 11 percent in 2004. This change is attributable to the growth of jobs in manufacturing, especially in the garment industry and construction. The share of manufacturing in total employment doubled from just 4 percent in 1993 to 8 percent in 2004, while construction increased from 2 percent to 3 percent.

FIGURE 4.4 **Structure of Employment, 1993–04**

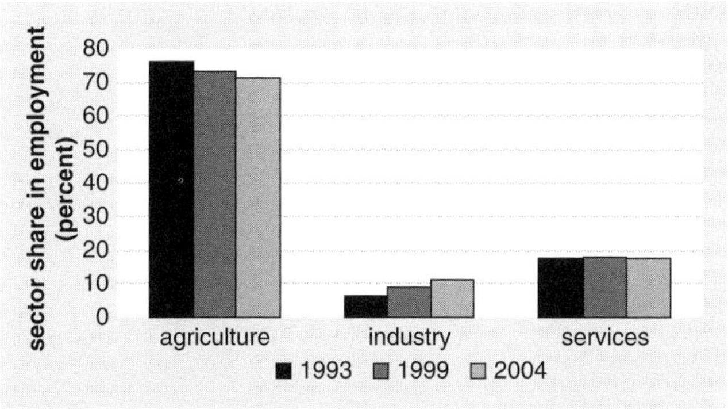

SOURCE: Economic Institute of Cambodia General Equilibrium Model, version 2006-05-17 (2006).

An employment shift from agriculture to other industries took place during the 10 years between 1994 and 2004, especially to the formal sector, principally garments, and informal sector, including the construction and services subsectors (transportation and restaurants). The garment and construction industries require low-skilled and unskilled workers and are accessible to rural job seekers. The share of women employed in agriculture declined significantly, from 71.1 percent in 1999 to 56.8 percent of total female employment in 2004, according to household surveys in 1999 and 2004 (National Institute of Statistics 1999, 2004). This declining share was largely attributed to the movement of rural women to the garment industry. About 85 percent of the 245,000–270,000 garment workers in 2004 were women who migrated from rural areas.

Globalization also fostered the tourism industry, which led to an increase in construction. Based on a 2005 EIC survey in a district[9] close to Siem Reap, which experienced a tourist boom as a result of its proximity to Angkor Wat, the district's villagers working in construction increased roughly sixfold from 1999 to 2005. This labor shift may have been seasonal, however, because workers were still engaged in farming activities during the crop-growing season.

The globalization process in Cambodia was very rapid, with trade and foreign investment expanding significantly following the adoption of a free-market economy in 1989. The impact on Cambodia has been increased FDI and exports, both primarily concentrated in the garment sector. Globalization seems to have facilitated a shift, especially of women, from employment in agriculture to manufacturing. Given this shift, the next two sections use a qualitative analysis and household data analysis to determine the impact on working conditions for Cambodian workers.

Globalization's Effects on Working Conditions: A Qualitative Analysis

Institutions and regulations have a significant effect on working conditions in Cambodia. These institutions have played a critical role in shaping globalization's effect on working conditions. Therefore, this section describes the major institutional forces affecting working conditions and how they have affected the influence of globalization.

REGULATIONS AND ACCORDS AFFECTING WORKING CONDITIONS

This section defines working conditions, using the core labor standards set forth by the International Labour Organization (ILO): (i) freedom of association and the right to organize, (ii) freedom from forced labor, (iii) elimination of child labor that is harmful to the child or interferes with schooling, and (iv) nondiscrimination in employment (Center for Global Development 2004).

Cambodia recognized basic human rights in its 1993 constitution, which grants basic rights to everyone. These rights include the right to choose employment, the right to equal pay for equal work, equality of work outside and inside the home, the right to form and join unions, the right to strike and to hold nonviolent demonstrations, the abolition of all forms of discrimination against women (with a particular prohibition of the exploitation of women in employment), the guarantee of women's job security during pregnancy, and the right to maternity leave. The 1997 Labor Code provides the legal and regulatory framework for worker protection.

Cambodia's normalization of relations with other countries included becoming a member of major international and regional organizations, such as the ILO. As a result of ILO membership and the country's commitment to basic human rights, Cambodia ratified major ILO conventions on core labor rights and standards. In 2000, the government of Cambodia and the parliament approved the conventions on forced or compulsory labor, abolition of forced labor, freedom of association, the application of the principles of the right to organize and to bargain collectively, equal remuneration for men and women workers for work of equal value, and minimum age for admission to employment. Table 4.2 shows Cambodia's ratification of the fundamental ILO conventions.

TABLE 4.2 **Fundamental ILO Conventions Ratified by Cambodia**

Convention number	Convention	Date of ratification
29	Forced Labour Convention	1970
105	Abolition of Forced Labour Convention	2000
87	Freedom of Association and Protection of the Right to Organise Convention	2000
98	Right to Organise and Collective Bargaining Convention	2000
100	Equal Remuneration Convention	2000
111	Discrimination (Employment and Occupation) Convention	2000
138	Minimum Age Convention	2000

SOURCES: ILO 2006; UNHCR 2005.

Because globalization has been concentrated in the garment and hotel sectors, the next subsections analyze working conditions in those sectors in the context of these labor standards. The analysis focuses on how growth in these sectors has affected the four core labor standards.

GARMENT INDUSTRY AND WORKING CONDITIONS

The garment industry, an example of success in Cambodia's trade openness, was the fastest growing export sector and has been an engine of economic growth since 1996. Table 4.3 contains some of the key descriptive statistics for Cambodia's garment industry. The industry's exports accounted for more than 75 percent of total national goods exports in 2005; it remains one of the significant FDI recipients despite decreasing overall FDI

TABLE 4.3 **Evolution of the Garment Industry in Cambodia**

Indicator	1996	1998	2000	2002	2003	2004	2005
Exports (US$ million)	106	355	925	1,291	1,580	1,969	2,197
Investment flow[a] (US$ million)	157	92	26	14	16	40	54
Number of factories (cumulative)	24	129	190	188	197	206	250
Number of workers (thousand)	24	79	123	210	234	246	300

SOURCES: USAID 2005; EIC database.
NOTE:

a. Data on investment is registered capital with the Council for the Development of Cambodia; , some of the registered projects might not have been implemented.

inflow. Furthermore, this industry is the only formal manufacturing sector that provides as many as 300,000 jobs (as of 2006) to the minimally educated labor force from rural areas, of which more than 80 percent are female.

In addition to its significant role in the domestic economy, the garment industry is considered a key driver of Cambodia's integration into the global and regional economies. The sector's working conditions have attracted much attention since the government's implementation of the 1997 Labor Code and its ratification of the major ILO conventions (table 4.2).

Considerable evidence demonstrates that Cambodia has improved its compliance with ILO core labor standards. Quarterly synthesis reports from the ILO Better Factories Cambodia project indicate that the industry generally complies with core labor standards despite some shortfalls in such areas as wages, working hours, and strikes. The common infractions include delayed payment of wages, excess overtime, and illegal strikes (see the annex to this chapter for details). A 2004 World Bank Foreign Investment Advisory Service survey of the 15 top international buyers of textiles and garments, accounting for 45 percent of Cambodian garment exports, rated Cambodia first in compliance with labor standards (World Bank 2004). An analysis by the Ministry of Commerce of Cambodia and the Asian Development Bank in 2004 pointed out that labor compliance is one of the strengths of the Cambodian garment industry. Another study also argued that Cambodia was maintaining its market niche in "sweat-shop-free" garment products (USAID 2005).

Yet, good labor standards in this industry cannot automatically be linked back to globalization. Good labor standards are perhaps more accurately attributable to globalization-driven government intervention, regulation, and monitoring. Regulation and monitoring possibly distinguish Cambodia from the other countries in this volume more than any facet of globalization. While increased monitoring did play a role in the Central American Free Trade Agreement that affected Honduras and El Salvador, Cambodia's trade agreement specifically tied U.S. market access to improvements in working conditions. As part of the labor program initiated by the government of Cambodia, the U.S. government agreed in 2001 to hire the ILO to undertake a monitoring program (Better Factories Cambodia) to detect core labor standards violations in exchange for annual increases in quota access. The Cambodian government agreed to rigorously enforce the Cambodian

Labor Law by creating the Arbitration Council and facilitating the establishment of trade unions and associations of garment makers. As of the end of the Multifibre Arrangement in 2004, the Cambodian garment sector's international buyers, the government, factory owners, and trade unions were all strongly committed to maintaining the good reputation for labor compliance in the country's clothing export niche market.

These complementary institutions and programs enhanced Cambodia's ability to adhere to internationally recognized labor rights. For instance, the Better Factories Cambodia program carries out surprise visits to check working conditions with regard to child labor, freedom of association, employee contracts, wages, working hours, workplace facilities, noise control, and machinery safety in each factory at least once a year. After the visits, the program reports its findings to factory owners. Quarterly Synthesis Reports, summarizing compliance for all participating factories, are then publicly released. The other three parties to the program—the Garment Manufacturers Association in Cambodia (GMAC), the Arbitration Council, and labor unions—have also helped to facilitate improved working conditions through mediation, negotiations, and strikes. See box 4.2.

BOX 4.2 **About Better Factories Cambodia**

The ILO program Better Factories Cambodia, also known as the ILO Garment Sector Project, was established in 2001 after Cambodia signed a deal with the United States to improve working conditions in exchange for better access to the U.S. market. This program aims to oversee labor compliance to ensure a "sweatshop-free" industry in the country. In 2005, Better Factories, formerly funded only by USAID, became jointly funded by the Cambodian government, GMAC (the association of apparel manufacturers), international buyers, USAID, and the French development agency AFD.

GMAC was established in March 1996. As of August 2006, there were 278 active members. GMAC plays an important role in the development of the garment industry through lobbying the government to seek GSP and MFN status and advising the government about relevant policies to promote the industry. GMAC and the government also lobbied the U.S. Congress to pass the Tariff Relief for Developing Economies Act, which would have allowed Cambodia to export clothing without tariffs and quotas.

The Arbitration Council, whose members are representatives nominated by trade unions, GMAC, and the Ministry of Social Affairs, Veterans, and Youth Rehabilitation, was established in 2003. The council's main function is to resolve collective labor disputes that cannot be resolved through negotiation or conciliation.

Labor unions also play an active role in ensuring compliance with the ILO core labor standards and Cambodian labor law. There have been many complaints, strikes, and demonstrations facilitated or organized by trade unions. In 2005, there were an estimated 823 labor unions under 24 labor federations, according to records provided by the Ministry of Social Affairs, Veterans, and Youth Rehabilitation.

SOURCE: Authors' compilation.

Conditions in the garment industry may be better than in other sectors that receive less international attention. For example, of working conditions in the brick and tile and salt manufacturing industries, which have a high degree of informality, have suggested that it is common practice in these industries to employ underage labor, violating ILO conventions related to child labor (Monyrath 2005). The Ministry of Labor and Vocational Training and the ILO are implementing social programs to reduce child labor. Although the garment industry provides relatively good working conditions compared with the same industries in other countries and other industries within Cambodia, the authorities are not suggesting that there have been no incidents of labor standard violations. Strikes frequently are organized by trade unions to demand better working conditions—there were approximately 90 strikes in 2000, and as many as

FIGURE 4.5 **Trade Unions and Strikes in the Cambodian Garment Industry**

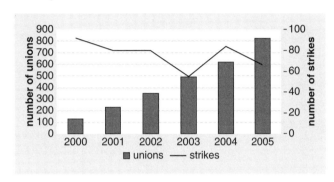

SOURCES: Garment Manufacturers Association of Cambodia (http://www.gmac-cambodia.org/members.asp) and personal communication with Ministry of Labor and Vocational Training.

66 in 2005. As figure 4.5 shows, however, the rise in unionization did not coincide with an increasing number of strikes. If anything, the relationship between the number of unions and the number of strikes seems to be negative.

HOTEL INDUSTRY AND WORKING CONDITIONS

The hotel industry, another leading FDI recipient, also grew rapidly during the globalization process. This tourist-oriented industry was chiefly driven by the sharp increase in the number of foreign visitors from Asia (especially from the Republic of Korea, Japan, China, and Malaysia), North America (especially from the United States), and Europe (especially from Germany, France, and the United Kingdom). As shown in table 4.4, the number of tourists reached more than 1 million in 2004, with a continued rise in arrivals to a record of nearly 1.5 million in 2005.

Tourism is one of the few leading formal sectors that provide jobs. According to data provided by the Cambodian Tourism and Service Worker Federation (an umbrella organization of unions in 18 hotels), approximately 3,000 workers were employed in hotels in 2005. This figure is well below the actual number of workers in the more than 300 hotels in Cambodia. These additional hotels, however, are small and thus employ fewer than the main large hotels.

Working conditions in the hotel industry are relatively good when compared with informal industries or with formal micro, small, or medium enterprises (such as brick and tile manufacturers, and salt producers, which have employed child workers). The industry's employer-employee relationships are relatively more stable than those in the garment industry, which experiences numerous strikes every year. In 2006 there was only

TABLE 4.4 **Hotel Industry in Cambodia**

Indicator	1996	1998	2000	2002	2003	2004	2005
Number of tourists (thousand)	260	287	466	787	701	1,055	1,422
Investment flow (US$ million)	43	58	34	22	25	4	16
Number of hotels (cumulative)	—	216	240	267	292	299	317
Number of workers[a] (cumulative)	—	—	—	—	—	—	3,226

SOURCES: Cambodian Investment Board and Council for the Development of Cambodia 2006; Ministry of Tourism various years; Cambodian Tourism and Service Workers Federation 2006.

NOTE: — = Not available.

a. Data are available for 2005 only and from the 18 main hotels in Phnom Penh and Siem Reap.

FIGURE 4.6 **Trade Unions and Trade Union Membership in the Hotel Industry, 2002–05**

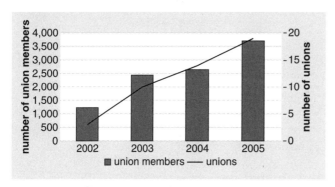

SOURCE: Cambodian Tourism and Service Workers Federation 2006.

one strike at one hotel, despite the dramatic rise in both the number of unions and union membership in the industry, shown in figure 4.6.

Household Survey Analysis

Globalization may have statistically identifiable effects on working conditions. Evidence of the effects of globalization may be evident from worker-level data. This section applies established econometric techniques to Cambodian worker-level data to identify some of the possible effects of globalization.

DATA

The analysis of the relationship between globalization and working conditions in Cambodia uses the 2003–04 Cambodia Socio-Economic Survey conducted by the Cambodian National Institute of Statistics. In addition to basic socioeconomic variables, this extensive survey covers housing conditions, expenditures, employment information, and industry-level information on accidents and disabilities.

The survey covered 74,808 individuals of all ages, with approximately 51 percent female respondents. To focus on the working population, the sample for this analysis was limited to people between 10 and 65 years of age, inclusive. The educational distribution, presented in figure 4.7, is similar to that found in many developing countries and indicates that workers with a high school education (12 years of education) are considered high-skilled workers.

FIGURE 4.7 **Educational Distribution in Cambodia Socio-Economic Survey, 2003–04**

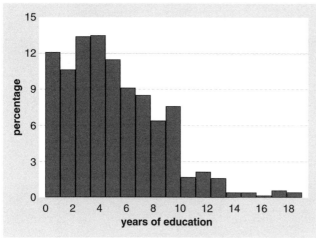

SOURCE: National Institute of Statistics of Cambodia 2004.

Table 4.5 illustrates some of the sample demographic characteristics by sector. About 58 percent of workers are employed in primary industries (agriculture, forestry, husbandry, and fishing). Just over 4 percent work in textiles and apparel, making it the largest manufacturing industry in the sample. Average education levels for each sector are shown in the second column of table 4.5. All of the primary industries (except other agriculture) have below-average education levels, as do the manufacturing industries food (with beverages and tobacco) and wood. The textiles and apparel sector, however, has slightly above the average education level.

Perhaps the least surprising yet most striking characteristics are found in the last two columns, which show the percentage female and average age in each sector. In the survey, 81 percent of the workers in textiles and apparel are female, far more than any other sector. The sales sector has the next highest share of female employment at just over 67 percent. Textiles workers are also much younger than workers in most other industries, with an average age of about 26 years. Thus, these survey data confirm a finding in other countries and throughout the literature: textiles and apparel workers are generally young females. Somewhat unexpected is that they are generally more educated than workers in other sectors.

WAGE DIFFERENTIALS

One measure of working conditions is the interindustry wage differential (IIWD), which is calculated using the difference between the wage earned in the worker's industry of employment and the wage the worker would earn if employed in another sector. IIWDs are not usually explained by differences in demographic characteristics, such as gender, age, and education, and seem to represent a benefit to workers who can get jobs in high-wage industries. Because globalization in Cambodia has been concentrated in the textiles and apparel sector, it is important to first compare wages in that sector with wages in other sectors within Cambodia. Using data from the socioeconomic survey, the analysis focuses on wage income reported as monthly income from remunerated employment.

The natural log of monthly income is used to measure IIWDs across industries. The first column of table 4.6 presents the overall average of log wages and the percentage difference from this overall average (wage differential or wage premium) that workers earn in each industry.[10]

TABLE 4.5 **Survey Demographic Characteristics**

Sector	Share (%)	Average education (years)	Percentage female	Average age
Primary sectors				
Agriculture, food	42.67	6.06	52.0	33.00
Agriculture, other	0.64	6.64	59.3	28.38
Husbandry and fishery	15.40	5.48	41.9	24.86
Forestry	2.06	5.89	50.1	27.72
Mining	0.21	4.48	44.4	31.21
Manufacturing				
Food, beverages, and tobacco	1.64	5.58	46.4	32.06
Textiles and apparel	**4.26**	**6.92**	**81.0**	**25.99**
Wood	2.53	5.54	61.5	34.08
Manufacturing, other	0.80	7.23	29.1	33.16
Utilities and construction				
Utilities	0.19	7.60	21.0	31.21
Construction	2.49	7.31	12.5	30.90
Services				
Sales	14.99	7.11	67.2	33.57
Transport	2.65	7.37	7.1	34.22
Finance, insurance, and real estate	0.49	7.74	46.9	37.53
Public administration	2.74	10.07	14.7	40.36
Social services	2.57	11.22	38.2	37.40
Other services	3.66	8.11	45.2	31.23
Average	n.a.	6.63	50.0	31.65

SOURCE: National Institute of Statistics 2004.

NOTE: n.a. = Not applicable. This table is based on 42,520 observations in the survey.

The first column of table 4.6 shows that the overall average log wage is 11.74. The primary industries (food agriculture through mining) all earn less than this average. Food agriculture workers, for example, earn nearly 52 percent less than the average wage.[11] This is comparable to the results found in Indonesia, El Salvador, and Honduras: workers in agriculture earn significantly less than the national average. Workers in two of the manufacturing industries, food (with beverages and tobacco) and wood products, also earn

TABLE 4.6 **Monthly Wage Differentials without and with Demographic Characteristics**

	Without demographic controls	With demographic controls
Mean log wage across all sectors per month	11.74	10.52
Sector	**Differentials**	
Agriculture, food	−0.52*	−0.52*
Agriculture, other	−0.83*	−0.72*
Husbandry and fishery	−0.27*	−0.25*
Forestry	−0.29*	−0.35*
Mining	−0.33*	−0.32
Food, beverages, and tobacco	−0.13	−0.03
Textiles and apparel	0.67*	0.80*
Wood	−0.27*	−0.29*
Manufacturing, other	0.27*	0.22*
Utilities	0.92*	0.58*
Construction	0.23*	0.12*
Sales	0.13*	0.13*
Transport	0.21*	0.13*
Finance, insurance, and real estate	0.01	−0.08
Public administration	−0.11*	−0.28*
Social services	0.09*	−0.10*
Other services	0.19*	0.27*
Effects of demographic characteristics		
Female		−0.13*
Age		0.07*
Age squared		0.00
Education		0.01*

SOURCE: Authors' calculations based on National Institute of Statistics (2004).

NOTE: The mean log wage is the natural log of monthly wage earnings. Wage differentials represent the percentage (log) difference from the mean wage for each sector. For example, −0.52 means 52 percent less than the overall mean wage. The percentage changes reported here are obtained by raising e to the estimated coefficient and subtracting 1, because the model is log-linear.

* indicates statistically significant difference from the overall mean wage at the 5 percent level.

below-average wages. Workers in utilities, construction, and sales, however, earn above-average wages.

Workers in textiles and apparel earn about 67 percent more than the average wage. This is a significant positive premium for these workers, and is larger than nearly every other positive premium. Only the utilities sector has a larger positive differential. This large differential is somewhat surprising given the gender composition of these workers (young females) found in table 4.5.

Differences in demographic composition could possibly affect average wages. For example, if a sector hires more-educated workers on average, and workers with more education earn higher wages, then wages in that sector will be higher than average. To control for this, the analysis estimates a regression that controls for demographic characteristics (gender, age, age squared, and years of education). After controlling for these characteristics, the IIWDs can be recalculated and compare with average wages.

The second column in table 4.6 illustrates the results. The wage differentials earned for different demographic characteristics are reported at the bottom of the table. Females, for example, earn about 13 percent less than other workers when controlling for sector, age, and education. Older and more-educated workers earn higher wages.

Once these demographic characteristics are controlled for, the IIWD in the textiles and apparel industry increases to nearly 80 percent. This increase over the regression that did not control for demographic characteristics is not surprising—the sector comprises primarily workers who are female and less educated. In fact, once these demographic characteristics are controlled for, these workers earn the largest positive differential of all sectors. In particular, the IIWD in the utilities sector falls because that sector tends to employ more-educated, older, male workers.

Working Conditions

Wages are just one measure of working conditions. Many other factors affect job quality. The Cambodian data analyzed here contain two main nonwage measures: hours and accidents. This section analyzes these two and relates them to estimates of the IIWDs.

HOURS

The large positive IIWD in the textiles sector could be compensating for adverse nonwage working conditions. One culprit could be long hours. Table 4.7 shows the differences in hours worked across industries. The overall average hours worked in the previous week, according to the survey, was nearly 49. Substantial variation in the number of hours worked occurs across industries. In particular, textiles employees work about 5.6 hours more than the average worker, which may result in higher monthly wage income. Workers in other manufacturing industries, except for wood products, also work more hours than the average worker.

To account for the differences in hours worked across industries, the analysis calculates the hourly wage by dividing the monthly wage by the number of hours worked the previous week and multiplies by 4.3 (the average number of weeks per month). These hourly wages are then used in the wage equation to estimate IIWDs. The results, without and with demographic characteristics, are shown in table 4.8.

TABLE 4.7 **Interindustry Differences in Hours Worked**

Overall mean hours worked	48.783
Agriculture, food	–2.007*
Agriculture, other	–2.783
Husbandry and fishery	2.189
Forestry	–7.369*
Mining	0.304
Food, beverages, and tobacco	3.863*
Textiles and apparel	5.627*
Wood	0.285
Manufacturing, other	7.005*
Utilities	–2.616
Construction	2.302*
Sales	4.869*
Transport	2.838*
Finance, insurance, and real estate	–3.205*
Public administration	–2.746*
Social services	–7.805*
Other services	–0.832*

SOURCE: Authors' calculations based on National Institute of Statistics (2004).

NOTE: Hours differentials represent the difference from the mean hours worked last week for each sector.

* indicates statistically significant difference from mean hours at the 5 percent level.

The first column of table 4.8 shows that the overall average hourly log wage is 6.637. Workers in the primary industries (food agriculture through mining) all earn less than average. Food agriculture workers, for example, earn nearly 54 percent less than the average wage. Workers in two of the manufacturing industries, food (with beverages and tobacco) and wood products, also earn below-average wages. Workers in utilities, transportation, and services, however, earn above-average wages.

Adjusting for hours worked reduces, but far from eliminates, the positive IIWD in the textiles sector. Table 4.8 shows that workers in textiles and apparel earn about 29 percent more than the average hourly wage, which is only surpassed by utilities.

The second column of table 4.8 contains the results when demographic controls are included. Females earn about 9 percent less in hourly wages than other workers when controlling for sector, age, and education. When demographic characteristics are controlled for, the textiles IIWD increases to 44 percent, again surpassed only by utilities. This is the highest wage differential found in any of the country studies in this volume. All countries find either high or rising differentials in the apparel industry, but the country with the most explicit and possibly most active monitoring program—Cambodia—also exhibits the highest wage premium in that sector.

If workers had higher monthly earnings only because they were working more hours, and their hourly wage was not different from the average, the argument could be made that working conditions are worse because, all else equal, workers are working more for no additional (per hour) pay. These results, however, do not support that argument. Textiles employees work 11.5 percent more hours than the average worker, but they are paid 44 percent more per hour than the average worker. Thus, hours of work only partially explain the observed differential.

TABLE 4.8 **Hourly Wage Differentials without and with Demographic Characteristics**

	Without demographic controls	With demographic controls
Mean log wage across all sectors per hour	6.637	5.774
Sector	**Differentials**	
Agriculture, food	−0.54*	−0.50*
Agriculture, other	−0.60	−0.58
Husbandry and fishery	−0.22*	−0.19*
Forestry	−0.34*	−0.35*
Mining	−0.37*	−0.30
Food, beverages, and tobacco	−0.21	−0.15
Textiles and apparel	0.29*	0.44*
Wood	−0.31*	−0.31*
Manufacturing, other	−0.01	0.01
Utilities	0.82*	0.66*
Construction	0.05	0.03
Sales	0.02	0.05
Transport	0.18*	0.13*
Finance, insurance, and real estate	0.08	0.03
Public administration	−0.10*	−0.19*
Social services	0.28*	0.16*
Other services	0.24*	0.25*
Effects of demographic characteristics		
Female		−0.09*
Age		0.046*
Education		0.014*

SOURCE: Authors' calculations based on National Institute of Statistics (2004).

NOTE: The mean log wage is the natural log of hourly wage earnings, estimated as monthly earnings divided by hours worked last week multiplied by 4.3. Wage differentials represent the percentage (log) difference from the mean wage for each sector. For example, −0.54 means 54 percent less than the overall mean wage. The percentage changes reported here are obtained by raising e to the estimated coefficient and subtracting 1, because the model is log-linear.

* indicates statistically significant difference from the overall mean wage at the 5 percent level.

ACCIDENTS

The Cambodian 2003–04 Socio-Economic Survey also contains information about accidents and disabilities. Workers were first asked if they either had had an accident in the past year or if they have a physical or mental disability. If respondents answer affirmatively to either question, they are then asked where the accident happened or if the disability was the result of an accident that happened at work.

The frequency of affirmative responses can be compared across sectors to get a crude measure of working conditions. Workers may be pressured (either directly or indirectly) not to report accidents in some industries but not so pressured in others. Furthermore, workers who have had accidents may not want to report their accidents accurately to government survey workers. Other concerns may apply as well; therefore, this measure should be taken with qualification. Nevertheless, given the survey design and the general lack of information about working conditions, this survey question represents a unique opportunity to get a glimpse into the differences in accident rates across industries.

To begin, the analysis defined a variable equal to 1 if the respondent reported having an accident at work or having a disability (physical or mental) that could be traced back to work. Physical disabilities include having problems seeing, hearing, moving, speaking, or feeling.

The first column of table 4.9 reports the raw accident rates by industry.

TABLE 4.9 **Accidents by Industry**

Sector	Accident rate (percent)	Probit
Agriculture, food	0.47	0.0074*
Agriculture, other	0.38	0.0122
Husbandry and fishery	0.30	0.0076
Forestry	0.23	0.0095
Mining	0.00	*dropped*
Food, beverages, and tobacco	0.29	0.0085
Textiles and apparel	0.06	*reference*
Wood	0.20	0.0073
Manufacturing, other	1.22	0.0171
Utilities	1.25	0.0346*
Construction	0.38	0.0073
Sales	0.26	0.0051
Transport	0.18	0.0004
Finance, insurance, and real estate	0.49	0.0104
Public administration	0.26	0.0038
Social services	0.09	0.0001
Other services	0.52	0.0113
Whole sample average	0.36	

SOURCE: Authors' calculations based on National Institute of Statistics (2004).

NOTE: The probit results include age, age squared, gender, and education controls. The dependent variable is the 0/1 variable indicating whether the respondent reported having an accident (= 1 if yes). The coefficient estimates report dF/dx for a discrete change of dummy variable from 0 to 1. The coefficient estimates, therefore, reflect the difference in the probability of having an accident relative to the textiles and apparel sector.

* indicates statistically different from zero at the 5% level, which indicates that the accident rates in these industries are statistically different from the accident rate in the textiles and apparel sector.

These accident rates are reported for all people in the survey, regardless of whether they reported having any earnings. There are some reasons to be suspicious of these data. First, no accidents were reported for mining. This may be partially due to the low sample size of mining, but the sample size of utilities was comparable, but has a relatively high accident rate. Second, the accident rate in finance, insurance, and real estate—usually considered relatively safe industries—was the fourth highest of the 17 reporting industries.

The accident rate in the textiles and apparel industry was relatively low. In fact, this sector had the lowest accident rate in the sample with the exception of mining (the accident rate for which is suspect). This low rate may have been due to textiles and apparel's relatively large size, pressure on workers not to report accidents, or because it is a very safe sector. It might also have been due to differences in demographic characteristics.

To assess the possibility that demographic characteristics affect the accident rate, the accident rate is formally compared across industries using a probit analysis. A probit analysis is similar to a regression analysis in that it allows comparisons to be made across industries while holding other variables constant. This analysis controls for the same demographic variables described above: age, education, and gender. The numbers in the second column of table 4.9 report the likelihood of having an accident in a particular sector relative to the textiles and apparel sector. A positive value indicates that having an accident is more likely.

Because all the coefficient estimates are positive, these results are consistent with the data in the first column and suggest that accidents are least likely in textiles and apparel as compared with the other industries. Formal statistical tests, however, suggest that the difference in the accident rate is not statistically significant in any industry except food agriculture and utilities (and marginally in other manufacturing). In any case, no evidence supports the notion that the large wage premium textiles and apparel workers earn is necessary to compensate them for the risk of accidents or work-related disabilities. A risk-associated compensating wage differential does seem to be present, however, in utilities. The utilities sector has both relatively high wages and a significantly higher accident rate. Conversely, food agriculture has both low wages and a high accident rate, suggesting relatively poor labor protections.

Conclusions

Globalization, defined as international trade and investment, in Cambodia seems to be primarily focused in the garment sector and, to a lesser degree, in the hotel sector. As globalization has advanced, employment in these sectors has increased while employment in the more traditional agriculture sector has contracted. Rising demand for workers caused by expanding export markets and FDI seems to have combined with international attention on the garment sector to generate relatively good working conditions as compared with other sectors in the economy. Relatively few accidents, and earnings that are up to 44 percent higher than the average Cambodian wage (controlling for demographic characteristics), in particular, characterize the garment sector. Working conditions and wages seem to be better in the garment sector than in agriculture, suggesting that the movement of workers from agriculture to apparel might be improving overall working conditions in Cambodia.

Notes

1. The Economic Institute of Cambodia examined the extent, key issues, and challenges of the informal economy in Cambodia in 2005. It estimated that approximately 85 percent of economic activity is informal and this activity contributed about 62 percent to GDP (Monyrath 2005).

2. Monyrath (2005) called for the extension of protection of labor to the informal economy workers.

3. The past conflict and genocide in the country cannot be neglected in coming to an understanding of the development and economy of Cambodia. The country was plagued by war from the 1970s through the 1990s, during which the genocide regime of 1975–79 resulted in nearly 2 million deaths from execution, starvation, and disease. Between 1979 and 1989, the country adopted a central planning economy, and only had economic and trade cooperation with members of the Council for Mutual Economic Assistance of former socialist countries such as Hungary, Bulgaria, the German Democratic Republic, the Soviet Union, and Vietnam.

4. In Cambodia, data records for periods before 1994 were largely lost or unreliable. Data on trade are probably much lower than actual trade flows because official data could not capture informal or illegal trade across borders. The underestimation of data still persists as a result of smuggling and tax evasion.

5. ASEAN was established on August 8, 1967, in Bangkok by its five original member countries, Indonesia, Malaysia, the Philippines, Singapore, and Thailand. Brunei Darussalam joined on January 8, 1984; Vietnam on July 28, 1995; the Lao Peoples Democratic Republic and Myanmar on July 23, 1997; and Cambodia on April 30, 1999. See http://www.aseansec.org/.

6. Australia, Austria, Belarus, Belgium, Bulgaria, Canada, the Czech Republic, Denmark, Finland, France, Germany, Hungary, Ireland, Italy, the Republic of Korea, Luxembourg, Japan, the Netherlands, New Zealand, Norway, Poland, Portugal, the Slovak Republic, Spain, Sweden, Switzerland, the United Kingdom, and the United States.

7. These countries include China, Cuba, India, Indonesia, the Lao PDR, Malaysia, the Philippines, Singapore, Thailand, Vietnam, the Russian Federation, and the members of OPEC. Some agreements give MFN treatment to Cambodia. Those agreements include Australia, Canada, Korea, Japan, and New Zealand.

8. Hong Kong, China, ranked first while the Democratic People's Republic of Korea ranked last. The Lao PDR, Thailand, and Vietnam stood at 149, 71, and 142, respectively.

9. A case study in Puok district, close to Siem Reap, a main destination for tourists, indicates that the tourism boom boosted hotel, guest house, and restaurant construction. In 1999, villagers coming to work in town as construction workers totaled 450 while in 2005 the figure was 3,300 (Visal 2006).

10. Normally, studies of wage differentials limit the sample to workers in the private sector (non-military and nongovernment), workers who are not self-employed, and workers who work a certain number of hours (for example, fulltime workers). Here the sample is limited to workers who are between 10 and 65 years of age, inclusive. We include all sectors because we are interested in the most comprehensive comparison.

11. This percentage change is calculated by raising e to the estimated coefficient and subtracting 1, because the model is log-linear.

References

Better Factories Cambodia. Various years. "Synthesis Report on Working Conditions in Cambodia's Garment Sector." Various issues. www.betterfactories.org.

Cambodian Investment Board and Council for the Development of Cambodia. 2006. Investment data for Cambodia.

Cambodia Tourism and Services Workers Federation. 2006. List of members.

Center for Global Development. 2004. "Global Trade, Jobs, and Labor Standards." Center for Global Development, Washington, DC.

IMF (International Monetary Fund). 2004. "Cambodia: Selected Issues." IMF Country Report No. 04/331, IMF, Washington, DC.

ILO (International Labour Organization). 2006. *Decent Work in the Informal Economy in Cambodia: A Literature Review.* Informal Economy, Poverty and Employment, Cambodia Series, No. 2. Bangkok: International Labour Office.

Ministry of Commerce and Asian Development Bank. 2004. "Cambodia's Garment Industry: Meeting the Challenges of the Post-Quota Environment." TA Report No. 4131-CAM, Ministry of Commerce, Phnom Penh.

Ministry of Tourism. Various years. "Tourism Statistical Report." Statistics and Tourism Information Department, Ministry of Tourism, Phnom Penh.

Monyrath, Nuth. 2005. "The Informal Economy in Cambodia: An Overview." *EIC Economic Review* 2 (1): 1–5. http://www.eicambodia.org/downloads/files/ER8_informal_economic.pdf.

National Institute of Statistics. 1999. "Cambodia Socio-Economic Survey 1999." National Institute of Statistics, Ministry of Planning, Phnom Penh.

———. 2004. "Cambodia Socio-Economic Survey 2003–2004." National Institute of Statistics, Ministry of Planning, Phnom Penh.

Royal Government of Cambodia. 1996. Socio-Economic Development Plan 1996-2001.

UNCTAD/ICC. 2003. "An Investment Guide to Cambodia: Opportunities and Conditions." UNCTAD/IEE/IIA/2003/6, United Nations, London and Geneva.

UNDP. 2004. "The Macroeconomics of Poverty Reduction in Cambodia." UNDP, New York.

UNESCAP. 2004. "Traders' Manual for Least Developed Countries: Cambodia." ST/ESCAP/2320, Trade and Investment Division, United Nations, London and Geneva.

UNHCR. 2005. "Khmer Law Compilation." Office of the United Nations High Commissioner for Human Rights in Cambodia, Phnom Penh. http://cambodia.ohchr.org/KLC_pages/klc_english.htm.

USAID (United States Agency for International Development). 2005. "Measuring Competitiveness and Labor Productivity in Cambodia's Garment Industry." USAID, Phnom Penh. http://www.nathaninc.com/nathan2/files/ccLibraryFiles/Filename/000000000029/Cambodia%20Garment%20Sector%20Main%20Report%20_Nathan.pdf.

U.S. Embassy, Cambodia. 2004. "Country Commercial Guide for Cambodia FY2004." U.S. Embassy, Phnom Penh, Cambodia. http://cambodia.usembassy.gov/uploads/images/_NSauSuPuw3T52JZEFXwBg/country_cguide04.pdf.

Visal, Lim. 2006. "Paths to Poverty Reduction in Cambodia: A Tale of Four Districts." *EIC Economic Review* 3 (1): 6–11.

World Bank. 2004. "Cambodia: Corporate Social Responsibility and the Apparel Sector Buyer Survey Results." Foreign Investment Advisory Service of the IFC and the World Bank, Washington, DC.

———. 2006. *World Development Indicators 2006.* Washington, DC: World Bank.

Annex A: Results of Monitoring from the ILO Better Factories Cambodia Project

Date of report and number of factories monitored	Findings
Nov 2001 (Report 1) 30 factories	• No evidence of child labor. • No evidence of forced labor. • Incorrect payment of wages occurs with some frequency. • Overtime work is not undertaken voluntarily, or not always undertaken voluntarily, in a substantial number of factories. • Overtime hours extend, either occasionally or frequently, beyond the legal limits in a substantial number of factories. • Freedom of association, including anti-union discrimination, is a problem in some factories. • Strikes are not organized in conformity with the legally required procedures.
Apr 2002 (Report 2) 34 factories	• No evidence of forced labor. • No evidence of discrimination, although three incidents of sexual harassment occurred. • No evidence of child labor with the exception of one minor incident. • Incorrect payment of wages occurs frequently. • Overtime work is not, or not always, undertaken voluntarily in a substantial number of factories. • Overtime hours extend, either occasionally or frequently, beyond the legal limits in a substantial number of factories. • Freedom of association, including anti-union discrimination, is a problem in some factories. • Strikes are not organized in conformity with the legally required procedures.

(continued)

ANNEX A **(continued)**

Date of report and number of factories monitored	Findings
	• No evidence of child labor.
	• No evidence of forced labor.
	• No evidence of sexual harassment.
Jun 2002 (Report 3) 29 factories	• Improvement in the correct payment of wages, though this remains a problem in a number of factories.
	• Improvement in ensuring that overtime work is undertaken voluntarily, though this remains a problem in a number of factories.
	• Improvement in ensuring that overtime hours are within legal limits, though this remains a problem in a number of factories.
	• Improvement in ensuring freedom of association, including protection against anti-union discrimination, though this remains a problem in a small number of factories.
	• Strikes are not organized in conformity with the legally required procedures.
	• No evidence of forced labor.
	• No evidence of child labor.
	• Some evidence of sex discrimination, including sexual harassment.
Sep 2002 (Report 4) 65 factories	• Incorrect payment of wages occurs frequently.
	• Overtime work is not, or not always, undertaken voluntarily in a substantial number of factories.
	• Overtime hours extend, either occasionally or frequently, beyond the legal limits in a substantial number of factories.
	• Freedom of association, including anti-union discrimination, is a problem in some factories.
	• Strikes are not organized in conformity with the legally required procedures.

(continued)

ANNEX A (continued)

Date of report and number of factories monitored	Findings
	• No evidence of forced labor.
	• No evidence of discrimination, although two new incidents of sexual harassment occurred.
	• Two minor incidents and one more serious incident of child labor.
Jun 2003 (Report 5) 30 factories	• Improvement in the correct payment of wages, though this remains a problem in a number of factories.
	• Some improvement in ensuring that overtime work is undertaken voluntarily, though this remains a problem in a number of factories.
	• Some improvement in ensuring that overtime hours are within legal limits, though this remains a problem in a number of factories.
	• Some improvement in ensuring freedom of association, including protection against anti-union discrimination, though this remains a problem in some factories.
	• Some improvement in ensuring that strikes are organized in conformity with the legally required procedures.
	• No evidence of child labor.
	• No evidence of forced labor.
	• No evidence of discrimination, although one incident of sexual harassment occurred.
Jun 2003 (Report 6) 30 factories	• Further improvement in the correct payment of wages, though this remains a problem in a number of factories.
	• Further improvement in ensuring that overtime work is undertaken voluntarily, though this remains a problem in a number of factories.
	• Further improvement in ensuring that overtime hours are within legal limits, though this remains a problem in a number of factories.
	• Improvement in ensuring freedom of association, including protection against anti-union discrimination, though this remains a problem in a small number of factories.
	• Some improvement in ensuring that strikes are organized in conformity with the legally required procedures.

(continued)

ANNEX A **(continued)**

Date of report and number of factories monitored	Findings
Oct 2003 (Report 7) 61 factories	• No evidence of forced labor.
	• No evidence of discrimination, although two incidents of sexual harassment occurred.
	• No evidence of child labor with the exception of two minor incidents.
	• Incorrect payment of wages occurs frequently.
	• Overtime work is not, or not always, undertaken voluntarily in a substantial number of factories.
	• Overtime hours extend, either occasionally or frequently, beyond the legal limits in a substantial number of factories.
	• Freedom of association, including anti-union discrimination, is a problem in some factories.
	• Strikes are not organized in conformity with the legally required procedures.
Feb 2004 (Report 8) 62 factories	• No evidence of forced labor.
	• Two incidents of sex discrimination including one minor incident of sexual harassment.
	• Four minor incidents and two more serious incidents of child labor.
	• Improvement in the correct payment of wages, though this remains a problem in a number of factories.
	• Some improvement in ensuring that overtime work is undertaken voluntarily, though this remains a problem in a number of factories.
	• Some improvement in ensuring that overtime hours are within legal limits, though this remains a problem in a number of factories.
	• Some improvement in ensuring freedom of association, including protection against anti-union discrimination, though this remains a problem in a small number of factories.
	• Some improvement in ensuring that strikes are organized in conformity with the legally required procedures.

(continued)

ANNEX A **(continued)**

Date of report and number of factories monitored	Findings
	• No evidence of forced labor.
	• No reported incidents of sexual harassment.
	• The factories at which pregnant workers were fired or forced to resign have discontinued this practice.
	• A small number of factories adversely altered the employment status of women upon their return from maternity leave.
	• One minor incident of child labor.
Jan 2005 (Report 9) 61 factories	• Improvement in the correct payment of wages, though this remains a problem in a number of factories
	• Some improvement in ensuring that overtime work is undertaken voluntarily and that overtime hours are within legal limits, though these issues remain a problem in a number of factories.
	• Some improvement in ensuring freedom of association, including protection against anti-union discrimination, though this remains a problem in a small number of factories.
	• No improvement in ensuring that strikes are organized in conformity with the legally required procedures.
	• Continuing problems associated with safety and health at work, including use of protective equipment and the installation of safety guards on machines, proper safety training, as well as issues such as inadequate ventilation and cleanliness of some workplaces.
	• No evidence of forced labor.
	• No incidents of discrimination reported in any of the factories.
	• Minor incidents of sexual harassment reported in one factory.
	• No confirmed cases of child labor.
	• Further improvement in the correct payment of wages, though this remains a problem in a number of factories.
	• Most factories that had problems ensuring that overtime work is undertaken voluntarily made improvements.
Mar 2005 (Report 10) 26 factories	• Further improvement in ensuring that overtime is exceptional, voluntary, and that overtime hours are within legal limits, but these issues remain a problem in a number of factories.
	• Every factory that had problems ensuring freedom of association, including protection against anti-union discrimination, made some progress in addressing these issues.
	• Workers in one factory made progress in organizing a strike in conformity with the legally required procedures.
	• Continuing problems associated with safety and health at work, including the provision and use of protective equipment, the installation of safety guards on machines, proper safety training, as well as issues such as inadequate ventilation and cleanliness in some workplaces.

(continued)

Date of report and number of factories monitored	Findings
	• No evidence of forced labor.
	• In six factories, management dismissed pregnant workers, or forced them to resign, and in one factory, management fired workers or changed their employment status during their maternity leave.
	• In one factory, management did not recruit any men, due to previous experience with men leading strikes.
	• More than half of the factories have problems with line supervisors failing to treat workers with respect.
Jun 2005 (Report 11) 50 factories	• Ten underage workers were found to be working in four factories.
	• Many of the factories monitored do not comply with minimum wage requirements; this problem is most prevalent among casual workers.
	• Most factories have problems ensuring that overtime work is voluntary, exceptional, and limited to two hours per day.
	• A few factories have significant problems ensuring freedom of association and refraining from anti-union discrimination.
	• None of the strikes that took place in this group of factories in the 12 months preceding the monitoring visits were organized in conformity with legal requirements.
	• Significant numbers of factories fail to meet safety and health standards, including the provision and use of protective equipment, the installation of safety guards on machines, proper safety training, and adequate ventilation.
	• No evidence of forced labor.
	• Two factories that had been altering the contractual status of workers when they returned from maternity leave have discontinued this practice. However, in another factory, management required workers to take an additional three months of maternity leave over that provided by law. The additional three months' leave was unpaid.
	• No underage workers were found in any of the factories.
	• About one-third of the factories monitored do not comply with minimum wage requirements for casual workers.
Aug 2005 (Report 12) 26 factories	• More than two-thirds of the factories monitored ensure that overtime work is not exceptional or limited to two hours per day.
	• Regarding freedom of association, one factory terminated several union leaders and union members after a strike, accusing them of inciting other workers to go on strike and of committing various serious offenses. The Arbitration Council ordered the factory to rehire these workers, but the factory objected to this award, and has appealed it in Court.
	• None of the six strikes that took place during the 12 months preceding the monitoring visits were organized in conformity with legal requirements, but all of the strikes were peaceful.
	• Progress in meeting health and safety standards was mixed. Most of the factories provide personal protective equipment to workers; however, workers in about 80 percent of the factories fail to use it. More than half of the factories also have failed to install safety guards on machines.

(continued)

ANNEX A (continued)

Date of report and number of factories monitored	Findings
	• No evidence of forced labor.
	• No evidence of discrimination, aside from anti-union discrimination (see below).
	• Eight factories that previously did not require workers to provide reliable age-verifying documents before hiring now require workers to do so. One factory still does not require casual workers to provide such documents.
	• About 20 percent of the factories monitored do not comply with minimum wage requirements for casual workers.
Aug 2005 (Report 13) 60 factories	• More than two-thirds of the factories monitored ensure that overtime work is voluntary. However, overtime work is not exceptional in two-thirds of the factories monitored, and about half of the factories do not limit overtime to two hours per day.
	• Six factories failed to ensure workers' freedom to organize and/or freedom from anti-union discrimination. However, seven factories made improvements in these areas.
	• Workers in two factories complied with some legal requirements before going on strike. All of the strikes covered by this report were peaceful.
	• Progress in meeting health and safety standards was mixed. Most of the factories provide personal protective equipment to workers. However, workers in about 77 percent of the factories failed to use it. More than half of the factories have also failed to install safety guards on machines.

(continued)

ANNEX A **(continued)**

Date of report and number of factories monitored	Findings
	• No evidence of forced labor.
	• Two factories dismissed pregnant workers or forced them to resign. One of these factories also discriminated against men during recruitment, out of concern that they could lead a strike. One factory that had adversely altered the employment status of workers returning from maternity leave has discontinued this practice.
	• Four factories that previously did not require workers to provide reliable age-verifying documents before hiring now require workers to do so. Two factories still do not require casual workers to provide such documents. No underage workers were found in any of the factories monitored.
	• Six factories failed to ensure workers' freedom to organize and/or freedom from anti-union discrimination.
	• All of the factories monitored pay regular workers the minimum wage for ordinary hours of work. However, approximately one-quarter of the factories do not comply with minimum wage requirements for casual workers. The level of compliance with wage payments for normal overtime work was 89 percent for both regular and casual workers.
Oct 2005 (Report 14) 46 factories	• About 85 percent of the factories monitored provide 18 days of paid annual leave. Some 63 percent pay the correct entitlement during maternity leave (noncompliant factories typically pay workers half their wages, but do not pay half of their other benefits). Only one-third of the monitored factories pay sick leave in accordance with MOLVT policy.
	• About 60 percent of the factories monitored ensure that overtime work is voluntary. However, overtime work is not exceptional in nearly three-quarters of the factories monitored, and nearly 60 percent of the factories do not limit overtime to two hours per day.
	• Workers in three factories complied with some legal requirements before going on strike. All of the strikes covered by this report were peaceful.
	• Progress in meeting health and safety standards was mixed. More than half of the factories provide personal protective equipment to workers. Nearly three-quarters of the factories failed to install safety guards on machines.

(continued)

ANNEX A (continued)

Date of report and number of factories monitored	Findings
	• No evidence of forced labor.
	• No evidence of discrimination, aside from anti-union discrimination (see below).
	• No indication of child labor in any of the factories.
	• Four factories failed to ensure workers' freedom to organize and/or freedom from anti-union discrimination.
	• Workers in two factories partially complied with some legal requirements before going on strike. All of the strikes covered by this report were peaceful.
Oct 2005 (Report 15) 24 factories	• All of the monitored factories pay regular workers the minimum wage for ordinary hours of work and correct wages for normal overtime work. For casual workers, about 83 percent of the factories comply with minimum wage requirements, and 96 percent are paying the correct rate for normal overtime work.
	• All of the monitored factories provide 18 days of paid annual leave. About 63 percent pay the correct entitlement during maternity leave (noncompliant factories typically pay workers half their wages, but do not pay half of their other benefits). Only half of the factories monitored pay sick leave in accordance with MOLVT policy.
	• About 71 percent of the monitored factories ensure that overtime work is voluntary. However, overtime work is not exceptional in three-quarters of the factories monitored, and two-thirds of the factories do not limit overtime to two hours per day.
	• Progress in meeting health and safety standards was mixed. Most of the factories provided some personal protective equipment to workers. However, about 62 percent of the factories failed to install safety guards on machines.

(continued)

ANNEX A (continued)

Date of report and number of factories monitored	Findings
	• Workers in one factory fully complied with legal requirements before going on strike, and workers in two factories partially complied with those requirements. Workers in four factories did not comply with applicable rules and procedures before going on strike. All but one of the strikes covered by this report were peaceful.
	• All but one of the monitored factories pay regular workers the minimum wage for ordinary hours of work. About 84 percent of the factories pay regular workers (including probationary workers, and workers paid by piece rate) correct wages for normal overtime work.
Mar 2006 (Report 16) 44 factories	• For casual workers, about 61 percent of the factories comply with minimum wage requirements, and 86 percent are paying the correct rate for normal overtime work.
	• About 82 percent of the monitored factories provide 18 days of paid annual leave. Some 59 percent pay the correct entitlement during maternity leave (noncompliant factories typically pay workers half their wages, but do not pay half of their other benefits). Less than one-quarter of the monitored factories pay sick leave in accordance with MOLVT policy.
	• Just over half of the monitored factories ensure that overtime work is voluntary. Moreover, overtime work is not exceptional in two-thirds of the factories monitored, and more than two-thirds of the factories do not limit overtime to two hours per day.
	• Progress in meeting health and safety standards was mixed. Nearly half of the factories provided some personal protective equipment to workers. However, about 70 percent of the factories failed to install safety guards on all machines.

SOURCE: Compiled from Better Factories Cambodia quarterly synthesis reports.

NOTE: MOLVT = Ministry of Labor and Vocational Training.

CHAPTER 5

The Effects of Globalization on Working Conditions: El Salvador, 1995–2005

Raymond Robertson and Alvaro Trigueros-Argüello

Like many other developing countries, including those featured in this volume, El Salvador's experience with globalization has been characterized by increasing foreign investment and total trade since 1990. Also like the other countries, these changes have been concentrated in relatively few sectors. Although an ambitious privatization program has attracted foreign direct investment (FDI) to several key nontradable sectors (banking and telecommunications, for example), much of the export-focused FDI has concentrated narrowly in the apparel sector. This sector generally imports intermediate inputs for assembly and re-export. Spanish-speaking developing countries often refer to this process of assembly for re-export as the *maquila* sector.

The discussion that follows first describes globalization in El Salvador, with a focus on the country's trade policies and related changes in both trade and investment. In particular, the sectors that seem to be most internationally engaged are identified. In addition to the usual experience with globalization, the relatively large role played by remittances has been unique to El Salvador. These remittances may have important, albeit indirect, effects on working conditions. They may increase reservation wages, effectively reducing labor supply and increasing market wages. They may also act as a form of insurance, making workers receiving remittances less dependent on social insurance programs linked to work—such programs being one possible measure of working conditions. These hypotheses are explored in the sections that follow.

The second section describes the institutional history of labor legislation and basic indicators of working conditions in the country. The third section uses El Salvador's extensive household surveys to estimate wage offer curves to lay the foundation for a more detailed study of the possible effects of remittances, controlling for selection bias, and of interindustry wage differentials (IIWDs) for the apparel sector. The fourth section examines nonwage working conditions through probit equations for indicators of working conditions in the country. The chapter closes with conclusions and public policy implications.

Globalization in El Salvador

Globalization has many facets. Globalization fosters rising values and volumes of trade in goods and services among countries. It also deals with the development of and the spread of technologies, especially information and telecommunication technologies, that allow access to information all over the world. The ability to connect with production, distribution, and knowledge networks rapidly increased the potential for worldwide economic development. Globalization is also intertwined with international migration, thus changing economic relations and structures among and within countries.[1] It is also linked to the spread of democracy and democratic institutions in the world. All these facets can affect the behavior and the structure of labor markets within a country. The effects depend on which of these features are more important for a particular country, and the particular characteristics of the country that determine how prepared it is to take advantage of the new opportunities and challenges posed by globalization.

Development is a process. Globalization interacts with evolving economic and political factors. During reform processes, legislative changes are only the first step. To construct economic and democratic institutions best suited to a country,[2] that country needs to make many changes that may not be immediately politically and economically feasible. Thus, implementation can be slow. Success depends on whether the country picks the right sequence for introducing its reforms and how fast it can implement this sequence. The way in which the country reacts to reform may be beyond the government's control, being the result of multiple interactions between society and the state. Therefore, the capacity of governance institutions to cope with differences among individuals and groups of individuals is also important. These features are important to any study of globalization.

Among Latin American countries, El Salvador implemented trade liberalization reform relatively eagerly. In the 2006 Index of Economic Freedom, El Salvador ranked second after Chile (Heritage Foundation and *Wall Street Journal* 2006). El Salvador is one of only three countries in Latin America that enjoy investment-grade risk rating in the region. BID (2006) presents a general index of quality of public policies.[3] Among 18 Latin American countries, only Chile falls in the "Very High" category. Six countries, including El Salvador, fall in the "High" category.[4] El Salvador enjoys a stable policy framework and compares favorably with regard to adaptability, efficiency, and implementation and effectiveness of application. For the coordination and coherence and public orientation indicators, El Salvador falls in the "Medium" category.

The making of a market economy in El Salvador. In 1989, El Salvador began constructing a market economy based on a democratic system and individual freedoms. The development agenda had two important components. The first was to find a peaceful way to resolve the 10-year civil war and to build the democratic institutions needed for effective governance. These efforts concluded with the signature of the Peace Accords in 1992, which included important reforms to the judiciary, the police, the army, and the electoral system, and disarmament and incorporation of guerrillas into the political system. This was just the beginning of a process to build democratic institutions. Since then there have been other reforms, and more will happen as the country realizes which ones work better than others.

The second component was the socioeconomic agenda. Its purpose was to build a market economy based on the principles of individual freedom, decentralization of decision-making processes, prices as basic economic signals, competition as a warranty of economic efficiency, and a supplementary role for the state.[5] The social agenda sought to make El Salvador a country of owners, prioritizing targeting social expenditure toward the poorest households, decentralization of social services, subsidies to demand, and private and communal participation in execution of projects.[6]

The remainder of this section discusses the trade liberalization program in El Salvador; determines the relevant sample period; then describes changes in trade volumes, tariffs, and FDI. Clearly for El Salvador, remittances-generating migration is a stylized fact of the economy with considerable impact on labor markets.

TRADE AND TARIFF POLICY

Within the context described above, El Salvador's trade liberalization program can be divided into two stages. The first stage began in 1989 as a predominantly unilateral liberalization process in which tariffs were reduced according to a particular schedule.[7] In addition to tariff reductions, most import and export licenses were eliminated. Some barriers remain, such as those protecting jute, henequen, imported salt, sugar, wheat flour, and saccharine. Tariff protection also remains in place for certain products such as sweetened drinks, alcoholic beverages, and tobacco. Rice still enjoys the protection of import quotas.

Import liberalization was accompanied by policies seeking to eliminate anti-export bias in the economy and to provide incentives for export promotion. To promote exports, legislation in 1991 created free trade zones for exporting firms that gave them a tariff-free area to produce for export. The legislation also included other tax incentives such as exemptions from income tax and local and municipal taxes for a minimum of 10 years. In addition, El Salvador adopted a policy of 6 percent drawback of value added to exports.

The reduction in tariff protection was dramatic. The average tariff fell from around 21.9 percent in 1991 to 5.7 percent in 1994. The percentage of revenue collected from import tariffs over the value of total imports of goods (an indirect measure of tariff protection) suggests that effective tariff protection actually increased between 1991 and 1994, even though nominal rates were falling (figure 5.1). Improvements in tax revenue management

FIGURE 5.1 **Tariff Revenue, 1990–2006**

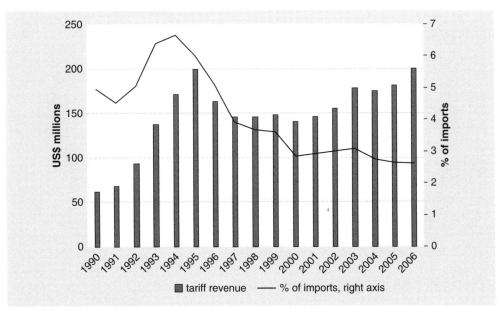

SOURCE: Central Bank of El Salvador.

TABLE 5.1 **El Salvador's Free Trade Agreements**

Country	Signed	Ratified	Published	Effective
Mexico	June 2000	December 2000	December 2000	March 2001
Dominican Republic	April 1998	April 1999	May 1999	October 2001
Chile	October 1999	October 2001	November 2001	June 2002
Panama	March 2002	October 2002	November 2002	November 2002
United States	August 2004	December 2005	January 2005	March 2006

SOURCE: Ministry of Economy.

NOTE: In negotiations for agreements with Canada, Colombia, the European Union, and Taiwan, China.

and customs explain this result. Since 1994, however, the tariff revenue ratio declined steadily from 6.6 percent of total imports in that year to 2.62 percent in 2006.

The second stage of trade liberalization sought to obtain better access to international markets, mainly through free trade agreements. El Salvador enjoyed preferential access to U.S. and European markets through the Caribbean Basin Initiative and the Generalized System of Preferences. El Salvador has signed five trade agreements, as illustrated in table 5.1.

The five Central American countries began negotiating the Central American Free Trade Agreement (CAFTA) in 2002 and signed the agreement with the United States on May 28, 2004. El Salvador was the first of those countries to ratify the treaty, bringing it into effect on March 1, 2006. One motivation El Salvador had in entering CAFTA negotiations was to protect its apparel sector after the end of the Multifibre Arrangement (MFA) in 2005. The goal was to lock in access to the U.S. market in a way that might survive the end of the MFA.

INVESTMENT REGIME

FDI has been an important component in El Salvador's development strategy, and a key factor in its globalization process. In 1990, legislation was passed giving foreign investment broad rights (Alas de Franco 2002).[8] In 1999, the government further revised the foreign investment law (FUSADES 2003), giving foreign companies the freedom to invest in almost all sectors of the economy. The new law granted the ability to repatriate profits, nondiscriminatory treatment to FDI, access to domestic financing, single-source registration to simplify paper work, intellectual property protection, tax incentives, and restrictions in very few activities.

The government also signed bilateral investment treaties with the United States, some European countries, and some South American countries. Several of these treaties were enhanced within the framework of free trade agreements. El Salvador is also a member of the Multilateral Investment Guarantee Agency.

TRADE AND FOREIGN DIRECT INVESTMENT

The public policy measures described in the previous section gave El Salvador a jumpstart to open the economy to free trade and free movement of capital with other countries.

Deep and profound structural changes began early in the 1990s and have continued until the present. The following paragraphs summarize the results in these areas.

Trade Trends

El Salvador's goods trade accelerated through the 1990s, increasing the ratio of exports to GDP from 10.8 percent in 1990 to 22.4 percent in 2000 (see figure 5.2). Since 2000, however, the rate of growth of exports has declined considerably: total exports remained close to 20 percent of GDP through 2005, falling to 18.8 percent in 2006. Conversely, trade liberalization and an abundance of foreign exchange (from remittances) have led to even faster growth in total imports. Imports as a percentage of GDP increased from 23.3 percent in 1990 to 40.9 percent in 2006.

Trends in the composition of exports. Since 1990, El Salvador has undergone important changes in the composition of its exports. In 1990, traditional exports, mainly coffee, sugar, cotton, and shrimp, amounted to nearly 51 percent of total exports. Their share in total exports declined steadily through 2006, ending with a share of 7.5 percent in that year. In the meantime, the role of maquila exports (mainly apparel) increased steadily, growing from US$137 million in 1991 to US$1.9 billion in 2004, reaching 58 percent of total exports. Nontraditional exports, including some agricultural products and many kinds of light manufacturing, also grew, from US$287 million in 1990 to US$1.65 billion in 2006 (see figure 5.3).

Apparel (maquila exports). Maquila, also known as export processing, refers to assembling imported intermediate inputs into finished goods, and then exporting those goods. For apparel, cut and uncut fabric are imported for assembly (sewing) into garments.

FIGURE 5.2 **Exports and Imports of Goods, 1990–2006**

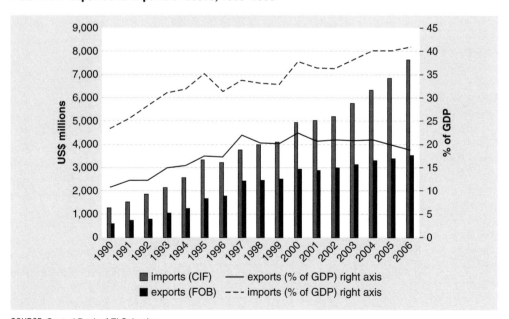

SOURCE: Central Bank of El Salvador.

NOTE: CIF = Cost, insurance, and freight; FOB = Free on board.

FIGURE 5.3 **Composition of Exports and Imports, 1990–2006**

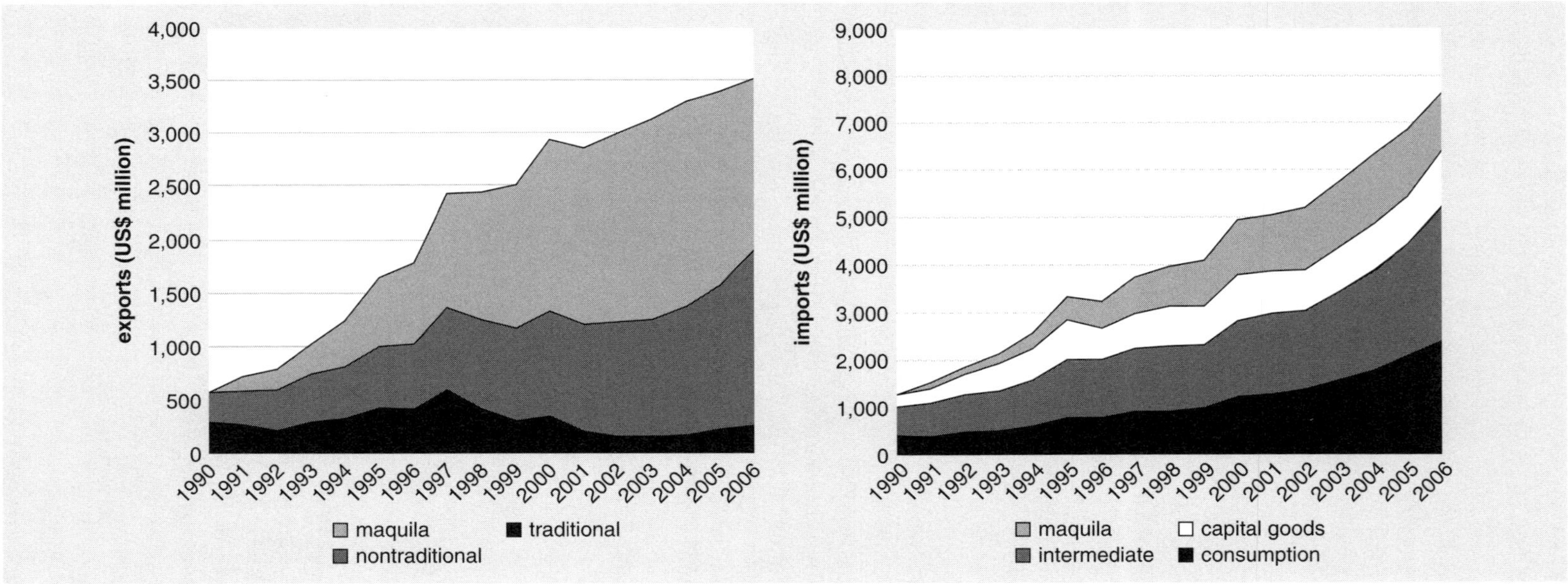

SOURCE: Central Bank of El Salvador.

In El Salvador and other countries of the region, including Mexico, the historical perspective is important to gaining an understanding of the evolution of maquila exports. The expiration of the MFA, which eliminated quotas regulating the flow in textiles around the world on January 1, 2005,[9] was a critical event in the development of the maquila sector. After the first round of economic reforms and liberalization in El Salvador, maquila exports took off, increasing from close to zero in 1990, to over US$1.6 billion in 2000. After that, growth in maquila (mostly apparel and textiles) slowed, reaching a peak in 2004 of nearly US$1.9 billion. Maquila decreased to US$1.6 billion in 2006. The resulting loss in employment was considerable. Employment growth fell each year from 2001 through 2005, suggesting that even before the expiration of the MFA, some companies had begun shifting production elsewhere.

India, Bangladesh, China, and perhaps Indonesia have lower wages and possibly higher productivity than El Salvador. Their rising participation in world trade may have contributed to the relative decline in El Salvador's maquila sector after 2000. If growth in the maquila sector improves or worsens working conditions, its contraction may have the opposite effect.

Trends in the composition of imports. Among the four major import aggregates—maquila, consumption, intermediate, and capital goods—imports of intermediate goods are the largest and increased from US$629 million in 1990 to US$2.8 billion in 2006. The second largest component comprises consumption goods imports, which increased from US$399 million in 1990 to US$2.4 billion in 2006, and increased their share of total imports from 24.6 percent in 1991 to 31.5 percent in 2006 (figure 5.3).[10] Similar to maquila exports, maquila imports increased rapidly from 1991 to 2000, but during 2000–05, maquila imports grew at a very mild rate, even reducing their share in total imports. Imports of capital goods increased rapidly between 1990 and 1995, stabilized between 1996 and 1999, and increased again in 2000. They stayed at similar levels until 2006, but have been decreasing in share overall since 1999.

Foreign Direct Investment

Systematic FDI data are available beginning with 1997, when the Central Bank adopted the standards of the International Monetary Fund's fifth edition of the Balance of Payments Manual. Between 1997 and 2006, FDI (not including intercompany transactions) increased ninefold, from US$480 million in 1997 to US$4.37 billion in March 2006 (tables 5.2 and 5.3). The dynamics of CAFTA and large investments in the banking sector created new opportunities that brought an additional US$1 billion in FDI between 2006 and 2007. Most of this increase came from the acquisition of controlling equity interests of the three largest banks in the country by Citibank, HSBC, and Bancolombia. The main FDI partner is the United States, followed by Mexico (with large investments in the telecom sector), and the British Virgin Islands.

FDI in El Salvador is biased toward the nontradable sector.[11] Privatization of electricity and communications attracted the first large inflows of FDI in 1998, bringing the total stock to US$1.6 billion in that year (table 5.3). The nontradable sector share in FDI went from 44.3 percent in 1997 to 71.1 percent in 1998, and remained close to 70 percent through 2004. Privatization of the banking sector and financial liberalization occurred in the early 1990s, but equity was mainly acquired by local investors. Since 2006, however, FDI has gone into the banking sector, with acquisitions of national and regional (Central

TABLE 5.2 **FDI Stocks in El Salvador by Country of Origin, 1996–2006**
(US$ millions)

Country	1998	1999	2000	2001	2002	2003	2004[a]	2005[b]	First quarter 2006[b]
United States	463.4	606.3	715.8	822.7	880.1	950.1	1,015.5	876.5	878.0
Venezuela, R. B. de	296.9	296.9	309.5	309.5	309.5	309.5	309.5	309.5	309.5
France	208.9	212.9	212.9	214.5	214.7	214.7	5.8	5.8	5.8
Chile	91.2	91.2	91.3	91.5	91.5	91.7	92.2	87.7	107.4
Mexico	80.5	66.7	66.7	69.0	72.7	84.7	616.3	647.8	647.8
Panama	66.0	72.6	79.6	85.6	100.7	102.3	105.1	144.5	216.7
Spain	29.3	68.4	68.4	120.5	159.0	161.4	194.9	195.2	195.2
Bahamas, The	63.0	64.5	64.8	65.2	71.4	72.8	74.2	68.6	68.6
Germany	41.9	41.9	44.0	75.7	78.7	84.8	84.9	89.4	92.1
Costa Rica	25.4	42.5	47.6	63.3	69.6	70.3	70.4	67.4	67.4
Singapore	32.1	32.1	32.1	32.1	32.1	32.2	32.5	36.5	37.3
Netherlands	26.1	26.1	32.2	32.2	34.8	39.1	39.1	55.0	56.3
Peru	17.1	22.2	22.2	22.3	22.3	22.3	22.3	22.3	22.9
Nicaragua	15.4	17.6	20.7	25.0	32.9	33.2	33.2	21.3	21.3
Ecuador	21.0	21.0	9.0	9.0	9.0	9.0	9.0	9.0	9.0
Canada	14.2	17.3	17.7	44.6	45.8	46.6	56.6	130.3	153.2

(continued)

TABLE 5.2 **(continued)**

Country	1998	1999	2000	2001	2002	2003	2004[a]	2005[b]	First quarter 2006[b]
Guatemala	10.7	15.2	25.5	32.0	38.7	48.2	52.1	70.4	76.2
Aruba	14.6	15.0	15.0	15.0	15.0	15.0	15.0	15.0	15.0
Korea, Rep. of	12.2	12.9	14.5	14.9	14.9	22.9	23.8	26.0	22.1
Switzerland	11.7	11.7	11.7	11.7	11.7	11.7	15.6	16.8	16.8
Japan	11.2	11.2	11.3	14.0	14.2	14.2	14.2	14.2	14.2
Bermuda	10.6	10.6	10.6	10.6	10.6	11.2	12.4	12.3	12.3
Taiwan, China	3.6	5.3	27.2	40.2	42.1	56.9	57.5	58.6	58.6
United Kingdom	4.8	4.8	6.4	6.4	6.4	6.4	7.4	8.2	9.4
Honduras	4.7	4.7	6.5	9.3	9.3	19.4	21.0	21.6	21.8
British Virgin Islands	4.2	4.2	4.2	4.2	23.1	29.2	56.2	356.2	356.2
Italy	3.3	0.0	0.0	0.0	26.6	26.6	26.6	26.6	26.6
Israel	0.0	0.0	0.0	0.0	8.5	10.4	22.9	1.0	1.5
Others	0.0	4.0	5.9	11.0	14.0	19.9	27.2	27.0	29.5
Total	1,583.9	1,799.7	1,973.1	2,252.1	2,460.0	2,616.5	3,113.1	3,420.2	3,548.5
Loans among FDI firms	—	—	—	—	673.6	686.2	659.4	752.7	820.2
Total	1,583.9	1,799.7	1,973.1	2,252.1	3,133.6	3,275.4	3,655.5	4,172.9	4,368.7

SOURCE: Department of Balance of Payments, Central Bank of El Salvador.

NOTE: — = Not available.

a. Revised figures.

b. Preliminary figures.

TABLE 5.3 **FDI Stocks in El Salvador by Industry, 1997–2005**
(US$ millions)

	1997	1998	1999	2000	2001	2002	2003	2004	2005
Total foreign investment	**480.1**	**1,583.9**	**1,799.7**	**1,973.1**	**2,252.1**	**3,133.6**	**3,275.4**	**3,655.5**	**4,172.9**
Equity capital and reinvested earnings	480.1	1,583.9	1,799.7	1,973.1	2,252.1	2,460.0	2,589.2	2,996.1	3,420.2
1 Industry	196.4	286.9	304.6	336.5	401.1	447.8	496.1	536.9	853.5
1.1 Manufacturing	196.4	286.9	304.6	336.5	401.1	447.8	496.1	536.9	853.5
2 Sales	106.0	124.6	142.0	169.1	190.2	225.9	239.2	278.3	305.0
3 Services	54.1	60.3	66.0	70.0	90.0	109.4	110.9	110.8	125.2
4 Construction	11.1	11.1	11.8	12.2	12.3	12.3	12.4	12.4	12.4
5 Communications	3.5	254.5	288.6	291.0	352.6	401.2	411.3	746.0	793.8
5.1 Telecommunications	1.2	251.1	285.1	287.4	338.4	379.3	386.8	722.3	766.1
5.2 Others	2.4	3.5	3.5	3.6	14.2	21.8	24.4	23.7	27.8
6 Electricity	0.0	598.4	723.5	806.9	821.5	848.2	848.2	800.2	712.3
6.1 Generators	0.0	3.4	128.5	199.0	213.6	240.3	240.3	192.4	104.4
6.2 Distributors	0.0	595.0	595.0	607.9	607.9	607.9	607.9	607.9	607.9
7 Agriculture and fishing		21.0	21.0	10.0	40.0	48.5	46.8	68.6	67.1
7.1 Agriculture				0.0	0.0	8.5	5.7	2.3	1.1
7.2 Fishing		21.0	21.0	10.0	40.0	40.0	41.1	66.3	66.0
8 Mines and "canteras"	14.0	15.6	0.0	0.0	0.0	0.0	0.0	0.0	1.5

(continued)

TABLE 5.3 **(continued)**

	1997	1998	1999	2000	2001	2002	2003	2004	2005
9 Financial	37.8	77.2	104.6	120.4	161.8	173.9	161.1	148.1	250.4
9.1 Pension fund managers		13.5	14.5	14.5	20.3	20.5	25.4	2.5	2.5
9.2 Banks	37.8	60.3	82.0	97.8	132.2	143.8	128.0	139.3	241.5
9.3 Insurance		3.4	7.9	7.9	9.0	9.4	9.4	7.9	8.1
9.4 Credit cards			0.3	0.3	0.3	0.3	-1.7	-1.7	-1.7
10 Maquila	57.2	134.4	137.6	156.9	182.6	192.7	263.3	294.7	298.9
10.1 Apparel	31.6	104.1	107.3	126.0	151.7	161.8	232.4	263.8	263.1
10.2 Electronic chips	25.6	30.2	30.2	30.8	30.8	30.8	30.8	30.8	34.8
10.3 Others	0.0	0.0	0.0	0.0	0.0	0.0	0.0	0.0	0.9
	480.1	1,583.9	1,799.7	1,973.1	2,252.1	2,460.0	2,589.2	2,996.1	3,420.2
Change over previous year		1,103.7	215.8	173.4	279.0	207.9	129.2	406.9	424.1
Intercompany transactions						673.6	686.2	659.4	752.7
	480.1	1,583.9	1,799.7	1,973.1	2,252.1	3,133.6	3,275.4	3,655.5	4,172.9
Tradable and nontradable grouping									
Tradable sector	267.6	457.8	463.2	503.5	623.7	689.0	806.2	900.2	1,221.1
Nontradable sector	212.5	1,126.1	1,336.5	1,469.6	1,628.4	1,771.0	1,783.0	2,095.8	2,199.1
Shares (%)									
Tradable sector	55.7	28.9	25.7	25.5	27.7	28.0	31.1	30.0	35.7
Nontradable sector	44.3	71.1	74.3	74.5	72.3	72.0	68.9	70.0	64.3

SOURCE: Central Bank of El Salvador.

American) banks by General Electric Finance, Scotia Bank, and HSBC. In 2006, Citibank and Bancolombia announced an offer to buy all equities of the two largest banks in El Salvador. By September 2007, FDI in the nontradable sector topped 74 percent after inclusion of new investments in the banking sector.

FDI in the tradable sector increased from US$266 million in 1997 to US$1.2 billion in 2005 (more than a fourfold increase). In the maquila sector, FDI grew from US$57.2 million in 1997 to US$299 million in 2005. FDI in manufacturing grew steadily from US$196.4 million in 1997 to US$853.5 million in 2005 (an increase of 4.3 times the initial value). Fishing is also worth mentioning; a Spanish investment in tuna fishing and canned tuna received preferential treatment with CAFTA, and FDI in this sector increased from zero in 1997 to US$66 million in 2005.

Investment in the services sector also increased. In 2006, Air Canada bought the airplane maintenance branch from the Salvadoran national company AEROMAN, which is the only company in Latin America certified to service Airbus (and has contracts with Jet Blue and America West). Call centers also represent an important area for FDI, with investments by Dell, Sykes, America Móvil, and others.

MACROECONOMIC IMPACT OF REMITTANCES AND MIGRATION

El Salvador and Honduras both continue to experience massive migration and flows of remittances. These remittances have had a major impact on macroeconomic conditions in both countries. In El Salvador, remittances reached almost 18 percent of GDP (totaling US$3.32 billion) in 2006 (see figure 5.4). This influx of income from abroad increases the demand for both tradable and nontradable goods. The price of tradable goods is checked by international prices, as in any open economy.[12] However, nontradable goods and services are not subject to international competition and supply is restricted by availability of

FIGURE 5.4 **Remittances, 1991–2006**

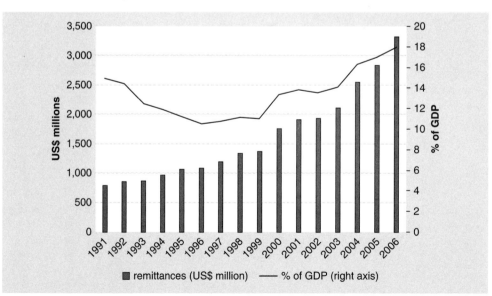

SOURCE: Central Bank of El Salvador.

resources (land, labor, capital). As a result, the relative price of nontradables goes up, leading to real exchange rate appreciation. In Honduras, the increase in remittances coincided with an appreciation of the real exchange rate. El Salvador had a similar experience: the relative price of tradable goods to nontradable goods decreased steadily from 100 in 1990 to 79.5 in 2005.[13]

Exchange rate appreciation makes exporting more difficult, and shifts investment incentives toward the nontradable sectors of the economy. The shares of both the tradable and nontradable sectors have evolved since the early 1990s: in 1991, the share of the tradable goods sector in GDP was 39.3 percent, and declined steadily to 32.5 percent in 2005. The decline was mainly due to the drop in the share of agriculture in total GDP; manufacturing maintained an average of 22.2 percent over the period, meaning that it managed to adapt to changes in international conditions and relative prices. The appreciation of the exchange rate (plausibly a result of remittances) creates a problem like Dutch Disease, that is, a fall in manufactured exports associated with a large inflow of money coming from exports of natural resources.

Exchange rate appreciation means that relative prices stimulate nontradable sectors. The finance and insurance sector increased its share from 2.2 percent of GDP in 1990 to 4.5 percent in 2005; the transportation, storage, and communications sector increased from 7.3 percent of GDP to 9.2 percent; sales, restaurants, and hotels from 18.1 percent to 19.4 percent; construction from 3.5 percent to 4.2 percent; other services from 6.1 percent to 7.7 percent; and real estate from 3.5 percent to 4.3 percent. Not all nontradable sectors moved in the same direction, however. Government services declined from 7.4 percent to 6.5 percent, reflecting the policy of minimizing state involvement in the economy. Housing rents' share also fell, from 11.3 percent to 7.4 percent.

Trejos and Gindling (2004) analyze changes in wage inequality in Central America during the 1990s. They find that the sign of the change in inequality between 1995 and 1999 depends on the measure of inequality. These results may signal significant changes in industry-specific wages. Formal sector workers in the two main tradable sectors, agriculture (at 12 percent of the total economy) and manufacturing (23 percent), have experienced falling real wages over the 1991–2004 period (figure 5.5). However, the trend of real wages within the nontradable sector varies over time. In electricity, gas, and water; transportation; and telecommunications the trend was positive until 2000 but was negative over the 2001–04 period. Although the financial sector has been one of the more dynamic sectors, real wages declined steadily from 1991 through 2004. Wages in the sales sector also fell, although at a slower rate. Real wages were stable in the personal services sector until 1996, but rose thereafter (figure 5.6). The change in real wages provides some support to the idea that remittances create a positive incentive to increase production in nontradable sectors and the opposite for tradable sectors.

Working Conditions in El Salvador

El Salvador's labor law is a direct product of its recent history. Civil war violently gripped El Salvador during the 1980s. The U.S. Department of State (2008) notes that human rights violations were rampant during the civil war. After the war's end in 1992, the United Nations helped supervise a truth commission to help deal with some of the worst

FIGURE 5.5 **Evolution of Real Wages in the Tradable Sector, 1991–2004**

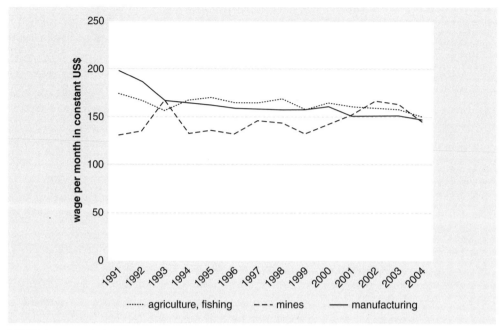

SOURCE: Central Bank of El Salvador.

FIGURE 5.6 **Evolution of Real Wages in the Nontradable Sector, 1991–2004**

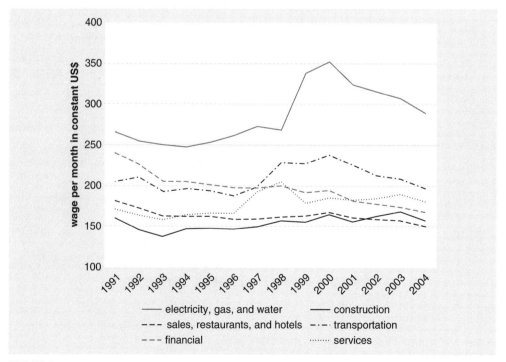

SOURCES: Social Security Institute of El Salvador and Central Bank of El Salvador.

offenses, and the accord stipulated that those responsible for human rights violations be removed from military and government posts.

The civil war provides an important context for reforms to labor law in El Salvador. Bronstein (1997) notes that several Latin American countries reformed labor laws and incorporated revisions into their constitutions in the late 1970s and early 1980s. In 1983, El Salvador implemented detailed constitutional reforms governing several aspects of working conditions, such as home work, domestic service, and protection against dismissal without good cause (Bronstein 1997). These reforms were generally considered to extend social protections and entitlements, but the context of the civil war made it difficult to enforce such provisions. After the peace accords, another comprehensive reform of El Salvador's labor law in 1994[14] extended social protections, especially in the areas of maternity protection, women's work, compensation for dismissal without just cause, and application of labor law to apprentices (Bronstein 1997). The reform was considered to be a significant improvement in worker protections compared with the previous code, and included mechanisms for inspection and monitoring, sanctions (civil, administrative, and penal), and tripartite discussion (for more information, see the NATLEX database at http://www.ilo.org/dyn/natlex/natlex_browse.country?p_lang=en&p_country=SLV). Significantly, this reform led to the ratification of 14 ILO conventions, as shown in table 5.4 (those ratified in 1995 and 1996).

TABLE 5.4 **ILO Conventions Ratified by El Salvador**

Convention	Description	Date ratified
12	Workmen's Compensation (Agriculture) Convention, 1921	October 1955
29	**Forced Labour Convention, 1930**	**June 1995**
77	Medical Examination of Young Persons (Industry) Convention, 1946	June 1995
78	Medical Examination of Young Persons (Non-Industrial Occupations) Convention, 1946	June 1995
81	Labour Inspection Convention, 1947	June 1995
87	**Freedom of Association and Protection of the Right to Organise Convention, 1948**	**September 2006**
88	Employment Service Convention, 1948	June 1995
98	**Right to Organise and Collective Bargaining Convention, 1949**	**September 2006**
99	Minimum Wage Fixing Machinery (Agriculture) Convention, 1951	June 1995
100	**Equal Remuneration Convention, 1951**	**October 2000**
104	Abolition of Penal Sanctions (Indigenous Workers) Convention, 1955	November 1958
105	**Abolition of Forced Labour Convention, 1957**	**November 1958**
107	Indigenous and Tribal Populations Convention, 1957	November 1958

(continued)

TABLE 5.4 **(continued)**

Convention	Description	Date ratified
111	**Discrimination (Employment and Occupation) Convention, 1958** .	**June 1995**
122	Employment Policy Convention, 1964	June 1995
129	Labour Inspection (Agriculture) Convention, 1969	June 1995
131	Minimum Wage Fixing Convention, 1970	June 1995
135	Workers' Representatives Convention, 1971	September 2006
138	**Minimum Age Convention[a], 1973**	**January 1996**
141	Rural Workers' Organisations Convention, 1975	June 1995
142	Human Resources Development Convention, 1975	June1995
144	Tripartite Consultation (International Labour Standards) Convention, 1976	June 1995
150	Labour Administration Convention, 1978	February 2001
151	Labour Relations (Public Service) Convention, 1978	September 2006
155	Occupational Safety and Health Convention[b], 1981	October 2000
156	Workers with Family Responsibilities Convention, 1981	October 2000
159	Vocational Rehabilitation and Employment (Disabled Persons) Convention, 1983	December 1986
160	Labour Statistics Convention[c], 1985	April 1987
182	**Worst Forms of Child Labour Convention, 1999**	**October 2000**

SOURCE: ILO.

NOTE: ILO "core" labor standards are in bold type. El Salvador has ratified all ILO core labor standards.

a. Specifies minimum age of 14.

b. Has ratified the Protocol of 2002.

c. Acceptance of all the Articles of Part II has been specified pursuant to Article 16, paragraph 2, of the Convention.

Ratification of these 14 conventions highlighted El Salvador's reluctance to ratify ILO conventions 87 (Freedom of Association and Protection of the Right to Organise) and 98 (Right to Organise and Collective Bargaining). Article 7 of El Salvador's constitution recognizes freedom of association, but this article did not apply to government workers. The government's main argument for refusing to ratify these conventions was that the constitution prohibited government workers from organizing unions on the grounds that public services were essential and therefore could not be interrupted. Throughout the 1990s and early 2000s, El Salvador faced increasing international criticism from labor groups for these provisions.

The Spanish tuna investment by Grupo Calvo played an important role in pressuring El Salvador to ratify ILO core conventions 87 and 98, as well as conventions

135 (Workers' Representatives) and 151 (Labour Relations [Public Service]). The European Union threatened to remove El Salvador from the European General System of Preferences if the country did not ratify these conventions; more importantly, Grupo Calvo (the tuna company) threatened to withdraw their investment from El Salvador because it would lose preferential treatment in the European Union. El Salvador did everything a country could do to avoid losing this preference and to continue negotiating an economic agreement with the European Union. On September 6, 2006, these four conventions were ratified, overcoming long-lasting prejudices against labor unions. At the end of October 2006, however, the Supreme Court of El Salvador ruled that allowing labor unions in public services was unconstitutional. Because addressing the issue requires a constitutional amendment, it has remained contentious into 2009.

On March 1, 2006, El Salvador became the first Central American country to approve, and thus bring into force, the CAFTA. In its 2006 report filed with the ILO, the government of El Salvador noted that it had begun to reform labor law to bring it into accordance with the provisions of the CAFTA. In particular, they noted that reforms of Articles 211 and 248 (of El Salvador's labor law) were in progress, with the goal of reducing from 35 the number of workers required to start a union and of reducing from six months the time required to wait to reapply for union status after an application had been rejected.

The timing of El Salvador's reversal of the ratification of the two remaining core ILO conventions (numbers 87 and 89) strongly suggests that international engagement played a significant role in El Salvador's decision, because it coincided with the CAFTA negotiations. International pressure increased during these negotiations and created an incentive to adopt these core conventions. Other international forces have played a role in changing labor standards in El Salvador. Frundt (2004) points out that the National Labor Committee (NLC) convinced the apparel company Gap to open its Salvadoran apparel contractor, Mandarin, in the 1995 holiday season to external monitors, thus opening the way for international pressure to affect labor standards. That action, the first example of independent (nongovernment) external monitoring in the world, resulted in the creation of the Grupo de Monitoreo Independiente de El Salvador (GMIES). Frundt (2004) notes that as a result, a union at Mandarin was recognized, fired workers were rehired, and workers reported improved conditions. Unfortunately, the union's efforts were reportedly undermined by another union, loyal to the company, that reversed previous changes. GMIES went on to monitor five other plants with mixed success. One plant closed to avoid unionization. In another, workers reported more success than at the Mandarin plant. In all cases, however, the monitoring brought attention to working conditions in these factories, a critical first step toward improvements.

During the CAFTA negotiations, El Salvador faced criticism for failing to enforce existing labor laws. In a 2006 report filed with the ILO (ILO 2006), the Office of the International Confederation of Free Trade Unions (ICFTU) repeated the concerns it had filed in previous years' reports about enforcement of labor laws, especially with respect to union activity. The ICFTU alleged that the right to collective bargaining had not been respected in export processing zones (EPZs), a criticism similar to those applied to Madagascar. The report also raised other concerns about the structure and application of labor law. In particular, it noted that the law requires that union leaders must be Salvadoran by birth and that trade unions are prohibited from political activities. These provisions have been used to minimize union power. Furthermore, they reflected the government's comments about legal obstacles to strikes, noting that 51 percent of workers must approve a strike, regardless of whether they are members of the union, and a strike is only legally recognized if it relates to a change in a collective agreement or defends workers' professional interests. The ICFTU's comments state that, under these conditions, the Ministry of Labor has considered all strikes in El Salvador illegal.

As in Honduras and Madagascar, El Salvador has wrestled with the problem of devoting resources to monitoring compliance by employers. This problem was obviated in Cambodia by directly tying market access to improvements in working conditions and by the presence of the ILO-affiliated monitors. In El Salvador, however, there is some indication that the government is increasing resources for enforcement. Enforcement was a specific topic in the CAFTA negotiations. The Office of the U.S. Trade Representative reported in February 2005 that El Salvador had increased the budget for the labor ministry by 20 percent. The Ministry of Labor increased the number of inspectors from 73 in 2002 to 171 in 2005 and cut the average time to hear a labor complaint in half (USTR 2005). In addition, the U.S. government allocated funds to support institutional capacity in Central America. While these are important steps, concerns persist about how long it takes the judicial process to follow up on workers' complaints and that law enforcement focuses mainly on medium to large firms, neglecting the broad scope of informal jobs in the country. Having signed CAFTA, the government faces the choice of enforcing compliance or risking trade sanctions.

Anecdotal evidence also suggests a lack of enforcement may not necessarily be due to a lack of government intent or ability. For example, a 2005 *New York Times* article described the experience of textiles workers whose (foreign) assembly plant had closed suddenly and pulled operations out of El Salvador (Thompson 2005). National law states that dismissed workers are entitled to compensation, but the government can do little to enforce these provisions when companies are no longer in the country. Foreign investment *leaving* El Salvador, therefore, may threaten working conditions.

Empirical Analysis

To complement the descriptive analysis above, this section presents a quantitative analysis of working conditions in El Salvador. The first part contains a description of the data. The second presents some basic statistics that illustrate the main changes in labor markets in El Salvador. The third part includes an econometric model of participation (Heckman's selection model) for labor conditions. The next part contains an analysis of IIWDs, and the last compares these directly to measures of FDI.

DATA

El Salvador has a history of collecting labor market and expenditure data through household surveys. El Salvador conducts the Encuesta de Hogares de Propósitos Múltiples (EHPM, or Multipurpose Household Survey) each year. The survey covers basic demographic information as well as labor market experience, housing, and other indicators.

While data are available roughly from 1989 through the present, survey and sample changes restrict the sample used here to 1995–2005. This period covers the rise of trade liberalization and globalization in El Salvador. The analysis focuses on workers with positive wage earnings (earnings from paid labor). The sample was further modified by several key variables: age, gender, education, occupation, sector of employment, geographic area, and remittances.

Table 5.5 contains sample characteristics. These sample statistics reveal several important features of the survey data. The first column displays the subsample size used in this chapter's analysis. The subsample consists of the number of workers in the sample who are between 10 and 65 years old (inclusive) and have positive earnings from wages. As the table clearly shows, the sample size varies greatly over the 1995–2005 period. Most notably, it increases significantly in 1998 over 1997, and again in 1999. The sample size falls back to 1998 levels in 2001 and rises closer to 1999 levels in 2002–05.

While mean age is relatively steady from 1995 to 2005, the female employment share falls through the sample, from just over 41 percent in 1995 to just under 37 percent in 2003, and around 30 percent in 2004 and 2005. Average education remains roughly constant through the sample period, although the average of the last two years is higher than the average of the first two years, possibly suggesting a gradual increase in average education levels.

TABLE 5.5 **Sample Characteristics for Employed Workers**

Year	Sample size	Mean age (years)	Female share (percent)	Mean education (years)
1995	10,703	33.97	41.53	7.20
1996	10,863	34.28	40.96	7.36
1997	7,859	33.72	38.40	8.08
1998	9,746	31.82	37.88	8.21
1999	13,736	31.31	36.13	7.90
2000	14,009	32.14	35.61	8.18
2001	9,973	32.93	34.99	7.76
2002	12,820	33.16	36.56	8.10
2003	12,769	32.54	36.89	7.53
2004	12,467	31.95	29.89	7.98
2005	12,721	32.51	30.72	8.25

SOURCE: Authors' calculations using Multipurpose Household Survey.

Table 5.6 contains sector employment shares for 1995, 2000, 2003, 2004, and 2005. If these samples are representative, they indicate significant changes in employment patterns in El Salvador. The share of workers in agriculture, particularly food agriculture, fell from nearly 25 percent to just over 16 percent. At the same time, the share of workers in sales rose from just over 22 percent to nearly 29.5 percent. For manufacturing, perhaps the most significant change was in the textiles and apparel sectors. The share of workers in textiles fell by nearly two-thirds, from 2.1 percent to 0.5 percent. This may have been due to rising imports of textile products for assembly. In contrast, the share in apparel rose from about 4.6 percent to 6.6 percent in 2003, but decreased to 4.7 percent in 2005. This fall coincides with the end of the MFA. These patterns are similar to those

TABLE 5.6 **Industry Employment Shares**

Industry	Employment shares (percent)				
	1995	2000	2003	2004	2005
Sales	22.2	26.3	27.4	29.3	29.5
Agriculture, food	25.0	20.8	17.4	18.4	16.1
Social services	5.3	6.7	6.0	6.8	6.9
Construction	6.8	5.1	7.1	6.4	5.7
Food, beverages, and tobacco	6.1	5.8	5.2	5.3	5.6
Manufacturing, other	5.3	5.4	4.3	5.1	5.0
Financial intermediation	0.0	3.8	0.0	4.1	4.7
Apparel	**4.6**	**6.0**	**6.6**	**5.5**	**4.7**
Transport	4.3	4.7	4.4	5.0	4.7
Domestic service	0.0	4.3	0.0	4.7	4.3
Public administration	4.1	5.3	3.9	3.9	3.9
Education	0.0	3.0	0.0	3.4	3.8
Agriculture, other	2.1	0.1	1.6	0.0	3.4
Textiles	2.1	1.0	0.7	0.5	0.5
Husbandry and fishing	1.3	0.7	1.5	0.7	0.5
Utilities	0.2	0.4	0.1	0.4	0.3
Wood	0.5	0.5	0.6	0.3	0.3
Mining	0.1	0.1	0.1	0.1	0.1
Others	0.0	0.1	0.0	0.0	0.0

Industry	Men			Women		
	2000	2004	2005	2000	2004	2005
Sales	17.9	20.3	20.8	38.5	42.3	41.7
Agriculture, food	32.7	29.0	24.7	3.6	3.2	4.0
Social services	3.6	4.4	4.4	11.1	10.3	10.5
Construction	8.5	10.6	9.5	0.2	0.5	0.2
Food, beverages, and tobacco	4.0	3.5	4.1	8.4	8.1	7.8

(continued)

TABLE 5.6 **(continued)**

	Men			Women		
Industry	**2000**	**2004**	**2005**	**2000**	**2004**	**2005**
Manufacturing, other	7.3	6.8	6.8	2.6	2.5	2.5
Financial intermediation	4.4	5.0	5.5	2.9	2.7	3.6
Apparel	**2.5**	**2.8**	**2.0**	**11.1**	**9.5**	**8.6**
Transport	7.3	7.5	7.2	0.9	1.3	1.1
Domestic service	0.5	0.7	0.7	9.9	10.5	9.3
Public administration	6.3	4.9	4.7	3.9	2.4	2.7
Education	1.9	2.0	2.1	4.6	5.5	6.1
Agriculture, other	0.1	0.0	5.3	0.0	0.0	0.7
Textiles	0.6	0.5	0.5	1.6	0.5	0.6
Husbandry and fishing	1.1	1.0	0.9	0.1	0.2	0.1
Utilities	0.6	0.6	0.4	0.0	0.1	0.1
Wood	0.5	0.3	0.3	0.5	0.4	0.3
Mining	0.1	0.1	0.2	0.0	0.0	0.0
Others	0.1	0.0	0.0	0.0	0.0	0.0

SOURCE: Authors' calculations based on Multipurpose Household Survey data.

in other small developing countries, particularly Honduras and Nicaragua, whose experiences with rising globalization coincided with the growth of apparel manufacturing. Note that other manufacturing sectors—food, beverages, and tobacco; wood; and other manufacturing—either contracted or remained steady.

The various industries have very different demographic characteristics. A closer snapshot shows that the average education level in the apparel sector is not statistically different from (and slightly above) the national sample average (table 5.7). Agriculture, as expected, has very low average education levels. Utilities, public administration, and social services have relatively high education levels, but apparel has the highest average education level of all manufacturing industries. As is evident in the studies of the other countries in this volume, one of the main characteristics of the apparel sector is the large concentration of women. Over 70 percent of employees in the sector are female. Only "Domestic Service" has a higher concentration of female employment, and the female share of employment in apparel is nearly double that in the other manufacturing industries. It may also not seem surprising that workers in apparel are younger than in other sectors: the average age in apparel is lower than in all other sectors. Thus, as in other countries in this volume, apparel in El Salvador is characterized by relatively young women. One key difference between El Salvador and the other studied countries is that education levels in apparel seem to be relatively high.

TABLE 5.7 **Share of Women's Employment by Industry, and Average Years of Education by Gender**

	Employment share of women	Years of education		
		Men	Women	Total
Sales	60.5	8.4	6.5	7.3
Agriculture, food	7.0	3.4	3.5	3.4
Social services	61.2	9.7	8.6	9.0
Construction	1.9	5.8	13.0	6.1
Food, beverages, and tobacco	61.0	7.9	5.6	6.5
Manufacturing, other	17.0	8.3	9.3	8.5
Financial intermediation	28.5	10.3	12.7	10.9
Apparel	70.8	9.3	7.7	8.2
Transport	8.1	8.1	12.0	8.5
Domestic service	87.7	5.5	4.4	4.5
Public administration	24.2	10.8	13.5	11.5
Education	64.7	14.2	14.6	14.4
Agriculture, other	—	—	—	—
Textile	44.4	8.1	4.5	6.5
Husbandry and fishing	10.4	3.5	3.3	3.5
Utilities	10.0	10.0	14.4	10.5
Wood	43.1	3.7	3.0	3.4
Mining	5.0	4.6	12.0	5.0
Others	20.0	12.0	6.5	11.0
TOTAL	**39.9**	**7.0**	**7.4**	**7.1**

SOURCE: Authors calculations based on Multipurpose Household Survey data.

NOTE: — = Data not available, because values too small.

GENERAL LABOR MARKET CONDITIONS

Given the trends described in the previous section of this chapter, attention will focus here on three specific periods:

1991–2000: Continuation of first phase of trade liberalization with unilateral tariff reductions, export promotion efforts, and beginning of privatization process, with large FDI in utilities sector, and some FDI in industry or manufacturing. Garment exports keep growing. Remittances, as a share of GDP, fall during this period.

2000–2004: Beginning of second phase of trade opening through signing of free trade agreements (Mexico, Dominican Republic, Chile, Panama). FDI flows into nontradable and tradable sectors. Maquila exports slow. This period also suffers many shocks: coffee price shock, 2001 earthquakes, oil price shock. Remittances increase from 13.3 percent of GDP to 16.3 percent.

2004–2005: Continuing efforts to sign a free trade agreement with the United States; incoming flows in FDI in financial sector. The end of MFA triggers a fall in maquila exports, dominated by garment industry. Nontraditional exports grow. Remittances keep increasing to 17 percent of GDP. Coffee prices recover.

Labor Force Participation

Labor force participation, defined as the economically active population 10 years old and older divided by total population in the same age range, was close to 50 percent in 1997 and from 2000 to 2005 remained around 52 percent, with little change. Labor force participation for men fell from 68.5 percent in 1997 to about 66 percent in 2000–05. Women's labor force participation, however, increased from 35.3 percent in 1997 to 38.7 percent in 2000, 38.6 percent in 2004, and 39.5 percent in 2005. The contraction of the agricultural sector (mainly male employment) and the gain in garment and sales employment (through 2003) help explain these trends.

A first approximation of the impact of remittances on labor markets and working conditions is shown by labor force participation. Labor force participation is compared between those living in households that do and do not receive remittances. In 2005, labor force participation was about 42 percent for those workers who resided in a remittances-receiving household. For those living in a household not receiving remittances, labor force participation was about 56 percent. Thus, the data suggest that remittances reduce labor force participation by 13 percentage points in the subset of the population that receives remittances. This could be biased if remittances are directed mainly to women, but specific calculations by sex show that for women and men, labor force participation is 12 percentage points and 13 percentage points smaller, respectively, for the subset of the population living in households that receive remittances.

Unemployment Rate

The unemployment rate declined between 1997 and 2000. Between 2000 and 2004, however, it remained close to 6.9 percent and increased to 7.2 percent in 2005. The most important changes occurred for women, where the unemployment rate declined steadily between 1997 and 2000, from 5.3 percent to 3.7 percent. After a jump to 5.2 percent in 2001, unemployment remained close to 3.5 percent through 2003, then increased to 4.8 percent in 2005. Given that women's participation in the garment industry was much larger than men's, it seems that women's unemployment rate followed a pattern set by occurrences in maquila exports, especially in 2004 and 2005, coinciding with the end of quotas associated with the MFA (figure 5.7).

Employment by Economic Sector

Employment opportunities in 2005 were concentrated in large sectors: sales with 29.5 percent of all employed, agriculture with 19.5 percent, and manufacturing (including food and beverages, garment and textiles, and other industry) with 16.4 percent. Women participate mainly in sales and services, but they also have high shares in manufacturing

FIGURE 5.7 **El Salvador: Unemployment Rate by Gender, 1992–2005**

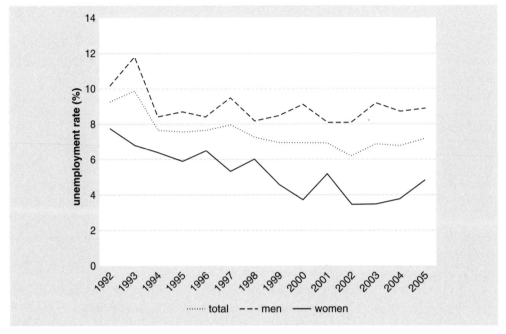

SOURCE: Ministry of Economy, General Directorate of Statistics and Census.

of food and beverages and garments and textiles. Men, however, participate more in agricultural activities and sales. (See table 5.6.)

Remittances do not change the overall pattern of distribution of employment by economic sector. Employment by firm size has a U-shaped distribution, where microenterprises generate 61.2 percent of employment, and large firms 29 percent. In the garment industry the employment share is larger in large firms, which tend to participate more in the regulated, or formal, segment of the labor market.

Average Hours per Week

The employed reported working 42.2 hours per week on average in their main job, with little difference between men and women: 42.6 hours compared with 41.7, but with variation across sectors. Women working as maids (with no contractual or legislative protections) had the longest work week. Those receiving remittances worked 40.2 hours per week; those not receiving remittances worked 42.7 hours. Average hours per week increased with firm size, from 39.3 for microenterprise to 47.3 hours for large firms. Generally, microenterprises represent the informal sector, where workers may enjoy more flexible hours, while large firms are subject to legislation offering less flexibility.

One of the distinguishing features of labor markets in El Salvador is rigidity in hours worked per week in the regulated segment of the market, determined by labor legislation. Density functions of the distribution of number of hours per week for the employed population in their main job show a concentration around 44 hours per week, which is the number of hours established in the labor code. However, there are differences between men and women. The distribution for women has two peaks, a small one at about 22 hours and another at 44 hours, suggesting that part-time work is important for many women. Workers living in households that receive remittances have more dispersed hours, showing less concentration at the 44-hour peak. Those not receiving remittances show a pattern similar to that of the general distribution, with a high concentration at 44 hours.

Wages and Wage Rates

The following analysis includes only those employed as wage laborers, whether temporary or permanent. It does not include the self-employed, employers, cooperativists, nonremunerated family members, trainees, or those who provide domestic services (maids).

The average wage per hour for those employed as wage laborers is US$1.51; the highest wage rate is found in the educational sector, followed by administration and defense, mainly reflecting jobs in the public sector. In the private sector, the highest wages are found in services and utilities (electricity, gas, and water), and the lowest wages in agriculture, at US$0.69 per hour. In the sales sector, where most people are employed, the wage rate is US$1.25 per hour. In manufacturing, the wage rate varies by subsector: US$1.08, US$1.48, and US$1.54, in garments, food and beverages, and other manufacturing, respectively. Therefore, it is important to note that apparel (the maquila-related sector) pays lower wages than do the other two subsectors. It is also true, however, that in this sector and in textiles, women's wage rates are lower than men's, while in other manufacturing, women's wage rate is higher.

Overall, workers receiving remittances have a higher wage rate per hour than those not receiving remittances: US$1.63 compared with US$1.49 per hour (although these differences may not be statistically significant). Remittances have a positive effect on wage rates in the garment and textiles industries but not in the food and beverage sector; in the other manufacturing sector, the impact is negative, contrary to expectations. In sales, one of the larger sectors, the average wage rate is also smaller for those receiving remittances.

The average hourly wage rate is almost twice as large in large firms compared with microenterprises, revealing that the quality of employment is better in the former.

HECKMAN SELECTION MODEL

The importance of remittances in El Salvador suggests they affect both labor market participation and the determination of wages. The Heckman selection model (Heckman 1979) provides a way to address labor market participation and wage determination. The decision to work or not work is made by individuals. Thus, those who are not working constitute a self-selected sample, not a random sample. It is likely that some of the individuals receiving remittances would earn low wages and thus choose not to work; this would account for part of the missing wage data belonging to those individuals that decide not to work. Because of this self-selection out of the workforce, it is likely that an analysis with employed individuals only will overestimate the wages of the workers in the population. The Heckman model accounts for information on the nonworking individuals.

The approach in this chapter assumes that there is one model predicting wages and one model predicting whether a person will be working. The identifying assumptions for the selection mechanism are that family characteristics and geographic location affect participation in labor markets. Plausibly, having young children at home (a family characteristic) may prevent or discourage parents from participating in labor markets, especially women. Two variables, the percentage of children less than 6 years old in the household, and the percentage of children between 6 and 12 years old, capture these effects. Multiplying each of these two variables by the dummy variable indicating the observation belongs to a woman (FEMALE) generates controls for whether the effects are different for women. With regard to geographic location, those located further from large markets are less likely to participate in labor markets because there are fewer employment opportunities. Regional dummies, excluding the reference location (the metropolitan area of San Salvador), capture this effect.

Table 5.8 reports results of the wage model (upper portion of table) and of the selection model (bottom portion) for three years: 2000, 2004, and 2005. The main determinants for sample selection are the female and remittances dummies; in both cases the probability of participation in labor markets is strongly reduced in all years. Education and age have a

TABLE 5.8 Heckman's Selection Model (Weighted One-Step)
Dependent variable: logwage

	2000		2004		2005	
Independent variable	**Coefficient**	**z**	**Coefficient**	**z**	**Coefficient**	**z**
Years of education	0.01	4.8*	0.07	32.5*	0.08	35.1*
Age	0.04	12.6*	0.04	13.2*	0.04	12.9*
Age squared	0.00	−10.6*	0.00	−10.1*	0.00	−9.8*
Urban dummy	0.40	26.6*	0.14	8.7*	0.10	6.0*
Public sector dummy	0.57	22.2*	0.45	12.4*	0.40	14.9*
Female	−0.09	−4.8*	−0.24	−12.6*	−0.21	−12.1*
Remittances	0.10	5.0*	0.07	3.0*	0.07	3.2*
Constant	1.14	16.7*	−1.56	−23.8*	−1.61	−25.5*
Selection						
Years of education	0.06	25.5*	0.02	6.4*	0.03	9.3*
Age	0.09	26.8*	0.00	−0.6	0.03	5.6*
Age squared	0.00	−24.8*	0.00	−3.9*	0.00	−8.6*
Female	−0.57	−20.1*	−0.33	−8.7*	−0.36	−8.9*
Urban dummy	−0.05	−2.9*	−0.09	−3.3*	−0.06	−2.0**
Remittances	−0.23	−9.9*	−0.20	−6.6*	−0.23	−7.6*
Public sector dummy	1.91	30.1*	1.05	17.0	1.58	18.4*
Percent of children 0 to 5 years old (g1)	0.69	8.7*	0.09	0.8	0.29	2.4**

(continued)

TABLE 5.8 **(continued)**

Independent variable	2000		2004		2005	
	Coefficient	z	Coefficient	z	Coefficient	z
Percent of children 6 to 12 years old (g2)	−0.50	−7.3*	−0.18	−1.9**	−0.60	−5.7*
g1*Female	−1.04	−9.2*	−0.61	−3.6*	−0.60	−3.2*
g2*Female	0.10	1.0	−0.09	−0.6	0.12	0.8
Region west	−0.22	−8.5*	−0.09	−2.2*	−0.14	−3.5*
Region central I dummy	−0.14	−5.3*	−0.03	−0.8	−0.10	−2.4**
Region central II dummy	−0.30	−10.6*	−0.28	−7.0*	−0.25	−6.4*
Region east dummy	−0.37	−13.2*	−0.29	−7.3*	−0.28	−6.8*
Region capital dummy (omitted)						
Constant	−1.80	−32.21*	0.7193	7.8*	0.0955	1.0
/athrho	−0.53	−16.7*	−0.29	−3.3*	−0.18	−5.0*
/lnsigma	−0.35	−28.0*	−0.53	−26.6*	−0.49	−32.2*
Wald test (rho = 0)		279.9*		10.80*		25.21*

SOURCE: Authors, based on Multipurpose Household Survey.
NOTE:
* significant at the 1 percent level.
** significant at the 5 percent level.

positive impact on labor force participation, although the latter may decrease as one grows older. Also, having children younger than age 6 reduces the probability of women's participation in labor markets, but not men's. However, having children between 6 and 12 years old seems to reduce the probability of labor market participation for both men and women. Regional controls are all statistically significant and show that in the capital city labor participation is higher. The Wald test for the importance of the sample selection mechanism is also significant, indicating an improvement over the linear regression for consistency and bias of the parameter estimators. The result for the remittances dummy provides evidence that those receiving remittances have more discretion in participation in labor markets; they can take longer to search for jobs because they have remittances as a cushion, or they simply have higher reservation wages and take more time to find jobs.

After considering sample selection, the results (upper portion of table 5.8) suggest that education has a positive effect on wages and age has a hyperbolic impact. Workers in urban areas and in the public sector enjoy much higher wages, while women have lower wages after controlling for other variables. Remittances have a positive effect on wages, indicating a positive impact on reservation wages. Remittances reduce labor market participation, but once a remittances-receiving worker decides to participate in the labor market, he or she closes the deal with a wage premium.

INTERINDUSTRY WAGE DIFFERENTIALS

One measure of working conditions is the difference between the wage a worker earns in the worker's industry of employment and the wage the worker would earn if employed in another sector, known as the interindustry wage differential (IIWD). IIWDs are not usually explained by differences in demographic characteristics, such as gender, age, and education, and seem to represent a benefit to workers who can get jobs in high-wage industries. Because globalization in El Salvador has been concentrated in the apparel sector, it is important to first compare wages in that sector with wages in other sectors in El Salvador. The household surveys contain information about monthly income from different sources. The analysis here focuses on wage income, which is reported as monthly wages from remunerated employment. Dividing the monthly wage by the number of hours that individuals worked during the month generates wage per hour. The dependent variable used in the subsequent analysis is the natural log of the hourly wage, which is customary in labor market analysis because the natural log of wages is approximately normally distributed.

Normally, studies of IIWDs limit the sample to workers in the private sector (nonmilitary and nongovernment), workers who are not self-employed, and workers who work a certain number of hours (for example, full-time workers). This study, however, includes all sectors in the interest of making the most comprehensive comparison. The minimum age of workers in the sample is 10 years old.

The first column of table 5.9 presents the percentage difference from the overall average that workers earned in each industry in 2000, after controlling for demographic characteristics and key variables for labor market participation.[15] This percentage difference (the log difference) is known as the IIWD (or wage

TABLE 5.9 **Percentage Interindustry Wage Differentials with Controls for Demographic Characteristics, 2000, 2004, 2005**

Independent variables	2000	2004	2005
Age	5.3*	3.6*	3.9*
Age squared	−0.1*	0.0*	0.0*
Years of education	1.3*	5.4*	5.5*
Urban dummy	11.5*	4.3*	5.3*
Female	−9.4*	−13.2*	−13.1*
Public sector dummy	83.0*	42.2*	47.3*
Remittances dummy	3.3**	2.7**	4.8*
Region west	−22.8*	−16.3*	−16.3*
Region central I	−17.4*	−11.7*	−9.8*
Region central II	−22.2*	−10.2*	−9.5*
Region east	−20.8*	−11.5*	−8.6*
Region capital city (omitted)			
Agriculture, food	−24.1*	−12.3*	−13.4*
Agriculture, other	9.0	23.1	−6.7**
Husbandry and fishing	13.7	36.8*	34.9*
Mining	24.4	31.8**	30.9
Utilities	62.0*	57.1*	37.8*
Construction	16.1*	18.6*	22.5*
Sales	−5.3*	−8.7*	−7.3*

(continued)

TABLE 5.9 (continued)

Independent variables	2000	2004	2005
Transport	32.0*	32.4*	23.3*
Financial intermediation	37.3*	6.7*	3.3
Public administration	16.9*	16.1*	5.8**
Education	84.9*	53.8*	49.0*
Social services	24.5*	16.9*	14.6*
Domestic service	–53.9*	–42.8*	–40.2*
Others	147.5*	41.3	0.0
Food, beverages, and tobacco	9.6*	0.2	0.7
Manufacturing, other	13.5*	2.5	6.6*
Textiles	–19.5*	–14.6*	–11.2
Apparel	10.8*	7.2*	7.5*
Wood	–33.5*	–33.6*	–26.3*
Constant	90.3*	–128.4*	–130.8*

SOURCE: Authors' calculations based on data from El Salvador's Multipurpose Household Surveys.

NOTE: Wage differentials represent the percentage (log) difference in each sector from the overall mean wage. The reported differentials are then calculated by raising e to the estimated coefficient and subtracting one because the model is log-linear.

* significant at the 1 percent level.

** significant at the 5 percent level.

premium) earned in each industry. The top of table 5.9 contains the IIWDs for different demographic characteristics. Females, for example, in 2000 earned about 9.9 percent less than other workers after controlling for sector, age, education, urban area, regional dummies, and whether the individual lives in a household receiving remittances.[16] Older and more-educated workers earn higher wages, as do those living in urban areas. Those receiving remittances have a slightly higher wages, indicating they have higher reservation wages.

As in other countries in this volume and elsewhere in the literature, industry-specific wage differentials are statistically and economically significant. Even after controlling for all demographic variables, work in the public sector has an IIWD of 83 percent in 2000. In food agriculture, workers earned 24 percent less than the average wage. Workers in the wood manufacturing industries earned below-average wages (–33.5 percent), while those in the food manufacturing industries (with beverages and tobacco) earned above-average wages (9.6 percent). Workers in utilities, construction, and finance, however, earned well-above-average wages, with percent differences of 62 percent, 16.1 percent, and 37.3 percent, respectively. These sectors are all considered nontradable sectors. Utilities and finance, in particular, have significantly important FDI shares. (See Communications, Electricity, and Financial in table 5.3.)

Workers in apparel earned about 10.7 percent more than the average wage in 2000. Average wages in apparel are low because they hire mostly young women; however, young women with similar characteristics are likely to earn more than the overall average if they work in the apparel sector, depending on the size of the wage premium in any other sector. The IIWD in the apparel sector is not large relative to other estimated differentials. In particular, workers in public administration and social services earn premiums of 16.9 percent and 24.5 percent, respectively. In fact, of all the positive wage premiums, only the food and beverage industry and other agriculture have smaller premiums in 2000.

The second and third columns in table 5.9 present the results for 2004 and 2005. In the agricultural food sector the wage differential, although still negative, rose considerably compared with 2000. The main reason behind the large negative number in 2000 was the drop in coffee prices—El Salvador's main agricultural export crop—during the period 1997–2001. Although 2004 and 2005 were recovery years for agriculture, the wage differential was still negative.

Before 2005, the MFA was in effect, favoring countries in Central America with preferential access to the U.S. market through the Caribbean Basin Initiative. On January 1, 2005, the MFA expired. The MFA's coming demise was known by 2004, and many firms in the sector began to move their operations to countries with comparative advantages after the elimination of quotas in the sector (mainly South Asian countries and China). Table 5.9 shows how the IIWD for apparel declined in those years, as did the industry's share in employment (shown in table 5.6). The rising wage premium (2004 to 2005) coincides with a falling female share of total employment in apparel.

THE RELATIONSHIP BETWEEN FDI AND IIWDS

Ideally, sufficient data would be available to allow IIWDs to be regressed on a full set of variables that characterize globalization. Such data are not available for El Salvador. This section presents some evidence about the link between globalization—as measured by FDI—and IIWDs.

The available FDI data are categorized by different industries that are used for the estimated IIWD results. These two data sets can be compared by reclassifying the industries in table 5.9 into the following 10 industries: agriculture, fishing, mining, apparel, nonapparel manufacturing, utilities, construction, sales, services, and financial. Estimating IIWDs, ω, for these 10 industries for each year from 1997 to 2005 (inclusive) creates a data set of 10 industries with 8 years of data that can be matched with the FDI data described earlier. These data represent FDI stocks, rather than flows. Differencing the FDI data captures the net effects of FDI flows. The following regression equation allows for the possibility that FDI flows take time (one year) to affect wages:

$$\omega_{it} = \alpha + \beta \Delta FDI_{it-1} + u_{it}. \tag{5.1}$$

The random-effects estimate for β is 0.0005628, which is significant at the 5 percent level. The standard deviation of the change in FDI is 106.8591, which implies that a one-standard-deviation change in FDI would lead to an increase in the IIWD of 0.06.

The estimated positive link between FDI and IIWDs is consistent with the literature that estimates the link between nonwage measures of working conditions and FDI (Daude, Mazza, and Morrison 2003; Mosley and Uno 2007). These and previous studies generally find nonnegative (either zero or positive) relationships between FDI and working conditions. (None of these studies, however, directly analyzes IIWDs.) There are still several reasons to interpret the results obtained here with caution. First, these results are estimated over very small samples (only seven time-series observations). Although these differentials are estimated controlling for demographic characteristics, they do not include other macroeconomic explanatory variables that might also contribute. Nevertheless, there is no evidence that increasing FDI lowers wage differentials.

Nonwage Aspects of Working Conditions in El Salvador

Wages are only one facet of working conditions. As in the Indonesia and Madagascar studies in this volume, the Salvadoran data include many nonwage measures of working conditions. This section uses probit models of nonwage working conditions (specifically, whether workers signed a contract or whether they registered for social security [mandatory health insurance]) to identify patterns across industries and to compare these with the pattern of wage differentials. This section also includes descriptive statistics for other nonwage working conditions for 2005.

CONTRACTUAL CHARACTERISTICS

Table 5.10 shows the main aggregates for working conditions in El Salvador in 2005 beyond wages. Overall, only 38.7 percent of wage laborers had signed a contract. The percentage was higher for women, for those receiving remittances, and for those working for larger firms. This same pattern holds for social security registration (with an overall average of 51.8 percent), and for receipt of the mandatory year-end payment. Both social security registration and receipt of the year-end payment increase with firm size, indicating that there are two segments in the market—those companies regulated by legislation, mainly large firms, and those mainly micro and small firms that are unregulated. Export-oriented firms tend to be large firms, and therefore are more prone to comply with labor regulation and provide better benefits to workers. The analysis that follows uses a probit model to test whether social security registration and signing of contracts are functions of individual characteristics, other control variables, and industry dummies. The other labor benefits and extra payments listed in table 5.10 are almost all voluntary; therefore, the percentage of workers who receive them is much smaller. Only 4.3 percent report receiving overtime pay.

Table 5.11 presents the percentage of the employed who had signed a contract or were registered for social security by industry for 2000, 2004, and 2005. In general, no major changes occur over time in the shares of workers with signed contracts or with registration for social security in an industry. On average, for 2005, close to 20 percent of workers had a signed contract and close to 30 percent were registered for social security. However, there are large differences across industries. For instance, workers in agricultural sectors were very unlikely to be registered for social security or to sign a contract, similarly, those in husbandry and fishing ; the percentages of construction and sales workers with signed contracts and social security were below average. Other manufacturing, textiles, and apparel sectors have above average percentages of workers with signed contracts and social security registration. Furthermore, workers in four key nontradable sectors had higher possibilities for signed contracts and registration for social security—utilities, education, public administration, and financial intermediation, which tend to be larger firms or organizations. It is clear that labor law enforcement and compliance is concentrated in large and formal sectors of society, and widely neglected in those sectors with an abundance of smaller and informal firms.

WORK ENVIRONMENT

The 2005 household survey introduced a new question about physical conditions in the workplace, including the presence of dust, smog, gas emissions, noise, or extreme temperatures; dangerous machinery, underground or height activities; insufficient

TABLE 5.10 **Working Conditions and Benefits for Wage Laborers in El Salvador, 2005**
(percentage with benefit)

Conditions or benefit	Sex		Remittances		Firm Size					All
	Male	Female	No	Yes	Micro	Small	Medium	Large		
Signed contract	32.1	52.5	38.3	40.6	38.7	24.4	31.6	69.4		38.7
Registered for social security	43.7	68.5	51.2	54.7	10.1	46.0	50.2	85.1		51.8
Received payment for end of year holiday	39.5	64.9	47.4	49.6	13.7	42.7	49.0	74.8		47.8
Received payment for vacations	11.1	18.3	13.4	13.5	2.6	16.1	15.5	20.6		13.4
Received payment for food or refreshments	8.4	14.7	10.6	9.7	17.0	8.0	7.2	6.5		10.4
Received payment for uniform	8.8	11.2	9.4	10.5	0.9	6.0	9.4	17.2		9.6
Received payment for bonus or commissions	5.7	10.3	6.6	10.0	1.4	7.1	5.9	11.7		7.2
Received payment for extra hours	3.3	6.2	4.2	4.5	0.5	1.7	4.2	7.8		4.3
Received payment for transportation	1.8	1.6	1.7	2.1	0.5	2.3	1.4	2.6		1.8
Received payment for housing	1.3	0.5	1.1	0.7	1.4	1.2	1.0	0.7		1.0
Received payments in kind	0.9	0.7	0.9	0.8	0.6	0.7	1.4	1.0		0.9
Received payment for private health insurance	0.0	0.1	0.0	0.1	0.0	0.0	0.3	0.1		0.0

SOURCE: Authors' estimates based on Multipurpose Household Survey data.

TABLE 5.11 **Percentage of Employed with Signed Contract and with Social Security, by Industry**

Industry	Percentage with signed contract			Percentage with social security		
	2000	2004	2005	2000	2004	2005
Agriculture, food	1.2	0.9	0.6	2.7	2.3	1.4
Agriculture, other	12.2	—	4.7	37.5	—	6.6
Husbandry and fishing	0.9	5.8	0.9	2.9	9.5	1.0
Mining	15.9	15.2	11.9	29.3	37.7	25.6
Utilities	39.8	35.0	78.7	86.6	84.2	90.4
Construction	11.1	8.0	10.8	26.1	18.0	19.0
Sales	8.6	7.8	9.3	18.2	19.3	18.0
Transport	14.0	13.3	17.1	28.7	29.4	30.0
Financial intermediation	37.4	32.2	42.7	66.3	65.4	67.8
Public administration	40.5	28.3	96.5	91.1	90.6	90.4
Education	42.6	28.9	84.6	83.9	85.0	87.4
Social services	19.2	16.7	34.3	39.4	38.3	40.1
Domestic service	0.0	—	0.0	0.0	—	0.0
Others	66.2	16.6	—	70.7	—	—
Food, beverages, and tobacco	17.2	12.7	12.9	27.5	25.7	23.4
Manufacturing, other	24.3	21.5	29.6	43.7	42.6	46.4
Textile	24.7	30.9	36.4	38.9	45.9	50.7
Apparel	32.4	33.5	38.0	60.5	65.5	60.2
Wood	1.1	—	4.2	2.3	4.7	13.5
Weighted average	14.6	12.1	20.2	29.0	29.7	29.3

SOURCE: Authors' estimates based on Multipurpose Household Survey data.

NOTE: — = Not available.

lighting; chemicals or heavy loads; and others not specified. Table 5.12 shows outcomes by industry. The most often reported negative labor condition was dust in the workplace, with 41.8 percent of workers reporting this problem. The problem was especially notice-able in construction, agriculture, and mining, as expected. The percentage was much lower in financial intermediation and the textiles and apparel sectors, close to 28 percent, showing they enjoy better conditions on average. In husbandry and fishing, only 6.2 per-cent reported dusty conditions.

Apparel sector workers reported better than average working environments with regard to dust, smog, gas emissions, carrying of heavy loads, and working with chemicals. However, an above-average percentage of apparel sector workers reported noisy conditions,

TABLE 5.12 **Percentage of Workers Who Reported Special Physical Conditions in the Workplace, by Industry**

Industry	Dusty	Smoggy	Gases	Noisy	Temperature	Machine	Underground	Heights	Poor light	Chemicals	Heavy Loads	Other
Agriculture, food	71.9	12.9	2.0	8.0	39.7	39.3	2.2	2.2	7.1	11.7	24.7	1.6
Agriculture, other	52.0	14.6	3.9	19.2	35.5	36.9	0.8	0.6	7.4	7.6	22.6	1.8
Husbandry and fishing	6.2	5.3	2.0	9.0	41.2	33.2	0.0	0.8	7.1	0.0	17.8	4.2
Mining	60.0	29.6	8.9	20.3	23.4	41.3	2.0	0.0	6.1	19.7	32.4	0.0
Utilities	34.5	24.1	11.1	26.1	22.4	15.4	3.0	11.0	9.1	10.3	8.7	1.8
Construction	73.6	19.4	7.5	29.0	30.2	39.7	6.1	13.6	8.8	8.5	39.5	1.7
Sales	32.4	27.7	15.5	27.2	18.1	15.8	0.3	0.9	8.7	6.0	15.6	0.9
Transport	51.2	46.8	19.9	31.7	21.6	13.5	0.9	1.8	9.3	2.8	17.8	1.0
Financial intermediation	23.1	14.3	5.1	13.8	10.8	21.2	0.3	1.7	9.0	3.0	3.3	1.3
Public administration	29.7	19.4	11.1	20.3	16.5	21.9	0.7	1.4	7.0	5.4	4.9	2.1
Education	27.4	8.3	3.4	30.3	11.9	2.8	0.2	0.7	8.2	1.1	0.4	1.1
Social services	20.3	12.0	6.0	17.4	13.7	11.6	0.4	0.3	8.9	9.3	3.8	0.6
Food, beverages, and tobacco	33.3	35.2	14.4	30.0	30.3	20.5	0.4	1.9	10.0	5.2	20.9	0.2
Manufacturing, other	43.8	27.2	15.4	42.8	32.5	40.6	1.0	1.4	10.7	18.7	20.0	0.4
Textiles	25.9	5.8	2.8	35.9	15.6	28.6	0.0	1.5	10.4	9.4	14.3	15.8
Apparel	28.3	14.1	4.9	44.9	25.5	31.9	0.6	0.7	13.8	4.3	8.0	16.5
Wood	45.7	10.2	0.0	39.8	32.7	65.8	0.0	4.0	0.0	9.5	14.9	0.0
Weighted average	**41.3**	**20.9**	**9.4**	**25.4**	**23.3**	**24.3**	**1.2**	**2.4**	**8.9**	**7.2**	**15.6**	**2.3**

SOURCE: Authors' estimates based on Multipurpose Household Survey data.

working with dangerous machinery, and insufficient lighting. The percentage of workers reporting extreme temperatures in the apparel sector was not different from the mean. These characteristics are what one would expect in this type of industry. Finally, the apparel and textiles industries had the highest percentages reporting "other, not specified" (16.5 percent and 15.8 percent, respectively), well above the other industries and the average, suggesting the presence of an additional unique condition that should be further investigated.

PROBIT MODEL FOR CONTRACTUAL ASPECTS OF LABOR

To test whether the differences in contract signing and social security registration are due to differences in worker characteristics, or differences in industry characteristics, the analysis uses probit estimations for both events as functions of individual characteristics such as education, age, and sex; other control variables such as area of residence (urban dummy); a public sector dummy; whether a worker's household receives remittances; and industry dummies, excluding the apparel sector, which serves as reference.

Table 5.13 presents the results for 2000, 2004, and 2005. Control variables have an impact similar to the impact they had on wages. The likelihood of signing a contract or participating in social security increased with age, education, living in urban areas, and working in the public sector, but decreased for women. Remittances has an unexpected sign, opposite from the one obtained in the wage regression. Those receiving remittances were less likely to sign a contract or register for social security. This requires further exploration. One possibility is that those receiving remittances were better able to negotiate higher wages, but are less demanding with regard to social security because remittances are a means of diversifying risk. If a need arises, the sending relative can provide a sort of insurance. This could explain why employers are willing to pay a premium to those receiving remittances: hiring remittances-receiving workers may reduce costs because the employer avoids making contributions to social security.[17]

After controlling for the previously mentioned variables, an interesting fact emerges in the pattern of industry differences. With very few exceptions, workers in almost all sectors are less likely to sign contracts and to register for social security than in the apparel sector. The only consistent exception is the textiles sector, where the difference from the apparel sector in the probability of signing a contract is not statistically significant.

PROBIT MODEL FOR WORKING ENVIRONMENT

Table 5.14 presents the marginal effect of being employed in a particular industry on the probability of working in an environment with some of the negative features reviewed above; marginal effects were calculated after controlling for age, education, and a female dummy. The omitted sector was the apparel industry so that coefficients in other industries represent the difference from this sector.[18] The outcomes are similar to the uncontrolled differences. For instance, in the apparel sector, the problems mentioned more often than in other industries were noisy environment, use of dangerous machinery, poor illumination, and "other." Similarly, the marginal effects results show that workers in the apparel sector were more likely to report a noisy environment than were workers in 15 other sectors; more likely to report working with dangerous machinery than workers in 14 sectors; more likely to report poor lighting than workers in 10 other sectors; and more likely to report "other" problems than workers in 14 sectors.

TABLE 5.13 **Probit Models for Signed Contract and Social Security Registration for Employed Workers (Marginal Effects)**
(percentage difference from apparel sector)

| | Dependent variables | | | | | |
| | Signed contract | | | Social security | | |
Explanatory variables	2000	2004	2005	2000	2004	2005
Years of education	0.7*	0.9*	1.9*	2.1*	3.3*	3.2*
Age	0.7*	0.3*	1.3*	1.3*	1.3*	1.6*
Age squared	0.0*	0.0*	0.0*	0.0*	0.0*	0.0*
Female	−2.7*	−2.3*	−3.3*	−7.5*	−7.4*	−6.6*
Urban dummy	6.3*	0.6*	3.1*	13.7*	4.0*	1.6*
Public sector dummy	11.6*	2.1*	90.2*	51.2*	43.8*	51.4*
Remittances dummy	−1.9*	−1.1*	−2.6*	−2.7*	−3.6*	−2.7*
Agriculture, food	−14.4*	−10.2*	−22.6*	−35.5*	−34.6*	−32.4*
Agriculture, other	−8.9*	−5.0*	−13.9*	−23.0*	−20.3*	−21.7*
Construction	−7.6*	−5.8*	−13.6*	−19.8*	−22.4*	−20.7*
Sales	−11.1*	−9.0*	−20.1*	−29.0*	−31.6*	−29.2*
Transport	−7.4*	−5.4*	−13.1*	−20.8*	−21.3*	−19.2*
Financial intermediation	0.1	−3.0*	−5.5*	−1.9*	−11.6*	−7.8*
Public administration	−4.6*	−4.6*	7.3*	−7.8*	−13.0*	−13.2*
Education	−0.6*	−4.9*	0.6*	1.1*	−13.7*	−10.1*
Social services	−6.3*	−5.2*	−13.1*	−18.7*	−21.4*	−19.8*
Domestic service	pp	−7.4*	pp	pp	pp	pp
Food, beverages, and tobacco	−5.2*	−4.8*	−12.1*	−17.9*	−19.4*	−18.2*
Manufacturing, other	−4.5*	−4.1	−7.4*	−14.4*	−16.8*	−13.2*
Textiles	0.0	0.0	0.3	−8.0*	−9.2*	−5.3*
Apparel (omitted)						

SOURCE: Authors' calculations based on Multipurpose Household Survey.

NOTE: pp = dropped because of perfect prediction.

Probit estimates a model where the dependent variable is the probability of an outcome, in this case, whether a worker signs a contract, or whether a worker contributes to social security. The model was estimated with the Stata command dprobit, which reports the marginal effect, or the change in probability for an infinitesimal change in the explanatory variable, if it is continuous, or a discrete change in the probability for dummy variables. The apparel sector was omitted for sectoral dummies; therefore, the percentage value tells whether that sector is below or above the apparel sector. Four sectors were dropped from the estimation—wood, mining, utilities, and others—because the sample size was too small to be representative. Domestic service was included in the estimation process but the dprobit command dropped it because prediction was perfect, with one exception.

*significant at 1 percent level.

TABLE 5.14 **Probit Models of Workers Who Declared Special Physical Conditions in the Workplace, by Industry after Controlling for Individual Characteristics (percentage difference from apparel sector)**

Explanatory variable	Noisy	Dusty	Smoggy	Gases	Temperature	Machine	Underground	Light	Height	Chemicals	Heavy Load	Others
Female	-6.2*	-15.6*	-7.5*	-4.5*	-6.6*	-14.0*	-0.58*	-0.1	-1.2*	-2.5*	-7.6*	-0.3
Age	0.4**	0.0	0.5*	0.3*	0.1	0.6*	0.1	0.1	0.1	0.3*	-0.1	0.0
Age squared	0.0*	0.0	0.0*	0.0*	0.0	0.0*	0.0	0.0	0.0	0.0*	0.0	0.0
Years of education	-0.2**	-1.4*	-0.5*	-0.1**	-0.8*	-1.1*	0.088**	0.1	0.0	0.0	-0.7*	-0.1*
Agriculture, food	-24.6*	29.9*	-3.0	-5.0*	3.0	-7.1*	0.6	-3.5*	1.4**	9.7*	4.1*	-1.9*
Agriculture, other	-17.4*	14.6*	-4.0	-2.0	-2.6	-10.3*	0.6	-3.5*	0.0	5.4*	2.9	-1.4*
Husbandry and fishing	-19.0*	-35.1*	-13.0*	-3.9	13.1**	-9.7**		-1.1	0.7		5.8	-1.2*
Mining	-11.6*	12.0	8.3	11.1	-1.3	-7.6	3.9	5.6		22.1*	13.6	
Utilities	-14.0*	3.4	2.5	4.7	-6.9	-14.3*	2.4	-2.7	12.4*	4.1	-0.4	-1.4*
Construction	-14.4*	35.9*	1.5	-1.8	0.1	-8.4*	2.78*	-2.3**	8.4*	3.4**	18.5*	-1.7*
Sales	-12.6*	4.6**	15.4*	8.8*	-6.0*	-15.6*	-0.4	-2.7*	0.3	1.8	5.0*	-2.3*
Transport	-10.0*	19.5*	32.3*	14.5*	-4.7**	-20.0*	-0.3	-2.8*	1.0	-2.3	4.9*	-1.7*
Financial intermediation	-19.7*	-6.8*	0.9	-0.7	-13.9*	-12.4*	-0.4	-2.3**	0.7	-1.9	-8.2*	-1.6*
Public administration and defense	-15.6*	6.4**	8.1*	6.0*	-6.7*	-9.6*	-0.1	-4.2*	0.4	-1.4	-4.5*	-1.5*

(continued)

TABLE 5.14 (continued)

Explanatory variable	Noisy	Dusty	Smoggy	Gases	Temperature	Machine	Underground	Light	Height	Chemicals	Heavy Load	Others
Education	−9.3*	14.9*	−1.1	−2.6**	−9.2*	−23.7*	−0.2	−3.8*	−0.6	−3.9*	−10.3*	−1.6*
Social services	−15.3*	−1.1	1.9	3.7**	−8.6*	−15.4*	−0.3	−2.9*	−0.8	5.2*	−4.6*	−1.7*
Domestic service	−24.8*	−11.7*	−5.4*	−3.8*	−19.7*	−16.1*	−0.6	−5.3*	−0.4	−0.2	−7.8*	−2.0*
Food, beverages, and tobacco	−12.2*	2.1	22.9*	8.0*	2.5	−14.8*	−0.5	−1.3	0.9	0.8	6.4*	−1.6*
Manufacturing, other	−6.8*	12.3*	13.0*	8.2*	−0.6	−2.6	0.3	−2.0	1.0	13.8*	7.2*	−1.7*
Textiles	−8.1*	−7.1	−11.1**	−1.0		−10.9*		−3.0	0.5	11.2*	2.8	0.2
Apparel (omitted)												
Wood	−8.2	8.3	−10.6		−7.7	14.8			3.4	3.0	−0.2	

SOURCE: Authors' calculations based on Multipurpose Household Survey.

NOTE: Not available.

* significant at the 1 percent level.

** significant at the 5 percent level.

Comparisons with other manufacturing sectors show that the differences in marginal effects depend on the specific sector. For instance, workers in food and beverages and other manufacturing were more likely to report dusty, smoggy environments, and gases in the workplace than were workers in apparel. In apparel, concerns about noise and "other problems" were more frequent than in food and beverages and other manufacturing. Working conditions seem to be worse in some sectors than in apparel. Positive marginal effects appear in eight sectors for dusty conditions, seven sectors for working with chemicals, six sectors for working with gases, and four sectors for working with heavy loads.

These results suggest that working in manufacturing generally is accompanied by several unpleasant characteristics as compared with nonmanufacturing employment. These differences may exist in every country as a result of the intrinsic nature of manufacturing. Among manufacturing industries, however, apparel has only two dimensions that suggest that conditions are worse (noise and "other"). Thus, the claim that conditions are particularly bad in apparel would depend on the weight given to these two dimensions (which could be subjective).

CORRELATIONS BETWEEN WORKING CONDITIONS AND IIWDs

Could positive wage differentials offset poor working conditions? This hypothesis, known as *compensating differentials*, has been often tested using risk as a measure of nonwage working conditions. In El Salvador, two possible measures of nonwage working conditions that relate to risk are having a contract (which reduces employment risk) and social security. The correlation between the propensity of each of these two benefits across industries and the corresponding IIWDs reveals whether the wage differentials are compensating for poor conditions.

The correlation between IIWDs (the estimated coefficients) in 2005 in table 5.9 and the percentage of workers with contracts in 2005 from table 5.10 is 0.37. The correlation between IIWDs in 2005 in table 5.9 and the percentage of workers with social security in 2005 from table 5.10 is 0.43. Both of these correlations are positive: industries with positive wage differentials tend to have better nonwage working conditions (although not tested against conditions intrinsic to industrial activity). These correlations suggest that the wage differentials in El Salvador are not consistent with the compensating differentials hypothesis (although the positive differentials could be compensating for other aspects of working conditions).

Conclusions

Globalization in El Salvador is characterized primarily by important efforts in trade liberalization, export promotion, and an attractive legal framework for FDI. Outward migration has been a widespread phenomenon in El Salvador, to the point that remittances play an important role in macroeconomic conditions and in individual decision-making processes. Remittances may affect labor supply, and by extension, working conditions, by increasing the reservation wage and by raising the prices of nontradables relative to tradable goods.

In the maquila sector, globalization effects exhibit several distinct periods. As liberalization progressed during the 1990s, the maquila sector expanded. The maquila sector leveled out beginning in 2000, and in 2004 began to contract, possibly because of the expectation that the MFA would expire. This chapter shows that before expiration of the MFA, the wage differential for the apparel sector was positive with respect to the average and maintained a positive trend, as it did in share of employment. But beginning in 2004, the trend changed—both employment share and the IIWD decreased. Regarding other working conditions, econometric results show that the percentage of workers in the apparel sector with signed contracts or with registration for social security was above average, after controlling for age, education, sex, public sector, and remittances. These results suggest that those keeping their jobs in the sector still enjoy these advantages as compared with working in other sectors, possibly because it is a regulated sector dominated by large exporting firms.

Because firms in the maquila sector are large and pay low average wages, they garner a lot of media attention. They are characterized as "sweatshops." International protests against the sector have created monitoring efforts, such as Grupo de Monitoreo Independiente de El Salvador, and lobbying to obtain greater compliance efforts and labor law enforcement in the sector. Such efforts, however, though positive for workers in that sector, ignore the fact that there is a positive wage premium for working in the sector—workers with similar characteristics earn lower wages on average in other sectors—and that labor conditions, as measured by signed employment contracts and social security registration, are better than in other sectors.

This analysis raises a rarely mentioned point. Qualitative and quantitative analyses suggest that, relative to other sectors (especially other manufacturing sectors), export-oriented, FDI-dominated apparel seems to have better conditions. As a globalized sector, it receives much international attention. Only about 5 percent of workers in El Salvador, however, work in apparel. Domestic service and agricultural workers represent 4.3 percent and 16 percent, respectively, of employment in El Salvador, and workers in these two sectors have far worse conditions and lower wages (40 percent and 13.3 percent below the mean, respectively, in 2005) than apparel workers. After controlling for individual and household characteristics, maids are very unlikely to enjoy a contract or contribute to social security, and agricultural workers are 17.4 percent less likely to have signed a contract and 20 percent less likely to contribute to social security. In El Salvador, it is almost impossible for a small, informal firm or a family to enroll a worker in social security. If efforts were made to change the rules for enrollment in social security, many workers could register for social security benefits. Rather than focusing efforts on 5 percent of workers, labor policy could obtain larger welfare gains by addressing the problems of the 20 percent in worse conditions. In other words, the purportedly positive effects of globalization do not seem to be reaching workers who are less exposed to international markets.

With regard to the impact of remittances on labor market in El Salvador, a sample selection model suggests that remittances have a negative impact on labor market participation, and that those that decide to work as wage laborers earn higher wages, indicating that remittances have a positive impact on reservation wages. However, when the impact of remittances on other working conditions, such as signing a contract or registering for social security, was tested, it was found that receiving remittances reduced the likelihood of receiving these benefits. A plausible explanation for this, from the perspective of workers, is that remittances are a sort of insurance and a means of risk diversification; therefore, remittances-receiving workers exhibit less demand for signing a contract or registering for social security. From the perspective of employers, the higher wages they pay to remittances-receiving workers are offset by lower requirements to register them for social security and provide the mandated contributions.

Notes

1. Williamson (2005) discusses the importance of migration and demographic transitions in the development process. He points out that when a demographic shock affects a specific group of the population (for example, young working-age people), and when this shock is big, it has a long-term impact on the economy.

2. Hausmann, Rodrik, and Velasco (2005) posed the problem of countries facing many policy goals against the feasibility of addressing all of them at once. Because this is not possible, they suggest that the best approach is to identify those constraints that have a bigger impact on development in a particular country, and to focus efforts on those constraints.

3. The index is the average of six indicators describing the quality of public policies: (i) stability, (ii) adaptability, (iii) coordination and coherence, (iv) implementation and effectiveness of application, (v) public interest orientation, and (vi) efficiency. The scale runs from 1 to 4; higher values indicate better quality of public policies.

4. Brazil, Colombia, Costa Rica, El Salvador, Mexico, and Uruguay.

5. See FUSADES (1989) for a proposal of an economic and social strategy for the country. The strategy proposed by FUSADES strongly influenced the agenda of the first government of the ARENA party, headed by President Alfredo Félix Cristiani in the 1989–94 period.

6. For a description of initial reforms, see Rivera-Campos (2000) and also Liévano (1996).

7. This part relies on Alas de Franco (2002).

8. The first FDI legislation was passed in April 1988. The law was reformed in January 1989 and again in December 1989.

9. For more information on the expiration of the MFA, see http://www.wto.org/english/tratop_e/texti_e/texintro_e.htm.

10. From 2003 to 2005, the increase in share of intermediate and consumption goods was strongly associated with the increase in oil prices.

11. Among others, see World Bank (1996), Rivera Campos (2000), and FUSADES (2003). For this section, the tradable sector includes Industry, Agriculture and Fishing, Mines, and Maquila; the nontradable sector includes Sales, Services, Construction, Communications, Electricity, and Financial.

12. Between 1991 and 2000, El Salvador fixed its exchange rate. Since January 1, 2001, the U.S. dollar has been the unit of exchange and legal tender, displacing the former currency, the *colon*.

13. GDP deflators were obtained by dividing GDP at current prices by GDP at constant prices for each sector. The relative price was obtained by dividing the GDP deflator for the tradable sector by the GDP deflator for the nontradable sector. GDP of the tradable sector is the addition of three sectors, as defined by national accounts in the Central Bank: (i) Agriculture, fishing, and hunting; (ii) Mines; and (iii) Manufacturing Industry. GDP of the nontradable sector is the addition of nine sectors, as defined by national accounts in the central bank: (i) Electricity, Gas and Water; (ii) Construction; (iii) Sales, Restaurants, and Hotels; (iv) Transportation, Storage, and Communications; (v) Finance and Insurance; (vi) Real Estate and Services;

(vii) Housing Rental; (viii) Communal, Social, Personal and Domestic Services; and (ix) Government Services. Data and estimation results are available upon request.

14. Decree No. 859 of April 21, 1994, as listed in the May 12, 1994, edition of the *Diario Oficial*.

15. As described in the annex to chapter 3 of this book, the appropriate standard errors for the differences from the mean are calculated following Haisken-deNew and Schmidt (1997).

16. The percentage change is obtained from the coefficient estimate by raising e to the coefficient estimate and subtracting 1, because the model is log-linear.

17. The authors thank Amy Damon for pointing out that there may be secondary effects on workers from changing the insurance pool if there are systematic differences between workers that stay in and leave the pool.

18. Note that the decision of which industry to exclude is arbitrary. The reported results (the coefficients) are basically transitive. That is, if industry A has better conditions than the omitted industry, and industry B has worse conditions, it can be concluded that industry A has better conditions than industry B. The formal tests of statistical significance of differences across industries are more straightforward when the industry of interest is omitted.

References

Alas de Franco, Carolina. 2002. "Política comercial y evolución del sector exportador durante los noventa en El Salvador." Serie de Investigación No. 2, FUSADES, DEES.

Bronstein, Arturo S. 1997. "Labour Law Reform in Latin America: Between State Protection and Flexibility." *International Labour Review* 136 (1): 5–27.

BID (Banco Interamericano de Desarrollo). 2006. "La política de las políticas públicas: Progreso económico y social de América Latina." Editorial Planeta.

Cox-Edwards, Alejandra. 2000. "Alternativas de política económica para agilizar la creación del empleo." Capítulo 3 en FUSADES (2000), 95–146.

Cox-Edwards, Alejandra, and Eduardo Rodríguez Oreggia. 2006. "The Effect of Remittances on Labor Force Participation: An Analysis Based on Mexico's 2002 ENET." Paper prepared for IZA/World Bank Conference "Employment and Development," Berlin, May 25–27.

Daude, Christian, Jacqueline Mazza, and Andrew Morrison. 2003. "Core Labor Standards and Foreign Direct Investment in Latin American and the Caribbean: Does Lax Enforcement of Labor Standards Attract Investors?" Inter-American Development Bank, Washington, DC.

Frundt, Henry J. 2004. "Unions Wrestle with Corporate Codes of Conduct." *Working USA* 7 (4): 36–69.

FUSADES (Salvadoran Foundation for Economic and Social Development). 1989. "Hacia una economía de mercado en El Salvador: Bases para una nueva Estrategia de Desarrollo Económico y Social." Departamento de Estudios Económicos y Sociales, El Salvador.

———. 2000. "Crecimiento con participación: una estrategia de desarrollo para el Siglo XXI." Volume II, Departamento de Estudios Económicos y Sociales.

———. 2003. Ley de Inversión Extranejera (Decreto Legislativo no. 732, Noviembre 1999).

Haisken-DeNew, J. P., and C. Schmidt. 1997. "Interindustry and Interregion Differentials: Mechanics and Interpretation." *The Review of Economics and Statistics* 79 (3): 516–21.

Hausmann, Ricardo, Dani Rodrik, and Andrés Velasco. 2005. "Growth Diagnostics." Unpublished, John F. Kennedy School of Government, Harvard University.

Heckman, James J. 1979. "Sample Selection Bias as a Specification Error." *Econometrica* 47 (1): 153–61.

ICFTU, WCL, and ETUC (International Confederation of Free Trade Unions, World Confederation of Labour, and European Trade Union Confederation). 2005. "Reports on Core Labor Standards in Countries Applying for the GSP-Plus." http://www.icftu.org/www/PDF/GSP.pdf.

Inter-American Development Bank. 2004. *Good Jobs Wanted: Labor Markets in Latin America.* 2004 Economic and Social Progress Report. Washington, DC: Inter-American Development Bank.

ILO (International Labor Organization). 2006 "Review of annual reports under the follow-up to the ILO Declaration on Fundamental Principles and Rights at Work Part II Compilation of Annual Reports by the International Labour Office," Geneva.

Liévano, Mirna. 1996. "El Salvador: un país en transición." San Salvador.

Mosley, Layna, and Saika Uno. 2007. "Racing to the Bottom or Climbing to the Top?" *Comparative Political Studies* 40 (8): 923–48.

Rivera Campos, Roberto. 2000. "La economía salvadoreña al final del siglo: Desafíos para el futuro." FLACSO-El Salvador.

Pagés, Carmen, and Alejandro Micco. 2006. "The Economic Effects of Employment Protection Laws." Paper presented at the IZA/ World Bank conference "Employment and Development," Berlin, May 25–27.

Robbins, Donald, and T. H. Gindling. 1999. "Trade Liberalization and Relative Wages for More Skilled Workers in Costa Rica." *Review of Development Economics* 3 (2): 140–54.

Robertson, Raymond. 2004. "Relative Prices and Wage Inequality: Evidence from Mexico." *Journal of International Economics* 64 (2): 387–409.

———. 2005. "Has NAFTA Increased Labor Market Integration between the United States and Mexico?" *The World Bank Economic Review* 19 (3): 425–48.

———. 2007. "Globalization and Working Conditions: A Guideline for Country Studies." Macalester College, St. Paul, MN.

The Heritage Foundation and *The Wall Street Journal.* 2006. "The 2006 Index of Economic Freedom."

Thompson, Ginger. 2005. "Fraying of a Latin Textile Industry." *New York Times*, March 25.

Trejos, Juan Diego, and T. H. Gindling. 2004. "Inequality in Central America in the 1990s." *CEPAL Review* 84: 175–96.

U.S. Department of State. 2008. "2008 Human Rights Report: El Salvador." Bureau of Democracy, Human Rights, and Labor, 2008 Country Report on Human Rights Practices. http://www.state.gov/g/drl/rls/hrrpt/2008/wha/119159.htm

USTR (Office of the United States Trade Representative). 2005. "CAFTA's Strong Protections for Labor Rights: A Comprehensive Strategy." CAFTA Policy Brief, February. http://www.ustr.gov/assets/Trade_Agreements/Regional/CAFTA/Briefing_Book/asset_upload_file652_7187.pdf.

Williamson, Jeffrey. 2005. "Las migraciones en masa, los mercados mundiales de capitales y las transiciones demográficas." *Cuadernos Económicos de ICE* 70: 11–24.

World Bank. 1996. *El Salvador: Meeting the Challenge of Globalization.* Washington, DC: World Bank.

CHAPTER 6

Globalization and Working Conditions: Evidence from Honduras

Douglas Marcouiller and Raymond Robertson

Honduras is one of the poorest Latin American countries, with a 2006 GDP per capita of approximately US$2,900. Although relatively small (a population of 7.3 million in 2006), Honduras attracted particular attention during the debate over the Central American Free Trade Agreement (CAFTA) between 2003 and 2005. Working conditions were one of the main concerns in the debate and continue to be an important issue in Honduran domestic and international relations.

In many ways, Honduras and El Salvador share similar experiences. They are both small Central American countries and both ratified CAFTA. Honduras ratified the agreement on April 1, 2006, taking a significant step along its path of trade liberalization. As in El Salvador, the years since Honduras's 1994 accession to the General Agreement on Tariffs and Trade have been a period of significant change in the country's exposure to foreign markets. Like many developing countries, Honduras began its transition from a relatively closed economy in the late 1980s.[1] And like many other Latin American countries, Honduras reduced its reliance on exports of primary products and increased exports in manufacturing. This switch induced a shift in employment from agriculture toward industry and services. The World Bank's World Development Indicators indicate that 59 percent of the population were engaged in agriculture in 1980, but that number fell to 39 percent by 2005. In particular, capital flows and trade liberalization caused a boom in apparel assembly, dramatically changing job prospects for young women. Emigration of workers has disrupted families but also spurred remittances that may well change consumption, labor supply, and investment (particularly in health, schooling, housing, and microenterprises).

One of the key differences between Honduras and El Salvador is income levels. Honduras is much poorer than El Salvador, and with that come the problems frequently encountered with development: fewer resources for infrastructure, monitoring, education, and transportation. These differences create an interesting comparison for relative wage levels and differentials between the two countries.

Like the other country studies in this volume, this chapter surveys various dimensions of globalization, concentrating on the combination of trade and investment. One of the dominant characteristics of Honduran trade is the importance of the *maquila* sector. From the Spanish word *maquilar*, which means to assemble, firms in the maquila industry import parts for assembly and re-export. In Honduras, the maquila sector primarily consists of apparel. The textiles and apparel sector has the highest rate of foreign investment after cigars. Enterprise surveys suggest that this foreign investment is led by exporting firms. Trade data sets that exclude maquila operations indicate that Honduras mainly exports agricultural goods and food products and imports fuels, machinery, and equipment. When assembly operations are included, however, apparel dominates the trade accounts. Morley (2006) shows that the ratio of maquila exports to total exports in 2002 was the highest (greater than 60 percent) in all of Central America.[2] Morley also states that in Honduras the maquila sector comprises 20 percent of industrial employment and 39 percent of GDP. Household surveys show employment in apparel rose dramatically between 1992 and 2004, coinciding with the decline in agricultural employment.

To analyze the link between globalization and working conditions, this chapter first describes the Honduran path of trade liberalization. The remaining sections focus on working conditions as determined by institutions and economics. The second section concentrates on institutions and nonwage aspects of working conditions in two parts. The first part is qualitative and provides an overview of labor law and the struggle over working conditions in Honduras. The second part uses an enterprise survey to analyze nonwage aspects of working conditions. This survey suggests that there is no systematic difference in nonwage pecuniary benefits across sectors.

The third and fourth sections consider the economic determinants of working conditions using a quantitative analysis of wages. Trejos and Gindling (2004) analyze wage inequality in Central America during the period of rising globalization and find mixed results for Honduras; their results are also sensitive to the choice of inequality measures. These results may imply that industry-specific wages play a significant role in explaining wage changes in Honduras. This chapter takes an alternative approach by focusing on economywide interindustry wage differentials (IIWDs). This approach pays particular attention to the textiles and apparel sector because it stands out as a large, growing, and internationally integrated sector. Controlling for personal characteristics, workers in textiles and apparel consistently earn an above-average wage. This premium has been maintained as employment in the sector has grown. Given the lack of evidence of significant differences in nonwage working conditions in the second section, it appears that the wage premiums apparel workers receive are not compensating them for worse working conditions.

The fourth section compares earnings of garment finishers with earnings of other workers in the manufacturing sector, excluding the self-employed and public sector workers. The results suggest that, after controlling for age, schooling, and gender, garment finishers earn significantly more than workers with the same characteristics in other sectors. That premium, however, vanishes when personal characteristics are not controlled for. In other words, apparel firms are paying relatively high wages to workers drawn from the low end of the wage distribution. The final section provides conclusions.

Globalization in Honduras

Because the globalization experience may be different in each country, this section describes what globalization has meant in Honduras by describing globalization policies, basic indicators, and trade flows.

OVERVIEW OF GLOBALIZATION POLICIES

Globalization can be measured by outcomes in trade, foreign investment, and remittances, but the notion of liberalization gives priority to changes in policy. Honduras had a relatively closed economy between the 1950s and 1970s, with the exception of its participation in the Central American Common Market, along with Costa Rica, El Salvador, Guatemala, and Nicaragua. Honduras joined the Central American Common Market in December 1960. However, the 1969 "Soccer War" between Honduras and El Salvador permanently disrupted the workings of that organization. Like the rest of Latin America, Honduras was significantly and adversely affected by the debt crisis of the 1980s.

Following the debt crisis, Honduras took its main steps toward an open-economy model in the 1990s. Honduras acceded to the World Trade Organization's (WTO's) General Agreement on Tariffs and Trade in 1994 and lowered most-favored nation (MFN) tariffs. Relative to its Central American neighbors, Honduras started the 1990s with both higher average tariff levels (41.9 percent) and higher tariff dispersion (21.8 percentage points). El Salvador, for example, had an average tariff level of 16 percent and dispersion of 8.6 percentage points in 1990. By 1997, however, Honduran average tariffs and dispersion were as low as or lower than those of other Central American countries (Morley 2006). The WTO documents a fall in the simple average applied MFN tariff from around 17 percent in 1993 to 6 percent in 2003 (WTO 2003).[3]

Perhaps as important as domestic tariff liberalization was the tariff treatment Honduras received from its trading partners (especially the United States). In 1982, U.S. president Ronald Reagan proposed the Caribbean Basin Initiative. These trade preferences were given to Caribbean Basin countries, including those in Central America, by the Caribbean Basin Economic Recovery Act starting January 1, 1984. While this act did not grant textiles tariff-free access to U.S. markets, it did exempt them from the Multifibre Arrangement (MFA)[4] as long as they were assembled using U.S. inputs. This system created incentives for the rapid growth of the maquila sector in Honduras. This act, and its extension (the Caribbean Basin Economic Recovery Expansion Act) in 1990, gave Central America a tariff advantage over Mexico that lasted until the emergence of the North American Free Trade Agreement in 1994. The U.S.-Caribbean Basin Trade Partnership Act (CBTPA) in 2000, granted the same duty-free access to U.S. markets as Mexico enjoyed under NAFTA (Morley 2006).

Perhaps in an attempt to solidify the benefits of the CBTPA beyond its planned expiration on September 30, 2008, Central America started negotiating CAFTA in 2002. The five Central American countries signed the agreement with the United States on May 28, 2004. Honduras ratified the treaty, thus bringing it into effect, on April 1, 2006. Several reports, such as Jansen et al. (2007), analyze the potential effects of CAFTA on Central American exports, especially in the maquila sector. While the maquila sector had preferential access to U.S. markets, restrictive rules of origin and other U.S. actions raised concerns among Hondurans.[5] One of the main concerns Jansen et al. (2007) focus on was whether the net effect of the end of the MFA in 2005 (which would potentially reduce Honduran textiles and apparel exports) and CAFTA (which would potentially increase Honduran textiles and apparel exports) was positive or negative. The report focuses on the maquila sector in Honduras because it has been one of the main sources, if not the main source, of employment growth in Honduras since the 1980s.[6]

Maquilas and export processing zones (EPZs) play a critical role in Honduras. Singa Boyenge (2007) reports that Asia and Central America lead employment generation in

EPZs and that Honduras in particular has 24 EPZs with total employment of 353,624. The 204 firms cited are divided among textiles and apparel, footwear, equipment assembly, services, food processing, and electronics. Of these, the textiles and apparel sector has the largest number of firms. UNCTAD (2005) notes that in 2003, only 17 percent of workers employed in garment factories in the country were employed in factories owned by Hondurans. The largest foreign employers were the United States (53 percent) and the Republic of Korea (15 percent). Maquila firms are generally large, formal-sector firms. As a result of preferential treatment for Honduran maquiladora production granted by the United States, the maquila industry is very closely integrated with the United States (Jansen et al. 2007). The U.S. programs, generally referred to as "807" programs because they fall under item 807 of the U.S. tariff code, encourage Honduran imports of U.S.-yarn-based cloth for assembly into clothing.

These statistics suggest that globalization in Honduras since 1990 has been dominated by the rise of foreign investment into the maquila sector (primarily textiles and apparel). The next section illustrates the importance of the textiles and apparel trade, foreign investment, and remittances as they have coincided with Honduran steps toward economic liberalization.

BASIC INDICATORS OF GLOBALIZATION

One way to gauge international economic integration is to measure outcomes: changes in trade, in foreign investment, and in remittances from workers abroad. Some results of the Honduran liberalization policy are shown in table 6.1, which presents relevant data drawn from the 2007 edition of the *World Development Indicators* (World Bank 2007). Several key aspects of the Honduran globalization experience are evident. The shares of both exports and imports rose significantly between 1990 and 2005, as would be expected during a transition from a relatively closed economy. Imports rose faster than exports, generating a growing trade deficit. These imports required financing with financial inflows. The two most significant of these inflows were foreign direct investment (FDI) and worker remittances.

Net inflows of FDI were significantly higher at the end of the period than at the beginning, with an upward spike in 2000. Both as a percentage of GDP and in millions of dollars, the rise in FDI was large (with nominal FDI increasing by a factor of near 10 between 1990 and 2005). The dramatic drop in 1998 was due to Hurricane Mitch, which lasted from October 22 to November 5, 1998. Following Mitch, however, foreign investment sharply increased. As mentioned earlier, much of this investment was targeted toward the maquila sector to create firms with the intention of producing for export.

Even more striking than FDI, however, was the dramatic rise in worker remittances. Real remittances in 2005 were 23 times larger than remittances in 1990. In 1991, remittances roughly equaled FDI, but by 2005 remittances were almost four times as great as FDI.

The effects of remittances are currently a subject of intense debate. One concern about rising remittances is their effect on the real exchange rate. Rising remittances increase the demand for the domestic currency, causing the real exchange rate to appreciate. An appreciation in the real exchange rate potentially depresses exports and increases imports. Figure 6.1 shows the change in the Honduran real exchange rate (calculated as the US$/lempira nominal rate multiplied by the ratio of the Honduran and U.S. current price

TABLE 6.1 **Basic Indicators of International Integration**

Year	Exports of goods and services (% of GDP)	Imports of goods and services (% of GDP)	Merchandise trade balance (constant US$ millions)	FDI net inflows (% of GDP)	FDI net inflows (constant US$ millions)	Worker remittances (constant US$ millions)
1990	36.60	39.95	−124.24	1.43	57.31	65.88
1991	33.50	37.58	−156.27	1.70	65.87	65.74
1992	30.63	36.28	−235.78	1.39	58.42	73.64
1993	35.70	43.70	−326.88	0.77	31.82	71.50
1994	40.32	49.86	−369.73	1.01	40.44	98.77
1995	42.43	48.08	−245.76	1.28	56.50	135.59
1996	44.31	51.97	−364.27	2.25	99.76	140.92
1997	45.22	51.82	−343.22	2.61	130.36	171.66
1998	46.55	54.08	−414.44	1.90	104.59	232.42
1999	41.45	55.98	−807.87	4.42	245.28	330.76
2000	42.09	55.22	−776.52	4.73	281.88	409.60
2001	38.72	54.27	−946.27	3.05	187.76	518.93
2002	39.06	53.32	−876.18	2.69	167.82	680.89
2003	39.47	54.43	−954.04	3.60	231.30	805.22
2004	42.18	60.09	−1,204.58	4.35	295.93	1,042.59
2005	41.80	61.41	−1,418.14	5.60	409.03	1,576.78
2006	—	66.79	—	—	—	—

SOURCE: World Bank 2007.

NOTE: — = Not available. Nominal values from the World Development Indicators (World Bank 2007) were converted to constant U.S. dollars using the U.S. Consumer Price Index for all Urban Consumers (base year 2000).

indexes). The data suggest a steady real appreciation since the mid-1990s, consistent with the rise in migration and remittances.

TRADE FLOWS BY SECTOR

The picture of Honduran trade patterns depends critically on the inclusion or exclusion of maquila statistics. The Honduran government's Instituto Nacional de Estadística (INE) aggregates trade volumes at the two-digit level of the Harmonized Commodity Description and Coding System (HS) of the World Customs Organization. Their export data[7] show significant export growth, perhaps in part reflecting recovery after Hurricane Mitch. Categories 01 through 04, covering animal and vegetable products and tobacco, account for over half of all exports in 2005. Reported exports of textiles and apparel are modest and apparently exclude maquila trade.

FIGURE 6.1 **Honduran Real Exchange Rate, 1991–2006**

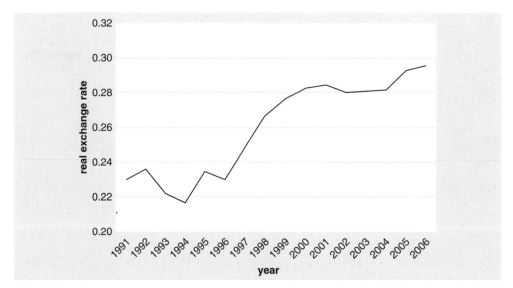

SOURCE: Authors' calculations using data from the World Development Indicators (World Bank 2007).

NOTE: The real exchange rate is calculated as the nominal exchange rate (in dollars per limpera) multiplied by the ratio of the Honduran and U.S. Current Price Indexes.

The data, while excluding maquila imports, show significant import growth, particularly in imports of mineral products, which include petroleum derivatives and fuels. These products have the largest shares of total imports, followed by machinery and equipment and then chemical products, a classification that includes pharmaceuticals, fertilizers, and dyes.[8] Again, the textiles and clothing category appears to be relatively insignificant. Data from the WTO paint a similar picture. WTO data suggest that food products dominate exports, although the share fell from 86.9 percent in 1995 to 63.1 percent in 2001. Coffee, bananas and other fruit, and shellfish are particularly important. Banana exports fell dramatically in the aftermath of Hurricane Mitch, but later recovered. Coffee exports are unstable.

The problem, of course, is that trade data that exclude maquila statistics are misleading. Possibly the most complete trade data are managed by the United Nations. The United Nations Commodity Trade Statistics Database (UN Comtrade) contains annual trade data that do not systematically exclude, or differentiate, maquila trade. The data are available at several different levels of aggregation, but for present purposes, industries are grouped into the principal HS categories.

Figure 6.2 contains constant-dollar (base year 2000) Honduran imports by sector from all countries for certain key sectors. Several trends are immediately apparent. First, Honduras principally imports capital-intensive goods (chemicals and machinery, including transportation equipment), as is expected for a labor-abundant country. Second, imports of foodstuffs significantly increased over the sample period, consistent with falling domestic value added (and employment share) in agriculture. Third, textiles imports remained relatively constant between 1995 and 2005, even while other sectors experienced a significant increase in imports. This is consistent with the hypothesis that textiles trade is not consumption-based.

Figure 6.3 displays Honduran exports, again from the UN Comtrade database, for several key sectors. In 1991, trade was dominated by the first three HS sectors (mainly vegetable products, including coffee). In 1991, these three sectors made up 68 percent of Honduran exports. The agricultural sectors grew slowly over time, more slowly than total exports, and by 2005 these three sectors made up only 26 percent of total exports. The main change over this period, of course, was the export of textiles (which, in these statistics, includes apparel). In 1991, the textiles sector made up 23 percent of total exports. By 2005, textiles made up 59 percent of total exports. Again, these changes did not occur because of the fall in agricultural exports: the real value of agricultural exports was 42 percent higher in 2005 than in 1991. The fall in agricultural share of total exports was due in large part to the 868 percent rise in the measured real value of textiles exports.

Because Honduras mainly trades with the United States, U.S. import

FIGURE 6.2 **Honduran Imports by Sector, 1995–2005**

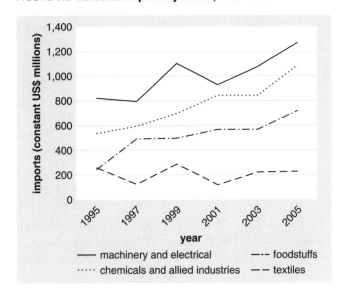

SOURCE: UN Comtrade database.

NOTE: Conversion to real values uses the U.S. Consumer Price Index for all urban consumers using 2000 as the base year.

FIGURE 6.3 **Honduran Exports by Sector, 1991–2005**

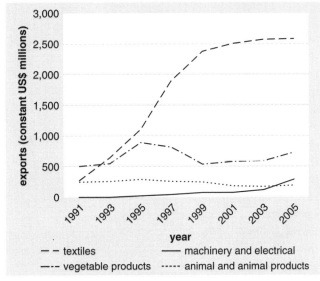

SOURCE: UN Comtrade database.

NOTE: Conversion to real values uses the U.S. Consumer Price Index for all urban consumers using 2000 as the base year.

data provide another view of Honduran trade. Table 6.2 presents U.S. imports from Honduras between 2002 and 2006. Just two end-use apparel sectors (apparel and household goods–cotton, and apparel and household goods–other textiles) made up 67 percent of

Honduran exports to the United States in 2006, down from 75.6 percent in 2002. This decline may have been partially due to the rise of China in the global textiles trade (Hanson and Robertson 2008). Nevertheless, Honduras remains the top CAFTA supplier of textiles to the United States.

Figure 6.4 illustrates changes in the textiles share of exports and FDI over time. Both shares rose significantly over the sample period, highlighting the fact that much of the Honduran globalization experience has been characterized by an increase in foreign investment. From 1990 to 2005, real dollar net FDI inflows quadrupled, passing $400 million. Most of the FDI is concentrated in the textiles and apparel sector. The World Bank's 2003 "Productividad y Ambiente de Inversión en Honduras: Encuesta Empresarial" (Investment Climate Assessment: Enterprise Survey) shows that, of the manufacturing firms in the survey, 40 percent of the apparel firms and 37.5 percent of the textiles firms reported that they were entirely owned by foreign capital. In all other sectors but tobacco products, fewer than 5 percent of firms were wholly foreign-owned. Furthermore, exports accounted on average for 57 percent of the sales of apparel firms and 46 percent of the sales of textiles firms, again far higher shares than those of all other surveyed sectors except tobacco products. Clearly,

TABLE 6.2 **Principal U.S. Imports from Honduras, 2002–06**

Year	Apparel and household goods–cotton		Apparel and household goods–other textiles	
	Value (constant US$)	Share (percent)	Value (constant US$)	Share (percent)
2002	1,735,765	53.2	730,321	22.4
2003	1,851,511	55.9	673,844	20.3
2004	1,954,899	53.7	745,627	20.5
2005	1,910,585	51.0	733,548	19.6
2006	1,810,574	48.7	679,981	18.3

SOURCE: FTD WebMaster, Foreign Trade Division, U.S. Census Bureau, Washington, D.C. 20233
Location: MAIN: STATISTICS:PRODUCT TRADE DATA: END-USE IMPORTS.
Created: March 15, 2007. Last modified: 15 March 2007 at 09:12:17 AM.

NOTE: Share represents portion of total U.S. imports from Honduras for each end-use category. Values are in constant (inflation-adjusted) dollars.

FIGURE 6.4 **Textiles Share of Total Honduran Exports and FDI Inflows, 1993–2005**

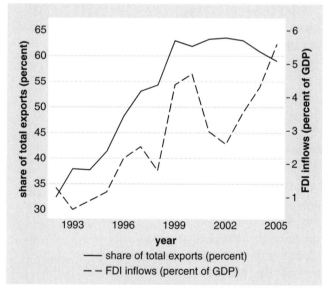

SOURCE: Authors' calculations using data from the UN Comtrade database for textile share of exports and UNCTAD 2008 Handbook of Statistics online for FDI inflows and GDP.

textiles and apparel are among the most internationally integrated sectors of the Honduran economy, at least in manufacturing.

Official trade statistics present Honduras as an exporter of agricultural and food products and an importer of fuels, machinery, and equipment. These statistics may be misleading, however, because when maquila operations are included in trade, clothing and accessories become by far the largest category for both imports and exports. During the 1990s, exports of clothing and accessories grew from $120 million to $2.3 billion, inducing a shift in resources toward textiles and apparel production and exports. These results suggest that it is important to be mindful of the textiles and apparel sector when analyzing working conditions in Honduras.

Working Conditions in Honduras

During the debate over CAFTA, working conditions in Honduras (and in Central America generally) attracted much attention. Any analysis of wages and working conditions in Honduras must clearly state the frame of reference. "Low" (as in wages) and "poor" (as in working conditions) are both relative terms. Two possible standards might be used in an evaluation of wages and working conditions: foreign or domestic. The discussion that follows uses the latter, thus focusing on wages and working conditions within Honduras rather than comparing wages and working conditions in Honduras with those in other countries. (Any attempt to address concerns about differences between countries would have to begin with changes within countries.) This focus acknowledges that domestic institutions play an important role. In fact, much of the debate about working conditions in Central America centered on the perceived difference between laws that were in place and enforcement of those laws. This section provides an overview of regulations currently in place in Honduras and places the debate over enforcement in the context of globalization.

WORK-RELATED LAWS AND REGULATIONS

In Honduras, institutions affecting working conditions comprise government regulation, enforcement, and foreign pressure from governments and nongovernmental organizations (NGOs). The roots of modern labor law in Honduras can be traced to the 1950s. In the context of a banana-workers' strike in 1954 and two authoritarian administrations, Honduras rejoined the International Labour Organization (ILO) in 1955. Soon after, Honduras adopted several labor codes, and established the Ministry of Labor in 1959. Table 6.3 shows the dates Honduras ratified the ILO core labor standards. The earliest were ratified in 1956 (Conventions 87, 98, and 100). The country ratified the core labor standards pertaining to child labor in 1980 and 2001. Over the years, the country adopted 14 additional ILO conventions, as listed in table 6.4. While most were adopted in the 1960s, several were adopted in the 1980s.

Together, ratification of these conventions, provisions in the Honduran Constitution, and the Honduran labor code form legal standards for working conditions that are considered relatively high for a developing country. Honduran law specifies freedom of association (in unions), a right to collective bargaining, and guaranteed rights to strike. Unlike all other Central American countries except Nicaragua, Honduras has no minimum percentage of workers that a union must represent to engage in collective bargaining. The minimum legal work age in Honduras is 16 (14 if in school), which is also the minimum age for hazardous or potentially unhealthy work. Minors may not work more than 30 hours per week, and Honduras has established programs to focus on child labor issues.

Labor law also includes minimum wages. In fact, minimum wages may be one of the most important labor market regulations in Honduras. Gindling and Terrell (2006, 2007) present two comprehensive studies of

TABLE 6.3 **Adoption of Core ILO Labor Standards by Honduras**

Convention	Description	Date ratified
87	Freedom of Association and Protection of the Right to Organise Convention, 1948	June 1956
98	Right to Organise and Collective Bargaining Convention, 1949	June 1956
29	Forced Labour Convention, 1930	February 1957
105	Abolition of Forced Labour Convention, 1957	August 1958
100	Equal Remuneration Convention, 1951	August 1956
111	Discrimination (Employment and Occupation) Convention, 1958	June 1960
138	Minimum Age Convention, 1973	June 1980
182	Worst Forms of Child Labour Convention, 1999	October 2001

SOURCE: ILOLEX, the ILO database of International Labor Standards (http://www.ilo.org/ilolex/english/).

the effects of minimum wages in Honduras. Honduras has more than 22 different minimum wages; although legally applicable to all private-sector employees, Gindling and Terrell (2006) find that compliance is limited to large private firms.

The effects of minimum wages in Honduras are significant. Gindling and Terrell (2006) find that a 10 percent increase in the minimum wage in Honduras reduces the probability of being in extreme poverty by 1.8 percent. The effect of minimum wages on poverty is concentrated in large, formal-sector firms, possibly because enforcement is concentrated on these firms. This is not to say that minimum wages come without costs, however. Gindling and Terrell (2007) find that there is a trade-off between employment and minimum wages in Honduras. Using data covering 1990–2004, they find that the minimum wage is correlated with a decline in employment. They find that the (negative) employment effect is greater than the (positive) wage effect, and thus conclude that minimum wages have resulted in a net welfare loss to workers. Enforcement of minimum wages plays a prominent role in the Gindling and Terrell (2206, 2007) studies, since a lack of enforcement reduces the effect of minimum wages.

Concerns about the efficacy of enforcement extend to other dimensions of working conditions as well. Misgivings about human rights and labor conditions are not limited to the export sector. The U.S. Department of State (2006) reports several human rights problems, including extrajudicial killings by members of the police, impunity for human rights violations, lack of government funding, institutional weakness, judicial corruption, and lack of enforcement of labor laws. These reports signal problems that probably exist irrespective of globalization.

TABLE 6.4 **Additional ILO Conventions Ratified by Honduras**

Convention	Description	Date ratified
45	Underground Work (Women) Convention, 1935	June 1960
78	Medical Examination of Young Persons (Non-Industrial Occupations) Convention, 1946	June 1960
95	Protection of Wages Convention, 1949	June 1960
106	Weekly Rest (Commerce and Offices) Convention, 1957	June 1960
108	Seafarers' Identity Documents Convention, 1958	June 1960
14	Weekly Rest (Industry) Convention, 1921	November 1964
32	Protection against Accidents (Dockers) Convention (Revised), 1932	November 1964
42	Workmen's Compensation (Occupational Diseases) Convention (Revised), 1934	November 1964
62	Safety Provisions (Building) Convention, 1937	November 1964
116	Final Articles Revision Convention, 1961	November 1964
27	Marking of Weight (Packages Transported by Vessels) Convention, 1929	June 1980
122	Employment Policy Convention, 1964	June 1980
81	Labour Inspection Convention, 1947	May 1983
169	Indigenous and Tribal Peoples Convention, 1989	March 1995

SOURCE: ILOLEX, the ILO database of International Labor Standards (http://www.ilo.org/ilolex/english/).

NGOs have made several attempts to address these issues. Frundt (2004) describes the experience of Equipo de Monitoreo Independiente de Honduras (EMI), a group formed by the National Labor Committee[9] that brought together the Honduran Committee for the Defense of Human Rights, the Honduran Women's Collective (Colective de Mujeres Hondurenas), and the Jesuits in El Progreso. The EMI was formed to address a struggle at Kimi, a plant that contracted with JCPenney. EMI had mixed success, apparently because of the way in which it handled the politics within the plant, but learned that success depends on widespread participation from several interested groups, including the government, NGOs, and the private sector.

International NGOs, such as the Maquila Solidarity Network, have also played an important role. For example, in December 2003, the Canadian Labor Congress (CLC) and the Independent Federation of Honduran Workers (FITH) filed a complaint against a Canadian factory for the unjust firing of workers possibly associated with union activity (Maquila Solidarity Network 2006). In 2006, the complaint was resolved enough for the CLC and FITH to drop their complaint, providing an example of international pressure on foreign factories to maintain working conditions at "acceptable" standards. The buyer-driven nature of the assembly chain in Honduras (Jansen et al. 2007) makes foreign firms susceptible to consumer pressure for acceptable standards in ways that do not apply to Honduran firms that do not participate in international markets.

Jansen et al. (2007) provide specific examples of the importance of international engagement in improving working conditions. They suggest that poor labor conditions in Honduran plants have led to boycotts by U.S. consumers. In response, U.S. employers have monitored plants and have responded to inadequate improvements in conditions by canceling contracts. Furthermore, Jansen et al. (2007) note that many employers believe that certification by the Worldwide Responsible Apparel Production organization increases orders and may help firms avoid damaging negative press coverage. This motivation for certification and concern about boycotts would not apply to Honduran firms not exporting to foreign markets.

NONWAGE CHARACTERISTICS OF EMPLOYMENT

One of the most significant problems with measuring nonwage working conditions in Honduras is the lack of systematic data, especially by industry.[10] One potential source of data is the World Bank's 2003 Investment Climate Assessment "Productividad y Ambiente de Inversión en Honduras: Encuesta Empresarial." Data are available from 450 firms spread across 11 manufacturing sectors. Table 6.5 notes particularly relevant variables and shows the mean response across firms in each sector. These firms are all considered formal-sector firms.

With the exception of the cigar industry (tobacco sector), apparel and textiles firms had the highest rates of foreign ownership and export sales. Apparel and textiles had the lowest percentage of temporary workers, either *eventuales* or on special contract. The survey defines eventuales as workers hired for less than one year with no guarantee of renewal. To the extent that temporary workers experience more job insecurity and are potentially more susceptible to employer demands (because of employment insecurity), these data do not support the hypothesis that these dimensions of working conditions are worse in textiles and apparel firms (although, of course, concerns could exist in less-measurable dimensions).

In addition, table 6.5 suggests that there is no systematic difference between apparel and textiles firms and others with respect to social benefits (13th month bonus, vacation, social security, and other benefits) as a percentage of total labor costs, either for skilled production workers or for unskilled production workers.

One concern that does emerge from table 6.5 is the low rate of unionization in textiles and apparel firms in the survey. When compared with firms in other Honduran industries, however, the textiles and apparel firms are not unusual. Low unionization may be a problem in Honduras, but it is not unique to globally engaged firms.

The apparel and textiles sectors are in the middle of the pack in offering formal training to employees. This training may complement other programs as well. Jansen et al. (2007) note that the Honduran Manufacturers Association provides training for managers and workers without charge. Training is important because wages are often based on productivity, and processes may change when styles change.

It is possible that the 450 firms in the survey are not representative. It is also conceivable that respondents in apparel and textiles are not representative or that responses from the sector are biased in some unknown way. At face value, however, little evidence suggests

TABLE 6.5 **Mean Responses of Manufacturing Firms to Productivity and Investment Climate Survey, 2003**

Sector	Total employees	Foreign ownership (%)	Exports as percentage of sales	Temporary workers (%)	Benefits to skilled workers (% of total labor costs)	Benefits to unskilled workers (% of total labor costs)	Workers in labor union (%)	Firms offering training (%)
Apparel	456	43	57	3	15	13	3	66
Textiles	308	37	46	4	14	14	0	56
Tobacco	278	57	99	11	14	5	17	45
Food products	158	5	15	21	11	11	1	49
Rubber and plastic	106	11	21	4	19	22	3	71
Wood products	52	3	16	16	13	9	0	42
Beverages	47	6	2	12	15	10	8	43
Chemical products	39	8	6	11	21	15	0	79
Furniture	38	2	9	11	11	7	0	39
Metal products	35	5	7	16	14	9	0	0
Nonmetal minerals	16	2	2	19	8	7	0	31

SOURCE: Authors' calculations based on data from World Bank (2003).

that garment workers have worse nonwage benefits than workers in other manufacturing sectors. If anything, the data raise concerns about the other highly internationalized sector—cigar-making.

Employment and Interindustry Wage Differentials

Trade changes an economy's output mix. Theory suggests that such change will raise the real return to the factors of production used intensively in the country's export sectors. When factors are not perfectly mobile across sectors, this may well lead to interindustry wage differentials (IIWDs)—differences across sectors in the wage paid to observationally equivalent workers. This section first examines trends in the composition of employment, and then estimates a full set of IIWDs, paying particular attention to wages in textiles and apparel (which is dominated by exports and FDI) and other, less globally engaged industries.

LABOR FORCE PARTICIPATION AND THE REMITTANCES EFFECT

Remittances can affect working conditions in several ways. By providing an alternative source of income, remittances can raise reservation wages, effectively reducing labor supply. As a result, firms would have to increase wages to attract workers. One key indicator of this effect would be a systematic difference in labor force participation between workers receiving remittances and those who do not.

The INE's Encuesta Permanente de Hogares de Propósitos Múltiples (Multi-use Permanent Household Survey) permits calculation of labor force participation rates for most years for the period 1990 to 2004. Figure 6.5 shows, separately for men and women, the proportion of those ages 16 through 65 who worked for compensation during the reference period ("employed") and the proportion who worked for compensation, worked without pay, had a job to which they expected to return, or looked for work ("active"). The percentages were calculated after applying the appropriate population weights to the individually reported data, so that the figures are nationally representative. Significant differences between the percentage active and the percentage employed should not be interpreted

FIGURE 6.5 **Labor Force Statistics by Gender, 1990–2004**

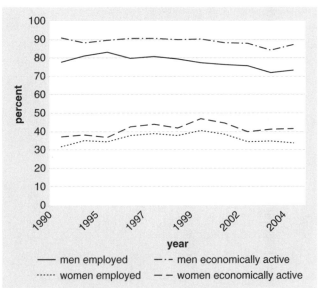

SOURCE: Authors' calculations from various years of the INE's Encuesta Permanente de Hogares de Propósitos Múltiples (Multi-use Permanent Household Survey).

NOTE: Population weight factors applied.

as open unemployment. Most of the difference is accounted for by people who report either working without pay or having a job to which they would soon return.

Evidence suggests that remittances from family members working abroad affect labor force participation. The effect is investigated here by estimating a probit model. The model estimates the impact of personal characteristics, including remittances, on the probability of being active in the labor force. The dependent variable is labor force activity, defined as above. The independent variables are being female, age and age squared, years of education, and monthly household income from remittances from abroad. All data come from the 2004 Permanent Household Survey.

Remittances are recorded as the total remittances received by the household each month in Honduran currency (lempiras). In general, household remittances are larger than a given household member's monthly earnings. In fact, 57.12 percent of workers in households receiving remittances reported a value of remittances greater than that worker's monthly income, and 41.18 percent reported receiving a value of remittances that are more than double that worker's wage.

Remittances might enter an estimation equation of the effect of remittances on labor force activity in several ways. Table 6.6 shows the marginal effects of the independent

TABLE 6.6 **Remittances and Labor Force Participation: Probit Results, 2004**
Dependent variable: Active

Independent variable	(1)	(2)	(3)	(4)
Female	−0.441	−0.441	−0.404	−0.404
	(54.37)**	(54.27)**	(17.39)**	(17.40)**
Age	0.052	0.052	0.058	0.059
	(28.17)**	(28.04)**	(11.17)**	(11.32)**
Age squared	−0.001	−0.001	−0.001	−0.001
	(25.60)**	(25.46)**	(10.24)**	(10.41)**
Years of schooling	0.008	0.008	0.012	0.012
	(7.83)**	(7.89)**	(3.74)**	(3.61)**
Monthly household income from remittances from abroad	−0.000			−0.000
	(3.99)**			(2.46)*
Ln(1 + remittances)		−0.006		
		(4.23)**		
Ln(remittances)			−0.027	
			(3.02)**	
Observations	15,317	15,317	2,053	2,053

SOURCE: Authors' calculations from various years of the INE's Encuesta Permanente de Hogares de Propósitos Múltiples (Multi-use Permanent Household Survey).

NOTE: Absolute value of z-statistics in parentheses. Coefficient estimates reflect the marginal effect on probability.

* significant at 5 percent level.

** significant at 1 percent level.

variables, with the absolute values of the z-statistics in parentheses, of four different specifications of remittances. Columns (2) and (3) use the natural log of remittances and columns (1) and (4) use the level value. Because there are many households receiving no
remittances, and the natural log of zero is not defined, column (2) includes the natural log
of (1+ remittances), which becomes zero for households without remittances. As an alternative, column (3) defines remittances as simply the natural log of remittances, dropping
all households with no remittances. Column (4) uses the same definition of remittances as
column (1), but restricts the sample to households receiving remittances.

In all specifications, all independent variables are statistically significant (with at least
95 percent confidence). The magnitude of the remittances effect in columns (1) and (4)
(when remittances are measured in levels) appears to be quite small, suggesting that remittances may have little meaningful effect on labor force participation.[11] When restricting
the sample to just households receiving remittances, however, the results are much larger,
as seen in table 6.6. The coefficient estimate increases by a factor of 4.5.

These results should not be taken as definitive, however, because endogeneity is a
potentially significant problem. Families with members who are unable to participate in
the labor market may be more likely to send someone abroad to work. Similarly, family
members may decide to send the "best" workers abroad where they could earn the highest
income. Nevertheless, these results are consistent with the literature that finds significant
negative labor force participation effects (see Acosta [2006]).

SECTORAL COMPOSITION OF EMPLOYMENT

Table 6.7 shows the sectoral composition of employment in Honduras in 2004. The data
come from the Permanent Household Survey, and the appropriate expansion factors have
been applied. The table includes all workers ages 16 through 65 who had some income
from labor in their principal occupation during the reference period. Some are in the private sector, others in the public sector. Some are wage workers, others are self-employed.

Note the importance of the textiles and apparel industry for employment of women.
More women are employed in this subsector than in all other manufacturing sectors combined. Moreover, the number of women in manufacturing is about as large as the number
in wholesale and retail trade (although this is not clear from table 6.7, where the industrial
classification adds employment in hotels and restaurants to employment in wholesale and
retail trade).

INTERINDUSTRY WAGE DIFFERENTIALS

Table 6.8 reports a complete set of wage regressions[12] for 2001 through 2004. As before,
workers ages 16 through 65 with some income from labor are included, whether they are
wage workers or self-employed, or private sector or public sector workers. Primary personal characteristics are included in the regression. The remaining coefficients measure
the unexplained log wage differential, above or below the sample mean, for workers in
each of the industries.

Six of the 17 industries have IIWDs significant at the 1 percent level in each of the
four years. Those who work raising food crops always earn less than the mean, controlling
for personal characteristics. It is not much of a surprise that workers in public administration, FIRE and business services, and transport and communications earn above the

TABLE 6.7 **Employment by Sector, 2004**

	Men		Women	
	Number	Percent	Number	Percent
Agriculture: food crops	431,891	34.5	26,470	3.9
Husbandry and fishing	47,805	3.8	5,470	0.8
Forestry	9,415	0.8	1,522	0.2
Mining and quarrying	5,706	0.5	216	0.0
Manufacturing				
Manufacture of food, beverages, and tobacco	49,849	4.0	65,387	9.6
Manufacture of textiles, apparel, and leather	58,326	4.7	86,724	12.7
Manufacture of wood products	12,206	1.0	2,113	0.3
Other manufacturing	62,591	5.0	11,325	1.7
Electricity, gas, and water	7,861	0.6	1,484	0.2
Construction	135,676	10.8	2,373	0.3
Wholesale and retail trade, hotels and restaurants	200,556	16.0	220,334	32.4
Transport, storage, and communications	69,864	5.6	7,553	1.1
FIRE and business services	41,737	3.3	25,048	3.7
Public administration	36,902	2.9	24,756	3.6
Other social services	68,188	5.4	163,661	24.0
Other services and n.e.s.	13,315	1.1	36,203	5.3
	1,251,888	100.0	680,639	100.0

SOURCE: Authors' calculations from various years of the INE's Encuesta Permanente de Hogares de Propósitos Múltiples (Multi-use Permanent Household Survey).

NOTE: Population weights applied. FIRE = Financial, insurance, and real estate; n.e.s. = Not elsewhere specified.

mean. Of more interest, workers in the wholesale/retail/hotels/restaurants group and in the apparel/textiles/leather group also consistently earn a premium above the average hourly wage, controlling for personal characteristics. Because the coefficient is a difference in the log of the hourly wage, a 0.188 coefficient for the apparel industry can be interpreted as a 21 percent wage premium.[13]

This IIWD is much larger than that estimated for El Salvador. The difference in the two estimated IIWDs may be consistent with the difference in the average wage levels. If apparel firms pay similar wages across countries, poorer countries like Cambodia and Honduras are likely to exhibit larger differentials relative to the overall mean wage. In fact, this seems to be the case.

TABLE 6.8 **Interindustry Wage Differentials**
Dependent variable: log of hourly labor income from principal occupation

Independent variable	2001	2002	2003	2004
Years schooling	0.103	0.101	0.101	0.104
	(46.43)**	(66.21)**	(65.07)**	(35.04)**
Age	0.054	0.052	0.055	0.046
	(12.72)**	(19.46)**	(20.18)**	(8.60)**
Age squared	−0.001	−0.001	−0.001	−0.0004
	(9.45)**	(14.02)**	(14.68)**	(6.24)**
Female	−0.303	−0.224	−0.191	−0.215
	(14.56)**	(17.10)**	(14.61)**	(8.36)**
Urban resident	0.248	0.142	0.201	0.241
	(11.33)**	(9.98)**	(14.16)**	(8.63)**
Agriculture: food crops	−0.627	−0.459	−0.490	−0.680
	(24.22)**	(32.41)**	(33.41)**	(22.71)**
Agriculture: other	−1.263	0.821		
	(14.28)**	(1.35)		
Husbandry and fishing	0.208	0.229	0.244	0.105
	(3.48)**	(6.62)**	(7.75)**	(1.42)
Forestry	0.070	−0.206	−0.158	−0.319
	(0.47)	(2.60)**	(1.92)	(1.90)
Mining and quarrying	0.390	−0.031	−0.335	−0.032
	(1.67)	(0.22)	(2.98)**	(0.16)
Manufacture of food, beverages, and tobacco	0.004	0.050	−0.059	0.125
	(0.11)	(2.18)*	(2.78)**	(2.86)**
Manufacture of textiles, apparel, and leather	0.188	0.180	0.109	0.215
	(5.98)**	(10.22)**	(6.25)**	(6.09)**
Manufacture of wood products	−0.416	−0.210	−0.208	0.100
	(4.53)**	(3.05)**	(2.90)**	(0.77)

The same regression cannot be run for earlier years because of a modification in the industrial classification. Table 6.9, however, shows IIWDs that are based on the earlier International Standard Industrial Classification (ISIC) rev.2 categories. Again, positive premiums were earned in both 1992 and 1996 by workers in textiles, apparel, and leather goods. This premium appears to be quite stable over time, which may seem at odds with rising foreign investment. One possible explanation could be that an important alternative sector—agriculture—collapsed during the sample period. Both in share of workers and in its IIWD, the agriculture sector demonstrates a significant decline over the sample period.

TABLE 6.8 **(continued)**

Independent variable	2001	2002	2003	2004
Other manufacturing	0.123	0.115	−0.017	0.080
	(3.13)**	(4.60)**	(0.70)	(1.58)
Electricity, gas, and water	0.320	0.216	0.435	0.412
	(2.37)*	(2.71)**	(6.01)**	(3.06)**
Construction	0.189	0.233	−0.000	0.103
	(5.59)**	(11.45)**	(0.02)	(2.53)*
Wholesale and retail trade, hotels and restaurants	0.095	0.078	0.210	0.061
	(6.34)**	(7.58)**	(20.60)**	(3.13)**
Transport, storage, and communications	0.248	0.154	0.101	0.213
	(5.88)**	(6.24)**	(4.09)**	(4.35)**
FIRE and business services	0.199	0.159	0.128	0.226
	(4.47)**	(6.12)**	(4.76)**	(4.44)**
Public administration	0.323	0.222	0.159	0.299
	(7.56)**	(8.38)**	(5.42)**	(5.55)**
Other social services	0.060	0.018	0.087	0.175
	(2.55)*	(1.14)	(5.58)**	(6.00)**
Other services and n.e.s.	0.034	0.025	−0.077	0.036
	(0.70)	(0.70)	(2.20)*	(0.51)
Constant	0.345	0.549	0.538	0.606
	(4.57)**	(11.59)**	(11.26)**	(6.43)**
Observations	9,878	25,427	24,622	8,817

SOURCE: Authors' calculations from various years of the INE's Encuesta Permanente de Hogares de Propósitos Múltiples (Multi-use Permanent Household Survey).

NOTE: t-statistics in parentheses. FIRE = Finance, insurance, and real estate; n.e.s. = Not elsewhere specified.

* significant at 5 percent level.

** significant at 1 percent level.

This could have created a significant supply shock for the maquila sector. As workers left agriculture and increased the supply of workers for apparel, the increase in supply could have offset the otherwise positive effect of rising demand for these workers.[14]

TRADE AND LABOR INCOME

The relatively constant wage premium in the textiles industry does not imply that trade and foreign investment have not affected workers. On the contrary, table 6.10 documents marked expansion of employment in the industry. The conclusion ought to be that

TABLE 6.9 **Interindustry Wage Differentials, Earlier Years**
Dependent variable: log of hourly earnings from principal occupation

Independent variable	1992	1996
Years schooling	0.108	0.116
	(36.53)**	(51.54)**
Age	0.064	0.059
	(9.91)**	(13.07)**
Age squared	−0.001	−0.001
	(6.86)**	(9.02)**
Female	−0.318	−0.273
	(10.94)**	(13.00)**
Agriculture, hunting, forestry, fishing	−0.266	−0.193
	(8.03)**	(8.81)**
Mining and quarrying	−0.241	
	(0.49)	
Manufactures: Food, beverages, tobacco products	0.128	0.058
	(2.28)*	(1.55)
Manufactures: Textiles, apparel, leather	0.223	0.324
	(4.51)**	(10.84)**
Manufactures: Wood and furniture	−0.080	0.109
	(0.99)	(1.89)
Manufactures: Other	0.162	0.171
	(3.24)**	(4.42)**

through globalization far more people were drawn into this group that consistently earns about a 20 percent wage premium. If these workers were drawn from agriculture (which is possible, given the marked decline in the share of the population in agriculture since 1990), workers would have moved from an industry that paid nearly 63 percent below the average wage to an industry that paid nearly 20 percent above the average wage. If nonwage working conditions were constant in these two

TABLE 6.10 **Employment in Textiles Manufacturing**

Year	Men	Women
1992	7,495	24,987
1996	15,424	39,245
2001	34,352	59,171
2004	46,713	76,082

SOURCE: Authors' calculations from various years of the INE's Encuesta Permanente de Hogares de Propósitos Múltiples (Multi-use Permanent Household Survey).

NOTE: ISIC rev.2, 3220, for 1992 and 1996; ISIC rev.3, 1810, for 2001 and 2004.

TABLE 6.9 **(continued)**

Independent variable	1992	1996
Electricity, gas, and water	0.270	0.268
	(2.32)*	(2.83)**
Construction	0.003	0.225
	(0.05)	(5.98)**
Wholesale and retail trade and restaurants and hotels	−0.022	−0.081
	(0.70)	(3.36)**
Transport, storage, and communications	0.126	0.009
	(2.27)*	(0.19)
Financing, insurance, real estate and business services	0.319	0.136
	(5.21)**	(3.28)**
Community, social, and personal services	−0.027	−0.063
	(1.43)	(4.31)**
Constant	−1.064	−0.402
	(9.87)**	(5.39)**
Observations	4,567	5,553

SOURCE: Authors' calculations from various years of the INE's Encuesta Permanente de Hogares de Propósitos Múltiples (Multi-use Permanent Household Survey).

NOTE: t-statistics in parentheses.

* significant at 5 percent level.

** significant at 1 percent level.

sectors, the move from agriculture to textiles would imply a significant improvement in working conditions (when wages are included as a measure of working conditions).[15]

A direct test for correlation between the estimated IIWDs would be useful, at least for those that are consistently statistically significant, as would be some appropriate measure of exposure to international trade. In principle, domestic industrial activity can be linked to trade in goods and services. The major problem with this approach for the Honduran case is the lack of sufficient years of data to generate a consistent series of IIWDs that would be required to match with trade or foreign investment data. This exercise is left for future work. Nevertheless, the results do paint a steady picture. The first section of this chapter documented the surge in exports from the Honduran garment industry. This section shows a corresponding boom in employment in the textiles and apparel industry. One major impact of globalization has been to draw workers into this industry, where, controlling for personal characteristics, workers earn about 20 percent more than average hourly earnings.

Low-Wage Work?

The previous section documented a persistent wage premium associated with work in the textiles and apparel industry. However, the industry also has an enduring reputation for paying low wages. For example, Jansen et al. (2007) note that the wages in maquilas are just enough to bring workers from "misery to poverty." Behind this apparent contradiction lies a crucial question: to whom should apparel workers be compared?

The wage regressions of the previous section compared average hourly earnings in the apparel industry with average hourly earnings of all workers in all sectors. The regressions also controlled for the individual's schooling, age, sex, and place of residence, which seems to be the appropriate comparison. It compares a worker's earnings in the internationally integrated apparel sector with the average earnings of similar workers across all other sectors. Comparing these workers to other manufacturing workers or not taking personal characteristics into account might generate contrary results.

ILLUSTRATING THE ISSUE: EARNINGS AND CHARACTERISTICS OF GARMENT FINISHERS

The point can be illustrated by isolating the earnings and personal characteristics of workers who list their occupation as *acabador(a) de prendas de vestir*, or garment finisher. These workers can be compared with other wage workers in the private sector, dropping out the self-employed and public-sector workers. The analysis considers only monetary earnings from the principal occupation, and is limited to manufacturing industries. Table 6.11 shows the result.

TABLE 6.11 **Descriptive Statistics: Garment Finishers and Other Manufacturing Workers**

	2001	2002	2003	2004
Acabadores(as)				
Median monthly earnings (lempira)	2,000	2,400	2,400	2,560
Mean monthly earnings (lempira)	2,338	2,487	2,496	2,773
Mean weekly hours	48	48	47	48
Mean years school	6.3	6.4	6.4	6.5
Mean age	24.7	25.0	25.5	26.2
Percent female	71	73	71	64
Other manufacturing workers				
Median monthly earnings (lempira)	2,400	2,400	2,400	2,800
Mean monthly earnings (lempira)	3,097	3,488	3,451	3,650
Mean weekly hours	49	51	48	50
Mean years school	7.0	7.7	7.6	7.8
Mean age	28.9	29.0	29.5	29.3
Percent female	29	32	28	31

SOURCE: Authors' calculations from various years of the INE's Encuesta Permanente de Hogares de Propósitos Múltiples (Multi-use Permanent Household Survey).

Median monthly earnings for garment finishers lag behind those of other manufacturing workers in two of the four survey years. Mean monthly earnings lag much farther behind. These statistics suggest that garment finishing is low-wage work. Of course, garment finishers are also on average younger, less schooled, and far more likely to be female than other manufacturing workers.

WAGE REGRESSION IN THE RESTRICTED SAMPLE

A series of wage regressions makes the point more succinctly. Data come from the 2004 Permanent Household Survey. The sample is limited to employees of private-sector firms that operate in the manufacturing sector. Self-employed workers are excluded as are nonmanufacturing workers. Only workers 16 though 65 years old are included. Two new dummies appear. "Garment finisher" takes the value 1 if the worker reported that his or her principal occupation is acabador(a) de prendas de vestir. "Cigar maker" takes the value 1 if the worker's principal occupation falls into the range 8282 to 8308 of the ISIC rev.3.

Regression (A) in table 6.12 shows that, controlling for personal characteristics, garment finishers earn a statistically significant wage premium of about 10 percent over all other manufacturing workers (the previous estimate was a 20 percent premium over the average wage of workers in all sectors). However, if the dummy for the worker's being female is dropped, the premium becomes statistically insignificant (regression (B)). If schooling and age are dropped as well (regression (C)), the sign of the point estimate becomes negative, although the negative estimate is significant only at the 85 percent level. Just for comparison purposes, a similar analysis was performed for cigar makers, who also work in an internationalized sector (regressions (D) through (F)). Unlike garment finishers, cigar makers earn lower wages than other manufacturing workers, even when controls are put in place for individual characteristics.

Perhaps the coefficients in table 6.12 can explain the contradiction between estimated wage premiums and the perception that garment work is low-wage. The wage premium emerges when controls are imposed for schooling, experience, and gender. Garment workers earn more in this industry than similar workers earn elsewhere. It is also true, however, that the garment industry draws workers whose personal characteristics are generally associated with low wages.

The previous section of this chapter documents a positive wage premium for work in the apparel, textile, and leather industries, but this positive premium does not sit well with the perception that the garment industry offers only low-wage work. This section of the chapter shows that, while garment finishers earn a wage premium relative to all workers with similar personal characteristics and even relative to other manufacturing workers with similar personal characteristics, the premium vanishes if controls are not implemented for personal characteristics. In bold strokes, young women with little schooling do better in the apparel industry than such workers do on average in the economy and even in manufacturing. Because the apparel industry employs many such people, however, its average wage could still be low relative to average wages in some other manufacturing sectors. This basic result emerges in the other countries in this book, especially Cambodia, in which apparel exports provide relatively well-paying opportunities for otherwise very low-earning workers (young women).

TABLE 6.12 **Wage Regressions Restricted to Manufacturing Workers, 2004**
Dependent variable: log hourly earnings

Independent variable	(A)	(B)	(C)	(D)	(E)	(F)
Years schooling	0.084 (17.43)**	0.083 (17.29)**		0.081 (17.18)**	0.080 (17.12)**	
Age	0.060 (5.47)**	0.060 (5.40)**		0.061 (5.50)**	0.060 (5.43)**	
Age squared	−0.001 (4.45)**	−0.001 (4.38)**		−0.001 (4.55)**	−0.001 (4.47)**	
Female	−0.072 (2.04)*			−0.047 (1.38)		
Garment finisher	0.097 (2.29)*	0.074 (1.81)	−0.066 (1.46)			
Cigar maker				−0.371 (3.13)**	−0.377 (3.17)**	−0.518 (3.83)**
Constant	0.936 (5.41)**	0.933 (5.39)**	2.643 (123.93)**	0.983 (5.68)**	0.980 (5.66)**	2.639 (139.66)**
Observations	1,226	1,226	1,226	1,226	1,226	1,226
R-squared	0.24	0.24	0.00	0.24	0.24	0.01

SOURCE: Authors' calculations from various years of the INE's Encuesta Permanente de Hogares de Propósitos Múltiples (Multi-use Permanent Household Survey).

NOTE: Absolute value of t-statistics in parentheses.

* significant at the X percent level.

** significant at the Y percent level.

Conclusion

Globalization in Honduras includes capital inflows, labor outflows, and exchange of goods. Dramatic growth in FDI, exports, and remittances all illustrate increasing globalization in the country. Increasing globalization can be linked to changes in institutions and economic conditions that affect working conditions. Anecdotal evidence and qualitative assessments suggest that increased attention to the apparel sector by foreign consumers, governments, and organizations seems to have led to improved conditions in exporting sectors. Relative to other sectors, the main exporting sector, apparel, pays a significant wage premium. Contraction in agriculture may have contributed to rising emigration and movement into apparel. The increase in FDI and export opportunities also drew workers into the apparel industry, where, controlling for personal characteristics, workers earn about 20 percent more than average earnings in other employment, suggesting that overall, globalization contributed to improvements in working conditions in Honduras.

If the apparel industry pays a wage premium, why is it perceived to offer low-wage jobs? The chapter has shown that garment finishers earn a wage premium relative to other manufacturing workers with similar personal characteristics. The premium vanishes, however, if controls for personal characteristics are not implemented.

Notes

1. It might be said that Honduras actually started its path toward liberalization in the 1970s when it established its first free trade zone. Country-wide liberalization measures, however, began in earnest in the 1980s.

2. El Salvador was second with just over 57 percent, and Nicaragua was last with just under 40 percent.

3. The WTO (2003) further notes this fall does not necessarily reflect an increase in the use of nontariff barriers.

4. Chapter 1 of this volume contains a brief history of the MFA.

5. For example, in testimony to the House Ways and Means Committee on March 12, 2003, Ambassador Mario M. Canahuati suggested that "protectionist companies and groups in the U.S. textile and apparel industry...undercut the pro-trade provisions [of the CBTPA]."

6. Indeed, Jansen et al. (2007, 1) write "The textile and clothing sector (often referred to as *maquila*)) has been responsible for most of the growth of manufactured exports and foreign exchange earnings, as well as for most of the employment generated since the late 1980s."

7. These data are available for download from http://www.ine-hn.org.

8. Although these may be used as inputs in maquila production, maquila inputs are usually officially separately registered.

9. The National Labor Committee is an NGO that focuses on improving working conditions in developing countries. See http://www.nlcnet.org/index.php.

10. For example, the ILO's LABORSTA database has very few observations at the 2-digit industry level for Honduras for injuries, days lost, and strikes.

11. Unfortunately, the surveys contain little additional information that would help identify the participation decision apart from factors that would also contribute to earnings, making selection corrections impossible in the subsequent analysis.

12. One might consider using a Heckman-style selection model to control for selection effects. As discussed in the annex to chapter 3 in this volume, this approach requires variables to identify the participation equation that are independent from the wage equation. The survey data used here do not contain data on good candidates for these variables, making the Heckman approach infeasible.

13. To interpret the estimated coefficients as percentage differences, raise e (about 2.718) to the estimated coefficient, then subtract 1.

14. This supply shock would be mitigated by the extent to which remittances reduced labor supply.

15. One might suggest that the gender differences between agriculture (mostly male) and apparel (mostly female) raise doubts that workers are leaving agriculture and moving to apparel. It is possible, however, that it is the women who are leaving agriculture in response to the increased demand for apparel workers, even if most of the workers in agriculture are male.

References and Other Resources

Acosta, Pablo. 2006. "Labor Supply, School Attendance, and Remittances from International Migration: The Case of El Salvador." Policy Research Working Paper No. 3903, World Bank, Washington, DC.

Feenstra, Robert C., Robert E. Lipsey, Haiyan Deng, Alyson C. Ma, and Hengyong Mo. 2005. "World Trade Flows: 1962–2000." NBER Working Paper No. 11040, National Bureau of Economic Research, Cambridge, MA. http://cid.econ.ucdavis.edu/data/undata/undata.html.

Frundt, Henry J. 2004. "Unions Wrestle with Corporate Codes of Conduct." *Working USA* 7 (4): 36–69.

Gindling, T. H., and Katherine Terrell. 2006. "Minimum Wages, Globalization, and Poverty in Honduras." IZA Discussion Paper No. 2497, Institute for the Study of Labor, Bonn.

———. 2007. "Minimum Wages and the Welfare of Workers in Honduras." IZA Discussion Paper No. 2892, Institute for the Study of Labor, Bonn.

Hanson, Gordon H., and Raymond Robertson. 2008. "China and the Recent Evolution of Latin America's Manufacturing Exports." In *China's and India's Challenge to Latin America: Opportunity or Threat*, ed. D. Lederman, M. Olarreaga, and G. Perry, 145–75. Washington, DC: World Bank.

Honduras, Instituto Nacional de Estadística. Sintesis del movimiento de comercio exterior 2001-2005. http://www.ine-hn.org/enconomica/comercioexterior1.htm.

———. Various years. *Encuesta Permanente de Hogares* (Permanent Household Survey).

Jansen, Hans G. P., Sam Morley, Gloria Kessler, Vakerua Piñeiro, Marco Sánchez, and Máximo Torero. 2007. "The Impact of the Central American Free Trade Agreement on the Central American Textile Maquila Industry." Discussion Paper 00720, International Food Policy Research Institute, Washington, DC.

Maquila Solidarity Network. 2006. "MSN Closes the Books on Honduras Complaint." http://en.maquilasolidarity.org/en/node/618/print.

Morley, Samuel. 2006. "Trade Liberalization under CAFTA: An Analysis of the Agreement with Special Reference to Agriculture and Smallholders in Central America." Development Strategy and Governance Division Discussion Paper No. 33, International Food Policy Research Institute, Washington, DC.

Singa Boyenge, Jean-Pierre. 2007. "ILO Database on Export Processing Zones (revised)." Sectoral Activities Programme, Working Paper 251, International Labour Office, Geneva.

Trejos, Juan Diego, and T. H. Gindling. 2004. "Inequality in Central America in the 1990s." *CEPAL Review* 84: 175–96.

UNCTAD (United Nations Conference on Trade and Development). 2005. *TNCs and the Removal of Textiles and Clothing Quotas*. UNCTAD/ITE/IIA/2005/1. New York and Geneva: United Nations.

U.S. Department of State. 2006. "Honduras." Country Reports on Human Rights Practices, Bureau of Democracy, Human Rights, and Labor, Under Secretary for Democracy and Global Affairs, U.S. Department of State, Washington, DC. http://www.state.gov/g/drl/rls/hrrpt/2005/61732.htm.

World Bank. 2003. "Productividad y Ambiente de Inversión en Honduras: Encuesta Empresarial." World Bank, Washington, DC.

———. 2007. *World Development Indicators 2007*. Washington, DC: World Bank.

WTO (World Trade Organization). 2003. "Trade Policy Review - Honduras - Report by the Secretariat." WT/TPR/S/120, World Trade Organization, Geneva. http://www.wto.org/english/tratop_e/tpr_e/tpr_e.htm.

CHAPTER 7

Globalization and Working Conditions: Evidence from Indonesia

Raymond Robertson, Sari Sitalaksmi, Poppy Ismalina, and Ardyanto Fitrady

With a population of over 220 million people, Indonesia is by far the largest country studied in this volume. Indonesia was also the most affected of those countries by the Asian financial crisis. Many people argue that the effects of the Asian crisis in Indonesia represent one of the greatest adverse consequences of globalization, because Indonesia may have been much less affected by the crisis if it had been isolated from the world economy. The crisis had direct implications for working conditions because of the significant macroeconomic contraction that ensued. As with most economic contractions, the Indonesian crisis was characterized by significant unemployment, falling wages, and possibly worsening working conditions for workers in firms seeking to cut costs in the face of the recession.

That macroeconomic contractions are bad for workers hardly seems debatable. To the extent that the Asian financial crisis represented a contraction linked to globalization, globalization certainly hurt workers. Rather than focus exclusively on macroeconomic fluctuations, however, this chapter focuses on the microeconomics of globalization and working conditions in Indonesia in the context of the country's broader globalization experience.

Since 1990, the Indonesian government has made a tremendous effort to integrate with the world economy. Indonesia's trade and investment policy transformed from an inward-looking import substitution strategy toward export promotion after the oil bust in the mid-1980s. Integration brought benefits and costs. While Indonesia was hit particularly hard by the 1997 Asian crisis, the move toward export promotion brought attention to Indonesia's working conditions in the 1990s (Manning 2003). Rather than retreat from globalization as a result of the crisis, the crisis was followed by substantive trade liberalization and labor regulation reform as part of meeting International Monetary Fund loan conditions, as stated in Indonesia's Letter of Intent. Indonesia was an active participant in the Uruguay Round negotiations, joined the World Trade Organization (WTO) at its inception on January 1, 1995, and agreed to one of the highest proportions of tariff bindings in the world.

This chapter examines globalization and working conditions in Indonesia in three sections. The first section describes Indonesia's globalization experience and the country's concerted efforts to move from import substitution toward export promotion. The second section provides an overview of working conditions in Indonesia first through a brief review of the academic literature, then by describing the evolution of labor regulations, providing some evidence of enforcement of labor laws, and presenting two firm-level case studies. These results suggest that problems with working conditions persist, but international pressure and exposure to international markets seem to be positively related to working conditions at the level of firms and workers, even while the Asian crisis induced significant job and wage loss. The third section analyzes working conditions by evaluating six measures of working conditions contained in the Indonesian National Labor Force Survey: income, facilities, medical benefits, safety, transport, and worker-based qualitative assessments of overall conditions. The results suggest that wages and nonwage working conditions are positively related and tend to be higher in exporting sectors receiving foreign direct investment (FDI).

Globalization in Indonesia

As in the other country studies in this volume, this first section mainly focuses on trade and foreign investment because these were the areas targeted by the government for liberalization. As in Cambodia, Madagascar, Honduras, and El Salvador, much of the foreign investment was industry specific. Indonesia, however, experienced two distinct phases of focused foreign investment: textiles and apparel dominated the first wave and chemicals and other manufacturing led later waves. Furthermore, as in many other developing countries, foreign investment had a distinctly outward focus with much of the foreign investment entering with the intention of producing for export.

During import substitution,[1] the government invested heavily in and controlled (through state-owned industries) heavy industries, petrochemicals, and mining. Falling oil revenues from 1982 to 1985 motivated a change away from import substitution toward export promotion. Indonesia's more recent liberalization period, starting around 1988, can be divided into four periods: the first wave, the second wave, the Asian crisis, and postcrisis recovery.

THE FIRST WAVE (MID-1980s TO MID-1990s)

The initial objective of Indonesia's trade liberalization effort was to attract foreign investment and promote exports to diversify from its heavy dependence on oil. The strategy consisted of three main components: trade liberalization, investment reform, and industrial policy changes. Together these are believed to have significantly contributed to Indonesia's strong economic growth in the late 1980s and early 1990s.

Although Indonesia joined several regional and global liberalization initiatives, such as AFTA[2] and the WTO, much of Indonesia's liberalization was unilateral (Ismalina 2002). In May 1986, the government deregulated tariff schemes and phased out several nontariff barriers. The government lowered tariff ceilings to 60 percent, reduced the number of tariff levels from 25 to 11, and converted several import licenses (which at their peak covered 43 percent of tariff lines) into tariff equivalents. Under the new system, the government also abolished some nontariff barriers such as import monopolies, simplified customs, and outsourced substantial customs responsibilities. The November 1988 deregulation package removed import monopolies for plastic and steel. Although the deregulation efforts seemed only partial, the psychological effect in business circles was strong and also increased confidence that the government was seriously committed to implementing deregulation. Figure 7.1 illustrates the change in Indonesia's average tariff rate relative to world tariff rates.[3]

The 1985 Plaza Accord quickly realigned industrial country currencies, resulting in a restructuring of southeast Asian manufacturing capacity. Japanese investment in Indonesia was joined in the late 1980s by labor-intensive garment and footwear firms

FIGURE 7.1 **Average Tariffs: Indonesia and the World**

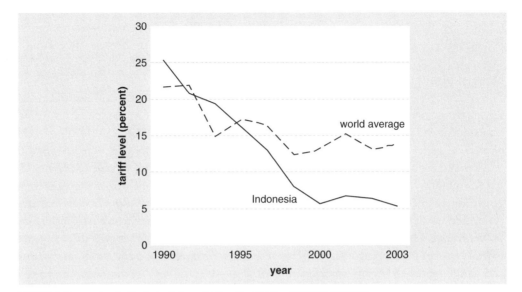

SOURCE: Authors, using the Trade Analysis and Information System (TRAINS) database.

NOTE: These are the overall average reported tariffs in the TRAINS database. These averages are the simple (unweighted) tariffs across all 10-digit Harmonized System entries.

from Hong Kong, China, the Republic of Korea, Singapore, and Taiwan, China (Pangestu 1996). The Indonesian government complemented these investments by relaxing trade barriers. In textiles and apparel, the government applied a more transparent quota allocation system (in 1987) and removed the import monopoly for cotton (in 1989). Furthermore, in May 1990, nontariff barriers for several commodities, such as consumer electronics and electronic components, were eliminated, allowing them to be imported under the nonrestrictive general importer license. The simple average tariff rate was reduced from 27 percent in 1986 to 20 percent in 1991. As a result, the spirit of liberalism that induced various deregulation policies boosted the export and import boom and eventually generated rapid economic growth during 1987–92. In addition to the increase in labor productivity, the liberalization-induced growth in manufacturing led to an increase of its share of value added from 12 percent during the late 1980s and early 1990s to 20 percent (Aswicahyono and Maidir 2003), representing a shift of resources toward sectors receiving FDI.

The influx of FDI, particularly from Hong Kong, China, Japan, Korea, Singapore, and Taiwan, China, brought the technical, managerial, and marketing skills needed to produce goods for world markets. These links connected Indonesia with the world trade system almost overnight by incorporating local producers into the manufacturing and trading chain of foreign buying agents and intermediaries. This increase in investment was followed by a threefold increase in garment (apparel) exports (World Bank 1996).

Trade liberalization was accompanied by other domestic economic reforms. Financial services were deregulated in the late 1980s and early 1990s. Competition was introduced in certain segments of the telecommunications and air transport market. In telecommunications, aviation, and financial services, Indonesia gradually reduced government control and public monopolies. These reforms set the stage for further diversification of foreign investment portfolios in the second wave.

THE SECOND WAVE

The second wave began with a surge of foreign investment approvals in 1994–95, the effects of which began to be realized in 1995 and 1996. This increase was mainly in chemicals. The World Bank (1996) reports that foreign investment became increasingly export oriented during the first half of the 1990s, reinforcing the earlier correlation between investment and exports.

Although foreign investment was increasing, the government made limited progress in removing an array of remaining nontariff barriers. Import monopolies, restrictive licensing, and export controls continued to affect up to 10 percent of imports, 40 percent of non-oil exports, and 30 percent of production. In the sectors concerned, nontariff barriers and export measures were often combined with other forms of assistance, including restrictions on domestic trade, price fixing, and subsidies, all of which were aimed at providing implicit or explicit protection on various grounds (including infant industry protection, security of food supply, resource management, and favoritism). As a result, the list of products benefiting from some form of protection or assistance was still extensive when the Asian crisis occurred in 1997, covering most strategic food commodities, mining and wood resources, key intermediate industrial goods (fertilizers, cement, iron and steel) and transport equipment. Notably, these were not the sectors that figured prominently in international trade and FDI inflows.

During the mid-1990s, FDI averaged US$4 billion a year. Indonesia ranked among the top 12 recipients of FDI inflows among developing and transition economies in the first half of the 1990s (UNIDO 1997). As seen in table 7.1, FDI accelerated in the second half of the 1990s. More than 250 new foreign establishments were added in 1996–97 alone—the year before the financial crisis—roughly equal to the total number of foreign firms in each of the two three-year intervals 1990–92 and 1993–95.

By the mid-1990s, foreign firms were operating in almost all subsectors, but were mainly concentrated in three: textiles, chemicals, and fabricated metal and machinery. The subsectoral composition of foreign establishments[4] also became more diversified after 1993. During 1990–93, most foreign establishments entered just two subsectors, textiles, garments, and footwear (46 percent) and fabricated metals and machinery (36 percent). After 1993, the proportion of new foreign firms entering the textile subsector fell to 10 percent in 1996–97 while that in the chemical subsector increased from 2 percent to 24 percent during 1993–96 and 10 percent in 1996–97.

Foreign firms also invested in wood manufacturing (furniture—from 1 percent to 6–10 percent) and basic metals (from 2 percent to 5 percent). Nevertheless, the textile subsector still attracted approximately 30 new foreign firms in each of these two periods, while the fabricated metal and machinery subsector continued to attract the most (more than 100 new firms, or 38 percent and 44 percent of the total during 1993–96 and 1996–97 periods).

As in many countries, foreign firms tend to be large. Foreign manufacturing establishments employed one in six workers in medium and large-scale establishments, or 0.8 percent of the 88 million Indonesian workers. Their labor productivity, as measured by value added per worker, was double that of domestic establishments, as seen in table 7.2. Higher productivity arises partly from economies of scale and division of labor, and partly

TABLE 7.1 **Subsectoral Composition of Foreign Manufacturing Establishments, 1990–98**

ISIC	Subsector	Cumulative 1997	Net changes in establishments				Subsectoral distribution (%)				
			1990–92	1993–95	1996–97	1997–98	1997	1990–92	1993–95	1996–97	1997–98
31	Food	154	12	25	24	7	11	5	9	9	−5
32	Textiles, garments, and footwear	277	113	38	26	−46	19	46	14	10	30
33	Wood	111	3	17	25	−27	8	1	6	10	18
34	Paper	33	−1	12	4	2	2	0	4	2	−1
35	Chemicals	277	5	65	26	−33	19	2	24	10	22
36	Nonmetal minerals	43	−13	6	16	−4	3	−5	2	6	3
37	Basic metals	44	6	10	13	3	3	2	4	5	−2
38	Fabricated metals and machinery	431	88	104	113	−50	30	36	38	44	33
39	Other manufacturing	52	31	−1	11	−4	4	13	0	4	3
	Total	1,422	244	276	258	−152	100	100	100	100	100

SOURCE: BPS various years.

NOTE: ISIC = International Standard Industrial Classification. A foreign establishment is any foreign establishment with foreign equity, either wholly owned or in joint venture with a domestic firm, private or government, and that benefits from an investment facility

TABLE 7.2 **Employment, Firm Size, and Value Added per Worker by Ownership, 1990–98**

Indicator	1990	1993	1996	1998
Total employment (million)	2.66	3.57	4.21	4.12
Share (percentage)				
Foreign	9	13	16	19
Domestic private	82	80	78	74
Public	9	7	6	7
Total	100	100	100	100
Workers per establishment				
Foreign	368	540	596	509
Domestic private	143	168	153	158
Public	432	734	585	494
Average	161	197	183	192
Value added per worker (million rupiah per year, current prices)				
Foreign	20	22	36	68
Domestic private	8	13	17	31
Public	8	13	51	29
Average in economy	9	14	22	38
Ratio foreign to domestic	2.4	1.7	2.1	2.2

SOURCE: BPS various years.

from concentrating in capital-intensive industries. Controlling for size, however, this labor productivity differential falls to zero in large textile firms.

Total employment in foreign manufacturing establishments grew by 20 percent per year, from 0.2 to 0.7 million between 1990 and 1996 (table 7.2), while the share increased from 9 percent to 16 percent of the total during the period. Domestic firms employed just under 80 percent of the total, while public firms employed the remaining 6 percent of total employment in 1996. The average foreign establishment and public-sector establishment employed about 600 workers, or four times as many workers as the average 150 workers per establishment in domestic firms in 1996.

The growth of the manufacturing sector and of manufacturing exports slowed down considerably as a result of structural and institutional weaknesses in the 1993–97 period, even before the financial crisis. Continued high dependence on imported raw materials and components, low value added in resource-based industries (for example, palm oil, wood, paper, and oil and gas), and a virtually nonexistent capital goods sector limited possibilities for upstream integration. Furthermore, limited range in export products and markets, singular specialization in labor-intensive products, and fierce international competition in the export markets from lower cost producers limited possibilities for expansion in export sectors. Firms also suffered from internal problems. Low productivity in small and medium industries, high market concentration in many segments of industry, weak human resources, weak technology support systems, and weak manufacturing capabilities in domestic firms also limited growth. Given the nature and extent of import dependence and low value added in the industrial sector, Indonesia ran a persistent deficit in manufacturing goods (US$5 billion per year) and an increasingly large deficit in the current account of the balance of payments (US$2 billion to $8 billion) in the 1985–86 to 1996–97 periods, which were offset by large inflows of private capital and external public borrowing.

THE ASIAN CRISIS

The Asian financial crisis, which marked the beginning of the third period, hit Indonesia very hard. In fact, the effects of the Asian crisis separate Indonesia in many ways from the other countries in this volume. Investment flows quickly and sharply reversed in 1997 and 1998. By 1999, gross domestic capital formation declined from 32 percent to 19 percent of GDP. FDI inflows fell from US$6.1 billion in 1996/97 to US$1.6 billion in 1997/98, and were negative in 1998/1999. Figure 7.2 shows the pattern of foreign investment and trade over the 1990–2004 period, in which the effects of the Asian crisis are clearly evident.

Manning (2000a) finds that the crisis induced significant interindustry shifts, specifically, a contraction of the manufacturing sector and a fall in real wages. At the same time, agricultural employment expanded. This result is important to the shift in globalization and working conditions, where FDI helped expand the manufacturing sector by drawing people out of agriculture before the crisis, and the reversal of foreign investment following the crisis sent people back to agriculture.

FIGURE 7.2 **Indonesian FDI and Exports**

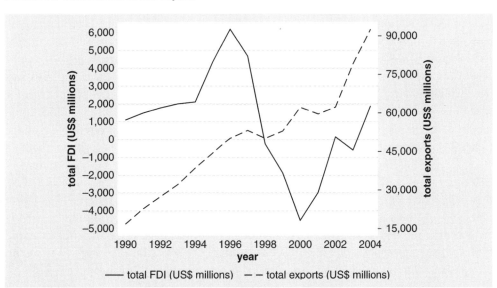

SOURCE: Authors' calculations using data from COMTRADE database (exports) and the 2007 World Investment Reports (FDI).

Large currency depreciations such as that experienced by Indonesia during the Asian crisis should increase exports within one or two years after the depreciation. Indonesia's export performance, however, remained anemic two years after the crisis began: exports collapsed at the start of the fall buying season in the second half of 1998 and showed almost no sign of recovery in 1999, while non-oil and gas exports for the first nine months of 1999 were down 9.1 percent compared with the same period the previous year. Exports resumed growth in 2002, as shown in figure 7.2.

The situation for Indonesian imports, mainly spare parts and industrial raw materials used for processing by Indonesian industries, was even worse. Imports began to decline immediately with the start of the crisis, and were about 60 percent of precrisis levels throughout 1998. Because of the lag time between the date raw materials are imported and the date finished goods are exported, imports serve as an indicator of future exports.

Abundant anecdotal information is available on why Indonesian exports were performing poorly during and after the crisis period. Among the problems mentioned in the press were the lack of trade finance, shortages of containers, and supply disruptions. However, the single most important factor causing Indonesia's weak export performance was probably declining international prices. After deflating by prices, Indonesian exports appeared to have been increasing at a healthy pace through mid-1998 when they went into decline for about six months. In March 1999, real exports recovered to above precrisis levels.

In early 1998, the government adopted the Program of Economic and Financial Reform and Restructuring covering financial sector restoration, fiscal consolidation, monetary issues, the exchange rate, and structural adjustment in the form of broadening and deepening the deregulation program. Domestic and international commerce, which had been relatively heavily regulated, were largely deregulated in late 1997 and early 1998. Imports were the most affected, with a large reduction in tariffs and the removal of the Bureau of Logistics' monopoly rights over all commodities under its control (except rice, for social reasons). During the crisis, the government also committed to removing all import licenses, including import licenses that fell outside previous WTO commitments. The Indonesian government's decision to reduce import barriers reflected a more fundamental policy goal of moving toward outward-oriented trade, and led to mounting concerns about increased imports resulting from the lack of competitiveness of Indonesian industries. A gradual reduction of import tariffs was undertaken, including those on chemical products and iron and steel, which settled at 10 percent in 2003. For a large number of chemical products tariffs were dropped from 10–20 percent to 5 percent in January 1998. In addition, various commodities such as wheat, wheat flour, soybeans, and garlic could be imported freely under General Importer status, and the administered retail price of cement was also abolished.

Sensitive products whose production was closely connected to the government—chemical raw materials, motor vehicles, and steel—continued to be largely untouched by the major trade liberalization (see table 7.3). Tariff peaks occurred in agriculture (food products) and manufacturing for different reasons. Agriculture protection reflected concerns over food security with the government aiming to achieve self-sufficiency in staple commodities, especially rice (WTO 2003). Agriculture was relatively important to the Indonesian economy, employing 45 percent of the labor force but producing only 17 percent of national output (Banerjee and Siregar 2002). Agricultural bound tariffs were very high, approximately 65 percent in trade-weighted terms, and significantly exceeded

TABLE 7.3 **Change in Tariff Protection in Sensitive Sectors, 1996–2002**

		1996		1998		2002	
ISIC	Sector	Simple average tariff (%)	Tariff range (%)	Simple average tariff (%)	Tariff range (%)	Simple average tariff (%)	Tariff range (%)
3121	Food products	15	5–170	13	5–170	6	5–170
3131	Distilling, rectifying, blending spirits	170	170–170	170	170–170	170	170–170
3132	Wine industries	135	5–170	137	5–170	137	5–170
3133	Malt liquors and malt	17	5–40	17	5–40	17	5–40
3511	Industrial chemicals	6	0–30	5	0–30	4	0–30
3513	Resins, plastics, and man-made fibers	13	0–40	12	0–35	8	0–30
371	Iron and steel	8	0–30	8	0–30	7	0–25
3819	Manufacture of fabricated metal products	14	0–30	13	0–25	10	0–20
3843	Manufacture of motor vehicles	48	0–200	52	0–200	21	0–80
3844	Manufacture of motorcycles and bicycles	42	0–150	42	0–150	19	0–60
3849	Manufacture of transport equipment	30	0–30	25	25–25	20	20–20

SOURCE: WITS/TRAINS 2003.

applied tariffs, which averaged 7 percent before the 2002 increases in sugar and rice. High applied tariffs pertained to rice (around 30 percent), meat (around 20 percent), bananas (20 percent), skimmed milk powder (25 percent), tomatoes (25 percent), and roasted coffee (25 percent) (UNCTAD 2003). Because bound tariffs were often more than twice applied levels, negotiated reductions of 50 percent or less were likely to have little economic impact in the agricultural sector. Changes in agriculture, therefore, were more likely to be the result of the indirect effects coming from changes in the manufacturing sector.

POSTCRISIS RECOVERY

The postcrisis years (2000–06) are the fourth period. After the crisis, Indonesia traded predominantly with developed countries. In 2006, about 38 percent of Indonesia's goods and services imports (non-oil and gas) and 74 percent of Indonesia's exports were from or to developed countries (BPS 2006). A consistent distinguishing feature of Indonesian trade—as compared with trade of other developing countries—was its reliance on the export of oil and gas. The only Southeast Asian member of OPEC, Indonesia exported US$21.2 billion oil and gas in 2006.

The crisis-led decline in international investment affected the textiles and apparel sector, but the sector remains important in Indonesian manufacturing. Indonesia imported about US$0.96 billion worth of textile products in 1990, US$1.6 billion in 2000, and US$0.9 billion in 2004. The share of imported textiles and textile products in total imports is relatively small, averaging 2.83 percent per year during 1986–05. In absolute terms, Indonesian textiles and textile product exports increased from US$3.6 billion in 1990 to about US$10.1 billion in 2000. Exports then decreased modestly to an estimated US$9.5 billion in 2005. The decline reflects higher competition in the textiles market, including that brought about by the end of the Multifibre Arrangement (MFA). Nevertheless, the textiles and apparel sector has always been a significant component of Indonesian exports, growing from 13.9 percent of total exports in 1990, to 16.2 percent in 2000, and 12.1 percent in 2005 (estimation). Textiles have consistently been the largest source of non-oil and gas foreign exchange for Indonesia.

Even with extensive reforms, investor confidence remained shaky for Indonesia. Not all investors' concerns were linked to the Asian crisis. Indonesia was poorly rated internationally, with its average number of days to start a business at a high 151 days (World Bank and the International Finance Corporation 2006). Indonesia's rank in the ease of doing business fell from 131 in 2006 to 135 in 2007 (World Bank and the International Finance Corporation 2007). Regional competition, delayed reform, and several high-profile investment disputes continued to inhibit investor confidence.

Net FDI was positive in 2004 for the first time since the crisis (ADB 2006). Although still only 22 percent of the precrisis record of US$4,677 million, both net and gross investment increased. The first-quarter year-on-year growth in foreign investment was 15.4 percent, increasing from US$2,609 to US$3,011 in 2006 (Indonesia's Investment Coordinating Board 2007). Overall investment (domestic plus foreign investment) also remained around 24 percent of GDP in 2006, far less than the consistent pre-Asian financial crisis level of 30 percent. Figure 7.3, however, shows that foreign investment outpaces domestic investment in level and manpower absorption, suggesting that changes in foreign investment continue to have important labor market effects.

As a result of these positive effects, the government continues to try to attract foreign investment. Under the terms of the Investment Law of 2007, the government treats foreign and domestic firms equally and provides better law enforcement and security from the startup stage to closing down a business. Small and medium enterprises, however, remain protected. In contrast with the previous law, the new law prohibits the government from nationalizing foreign firms. The new law also prioritizes and facilitates labor-intensive investment. Along with this development, the government plans to reduce investment that shows negative growth. Other concerns, however, such as reforming customs regulation, taxation, and manpower have yet to be addressed.

In short, Indonesia's globalization experience has several key characteristics. First, throughout the recent era of reform, trade and investment policies were designed to complement one another and to promote exports. Second, Indonesia experienced distinct periods of inflow and outflow of foreign capital, which can be contrasted to provide heuristic

FIGURE 7.3 **Investment and Manpower Absorption, 2001 through November 2006**

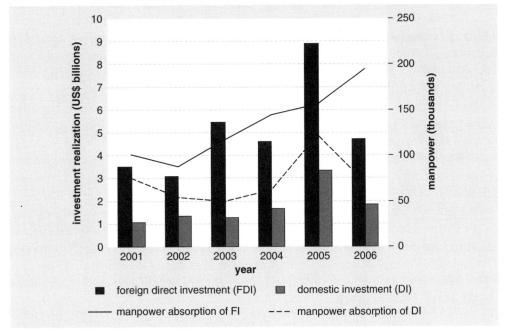

SOURCE: Data are from Indonesia's Investment Coordinating Board, http://www.bkpm.go.id and http://www.bkpm.go.id/index.php/main/statistik.

NOTE: The data do not include investment in oil and gas, finance, banking, nonbank finance, insurance, and leasing.

evidence of the effects of globalization on working conditions. The next section of this chapter analyzes factors that have shaped working conditions in Indonesia.

Working Conditions in Indonesia

Several papers have focused on Indonesia's globalization experience and, in particular, globalization's effects on wages and working conditions. Working conditions are affected by both economic and political factors, and the how these factors work in combination depends on the degree of enforcement at the firm level. The following discussion examines each of these aspects in turn. The section concludes with two case studies to illustrate the interaction of economic and political factors at the firm level.

ECONOMIC STUDIES

Perhaps because of its size, Indonesia has received much more attention in academic literature than have the other countries in this volume. Economic studies of Indonesia's experience tend to define globalization through either foreign direct investment or trade liberalization. The studies of FDI often focus on manufacturing and find that foreign investment increases wages because plants with some foreign capital pay higher wages than other firms (in particular, see Lipsey and Sjoholm [2004a, 2004b]). These results remain after controlling for size, industry, and other factors. To the extent that overall employment is not significantly affected (Sjoholm and Lipsey [2006] suggest that it is not), these results suggest that foreign firms increase labor demand.

Amiti and Konings (2005) and Arnold and Javorcik (2005) find that trade liberalization in Indonesia contributed to increased productivity in manufacturing plants. Productivity gains came from falling tariffs on imported inputs and the pressure of rising competition from falling tariffs on final goods. The former effect is more important. These results suggest that firms could share gains with workers through higher wages and better working conditions, although they may choose not to. Suryahadi (1999) finds that trade liberalization corresponded with a fall in wage inequality between skilled and less-skilled workers, which is predicted by the Heckscher-Ohlin framework.

Suryahadi, Chen, and Tyers (1999) show that trade liberalization led to an expansion of manufacturing, as resources shifted into the expanding sectors. Suryahadi (2003) shows that between 1988 and 1999, the share of workers in agriculture fell from 55.4 percent to 43.2 percent, while the share in manufacturing increased over the same period from 10 percent to 13 percent. During the Asian crisis, as foreign investment left and exports fell, the share employed in manufacturing fell and the share employed in agriculture rose. These shifts have implications for working conditions, as shown later in this chapter.

LEGISLATIVE FRAMEWORK

Indonesia's labor law has been described as one of the most labor-friendly in Southeast Asia (Caraway 2004). Indonesia's current labor law traces back to 1948, during Sukarno's regime (1945–67). Sukarno, the first president of Indonesia, codified many worker protections. These laws defined and established minimum working standards, including outlawing employment of children under 15 years old, limiting night work for women, allowing for maternity leave, and emphasizing job security (Kaur 2004).

Sukarno's successor Suharto (1967–98) was driven to eliminate communists, and union affiliation was a key component of his strategy to identify suspected communists. Rather than change the labor laws to achieve his goal, Suharto enacted 197 executive decrees, all favoring employers and business. Suharto's government also implemented minimum wage laws in the mid-1970s, thereby doubling real minimum wages between 1988 and 1995 (Cox Edwards 1996).

When Suharto stepped down, reversal of these decrees became an important part of the country's return to democracy. Reversing these decrees, however, reinstated the terms of labor-friendly labor laws established by Sukarno, giving labor unions, which were neither generally affiliated with political parties nor unified, strength in dealing with both the government and business, allowing them to achieve several victories. In particular, they were able to block moves to reduce employment protections that would have increased employer flexibility in the labor market (Caraway 2004).

As part of the return to democracy, the new government moved quickly to ratify all of the core International Labour Organization (ILO) conventions between June 1998 and May 1999. The government also enacted social protection programs, although these did not cover the majority of the poor (Suryahadi 2003).

International pressure played a significant role in the enactment of laws to improve working conditions in Indonesia. International pressure, mainly from the United States and the European Union, contributed to efforts to change legislation beginning in the late 1980s, when economic liberalization began. Both the ILO and the U.S. government criticized Indonesia for violating labor standards in the late 1980s, contributing to the country's move to increase workers' statutory rights and facilitate collective bargaining (Cox Edwards 1996). When Bacharuddin Jusuf Habibie succeeded Suharto in May 1998, he moved quickly to ratify ILO Convention 87 (Freedom of Association and Protection of the Right to Organise) in June 1998. Caraway (2004) suggests that this move was designed to signal meaningful reform to a world that was very wary following the Asian crisis in September 1997. The Habibie administration seemed resistant to additional labor reform, but the ILO, which had been advocating labor reform in Indonesia throughout the reform period, now had the backing of the international financial community, including the U.S. Treasury and the International Monetary Fund (Caraway 2004). Caraway (2004) attributes a significant portion of the force behind subsequent labor reforms, including the adoption of the rest of the core ILO conventions, to international pressure.

International pressure on specific firms may also have contributed to improving conditions. Harrison and Scorse (2004) use wages as a measure of working conditions. Their results suggest that external pressure on Indonesian manufacturing (both from the U.S. government and anti-sweatshop campaigns) led to a 50 percent increase in real wages for unskilled workers at targeted plants and the employment effects were limited or offset by expansions of other plants.

ENFORCEMENT

Labor-friendly laws do not improve working conditions if they are not enforced. Pangestu and Hendytio (1997) argue that the lack of effective trade unions and worker representation in the workplace led to a lack of enforcement and therefore poor conditions. To investigate the prevalence of enforcement (or lack thereof), Pangestu and Hendytio (1997) surveyed 300 women working in garments, textiles, and footwear. Their results reveal a significant difference in enforcement across firm sizes. In particular, small and medium enterprises seem to have less enforcement than large firms.

The pattern of compliance varies with the measure of working conditions. The study finds relatively high compliance for maternity leave (96 percent), hours worked per week (91 percent), compensated maternity leave (89 percent), access to clean water (97 percent), first aid (91 percent), sanitation facilities (82 percent), and training (76 percent). Other measures were not quite so high. Examples include fire drill training (17 percent) and safety equipment (64 percent). The main issue with low compliance, however, was that workers lacked knowledge of benefits. The minimum wage was most familiar to workers, but only 41 percent indicated accurate knowledge of minimum wage regulations. The authors suggest that compliance seemed to rise as workers were more informed about benefits.

CASE STUDIES

This section discusses two firm-level case studies: a textile company and a garment company. Both are located in Yogyakarta, a province in the middle part of Java, the most populated island in Indonesia. Yogyakarta's unemployment rate is the lowest among all provinces in Java, and easy mobility across the island has made working in this area highly desirable. The data were collected in January 2007 and are based on in-depth interviews with top management, trade union leaders, and labor activists.

A Textile Company

This company was selected because it appears to typify the experience of Indonesian textile firms responding to liberalization and how these changes have affected working conditions.

This company is a mid-size firm that began to operate in 1972 in Yogyakarta. It was established in response to Law No. 9/1969, which induced a rearrangement of state enterprises. With this law, overseas in-kind grants had to be owned by the state, which made contributions for joint ownership with a private entity. The grants to this company consisted of advanced spinning and weaving machinery, which were actually given to the partnering Indonesian entity as part of the Dutch government's effort to sustain domestic high-quality cambric from this former sole importer. Before becoming a state-owned enterprise, the organization was initially a sole importer of cambric from the Netherlands. Following the closure of the Dutch cambric firm and the announcement of Indonesia's Investment Law, the Dutch government granted the machineries to this Indonesian firm. The firm produces semi-finished products: yarn, grey fabric, and cambric. The imported raw material (cotton) is spun into yarn, which is all woven into grey fabric. Some of the grey fabric is sold in Indonesia as intermediate products and some is reprocessed to make cambric for export.

The firm has engaged in importing and exporting since its inception. Raw material is fully imported because of the limited supply of domestic cotton and because of quality requirements. Australia was the major source of imports in 2007 (nearly 50 percent of total imports of cotton), surpassing the United States and China. The firm exports 50 percent of its production and, similar to the trend in national exports, the main export destination for this firm is Japan. The United States was delisted from the firm's export destinations because of the increasing competition in the U.S. market following the end of the MFA in January 2005. This largely confirms Aswicahyono and Maidir's (2003) argument that Indonesia may have benefited from the MFA, particularly in the protections the MFA offered from established exporting countries.

The Japanese textile market, however, has been slowly eroded by imports from China and other emerging economies. Although struggling, the firm remains confident that its effort to move to serve the higher quality segment would prevent its downfall, because the new entrants are most competitive at the low end of the market. While struggling, the firm was clinging to its temporary competitive advantage of product quality at the high end of the market. In the domestic economy, the firm has to compete with illegal products from overseas that have worsened the already sluggish textile market.

The firm employs 1,150 workers (virtually all male). Because of the abundance of workers seeking jobs, the firm frequently hires overqualified workers. The firm's working conditions seem to be above the minimum standard. While many firms still pay less than the provincial minimum wage (which for Yogyakarta was about US$50 per month in 2006), this export-oriented, FDI-linked firm pays employees more than the minimum wage. The collective bargaining agreement between management and the trade union also guarantees inflation-based annual wage increases. In addition, permanent employment status provides employees with a set of relatively lucrative benefits, particularly in comparison with other domestic firms, especially those within the region (Yogyakarta and Central Java). For example, some elements of medical benefits are even extended to workers' families.

Problems began to arise when the firm's performance began to decline near the end of 2003. Finding credit for expansion became difficult, competition increased, the cost of living rose, and profits fell. Difficulties in obtaining credit are common for Indonesian companies because the banking sector fails to play its intermediary role. Lack of financing has created serious problems for the firm in renewing and replacing its assets, such as outdated machinery, while the firm must keep up with the technology in textile production to secure its position in the mid to upper segments of the market.

As China grew and the MFA ended in January 2005, pressure for efficiency increased. In response, management turned to the workers. National labor law makes layoffs unaffordable, so the company increased working hours. Industrial relations at the firm, which used to be harmonious, changed in January 2007. For the first time in company history, workers went on strike to protest this particular company policy. Although the company's ability to increase hours, especially during economic hardship, had been discussed and even stipulated in the collective agreement, the strike could not be averted.

In short, the firm's response to rising competition combined with constraints on its labor flexibility was to increase hours. No evidence was found that the firm attempted to adjust other dimensions of working conditions, but the fact that facilities and benefits have been stagnant since early 2000 has begun to raise concern among workers. It is possible that the firm may respond to increasing competition by not improving conditions at the same rate as it might have in the past.

A Garment Company

This company was established in the early 1980s as a fully domestic, privately owned firm. It exports 100 percent of its product and imports all of its raw materials. Its role is as a "tailor" (make-cut-trim): buyers carefully define product specifications and usually place their quality control officer at the firm. As of 2006, the company had been able to maintain its increasingly demanding customers. With the entrance into world markets of lower quality products from some developing economies, the firm had no choice but to push itself to serve a higher quality market segment—a similar phenomenon as that observed in the textile firm.

Unlike the previous firm, this garment company has a relatively stable number of customers, yet the firm faces a similar degree of uncertainty because long-term job orders have never been placed with this firm. Given this situation, the firm prefers to only hire contract workers. If workers fulfill the firm's requirements, they may be upgraded to permanent status. Production workers, however, are at the bottom of the list for consideration for permanent status. Production workers are hired based on the estimated length of time needed to fill particular orders.

The firm employed 1,900 workers in early 2007; 1,800 of these workers were females concentrated in the production department. Firms classically respond to increasing market competition by reducing labor costs. When demand rises again, the firm hires and trains new contract workers. This approach is cheaper than upgrading contract workers to permanent status because most of the work does not require advanced skills. Contract workers do not receive medical benefits, pension contributions, or job security.

Continually hiring new contract workers requires circumventing labor law. Workers are supposed to be considered permanent if they work for more than three years.

Law No. 13/2003 on manpower stipulates that a work agreement for a limited specified time is permitted if the work is temporary in nature, seasonal, can be completed in less than three years, or is related to new product development. The work agreement can last up to two years and only be extended for one year. The common practice in the industry is to claim that work is seasonal so that firms can avoid giving workers permanent status after the two-year contract and its one year extension. Even if the worker is a good performer, the firm still discontinues the contract. Individual workers are advised to "lapse" for some time before getting a job back at the firm. An implicit agreement seems to be in place with another similar firm to swap workers during their lapses.

Cutting labor costs, such as training, may adversely affect product quality. The firm admitted that reworking is becoming more frequent. In this situation, the firm has to bear the cost of sending the products by air to meet the agreed-on schedule. Management implicitly blames the lower skills of the average worker for its inability to increase product quality (that is, style, level of difficulty, finer finishing). At the same time, technical assistance from U.S. buyers has fallen in recent years.

These case studies reveal several important concerns. First, export-oriented firms are likely to offer higher wages, have better technology, and have better access to markets. These two firms are no exception. However, foreign exposure involves risk. The emergence of foreign competitors or changes in partners' trade policies (for example, ending the MFA) can pose serious threats to globally engaged firms. Such threats may exert downward pressure on working conditions, meaning that the future of the link between globalization and working conditions is far from certain.

Empirical Analysis of Working Conditions with Labor-Force Surveys

The previous sections suggest that Indonesia's trade liberalization induced a move from agriculture toward manufacturing, and, in particular, toward textiles, apparel, chemicals, and machinery. This move leads to improved working conditions on average if working conditions were better in these sectors than in agriculture. Changes in trade and foreign investment over time might also be linked to working conditions. While the previous literature review and case studies suggest that this is the case, empirical analysis of labor force surveys reveals more definitive results.

DATA

To measure unemployment, the government relies on the National Labor Force Survey (SAKERNAS), which contains demographic information (age, gender, education, and other variables) and employment-related statistics (employment status, industry, occupation, and wages). BPS-Statistics Indonesia, which collects the data, historically conducted the survey annually (every August) but increased to twice a year (February and November) in 2005. The available data cover 1989 to 2004, with the exception of 1995 and 1997. These surveys are similar to those used in the studies of El Salvador and Honduras in this volume.

Table 7.4 contains sample characteristics that reveal several important features of the survey data. The first column contains the sample size, which depicts much variation

TABLE 7.4 **Sample Characteristics**

Year	Sample size	Age	Female (%)	Education[a]
1991	46,000	32.63	30.47	4.50
1992	45,835	32.94	31.25	4.56
1993	47,126	33.17	31.18	4.56
1994	44,405	32.90	30.04	4.59
1996	41,338	33.91	28.82	4.81
1998	28,787	33.88	32.47	4.89
1999	27,546	34.02	32.03	4.90
2000	15,612	33.30	30.76	4.60
2001	18,630	32.41	29.89	5.14
2002	29,219	33.00	28.75	5.15
2003	33,538	32.97	28.68	5.47
2004	33,605	32.88	29.19	5.38

SOURCE: Authors' calculations based on the SAKERNAS, various years.

NOTE: The sample includes workers with positive earnings who are between 10 and 65 years old, inclusive.

a. The education variable takes on one of 10 values (1–10) with three representing primary education and six representing high school education: 1 = not yet in school; 2 = still in school; 3 = primary school; 4 = junior high school; 5 = vocational junior; 6 = senior high school; 7 = vocational senior high school; 8 = Diploma I and II; 9 = Academy/Diploma III; and 10 = University/Diploma IV.

by year, and indicates the number of workers from the survey who are between 10 and 65 years old (inclusive) and have positive earnings from wages. Starting with the Asian crisis in 1997, sample sizes fall, possibly reflecting the difficult economic times following the Asian crisis. The sample size is smallest in 2000, but increases thereafter. The average age is relatively constant. A very weak positive trend in age emerges, suggesting the lack of large waves of younger entrants into the labor force. The female share of the sample is relatively constant as well, hovering around 30 percent.

The main change over the sample period is the increase in average education levels. The education variable rises steadily through the sample period, along with the share of workers with at least a high school education. During the same period, the returns to education also increased, suggesting an overall increase in the demand for education.

These data also reveal other important trends in the Indonesian labor market. Figure 7.4 presents the evolution of the natural log of the average real wage from 1989 through 2004. The real wage rose over the sample period, possibly because of rising education levels (table 7.4), with the notable exception of 1996–98, the year of the Asian financial crisis. The data illustrate a relatively strong recovery in real wages by 2001, and depict a slowdown in the growth rate at the end of the sample.

The data also can be used to track employment shares within the survey over time. Figure 7.5 shows the employment shares of the three largest sectors in Indonesia: manufacturing, agriculture, and commerce (retail and wholesale trade).[5] The share of workers in manufacturing appears relatively constant over the sample period, rising from 1989 until 1999, and then falling. The share of workers in agriculture falls until the middle of the 1990s and rises afterward. These patterns reflect Manning's (2000a) findings of the postcrisis resurgence of agriculture following the crisis-induced contraction of FDI, exports, and employment in manufacturing.

FIGURE 7.4 **Mean Log Real Wage, 1989–2004**

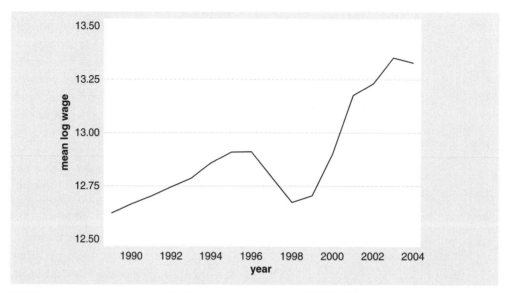

SOURCE: Authors' calculations based on the National Labor Force Survey (SAKERNAS).

NOTE: Real wages are calculated using the annual average of the current price index. The demographic-adjusted real mean log wage follows basically the same path.

FIGURE 7.5 **Labor Force Survey of Industry Employment Shares**

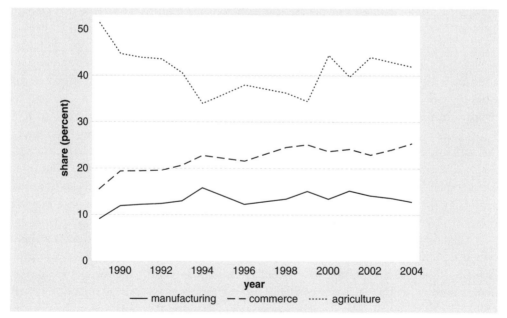

SOURCE: Authors' calculations based on SAKERNAS, various years.

NOTE: Employment shares of all workers. These categories are the three largest employment categories. Years 1995 and 1997 are excluded because of a lack of data.

The trends in figure 7.5 hide heterogeneity within manufacturing. Figure 7.6 shows the evolution of employment shares of sectors within manufacturing. These shares are each manufacturing sector's share of total paid employment (workers with positive earnings in the sample). Figure 7.6 shows sharply rising employment shares for textiles and "other manufacturing" (which includes machinery and chemicals) during the recovery period. Food products and the wood sector remained relatively constant or fell. After the initial sharp increase in 2000, the trend in the employment shares for textiles and other manufacturing was negative, mirroring the fall in manufacturing shown in figure 7.5. These trends have been the source of much concern in Indonesia, and seem to coincide with the rise of Chinese exports in the world economy.

The various industries have substantially different demographic characteristics. Table 7.5 contains the demographic characteristics broken down by industry for 1991 and 2004, and shows that, in particular, the average education level in textiles, apparel, and leather is below the national sample average. Agriculture has very low average education levels, as is typical. Utilities, public administration, and FIRE (finance, insurance, and real estate) have relatively high education levels.

As in the other countries in this volume, employment in textiles, apparel, and leather is characterized by a large concentration of women: over 52 percent in 1991 with a slight decrease to 50 percent in 2004. The female share of employment in textiles, apparel, and leather is nearly double that in the other manufacturing category, and the

FIGURE 7.6 **Within-Manufacturing Employment Shares**

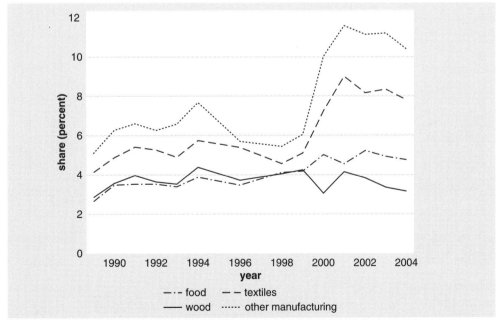

SOURCE: Authors' calculations based on SAKERNAS, various years.

NOTE: Employment shares of all workers with positive earnings. Years 1995 and 1997 are excluded because of a lack of data. "Food" is the manufacturing industry that includes food, beverages, and tobacco.

TABLE 7.5 **Sample Characteristics by Industry, 1991 and 2004**

Sector	1991			
	Frequency (%)	Age	Female (%)	Education[a]
Food agriculture	7.80	36.42	41.89	2.29
Other agriculture	7.32	32.91	26.95	2.77
Mining and quarrying	1.52	34.91	9.57	4.60
Food, beverages, and tobacco	3.54	29.56	45.82	3.51
Textiles, apparel, leather	5.43	26.82	52.98	3.90
Wood	3.98	29.26	20.93	3.95
Other manufacturing	6.62	29.89	25.43	4.39
Electric, gas, water	0.65	33.61	8.00	5.71
Construction	8.69	32.82	4.20	3.59
Retail, wholesale, hotels	6.65	29.48	33.29	4.68
Transportation, storage, communications	4.80	32.84	4.57	4.24
FIRE and business services	2.49	32.33	26.14	6.35
Public administration	19.42	36.50	27.31	6.51
Other services	21.08	31.79	43.93	4.66
Average (whole sample)		32.63	30.47	4.50

Sector	2004			
	Frequency (%)	Age	Female (%)	Education[a]
Food agriculture	4.46	35.14	28.50	3.53
Other agriculture	3.38	31.56	12.49	3.63
Mining and quarrying	2.23	33.81	6.13	4.80
Food, beverages, and tobacco	4.76	31.81	40.90	4.64
Textiles, apparel, leather	7.82	30.05	49.45	4.84
Wood	3.15	30.77	20.38	4.69
Other manufacturing	10.39	32.20	21.51	5.56
Electric, gas, water	0.82	36.94	10.11	6.58
Construction	7.34	35.26	4.79	4.76
Retail, wholesale, hotels	20.29	29.59	35.58	5.83
Transportation, storage, communications	7.32	34.84	10.89	5.39

(continued)

TABLE 7.5 **(continued)**

Sector	1991			
	Frequency (%)	Age	Female (%)	Education[a]
FIRE and business services	5.89	33.86	26.91	7.31
Public administration	11.80	39.39	21.94	7.04
Other services	10.33	31.20	58.51	4.13
Average (whole sample)		32.88	29.19	5.38

SOURCE: Authors' construction using SAKERNAS, given years.

NOTE: FIRE = Finance, insurance, and real estate.

a. The education variable takes on one of 10 values (1–10) with three representing primary education and six representing high school education: 1 = not yet in school; 2 = still in school; 3 = primary school; 4 = junior high school; 5 = vocational junior; 6 = senior high school; 7 = vocational senior high school; 8 = Diploma I and II; 9 = Academy/Diploma III; and 10 = University/Diploma IV.

workers in textiles, apparel, and leather are younger than in all other sectors except retail, wholesale, and hotels in 2004. Thus, as in other countries, apparel employment in Indonesia is typified by relatively young women.

Table 7.5 also shows several changes occur over time. First, the share of employment in textiles, apparel, and leather rose from approximately 5.4 percent to 7.8 percent. The share of employment in other manufacturing, which includes chemicals and other FDI-intensive sectors, rose from about 6.6 percent to nearly 10.4 percent. The average age and education level rose relative to the mean, and the share of females fell relative to the mean. The first two seem consistent with an increase in demand for skill in FDI-intensive manufacturing industries. Of interest is the fact that the relative shares of non-FDI intensive sectors did not change as much as textiles, apparel, and leather and other manufacturing. Construction, for example, fell slightly—from 8.69 percent to 7.34 percent. Employment shares in wood fell from 3.98 percent to 3.15 percent. Finally, the sample share of food agriculture fell from 7.80 percent to 4.46 percent. Again, these shifts are consistent with Manning (2000a) and the hypothesis that FDI induced a between-industry shift.

INTERINDUSTRY WAGE DIFFERENTIALS

Globalization in Indonesia coincided with an expansion of sectors that attracted export-oriented FDI, so it is important to first compare wages in these sectors with wages in other sectors within Indonesia. The National Labor Force Surveys contain information about monthly income from different sources. Wage income, which is reported as monthly income from remunerated employment, is analyzed here. Monthly wage income is divided by hours worked in the week before the survey (the only measure of hours available in the survey) then divided by 4.3 to get an estimate of the hourly wage.[6]

To get an idea of how wages differ across industries, the natural log of hourly earnings is chosen as the wage variable, which is customary in labor market analysis because the natural log of wages is usually approximately normally distributed. The technical details of the estimation of interindustry wage differentials (IIWDs) are found in the annex to chapter 3. The first column of table 7.6 presents the overall average of log wages and the percentage difference from this overall average that workers earn in each industry, using 1991 data. This percentage difference is the wage differential (or wage premium) earned in each industry. The corresponding results for 2004 are presented in column three.

Normally, studies of wage differentials limit the sample to workers in the private sector (nonmilitary and nongovernment), workers who are not self-employed, and workers who work a certain number of hours (for example, full-time workers). Here the sample is limited to workers who are between 10 and 65 years of age, inclusive, and have positive earnings. All sectors are included to obtain the most comprehensive comparison.

The first column of table 7.6 shows that the overall average log wage was 7.48 in 1991. Food agriculture and other agriculture earned less than average. Food agriculture workers, for example, earned nearly 41 percent less[7] than the average wage (without controlling for demographic characteristics). Workers in food, beverages, and tobacco (which is a manufacturing industry) also earn below-average wages. Workers in utilities (electric, gas, and water), construction, FIRE and business services, and public administration, however, earn above-average wages.

Workers in textiles, apparel, and leather earned about 26 percent less than the average wage in 1991. Because that sector generally has more female workers and relatively less-educated workers, it is likely that differences in demographic composition affects these average wages. For example, if a sector hires more-educated workers on average, and workers with more education earn higher wages, then wages in that sector will be higher than average. A second regression that controls for demographic characteristics (gender, age and age squared, region, and a dummy for urban areas, and years of education) is estimated, and wage differentials, after controlling for demographic characteristics, are recalculated for each sector and compared with the average wage.

The second column in table 7.6 illustrates the wage differential results after controlling for demographic characteristics. The impact of demographic characteristics presented in table 7.6 indicate that in 1991 females earned about 24 percent less than other workers when controlling for sector, age, and education, while older and more-educated workers earned higher wages when controlling for other characteristics.

Once these demographic characteristics are controlled for, the wage premium in the textiles, apparel, and leather industry in 1991 increases to about 3.6 percent, and is not statistically different from the overall mean wage. This is not surprising given the fact that the sector primarily comprises workers who are less educated than average. Workers in food agriculture, however, still earned significantly less than other workers, even after demographic controls are included. Furthermore, the large premiums in other sectors, such as public administration, fall, because these sectors tend to employ more-educated, older, male workers.

Although the workers in textiles, apparel, and leather do not seem to have earned any significant wage premium in 1991, it is possible that they have been affected by the rise in foreign investment and exports in the apparel sector since that time. A similar possibility exists for the other manufacturing sectors that have attracted FDI. To get an idea of how these premiums have changed over time, the same regression is estimated for each year between 1991 and 2004, including the same demographic controls described above.[8] The results for 2004 are illustrated in the last two columns of table 7.6.

TABLE 7.6 **Interindustry Wage Differentials without and with Controls for Demographic Characteristics, Indonesia, 1991 and 2004**

	1991		2004	
	(1) Without controls for demographic characteristics	(2) With controls for demographic characteristics	(3) Without controls for demographic characteristics	(4) With controls for demographic characteristics
Mean log wage	7.48	5.64	8.00	6.29
Sector	**Differentials**			
Food agriculture	−0.409*	−0.150*	−0.326*	−0.105*
Other agriculture	−0.305*	−0.106*	−0.259*	0.000
Mining and quarrying	0.731*	0.440*	0.423*	0.405*
Food, beverages, and tobacco	−0.343*	−0.118*	−0.211*	−0.010
Textiles, apparel, leather	−0.257*	0.036	−0.079*	0.074*
Wood	−0.024	0.059	−0.108*	0.057*
Other manufacturing	−0.007	0.079*	0.171*	0.118*
Electric, gas, water	0.580*	0.188	0.618*	0.225*
Construction	0.042*	0.124*	0.065*	0.102*
Retail, wholesale, hotels	−0.075*	−0.028	−0.090*	−0.115*
Transportation, storage, communications	0.183*	0.115*	0.119*	0.041*
FIRE and business services	0.785*	0.306*	0.719*	0.173*
Public administration	0.704*	0.102*	0.765*	0.284*
Other services	−0.155*	−0.131*	−0.503*	−0.365*
Demographic characteristics	**1991**		**2004**	
Age	0.060*		0.045*	
Age squared	−0.001*		0.000*	
Female	−0.230*		−0.162*	
Education	0.151*		0.142*	

SOURCE: Authors' calculations using SAKERNAS. Regional and urban controls were also included but are not reported.

NOTE: FIRE = Finance, insurance, and real estate. The percentage changes for dummy variables (industries and female) shown in this table are calculated by raising e to the power of the estimated coefficient and subtracting 1 because the model is log-linear.

* = significant at the 1 percent level.

Although the economics literature on IIWDs suggests that they are "remarkably stable" over time (especially in developed countries), the last two columns of table 7.6 show important changes in wage differentials since 1991. In particular, the negative unadjusted differential in textiles, apparel, leather is now much closer to zero. More important, however, the adjusted differential is positive and significant. The adjusted wage differential (coefficient estimate) for other manufacturing increases from 0.050 to 0.121. The increase in relative employment in these sectors coincided with a rise in their average wage, which suggests that the demand for these workers increased. The IIWD for workers in food agriculture also rose (but stayed negative). However, because this increase coincided with a fall in relative employment share, the changes for food agriculture are most consistent with a fall in the supply of labor. These results are consistent with the hypothesis that export-oriented FDI increased the demand for manufacturing workers and, as workers left agriculture, the supply of workers in agriculture fell.

To provide an idea of how the differential has changed over the entire sample period, figure 7.7 illustrates the results by graphing the annually estimated apparel IIWD and the share in total employment of the textiles, apparel, and leather sector. The two rise together, suggesting an increase in demand for these workers, which seems to have resulted in a rising wage premium as the sector has expanded.

WAGE DIFFERENTIALS AND FOREIGN DIRECT INVESTMENT

Ideally, an analysis would formally test the hypothesis that the wage differentials are related to globalization measures. One problem in the Indonesian case is that the main

FIGURE 7.7 **Apparel Sector Employment Share and Wage Premium, Indonesia, 1991–2004**

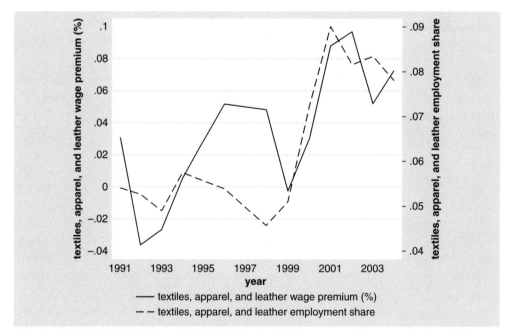

SOURCE: Authors' calculations based on SAKERNAS, various years.

NOTE: The textile wage premium is the percentage difference from the overall mean wage, as described in the text.

liberalization period spanned 1988–96, and globalization measures for that country that vary by year and industry from that period are difficult to find. One measure that is available, however, is approvals of FDI. Presumably, all or less than the approved amount of FDI was actually realized in the years following approval. Table 7.7 contains the available data for FDI approvals by industry and year, showing significant variation across industry and time.

The Capital Investment Coordinating Board (BKPM) is the central processing point for most investment applications, and is the source for these data. The data do not include investments in the following sectors: oil and gas, finance (including banking and nonbank finance) and insurance. BKPM approval reports should be treated with caution, because the agency performs little monitoring of investment project implementation. Some investors may inflate the value of their investments to maximize government incentives. For example, the mid-1990s approvals were inflated for several years by a surge of interest in oil product refineries, most of which were never constructed. In addition, year-on-year comparisons of domestic approvals after the rupiah began to decline in mid-1997 are difficult because of the currency's fluctuating value.

As a test of the hypothesis that FDI has a positive effect on IIWDs, a panel of IIWDs (the difference in average wage in each industry from the mean, controlling for demographic characteristics) is first constructed. Using these differentials as the dependent variable, three regressions are estimated using the natural log of FDI approvals as the independent variable differentiated by specification.

The results from this first-pass estimation are shown in table 7.8. Log FDI approvals are included as the current period and four lagged values. The lagged values are important because current FDI approvals should not affect differentials. Indeed, it could take several years for approved FDI to be implemented to the point it could affect wages. The three specifications vary in their inclusion of fixed time and industry effects.

In all three specifications, the third lag of FDI approvals is statistically significant and positive, which is a reasonable result. These results suggest that inflows of FDI increase the sector-specific IIWD, which is consistent with the descriptive evidence presented in the previous sections. To the extent that working conditions are positively correlated with wages, the shift into industries with better working conditions suggests that FDI positively contributed to rising working conditions.

Qualitative Measures of Working Conditions

The results of the previous section are consistent with the idea that export-oriented FDI induced a between-industry shift out of agriculture and into certain manufacturing sectors. The effect that this movement has on nonwage working conditions, however, depends on whether conditions are better in manufacturing or in agriculture. If conditions are worse in manufacturing, then an export-oriented, FDI-induced shift from agriculture to manufacturing cannot be said to improve working conditions in Indonesia. This section compares nonwage measurements of working conditions across industries and compares the differences across industries with the estimated wage differentials.

The SAKERNAS surveys began to contain specific questions about working conditions in 1998. These conditions include income, facilities, medical benefits, safety, transport, and an overall assessment. The survey offers workers four categories with which to assess

TABLE 7.7 Approved FDI by Industry
(US$ millions)

Year	Food agriculture	Other agriculture	Mining and quarrying	Food, beverages, and tobacco	Textiles, apparel, leather	Wood	Other manufacturing	Electric, gas, water	Construction	Retail, wholesale, hotels	FIRE and business services[a]
1992	65.9	165.4	2,313.0	212.7	584.3	31.5	3,164.3	417.1	20.2	847.8	475.6
1993	131.9	21.3	0	141.3	423.0	50.4	2,909.6	3,411.7	103.2	394.4	579.0
1994	689.4	39.5	0	1,240.5	396.5	68.0	17,210.8	892.1	76.6	343.6	1,029.4
1995	1,074.1	227.3	37	1,293.2	471.1	263.0	30,363.6	3,704.2	205.8	1,797.9	1,191.8
1996	1,296.8	215.2	1,696.8	692.0	513.8	101.0	15,350.7	4,890.3	295.8	1,716.5	3,007.5
1997	436.4	27.2	1.9	575.9	333.4	69.9	27,232.6	2,344.5	306.7	400.8	1,397.6
1998	965.3	33.1	0.3	335.7	217.0	70.7	7,837.2	2,177.6	197.8	450.9	1,270.9
1999	412.5	78.5	14.2	680.7	240.4	113.1	5,997.8	2,792.8	153.3	228.6	179.5
2000	389.1	54.6	1.1	701.3	400.4	156.9	10,588.2	2,303.4	125.3	257.2	301.5
2001	284.2	107.5	118.7	289.2	330.0	21.4	4,877.1	1,899.1	47.6	6,891.6	177.5
2002	446.3	12.6	49.2	267.3	89.9	30.4	6,533.8	1,764.9	287.7	254.6	7.4
2003	57.2	121.7	17.8	408.5	123.1	235.0	9851.0	1,106.7	787.2	488.2	10.3
2004	196.9	132.8	66.3	721.8	407.9	15.5	5,775.6	1,079.7	954.0	587.2	339.6
2005	462.0	144	775.9	642.6	139.5	102.2	8,251.0	901.0	1,777.2	259.1	124.8
2006	673.1	109.1	285.6	920.5	139.6	57.4	6,738.8	2,568.2	2,121.8	235.1	40.1

SOURCE: Indonesia's Capital Investment Coordinating Board (BKPM), various years. See http://www.bkpm.go.id/.

NOTE:

a. FIRE = Finance, insurance, and real estate, but the investment approval statistics exclude Finance and Insurance and only include Real Estate and Business Services.

TABLE 7.8 **Estimation of Correlation between Interindustry Wage Differentials and FDI Approvals**

	(1) Wage differential	(2) Wage differential	(3) Wage differential
Log FDI	0.001 (0.004)	0.002 (0.004)	0.001 (0.004)
Log FDI T-1	0.003 (0.004)	0.003 (0.004)	0.003 (0.004)
Log FDI T-2	−0.000 (0.004)	0.001 (0.004)	0.002 (0.004)
Log FDI T-3	**0.007 (0.003)***	**0.008 (0.003)***	**0.011 (0.004)****
Log FDI T-4	−0.001 (0.004)	−0.000 (0.004)	0.003 (0.005)
Constant	0.009 (0.061)	−0.218 (0.050)**	−0.259 (0.061)**
Industry?	No	Yes	Yes
Year?	No	No	Yes
Observations	86	86	86
Number of industries	11	11	11

SOURCE: Authors' calculations based on foreign investment approval data from BKPM and estimated wage differentials from table 7.6.

NOTE: Standard errors in parentheses.

* significant at the 5 percent level.

** significant at the 1 percent level.

working conditions in their jobs; they are asked whether each condition is better, just as good, just as bad, or worse than the condition a year ago.

The strategy is to estimate an ordered probit, described in the annex to chapter 3, using industry dummy variables and the demographic characteristics that were included in the wage differential analysis. The main concern about this approach is the ranking of the responses. In particular, "better" than a very bad situation a year ago is not necessarily "better" than "just as good" as a year ago. A more complete analysis of the comparison of these choices would be relevant for future research. Here, however, it is useful to apply these given categories under the possibly contestable assumption that the given ordering is meaningful. The years 1998–2004 are pooled and a linear time trend is included to control for overall changes in attitude.

Table 7.9 contains the ordered probit estimates. All of the industry coefficient estimates represent the difference between that industry and the textiles, apparel, and leather sector. Positive coefficients suggest that workers in that sector were more likely to respond with a higher ranking than workers in the textiles, apparel, and leather industry, and is interpreted to suggest that conditions in that industry are better than in the textiles, apparel, and leather industry. Although the ordering is certainly subject to discussion, the overall results seem sensible. For example, relative to textiles, apparel, and leather, agriculture workers are much more likely to rank "income" lower. Workers in FIRE are much more likely to rank facilities higher. Construction workers and mining workers are more likely to rank safety lower than textiles, apparel, and leather workers. Of some interest is that workers in the other manufacturing sector rank conditions in their industries above textiles, apparel, and leather in every dimension, and the differences are statistically significant in all but one dimension (safety). These results suggest that conditions are better in other manufacturing sectors than in agriculture.

TABLE 7.9 **Ordered Probit Estimation of Working Conditions**

Sector	(1) Income	(2) Facilities	(3) Medical benefits	(4) Safety	(5) Transport	(6) Overall
Food agriculture	−0.204 (0.000)**	−0.528 (0.000)**	−0.395 (0.000)**	−0.419 (0.000)**	−0.169 (0.000)**	−0.285 (0.000)**
Other agriculture	−0.046 (0.003)**	−0.254 (0.000)**	−0.179 (0.000)**	−0.233 (0.000)**	−0.053 (0.001)**	−0.099 (0.000)**
Mining and quarrying	0.096 (0.000)**	−0.151 (0.000)**	−0.110 (0.000)**	−0.095 (0.000)**	0.138 (0.000)**	0.018 (0.437)
Food, beverages, and tobacco	0.072 (0.000)**	0.042 (0.011)*	0.055 (0.000)**	0.039 (0.014)*	0.039 (0.012)*	0.069 (0.000)**
Wood	0.046 (0.005)**	−0.035 (0.047)*	−0.081 (0.000)**	−0.072 (0.000)**	−0.010 (0.540)	−0.004 (0.812)
Other manufacturing	0.065 (0.000)**	0.042 (0.002)**	0.033 (0.012)*	0.014 (0.287)	0.041 (0.002)**	0.071 (0.000)**
Electric, gas, water	0.131 (0.000)**	0.104 (0.006)**	0.144 (0.000)**	0.132 (0.000)**	0.187 (0.000)**	0.163 (0.000)**
Construction	−0.074 (0.000)**	−0.362 (0.000)**	−0.446 (0.000)**	−0.404 (0.000)**	−0.069 (0.000)**	−0.146 (0.000)**
Retail, wholesale, hotels	−0.005 (0.690)	0.018 (0.152)	−0.155 (0.000)**	−0.157 (0.000)**	0.009 (0.474)	0.033 (0.008)**
Transportation, storage, communications	−0.028 (0.048)*	−0.058 (0.000)**	−0.102 (0.000)**	−0.107 (0.000)**	0.152 (0.000)**	0.018 (0.237)
FIRE and business services	0.163 (0.000)**	0.214 (0.000)**	0.152 (0.000)**	0.093 (0.000)**	0.180 (0.000)**	0.210 (0.000)**
Public administration	0.242 (0.000)**	0.214 (0.000)**	0.170 (0.000)**	0.041 (0.002)**	0.197 (0.000)**	0.232 (0.000)**
Other services	−0.004 (0.760)	0.039 (0.003)**	−0.066 (0.000)**	−0.123 (0.000)**	−0.032 (0.008)**	0.047 (0.000)**
Linear time trend	0.051 (0.000)**	0.011 (0.000)**	−0.006 (0.000)**	−0.005 (0.000)**	−0.020 (0.000)**	0.045 (0.000)**
Female	−0.005 (0.431)	0.044 (0.000)**	0.030 (0.000)**	0.009 (0.136)	−0.050 (0.000)**	0.023 (0.000)**
Observations	186,937	186,937	186,937	186,937	186,937	186,937

SOURCE: Authors' calculations using SAKERNAS.

NOTE: Standard errors in parentheses.

* significant at the 5 percent level.

** significant at the 1 percent level.

One concern is whether the wage differentials analyzed earlier represent compensating differentials. That is, are wages higher in textiles, apparel, and leather to compensate workers for worse conditions? If wages compensate workers for poor working conditions across industries, the correlation between wage differentials and the estimates in table 7.9 would be negative. Conversely, wage differentials may be positively correlated with working conditions, suggesting that wages may not be a poor proxy for overall working conditions.

Table 7.10 contains the comparison of the ordered probit coefficients in the "overall" column of table 7.9 and the estimated IIWDs (both numbers relative to textiles, apparel, and leather). This comparison yields two main results. First, in general, the numbers seem to be positively correlated, with an overall correlation coefficient of 0.443. The correlation between wage differentials (estimated coefficients) and every measure of working conditions is positive, ranging from just under 0.25 for facilities to over 0.70 for transportation. This result suggests that, in fact, wage differentials are positively correlated with working conditions and that higher wages do not serve as compensating differentials in Indonesia.

The second, relatively minor, result is that there is some evidence that wages do compensate for adverse conditions within manufacturing. In particular, wages in textiles, apparel, and leather are higher than in food, beverages, and tobacco (table 7.6), but working conditions are worse (table 7.7). In the other manufacturing sector, however, working conditions and wages are both higher than in textiles, apparel, and leather; but these differences are small relative to the overall strong positive correlation between wages and working conditions. This result is also similar to those obtained in the studies of El Salvador, Cambodia, and Madagascar in that they all found relatively better conditions in high-wage industries characterized by foreign investment.

Manufacturing industries that have expanded (textiles, apparel, and leather and other manufacturing) have much higher wages and much better working conditions than food agriculture. To

TABLE 7.10 **Comparison of Wages and Working Conditions**

Sector		Wages	Working conditions
1	Food agriculture	−0.230	−0.285
2	Other agriculture	−0.070	−0.099
3	Mining and quarrying	0.323	0.018
4	Food, beverages, and tobacco	−0.136	0.069
5	Wood	−0.014	−0.004
6	Other manufacturing	0.030	0.071
7	Electric, gas, water	0.145	0.163
8	Construction	0.002	−0.146
9	Retail, wholesale, hotels	−0.172	0.033
10	Transportation, storage, communications	−0.021	0.018
11	FIRE and business services	0.130	0.210
12	Public administration	0.135	0.232
13	Services (private)	−0.357	0.047

SOURCE: Authors' calculations using SAKERNAS.

NOTE: The simple correlation between the two series is 0.443. The correlation of the ranks is 0.450. Eight of the 13 signs agree.

the extent that export-oriented FDI induced a shift out of agriculture into these industries, no evidence supports the hypothesis that globalization has made working conditions worse for Indonesian workers. On the contrary, it seems likely that conditions improved for workers who changed industries, as supported by the results of the comparison of changes in wage differentials with approved FDI.

Conclusions

This chapter focuses on two specific aspects of working conditions: interindustry wage differentials and qualitative measures of working conditions. The chapter finds that reform policies successfully attracted export-oriented foreign investment, and the resulting investment concentrated in a limited number of manufacturing sectors. As FDI increased, the employment shares and IIWDs in these industries increased relative to other manufacturing sectors and, most important, relative to agriculture. An analysis of working conditions in these sectors suggests that conditions in the expanding sectors are better than in agriculture, which is often the relevant alternative for many Indonesian workers. When the Asian financial crisis hit, these results reversed: as FDI fell, wages in FDI-linked sectors fell and the share of employment in agriculture rose. Overall, these results are consistent with the hypothesis that FDI and liberalization contributed to a shift in workers from low-wage, poor-condition sectors to high-wage sectors with better conditions.

Notes

1. According to Pangestu (1996), the new government in 1960 implemented liberalization reforms. The first phase was between 1966 and 1972. During this period, Law 1/1967 on Foreign Investment was passed, marking the beginning of the Indonesian investment regime. While the law was intended to attract foreign investors, it was still viewed as having too many restrictions. In addition to prohibiting foreign capital to enter several strategic and basic industries, foreign capital did not receive the same treatment as domestic capital in many cases. Import licensing was dismantled and a new "export bonus" scheme was introduced. In 1970, the government introduced a major trade policy package that included simplification of exports and import procedures. The elimination of international capital controls marked an important change in Indonesia's capital account policy (Aswicahyono and Feridhanusetyawan 2003). In the second phase, from 1973 to 1981, the government received great windfall profits from the oil boom. The government was unwilling to institute further trade liberalization reforms because its own increased foreign exchange reserves could be used to finance development. The protective regime emphasized self-supply domestic consumption by adopting an import-substitution policy.

2. The Association of East Asian Nations (ASEAN) began moving toward the ASEAN Free Trade Area (AFTA) at the fourth ASEAN summit in Singapore in January 1992. When the AFTA agreement was originally signed, ASEAN had six members (Brunei, Indonesia, Malaysia, the Philippines, Singapore, and Thailand). Four countries subsequently joined: Vietnam (1995), the Lao People's Democratic Republic (1997), Myanmar (1997), and Cambodia (1999).

3. These falling tariffs seem to be broad-based. Fane and Condon (1996) use real effective rates of protection (RERP) to quantify Indonesian trade liberalization between 1987 and 1995. The RERP for manufacturing, including oil refining, fell from 27 percent in 1987 to 11 percent

in 1995, and from 59 percent to 16 percent, excluding oil refining. For agriculture, RERP fell from 9 percent to 4 percent over the same period.

4. Here "foreign" is defined as in the BPS-Statistics Indonesia manufacturing surveys, that is, any establishment with foreign equity, either wholly foreign owned or in joint venture with domestic private or government firms.

5. The workers included in figure 7.5 are all those included in the survey, regardless of earnings. Many of the workers in agriculture are not formally remunerated.

6. The results presented here are robust to using monthly earnings (not adjusted for hours) as the earnings variable. The correlation between differentials estimated with monthly earnings and differentials estimated with hourly earnings is above 0.9.

7. The percentage difference from the mean wage using the coefficient estimates in table 7.6 are obtained by raising the value e (about 2.7183) to the coefficient estimate and subtracting 1 because the estimated equation is log linear, implying a multiplicative relationship between the industry dummy variables and the intercept.

8. The analysis excludes 1995 and 1997 because of a lack of data for those years.

References

ADB (Asian Development Bank). 2006. *Key Indicators 2006: Measuring Policy Effectiveness in Health and Education.* Manila: Asian Development Bank. http://www.adb.org/Documents/ Books/Key_Indicators/2006/xls/INO.xls.

Amiti, Mary, and Jozaf Konings. 2005. "Trade Liberalization, Intermediate Inputs, and Productivity: Evidence from Indonesia." IMF Working Papers No. 05/146, International Monetary Fund, Washington, DC.

Arnold, Jens, and Beata Smarzynska Javorcik. 2005. "Gifted Kids or Pushy Parents? Foreign Acquisitions and Plant Performance in Indonesia." CEPR Discussion Paper No. 5065, Centre for Economic Policy Research, London.

Aswicahyono, H., and T. Feridhanusetyawan. 2003. "Indonesia's Strategy for Industrial Upgrading." Paper presented at the conference "Why Trade and Industry Policy Matters," Jakarta, January 14–15.

Aswicahyono, H., and I. Maidir. 2003. "Indonesia's Textiles and Apparels Industry: Taking a Stand in the New International Competition." Working Paper No. WPE064, Centre for Strategic and International Studies, Jakarta.

BPS (Badan Pusat Statistik). 2002. "Welfare Indicators." BPS-Indonesia.

———. 2006. "Statistik Indonesia." BPS-Indonesia.

Banerjee, S., and H. Siregar. 2002. *Agriculture as the Leading Sector: An Industrial Policy Framework.* Jakarta: UNSFIR.

Bank of Indonesia. 2007. Statistics. Jakarta. www.bi.go.id. Accesssed March 29, 2007.

BPS-Statistics Indonesia, Bappenas, and UNDP. 2001. *Towards a New Consensus: Democracy and Human Development in Indonesia.* Jakarta: UNDP.

Brown, Drusilla K. 2007. "Globalization and Employment Conditions Study." Social Protection Discussion Paper No. 0708, World Bank, Washington, DC.

Caraway, Teri L. 2004. "Protective Repression, International Pressure, and Institutional Design: Explaining Labor Reform in Indonesia." *Studies in Comparative International Development* 39 (3): 28–49.

Cox Edwards, Alejandra. 1996. "Labor Regulations and Industrial Relations in Indonesia." Policy Research Working Paper No. 1640, Poverty and Social Policy Department, World Bank, Washington, DC.

Fane, George, and Timothy Condon. 1996. "Trade Reform in Indonesia, 1987–95." *Bulletin of Indonesian Economic Studies* 32 (3): 33–54.

Gittleman, M., and E. Wolff. "International Comparisons of Inter-Industry Wage Differentials." *Review of Income and Wealth* 39 (3): 295–312.

Harrison, Ann, and Jason Scorse. 2004. "Moving Up or Moving Out? Anti-Sweatshop Activists and Labor Market Outcomes." NBER Working Paper No. 10492, National Bureau of Economic Research, Cambridge, MA

Helwege, J. 1992. "Sectoral Shifts and Inter-Industry Wage Differentials." *Journal of Labor Economics* 10 (1): 55–84.

Ismalina, P. 2002. "How to Sustain Indonesia's Economic Development through Export-Led Growth Strategy: Building Productive Capacity and Equal Economic Opportunity." Paper presented at conference Seminar Nasional "Peningkatan Daya Saing Ekspor Non-Migas" (Improving the export competitiveness of non-oil and gas) Dies Natalis ke-43 Fakultas Ekonomi Universitas Diponegoro in collaboration with Bank of Indonesia. Semarang, April 3.

Indonesia's Investment Coordination Board. 2006. Annual Report.

Katz, L. F., and L. H. Summers. 1989a. "Can Inter-Industry Wage Differentials Justify Strategic Trade Policy?" In *Trade Policies for International Competitiveness*, National Bureau of Economic Research Conference Report, ed. Robert C. Feenstra, 85–116. Chicago and London: University of Chicago Press.

———. 1989b. "Industry Rents: Evidence and Implications." *Brookings Papers On Economic Activity, Microeconomics*: 209–75.

Kaur, Amarjit. 2004. "Workers, Employment Relations, and Labour Standards in Industrialising Southeast Asia." In *Asia Examined: Proceedings of the 15th Biennial Conference of the ASAA*, ed. Robert Cribb. Canberra: The Australian National University.

Kühl, Bianca. 2003. "Social Standards in Indonesia: A Review of Existing Tools and Regulations." Occasional Papers, International Development Cooperation, Global Trade Union Program, Bonn.

Lipsey, Robert E., and Fredrik Sjoholm. 2004a. "FDI and Wage Spillovers in Indonesian Manufacturing." *Review of World Economics/Weltwirtschaftliches Archiv* 140 (2): 321–32.

———. 2004b. "Foreign Direct Investment, Education and Wages in Indonesian Manufacturing." *Journal of Development Economics* 73 (1): 415–22.

Manning, Chris. 1998. *Indonesian Labour in Transition: An East Asian Success Story?* Cambridge: Cambridge University Press.

———. 2000a. "Indonesian Labour Markets: Adjusting to Crisis and Slow Recovery." *Indian Journal of Labour Economics* 43 (3): 545–64.

———. 2000b. "Labour Market Adjustment to Indonesia's Economic Crisis: Context, Trends and Implications." *Bulletin of Indonesian Economic Studies* 36: 105–36.

————. 2003. "Labor Policy: Lessons from East Asia." In *The Impact of Trade on Labor: Issues, Perspectives, and Experiences from Developing Asia*, ed. R. Hasan and D. Mitra, 159–85. Amsterdam: North Holland/ Elsevier.

Pangestu, Mari. 1996. *Economic Reform, Deregulation and Privatization: The Indonesian Experience*. Jakarta: Centre for Strategic and International Studies.

Pangestu, Mari, and Medelina Hendytio. 1997. "Survey Responses from Women Workers in Indonesia's Textile, Garment, and Footwear Industries." Policy Research Working Paper No. 1755, World Bank, Washington, DC.

Papola, T., and W. Bharadwaj. 1970. "Dynamics of Industrial Wage Structure: An Inter-Country Analysis." *The Economic Journal* 80: 72–90.

Robertson, Raymond. 2007. "Globalization and Working Conditions: A Guideline for Country Studies." Unpublished, World Bank, Washington, DC.

Sjoholm, Fredrik, and Robert E. Lipsey. 2006. "Foreign Firms and Indonesian Manufacturing Wages: An Analysis with Panel Data." *Economic Development and Cultural Change* 55 (1): 201–21.

Suryahadi, Asep. 1999. "Wage Inequality between Skilled and Unskilled Labor in Indonesian Manufacturing." *Economics and Finance in Indonesia* 47: 271–88.

————. 2003. "International Economic Integration and Labor Markets: The Case of Indonesia." In *The Impact of Trade on Labor: Issues, Perspectives, and Experiences from Developing Asia*, ed. R. Hasan and D. Mitra, 275–302. Amsterdam: North Holland/ Elsevier.

Suryahadi, Asep, P. Chen, and R. Tyers. 1999. "Openness, Technological Change, and Labor Demand in Pre-Crisis Indonesia." Working Papers in Economics and Econometrics No. 377, Australian National University, Canberra.

Tobing, E. 1993. *Masalah struktural peningkatan kesempatan kerja*. Jakarta: Bisnis Indonesia.

UNCTAD. 2003. *World Investment Report 2003-FDI Policies for Development: National and International Perspective*. New York and Geneva: UNCTAD.

UNIDO. 1997. *Annual Report*. Geneva and New York: United Nations Industrial Development Organisation.

WITS/TRAINS. 2003. Database on International Trade and Tariffs. UNCTAD, World Bank, Geneva, and Washington, DC.

World Bank. 1996. "Indonesia Dimensions of Growth." Report No. 15383-IND, World Bank, Washington, DC.

————. 2005. *Doing Business in 2005: Removing Obstacles to Growth*. Washington, DC: World Bank.

World Bank and the International Finance Corporation. 2006. *Doing Business in 2006: Creating Jobs*. Washington, DC: World Bank.

————. 2007. *Doing Business in 2007: How to Reform*. Washington DC: World Bank.

WTO (World Trade Organization). 2003. "Trade Policy Review: Indonesia." Report by the Secretariat, WT/TPR/S/117, Geneva.

CHAPTER 8

Export Processing Zones in Madagascar: The Impact of the Dismantling of Clothing Quotas on Employment and Labor Standards

Jean-Pierre Cling, Mireille Razafindrakoto, and François Roubaud

Any description of Madagascar's globalization experience must focus on export processing zones (EPZs), known as Zone Franche in Madagascar. While EPZs play a prominent role in other countries in this book, such as Honduras and El Salvador, the predominance of EPZs in Madagascar distinguish it from the rest of Africa. With the possible exception of Mauritius, there is no other African country in which EPZs play a more significant role. The Zone Franche has had a significant macroeconomic impact on both exports and jobs, and, as in the other countries in this book, these exports and jobs are primarily concentrated in the apparel sector. The growth of the EPZs helped Madagascar become the second largest clothing exporter in Sub-Saharan Africa. At its peak in 2004, the Zone Franche employed 100,000 employees, but the final phase-out of the Multifibre Arrangement (MFA) in 2005 had a negative impact. Export and employment growth have come to a halt, and the econometric estimates presented in this chapter indicate that average wages in the Zone Franche have become lower than in the formal industrial sector, other things being equal; other labor standards are higher than average but are progressively being reduced in a context of increased international competition. As the example of Madagascar shows, the end of the MFA's clothing quotas meant that EPZs can no longer be placed at the core of development and employment policies in Africa, although no alternative strategy has yet emerged.

In a purely economic sense, globalization is usually defined as a process of simultaneous expansion of international trade and financial flows, as well as flows of production factors (capital through foreign direct investment [FDI]; labor through migrations). Within this process, the production of labor-intensive goods has gradually shifted to developing countries, which export these products worldwide. Globalization, therefore, increases competition between developing countries for attracting FDI, especially for manufacture of consumer goods. Facing this competition, some developing countries have tried to increase their competitiveness by providing tax holidays for investors establishing operations in EPZs.

According to the International Labour Organization (ILO), total employment in EPZs worldwide, excluding China, amounted to 26 million in 2006 (Singa Boyenge 2007). EPZs are mostly established in developing countries and generally specialize in the production of labor-intensive consumer goods, mainly clothing. As pointed out by

Jayanthakumaran (2003), over the decades until 2005, investment in these zones served to circumvent textiles quotas imposed on Asian exports by the MFA.

Most of the economic debate on EPZs focuses on the question of labor standards. Following international conventions set by the ILO, labor standards are defined here as including all aspects of wages, working conditions, and labor markets (trade unions, discrimination, and so forth). Indeed, the main motivation for investing in EPZs is to minimize the costs of producing labor-intensive consumer goods, thanks to the combination of tax exemptions and low wages. Because of these characteristics, foreign firms in EPZs have often been accused (especially by labor unions) of being "sweatshops" exploiting a low-paid, unskilled labor force and eventually encouraging a "race to the bottom" in labor standards.

Many studies have compared wages paid by firms in EPZs with the rest of the economy. These studies all agree that the situation varies enormously from one country and sector to the next. Limiting the study to the textiles and clothing sector, Romero (1995) and Kusago and Tzannatos (1998) conclude there are no significant differences between the wages paid by firms in Asian EPZs and those paid by other companies in the same sector. Economic literature on the subject suggests that because most of the labor is female, low average wages can be explained by women's low skills and the wage discrimination generally suffered by women, without firms in EPZs appearing to practice a systematic policy of specific remuneration for given jobs (Madani 1999). However, none of the abovementioned studies is based on individual wage data, but on average sector wages.[1]

The studies agree that firms in EPZs do not practice specific wage discrimination—their poor image stems mainly from the fact that working conditions are generally deemed harder than in other economic sectors. EPZ factories are often accused of violating core labor standards (ILO 2003; ICFTU 2003); labor legislation is not applied as strictly as elsewhere, and sometimes not at all; working hours are longer and the pace of work is faster; trade unions are often discouraged or forbidden; and gender discrimination is worse than in the rest of the economy.

Madagascar is one of only two examples, alongside Mauritius (and Kenya since the beginning of the 2000s, but on a smaller scale), of significant EPZ success in Sub-Saharan Africa, where all other free zone initiatives have failed despite numerous attempts. The example of Mauritius is well known, but not so the Malagasy EPZs, otherwise known as the Zone Franche.[2] The Zone Franche developed quite remarkably in just one decade: it has gained considerable ground in exports and formal employment, making a significant contribution to the economic upturn observed in Madagascar since the mid-1990s.

The objective of this chapter is to determine whether the characteristics of labor standards generally observed in the rest of the world hold in the case of the Malagasy Zone Franche. The study draws on some national statistical sources with no other equivalent in Sub-Saharan Africa: labor force surveys (LFSs) conducted annually at the authors' initiative since 1995 in the Malagasy capital of Antananarivo, where most Zone Franche companies are located. To the authors' knowledge, this is the first study to make an assessment of the impact on African labor markets of the dismantling of international clothing quotas (the MFA) using econometric estimates based on individual wage data.[3]

The first section describes the Zone Franche's booming growth up to 2005 (temporarily interrupted by the political crisis in 2002) and its difficulties since the end of the MFA, and assesses its contribution to the country's performance in exports and employment. The second section briefly reviews the evolution of regulations and ILO conventions affecting working conditions in Madagascar. The third section analyzes the Zone Franche's impact on earned income using estimated earnings equations to compare wages paid in Zone Franche companies with other sectors of the economy. The fourth section compares Zone Franche working conditions and other labor standards with those in other companies. The final section provides conclusions.

Globalization in Madagascar: The Growth of the Zone Franche

The introduction of a special scheme for free-zone companies in Madagascar in 1990 followed the government's decision to opt for an export-led growth strategy under the structural adjustment policies adopted in the late 1980s in compliance with Bretton Woods Institution recommendations. Generous tax breaks, combined with low wages and trade preferences granted on the U.S. and European Union (EU) markets, triggered strong and continuous growth of the Malagasy Zone Franche. According to the Zone Franche association, 180 firms were in business, employing more than 100,000 workers at the end of 2004. However, this boom was interrupted by the final dismantling of the quotas on clothing products at the beginning of 2005.

A COMBINATION OF TAX BREAKS, LOW LABOR COSTS, AND TRADE PREFERENCES

Legislation enacted in 1991 defined the scheme's scope and the tax incentives granted to Zone Franche companies, which are under no obligation to set up in specific geographic areas. Companies wishing to be part of the free zone scheme must intend to export at least 95 percent of their production. Companies providing services to the Zone Franche can also benefit from the free zone scheme.

Zone Franche companies are exempt from all duties and taxes on exports and imports alike. They are also exempt from domestic excise taxes, but have been liable for value added tax (VAT) on imported inputs since 1997, although VAT payments can be refunded at a later date against proof of export. The VAT measure was introduced to curb tax evasion and prevent companies supplying the local market from setting up as Zone Franche companies. The Zone Franche scheme grants total exemption from taxes on profits for an initial grace period of two years for labor-intensive farming and fishing companies and four years for industrial and services companies. These companies become liable for a fixed rate of 10 percent thereafter, which is far lower than the general rate of 35 percent. They are also eligible for profits tax breaks equal to 75 percent of the cost of new investments. Last, Zone Franche companies are granted special access to foreign currency and total freedom for capital transfers.

The success of the Zone Franche was initially due to French investors attracted by a French-speaking environment, where a large number of their compatriots had already set up business (Madagascar has the largest French community in Sub-Saharan Africa). Investors gradually became more diverse. No recent precise breakdown of the country origin of investors is available. Most of them are French, Mauritian (Madagascar's next door neighbor), or Asian.[4]

Investors sought primarily to take advantage of low labor costs in Madagascar. Cadot and Nasir (2001) report that the monthly wage for an unskilled textiles industry machine operator is less than one-third of the equivalent wage in Mauritius, around half that in China, and only about 60 percent of the average wage in India. Although labor productivity is apparently much lower in Madagascar than in Mauritius or China (and equal to that in India), unit production costs are among the lowest in the world and lower than in the other three countries.

Because many Asian countries had already saturated their quotas under the MFA, producing in Madagascar also helped circumvent the textiles quotas imposed by developed countries under the MFA. Hence, the Central Bank of Madagascar (Banque central de Madagascar 2002) reported that clothing accounted for 90 percent of the Zone Franche's production in 2001. Madagascar enjoys duty-free access to the European and U.S. markets.

Madagascar has been AGOA (African Growth and Opportunity Act) eligible since 2001. AGOA, launched in 2000 toward African countries, is a unilateral U.S. initiative that authorizes duty-free access to the U.S. market for the products it covers, subject to quotas. Starting in 1997–98, investments were made in the Zone Franche in anticipation of AGOA (Gibbon 2003). However, AGOA imposes restrictive conditions on inputs ("third-party fabric provision"), which must come either from the United States or other countries benefiting from the agreement (Mattoo, Roy, and Subramanian 2003). This provision excludes Asian fabrics, which are much cheaper than fabrics from Africa or the United States. However, Madagascar was granted a dispensation within AGOA for its clothing sector to use inputs from other countries. In 2006, this was extended through 2012.

Madagascar also benefits from tax-free and quota-free access to the European market under the terms of the Cotonou Agreement signed in 2000 between the EU and the ACP (Africa-Caribbean-Pacific) States and, since 1999, under the Everything But Arms (EBA) initiative covering all LDCs (least developed countries). Under the Cotonou Agreement, the rules of origin are as strict as under AGOA, but without any dispensation for third-party imports (and even stricter for EBA); this greatly reduces the benefits of this agreement for clothing exports.

Clothing exports are concentrated toward the U.S. and European markets, which are the top two markets worldwide for these products. Although trade preferences played an important role in the success of the Zone Franche, these preferences would not have been taken advantage of had it not been for the tax breaks granted under the Zone Franche scheme. Zone Franche managers interviewed by several surveys clearly state that they would not have invested in Madagascar had it not been for these tax advantages (Cadot and Nasir 2001; Razafindrakoto and Roubaud 2002).[5]

REMARKABLE EXPORT GROWTH

Starting from negligible amounts at the beginning of the 1990s, growth in Zone Franche exports has been remarkable[6] (figure 8.1). Sales to the U.S. market, which were marginal until 2000, drove growth over the next few years until 2005 as a result of AGOA. In 2006, the European Union and the United States absorbed half of the Zone Franche exports each. The share of the Zone Franche in total exports rose steadily to reach nearly 50 percent in 2005–06, a proportion unequalled in any other LDC.

FIGURE 8.1 **Malagasy Exports, 1995–2006 (US$ millions)**

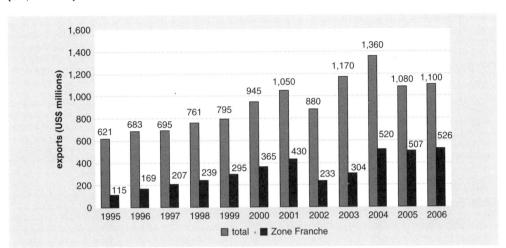

SOURCES: International Trade Centre PC-TAS database for total exports; Eurostat and U.S. Department of Commerce Office of Textiles and Apparel for Zone Franche exports (clothing products).

The Zone Franche accounted for most of the boom in Madagascar's goods exports from 1995 to 2006. The Zone Franche made Madagascar the only successful new African exporter of manufactured goods, except Lesotho, in that period. The breakdown of exports changed considerably with export growth (Cling, Razafindrakoto, and Roubaud 2005). At the beginning of the 1990s, Madagascar exported almost exclusively agricultural products (mainly coffee, vanilla, cloves, and shrimp). The share of these products subsequently fell to less than half of total exports. Conversely, the share of manufactured products was negligible at the beginning of the period, but grew steadily to half of total exports. This growth consisted mainly of exports of clothing products, that is, exports from the Zone Franche. Although the total amount (US$500 million in 2006) might seem relatively modest by world standards, by 2001 Madagascar had become the second largest clothing exporter in Sub-Saharan Africa behind Mauritius, and it still held that position in 2006.

The Malagasy economy was hard-hit by the 2002 political crisis, which took a heavy toll on Zone Franche companies. Missed contract deadlines resulting from the crisis prompted international buyers to cancel their orders and, given the political instability, turn to more reliable suppliers. Foreign trade figures show the Zone Franche's extreme vulnerability to the crisis and its remarkable responsiveness once the crisis was over. Total clothing exports were practically halved in 2002 but climbed back up in 2003 and topped precrisis levels in 2004. However, some companies that had shifted their textiles production facilities to Madagascar for export to the United States or the European Union did not return after the crisis.

As shown in figure 8.1, Zone Franche export growth came to a halt in 2005, with the end of the MFA and the quotas imposed on Asian exports of clothing products. This situation is far from unique: although the United States and the European Union almost immediately imposed new temporary quotas on China's exports of textiles and clothing products through the end of 2008, exports from China continued to swell, while exports from most other developing countries stagnated or decreased. All major African exporters such as Mauritius, Madagascar, Lesotho, and Kenya (table 8.1) exemplify this dormancy.

TABLE 8.1 **Clothing Exports of Major African Exporters Compared with Selected Asian Countries, 2003–06**
(US$ millions)

Country and export destination	2003	2004	2005	2006	Change, 2004 to 2006 (%)
Mauritius					
Total	896	865	712	721	−16.6
European Union	627	638	555	602	
United States	269	227	167	119	
Madagascar					
Total	347	520	506	526	1.2
European Union	151	197	229	288	
United States	196	323	277	238	
Lesotho					
Total	394	457	392	388	−15.1
European Union	1	1	1	1	
United States	393	456	391	387	
Kenya					
Total	192	280	278	265	−5.4
European Union	4	3	7	1	
United States	188	277	271	264	
China					
Total	23,970	28,288	45,365	49,981	76.7
European Union	12,361	13,730	22,960	22,974	
United States	11,609	14,558	22,405	27,067	
Vietnam	3,115	3,478	3,793	4,611	32.6
Total	631	758	912	1,215	
European Union	2,484	2,720	2,881	3,396	
United States					
Cambodia					
Total	1,726	2,085	2,319	2,841	36.3
European Union	475	643	592	690	
United States	1,251	1,442	1,727	2,151	

SOURCES: Office of Textiles and Apparel of the US Department of Commerce (US) and Eurostat (EU).

NOTE: Total is total exports to the European Union and the United States.

A MAJOR CONTRIBUTION TO JOB CREATION

The labor force surveys used in this study correspond to the first phase of the *1-2-3 surveys,* which also cover the informal sector (second phase) and consumption (third phase) and have been conducted in a number of developing countries in Africa and Latin America (Razafindrakoto and Roubaud 2003). This system of household surveys was introduced in Madagascar in 1995 (Rakotomanana, Ramilison, and Roubaud 2003). The National Statistical Office of Madagascar has repeated the operation every year since then. The sample, drawn from a stratified, two-stage, area-based survey plan, is representative of all ordinary households in Antananarivo. In each household, all individuals age 10 and over—all individuals of working age as defined by the official nomenclature—were asked about their labor market participation. The definitions used (employment, unemployment, and so forth) observed the international standards recommended by the ILO. In addition to the general purpose of analyzing labor market dynamics, one of the strong points of the Malagasy survey is that the questionnaire includes a specific question to single out employment in the Zone Franche (Razafindrakoto and Roubaud 1997).

The LFSs confirm the Zone Franche's exceptional buoyancy. From 1995 through 2004 (that is, until the end of the MFA), the rate of job creation in the Zone Franche was almost four times higher than in Antananarivo's labor market as a whole. The average annual employment growth rate exceeded 15 percent compared with less than 4 percent for the market as a whole (table 8.2). This is by far the best performance among all sectors. Even though the informal sector is the main job provider, it is far behind in the job growth rate. Over the period 1995–2001 (before the political crisis), the Zone Franche's contribution to job creation was as strong as that of the informal sector. The contribution is still significant for the period 1995–2004: of a total 195,000 new jobs, 65 percent could be attributed to the informal sector whereas the Zone Franche generated 62 percent of the new jobs in the formal sector, tripling its share of total employment from an initial 3 percent to 9 percent in 2005. In the formal private sector, nearly one-third of all employees worked in the Zone Franche in 2004 compared with barely 1 in 10 in 1995. There were more women employed in the Zone Franche than in the rest of the formal private sector in 2004.

As with the foreign trade statistics, the employment data highlight that the Zone Franche was extremely vulnerable to the political crisis in 2002. Employment fell by 60 percent, wiping out in one fell swoop the huge progress made in previous years. The informal sector acted as a safety net for employees who had been made redundant and for new arrivals. The number of jobs in the informal sector grew by 12 percent. As with exports, employment in the Zone Franche quickly recovered and in 2004 almost reached precrisis levels. Between 2004 and 2006, employment decreased by 6 percent.

Labor Law and Working Conditions

The focus of this chapter is on wages and working conditions in Madagascar's Zone Franche, which are a function of conditions in Madagascar generally and deviations from these conditions that appear in the Zone Franche. This section describes labor law and working conditions generally in Madagascar to provide a point of comparison and reference for understanding conditions within the Zone Franche.

TABLE 8.2 **Change in the Employment Breakdown by Institutional Sector in Antananarivo, 1995–2006 (percent)**

Sector	Growth period (1995–2001)				Crisis period (2001–02)		Recovery period (2002–04)		Growth period (1995–2004)				End of quotas (2004–06)	
	Average annual growth rate 1995–2001	Contribution 1995–2001	Structure 1995	Structure 2001	Growth rate 2001–02	Structure 2002	Growth rate 2002–04	Structure 2004	Average annual growth rate 1995–2004	Contribution 1995–2004	Structure 1995	Structure 2004	Growth rate 2004–2006	Structure 2006
Public administrations	-1.4	-3	11.6	8.1	2.3	8.3	11.0	8.3	0.4	1	11.6	8.3	-3.9	7.5
Public companies	4.1	2	2.7	2.6	7.1	2.8	-12.4	2.2	1.8	1	2.7	2.2	-39.1	1.3
Formal private companies	9.1	61	26.7	34.6	-20.0	33.0	25.9	30.0	5.0	37	28.1	30.0	10.3	31.4
Zone Franche	27.2	34	3.1	10.2	-60.0	4.1	146.5	9.0	15.4	22	3.1	9.0	-6.0	8.0
Informal private companies	3.1	38	57.6	53.1	12.2	59.9	9.7	58.4	4.0	65	57.6	58.4	4.5	58.0
Total	4.5	100	100	100	-0.4	100	12.3	100	3.8	100	100	100	2.6	100

SOURCE: Authors' calculations based on INSTAT/MADIO's 1-2-3 Surveys, phase 1 (employment), 1995–2006.

Labor law in Madagascar shows nominal adherence to international labor standards: all eight of the ILO conventions regarding the core labor standards[7] have been ratified, and the Constitution promises freedom of association and collective bargaining, and freedom from child labor, forced labor, and discrimination. These rights, however, may be taken away by decree, and institutions to oversee the protection of many basic rights are nonexistent; for instance, discrimination is condemned by Malagasy law, ratified ILO conventions, and the Malagasy Constitution, but no agency exists to handle charges of discrimination (ITUC 2008). The Zone Franche adds a layer of complexity to the legal framework by allowing for differing tax rates and lower wages (ITUC 2008).

The ITUC (2008) report for the ILO on core labor standards in Madagascar suggests that the Malagasy government is violating all four of the ILO's core labor standards, either by neglect or by conflicting law, both inside and outside the Zone Franche. The results of these violations are discrimination, sexual harassment, child labor, decreased ability to form and maintain unions, human trafficking, and forced labor. Because the government was paralyzed by the political crisis in 2002, and the recovery has been slow, it is possible that government resources and organization are insufficient to cope with the problems facing Madagascar's workers; however, this does not explain the legal framework that allows for violations of the ILO core labor standards.

RATIFICATION OF ILO CONVENTIONS

There were three main waves of adherence to ILO core conventions. The first came in the 1960s, the second around 2000, and the third in 2007. Each of the three waves is separated from the others by economic, social, and political changes. Table 8.3 contains

TABLE 8.3 **ILO Conventions Ratified by Madagascar**

Number	Description	Date ratified
14	Weekly Rest (Industry) Convention	November 1960
29	Forced Labour Convention	November 1960
81	Labour Inspection Convention	December 1971
87	Freedom of Association and Protection of Right to Organise Convention	November 1960
95	Protection of Wages Convention	November 1960
97	Migration for Employment Convention (Revised)	June 2001
98	Right to Organise and Collective Bargaining Convention	June 1998
100	Equal Remuneration Convention	August 1962
105	Abolition of Forced Labour Convention	June 2007
111	Discrimination (Employment and Occupation) Convention	August 1961
118	Equality of Treatment (Social Security) Convention	June 1964

(continued)

TABLE 8.3 (continued)

Number	Description	Date ratified
120	Hygiene (Commerce and Offices) Convention	November 1966
122	Employment Policy Convention	November 1966
124	Medical Examination of Young Persons (Underground Work) Convention	October 1967
129	Labour Inspection (Agriculture) Convention	December 1971
138	Minimum Age Convention	May 2000
144	Tripartite Consultation (International Labour Standards) Convention	April 1997
159	Vocational Rehabilitation and Employment (Disabled Persons) Convention	June 1998
173	Protection of Workers' Claims (Employer's Insurance) Convention	June 1998
182	Worst Forms of Child Labour Convention	October 2001
185	Seafarers' Identity Documents Convention (Revised)	June 2007

SOURCE: International Labor Organization.

the ILO conventions ratified by Madagascar. Like the other countries in this volume, Madagascar has adopted many of the ILO labor conventions; and like El Salvador, ratification has continued into the last several years.

The first wave began in 1960, the year that Madagascar formally declared independence. ILO conventions 87 (Freedom of Association and Collective Bargaining) and 29 (Forced or Compulsory Labor) were ratified in late 1960. In 1961, Madagascar ratified Convention 111 (Discrimination in Occupation and Employment), and in 1962 Convention 100 (Equal Remuneration for Work of Equal Value) was ratified.

Madagascar established Zone Franche in 1990, but experienced stagnant growth through 1996, prompting structural reforms. This may have sparked the second wave of ratifications, which began in 1998, when Convention 98 (Right to Organise and Collective Bargaining) was ratified. In 2000, Convention 138 (Minimum Age for Admission to Employment) was ratified, and in 2001 Convention 182 (Worst Forms of Child Labor) was ratified. Madagascar's political crisis and slow recovery occurred following the second wave of ratifications. Convention 105 (Abolition of Forced Labor) was ratified in 2007.

WORKING CONDITIONS IN MADAGASCAR

Madagascar ratified ILO conventions on each of the four core labor standards but has devoted few or no resources to enforcement of the labor standards, either inside or outside of the Zone Franche. For forced labor and child labor, it seems that Madagascar either lacks the necessary resources to combat the problem, or is unwilling to devote sufficient resources. A U.S. Bureau of International Labor Affairs report from 2002 suggests that Madagascar had made efforts to educate children and reintegrate them into the education system, but did not have enough trained inspectors to handle reports of child labor. Furthermore, "where violations are found, the fines reportedly are low, and employers are not jailed" (U.S. Bureau of International Labor Affairs 2002, Madagascar Country Profile http://www.dol.gov/ILAB/media/reports/iclp/TDA2001/madagascar.htm).

There are two main sources of forced labor: human trafficking and prison labor. Children are the primary targets of trafficking, most working as prostitutes or domestic servants, or in the southern mining regions; women are also trafficked to other countries. ITUC (2008, 8) suggests that "human traffickers enjoy a high level of impunity," and notes that there have been no recent arrests, suggesting that the trend the Bureau of International Labor Affairs noticed in 2001 has continued. In 2006, the Malagasy government abolished the use of forced labor for prison inmates (U.S. Department of State 2006), excepting those condemned to forced labor, although the ITUC report suggests that the government is still tolerant of the practice.[8]

Discrimination is prohibited in all forms by the Malagasy Constitution. High levels of sexual harassment, however, are reported, with higher levels in the Zone Franche. Provisions in the January 2008 export processing zone law pertaining to work undertaken within the Zone Franche are discriminatory to migrant workers, allowing lower wages and social security coverage (ITUC 2008).

Freedom of association and collective bargaining are theoretically ensured by the Malagasy Constitution, but are limited by the legal code; specifically, workers in essential services (including the military and the police) are prohibited from forming unions, and seafarers are not covered by the law at all. Despite the fact that, "registration [of unions] was granted routinely," the U.S. Department of State (2006) quotes the Ministry of Civil Services and Labor and estimates that only 14 percent of workers in Zone Franche companies and 10 percent of workers in the rest of Madagascar are unionized. The U.S. Department of State (2006) also notes that "before resorting to a strike, the law calls for workers to exhaust all other options."

The seeming conflict between legal protections and possibly low enforcement raises the question of how wages and working conditions in the Zone Franche compare with the rest of the country. This question can only be addressed with empirical analysis. The next section, therefore, provides an empirical analysis of a unique data set of wages and working conditions in and out of the Zone Franche.

Empirical Analysis of Remuneration in the Zone Franche

There are usually two ways of comparing wages across the different sectors of the economy: comparing overall wages by sector, and comparing averages controlling for socio-demographic characteristics. This section uses both methods:

- A simple comparison of wages paid across all sectors of activity shows that wages in the Zone Franche are lower than in the rest of the economy, especially compared with the formal industrial sector.

- To go further and to check structural effects resulting from the composition of the labor force, some econometric wage equations are also estimated.

WAGES IN THE ZONE FRANCHE ARE LOWER ON AVERAGE

The LFS data clearly show the structural weakness of wages in the Zone Franche (table 8.4). Not only was the average monthly wage 34 percent lower than that paid

TABLE 8.4 **Labor Force Characteristics in the Zone Franche Compared with the Other Sectors, Antananarivo, 2006**

Indicator	Public sector	Formal private sector, total	Formal private sector, industrial, excluding Zone Franche	Zone Franche	Informal sector	Average
Monthly income (US$)	95	57	61	40	33	46
Hours worked per week	44.0	48.0	47.5	53.9	44.0	45.6
% women	35.5	43.9	31.8	70.5	50.6	47.0
% managerial staff	34.5	11.4	10.8	6.8	0.2	7.0
% trade union presence	44.4	25.0	26.4	54.6	0.2	12.4
Years of schooling	11.8	9.2	9.0	7.6	6.2	7.8
Professional experience (years)	26.2	19.1	20.0	16.1	22.6	21.8
Seniority (years)	11.9	5.7	6.3	3.8	7.7	7.4
Size of company (% ≥100 employees)	100	36.8	30.8	87.5	0	20.9

SOURCE: Authors' calculations based on INSTAT/DIAL's 1-2-3 Survey, phase 1, 2006.

by other types of industrial companies in 2006, but it was also one of the lowest on the market—compared with the average earnings for gainfully employed workers in all sectors of the economy, the gap amounted to 13 percent in 2006. Only the informal sector paid its workers less. These findings are somewhat tempered if median monthly wages (which have the advantage of being less sensitive to extreme values) are compared: the median monthly wage in the Zone Franche was equivalent to that for all gainfully employed workers together, but was still lower than that found in other industrial firms.[9]

Zone Franche companies appear to have granted more generous wage increases than others from 1995 to 2006. Whereas the purchasing power of monthly earnings grew an average 4.0 percent per year for all gainfully employed workers, the rate was 5.3 percent in the Zone Franche. However, this positive finding is partly due to increasingly long working hours, which tended to raise monthly earnings compared with other sectors: in 2006, Zone Franche employees worked six hours longer on average per week than their counterparts in non-Zone Franche private industrial companies (53.4 hours and 47.5 hours per week, respectively). Hence, the diagnosis is reversed when comparing hourly earnings. Although growth in real median hourly earnings per Zone Franche worker is appreciable (2.4 percent per year), it is among the lowest when compared with the labor market as a whole, where it comes to 3.2 percent per year. Furthermore, real wages (hourly wages as well as monthly earnings) in the Zone Franche decreased in 2006, after the dismantling of the MFA.

However, these differences in average and median earnings are misleading for two reasons. First, the remuneration taken into account in table 8.4 does not include benefits, in money or in kind (bonuses, paid holidays, and miscellaneous benefits). These benefits add to basic earnings to form total earnings. Second, as shown in table 8.4, job characteristics and wages are not identical across sectors. Some characteristics weigh negatively on Zone Franche earnings, such as the low percentages of managerial staff, the lack of seniority and professional experience, and the preponderance of female staff. All of these characteristics are common to most EPZs worldwide (Madani 1999). In 2006, women represented over 70 percent of the labor employed by the Zone Franche as opposed to 31.8 percent in formal industrial jobs outside the Zone Franche.[10] However, other characteristics work in favor of earnings in the Zone Franche. For example, the rate of trade union presence is higher than in the public sector and double the rate observed for the rest of the industrial sector (this characteristic can be linked, in particular, to the large average size of Zone Franche companies compared with other industrial companies).

ALL OTHER THINGS BEING EQUAL, WAGES ARE LOWER IN THE ZONE FRANCHE THAN IN THE REST OF THE INDUSTRIAL SECTOR

Fine-tuning the calculations entails checking all these "structural effects" to measure earnings levels for comparable jobs and human capital assets. These estimates are made first for basic earnings and then for total job earnings. In both cases, the positive or negative premium earned by Zone Franche employees is compared with the labor force as a whole and with employees in the non-Zone Franche formal private industrial sector. The analysis estimates extended Mincerian earnings functions for each year from 1995 through 2006 to explain the level of hourly earnings (both basic earnings and total earnings)[11]:

$$\ln W_{it} = a_t + b_t GEN_i + c_t SCO_{it} + d_t EXP_{it} + e_t S_{it} + f_t S_{it}^2 + g_t SEC_{it} + DUMMY\ EPZ + \varepsilon_{it} \tag{8.1}$$

Independent variables are the usual explanatory factors: gender (GEN), number of years of schooling (SCO) and potential professional experience (EXP). Seniority (S) and seniority squared (S^2) are also included in the explanatory variables.[12]

Socioeconomic group (SEC) is broken down into eight groups, including five categories of wage earners: the latter consist of managers (senior and middle), employees (skilled and unskilled), and laborers; the three categories of nonwage workers consist of employers, self-employed, and family help and apprentices. Socioeconomic group is alternatively included and excluded from the regressions to take account of its potential endogeneity. This concept mixes skills and job status, and is inspired by the French experience (Desrosieres and Thevenot 2002), adapted to the Malagasy context. It allows the analysis to go deeper than the usual breakdown based on skills only, and has been used in all 1-2-3 surveys in Madagascar since 1995. Last, a dummy Zone Franche variable ($DUMMY\ EPZ$) is introduced to estimate the earnings premium associated with this sector. Each of these estimations is made first for all gainfully employed workers and then for wage earners (excluding nonwage earners such as the self-employed) in the formal industrial sector. Both ordinary least squares (OLS) estimates and Heckman estimates selection-corrected for participation and sector choice (Zone Franche versus non-Zone Franche) were obtained. Because the results are very similar and the database does not provide any credible instruments for correcting potential selection biases, only the OLS estimates are presented.

At the same time, a single model using pooled data from 1995 to 2006 is estimated. The dependent variable is real hourly earnings at 1995 prices[13] and dummies are introduced for each year (*DATE*):

$$\ln Wr_{it} = a + bGEN_i + cSCO_{it} + dEXP_{it} + eS_{it} + fS_{it}^2$$
$$+ g\Sigma SEC_{it} + h_t \Sigma DATE_t + DUMMY\ EPZ + \varepsilon_{it}. \tag{8.2}$$

Table 8.5 presents the results of estimates of the real hourly wage in the formal industrial sector using pooled data, excluding bonuses (models 1 and 2) and including bonuses (models 3 and 4), and excluding socioeconomic group (models 1 and 3) and including socioeconomic group (models 2 and 4). The quality of the regressions is good and in keeping with international literature on the subject (R^2 from 0.35 to 0.43), and the coefficients for the four chosen models are close to and comply with the theory. Remuneration, regardless of whether the different types of bonuses are taken into account, is a growing function of the level of education, seniority, and professional experience. For example, each additional year of schooling is equivalent to a net wage increase of approximately 10 percent when the socioeconomic group is not taken into account, whereas gains from seniority and professional experience are less marked (about 2 percent and 1 percent respectively).

Growth in average hourly wages is not due solely to improved skills over the period, as is shown by the significant positive trend of the year dummies.[14] Madagascar also experienced unprecedented dynamic endogenous urban growth (Razafindrakoto and Roubaud 2000). The hourly wage is also closely correlated with position in the company, in keeping with a strict wage scale ranging from senior management to unskilled workers. When the socioeconomic group is taken into account, it partially absorbs the return to human capital, highlighting the two-stage mechanism whereby the latter is beneficial to employees: first, by giving them access to jobs that require higher skills and second, by giving them additional income in a given job. Hence, the return on education is reduced by approximately one-third (from 10 percent to 7 percent) when the socioeconomic group is included in the equation. Finally, women appear to be subject to a form of wage discrimination, earning between 12 percent and 14 percent less in the industry. Nicita and Razzaz (2003) observe an even higher level of discrimination in the Malagasy textiles industry (whose coverage is similar to, but not exactly the same as the Zone Franche) using the same kind of wage equations.

The variable of interest here, the Zone Franche dummy, is not significant in the models estimated with wages including bonuses (3 and 4). It is significant and slightly negative (3 percent) in the models excluding bonuses (1 and 2): this wage gap is thus compensated for with the addition of bonuses, which correspond to payment for extra hours and other individual remuneration. Whereas Zone Franche employees were paid nearly 30 percent lower hourly wages on average than their counterparts in the non-Zone Franche private formal industrial sector over the 1995–2006 period, most of this gap can be attributed to labor force composition differences between the two sectors.

Table 8.6 presents the results of the same estimates for all gainfully employed (wage and nonwage) workers. This case refers to earnings rather than wages because some workers are nonwage workers. The quality of the adjustments is slightly better than for the estimates commented on above, for relatively similar results. Gender discrimination is the most notable exception: it is approximately twice as high in the economy as a whole as its

TABLE 8.5 **Equation of Zone Franche Hourly Wages Compared with the Rest of the Formal Industrial Sector, 1995–2006**

	Wages (excluding bonuses)		Wages (including bonuses)	
	Model 1	Model 2	Model 3	Model 4
Intercept	−1.560 (44.77)**	−1.470 (41.68)**	−1.551 (42.38)**	−1.468 (39.64)**
Sex (male = 1)	0.123 (8.74)**	0.109 (8.26)**	0.129 (8.75)**	0.114 (8.26)**
Years of schooling	0.095 (47.16)**	0.066 (31.26)**	0.097 (46.04)**	0.067 (30.13)**
Seniority	0.018 (6.58)**	0.017 (6.61)**	0.026 (8.89)**	0.025 (8.97)**
Seniority squared	−0.0003 (3.15)**	−0.0003 (3.38)**	−0.0004 (4.68)**	−0.0005 (4.96)**
Experience	0.011 (13.00)**	0.008 (10.43)**	0.011 (12.66)**	0.008 (10.08)**
Year				
1995	−0.452 (15.06)**	−0.398 (13.98)**	−0.422 (13.39)**	−0.360 (12.04)**
1996	−0.264 (8.99)**	−0.195 (7.01)**	−0.216 (7.02)**	−0.138 (4.73)**
1997	−0.161 (5.56)**	−0.122 (4.47)**	−0.077 (2.54)*	−0.034 (1.18)
1998	−0.102 (3.56)**	−0.050 (1.83)	−0.047 (1.58)	0.013 (0.47)
1999	−0.040 (1.43)	−0.003 (0.10)	0.028 (0.94)	0.070 (2.52)*
2000	0.016 (0.60)	0.021 (0.83)	0.062 (2.16)*	0.068 (2.53)*
2001	0.037 (1.36)	0.023 (0.90)	0.085 (2.97)**	0.070 (2.63)**
2002	0.003 (0.10)	0.003 (0.09)	0.020 (0.58)	0.014 (0.43)
2004	0.009 (0.33)	0.002 (0.09)	0.025 (0.83)	0.016 (0.59)
2006	—	—	—	—

(continued)

TABLE 8.5 **(continued)**

Socioeconomic group	Wages (excluding bonuses)				Wages (including bonuses)			
	Model 1		Model 2		Model 3		Model 4	
Senior managers			1.352	(26.33)**			1.391	(25.79)**
Middle manager			0.566	(18.95)**			0.614	(19.58)**
Empl., skilled workers			0.195	(10.14)**			0.227	(11.23)**
Empl., unskilled workers			0.0879	(4.33)**			0.100	(4.58)**
Laborers			–				–	
Dummy EPZ (=1)	−0.028	(−1.84)	−0.029	(2.06)*	−0.010	(0.65)	0.022	(1.24)
Number of observations	6,352		6,352		6,352		6,352	
R-squared	0.35		0.43		0.35		0.43	

SOURCE: Authors' calculations based on INSTAT/MADIO's 1-2-3 Surveys, phase 1, 1995–2006.

NOTE: The survey was not conducted in 2003 or 2005; 2006 is the reference year. The absolute values of the t-statistics are in parentheses.

The dependent variable is a logarithm so the coefficients cannot be read directly. For example, in model 1, a man's average hourly wage exceeds that of a woman by 13.1 percent (coefficient 0.123), all other things being equal. The percentage change from the coefficient estimate is obtained by raising e to the coefficient estimate and subtracting 1, because the model is log-linear.

* significant at the 5 percent level.

** significant at the 1 percent level.

TABLE 8.6 **Equation of Hourly Earnings in Zone Franche Compared with the Rest of Labor Market, 1995–2006**

| | Earnings (excluding bonuses) | | | | Earnings (including bonuses) | | | |
	Model 1		Model 2		Model 3		Model 4	
Intercept	-2.149	(129.54)**	-1.093	(35.49)**	-2.116	(127.21)**	-0.944	(30.51)**
Sex (man = 1)	0.257	(35.21)**	0.225	(31.81)**	0.256	(34.95)**	0.216	(30.38)**
Years of schooling	0.136	(153.52)**	0.103	(99.81)**	0.137	(155.19)**	0.102	(98.31)**
Seniority	0.028	(27.69)**	0.022	(21.89)**	0.030	(29.54)**	0.024	(23.76)**
Seniority squared	-0.0006	(19.86)**	-0.0004	(16.70)**	-0.0006	(20.71)**	-0.0005	(17.59)**
Experience	0.013	(37.89)**	0.010	(27.92)**	0.013	(35.19)**	-0.009	(26.13)**
Year								
1995	-0.300	(18.31)**	-0.270	(17.12)**	-0.236	(14.36)**	-0.212	(13.37)**
1996	-0.284	(17.57)**	-0.267	(17.24)**	-0.252	(15.58)**	-0.236	(15.20)**
1997	-0.185	(11.59)**	-0.190	(12.38)**	-0.134	(8.38)**	-0.141	(9.14)**
1998	-0.093	(5.82)**	-0.084	(5.47)**	-0.054	(3.40)**	-0.049	(3.15)**
1999	-0.024	(1.46)	-0.010	(0.66)	-0.009	(0.58)	-0.019	(1.23)
2000	-0.038	(2.38)*	-0.026	(1.71)	-0.077	(4.80)**	-0.065	(4.23)**
2001	0.092	(5.68)**	0.071	(4.55)**	0.121	(7.45)**	0.099	(6.37)**
2002	0.032	(1.97)	0.034	(2.18)*	0.039	(2.36)*	0.044	(2.77)**
2004	0.017	(1.04)	0.012	(0.74)	0.034	(2.08)*	0.031	(1.96)
2006	–		–		–		–	

(continued)

TABLE 8.6 (continued)

	Earnings (excluding bonuses)		Earnings (including bonuses)	
	Model 1	Model 2	Model 3	Model 4
Socioeconomic group				
Senior managers		—		—
Middle managers		-0.258 (10.33)**		-0.264 (10.49)**
Empl., skilled workers		-0.539 (23.83)**		-0.590 (25.99)**
Empl., unskilled workers		-0.746 (30.43)**		-0.820 (33.30)**
Laborers		-1.111 (44.60)**		-1.145 (45.76)**
Employers		-0.140 (5.39)**		-0.294 (11.26)**
Self-employed		-0.668 (28.80)**		-0.828 (35.57)**
Family help and apprentices		-1.005 (27.06)**		-1.132 (30.34)**
Dummy EPZ (=1)	0.106 (7.26)**	0.034 (2.29)*	0.146 (9.98)**	0.033 (2.24)*
Number of observations	50,010	50,010	50,010	50,010
R-squared	0.40	0.45	0.40	0.45

SOURCE: Authors' calculations based on INSTAT/MADIO's 1-2-3 Surveys, phase 1, 1995–2006.

NOTE: The survey was not conducted in 2003 or 2005. "Senior managers" is the reference group. The absolute values of the t-statistics are in parentheses.

The dependent variable is a logarithm so the coefficients cannot be read directly. For example, in model 1, a man's average hourly wage exceeds that of a woman by 29.3 percent (coefficient 0.257), all other things being equal. The percentage change from the coefficient estimate is obtained by raising e to the coefficient estimate and subtracting 1, because the model is log-linear.

* significant at the 5 percent level.

** significant at the 1 percent level.

estimation for formal industry. This result can be attributed mainly to the presence of the informal sector, where highly significant differences between men and women are found. The return on human capital is higher than that observed in the model limited to the industrial sector, whereas the time trend is flatter. The models including socioeconomic group find the same wage scale as observed earlier, with nonwage groups being inserted into the scale.[15] Hence, employers' earnings appear to be lower than senior managers' earnings, but higher than middle managers' earnings, whereas self-employed workers earn the same as unskilled employees, with apprentices and family workers coming last.

However, contrary to the estimates for the formal industrial sector alone, employees in the Zone Franche always have a significant premium, varying from 3 percent to 16 percent depending on the model. Introducing the socioeconomic group into the regression sharply reduces the earnings premium secured by Zone Franche employees, by nearly two-thirds in the model excluding bonuses and by nearly three-quarters in the model including all elements of remuneration. For an equivalent level of human capital, Zone Franche employees have lower level jobs. This phenomenon can be partly explained by the specific labor organization (low percentage of managerial staff and little job differentiation). It could also be due to a deliberate policy by employers to hire over-qualified workers. Estimates broken down by the different institutional sectors[16] show that the premium for Zone Franche workers is always significantly lower than for workers in the public sector (administration and public enterprises) and higher than in the informal sector, and is not significantly different from that secured by other employees in the formal private sector.

THE WAGE GAP IS INCREASING

A study of the time trend for the premium for Zone Franche workers can take the analysis beyond the average effects for the period as a whole (figures 8.2 and 8.3). The comparison of wages in the formal industrial sector shows that the average income gap widens,

FIGURE 8.2 **Change in Relative Wages and Wage Premium in the Zone Franche from 1995 to 2006: Zone Franche versus Non-Zone Franche Formal Industrial Private Sector**

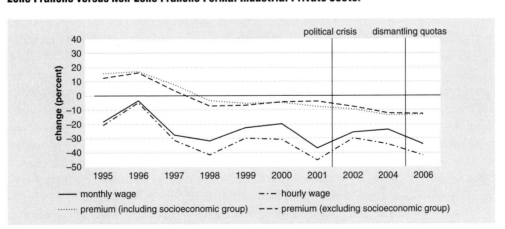

SOURCE: Authors' calculations based on INSTAT/MADIO's 1-2-3 Surveys, phase 1, 1995–2006.

NOTE: Remuneration excludes bonuses. The monthly and hourly wage curves correspond to the ratio of wages in the Zone Franche compared with the other sectors. The premium corresponds to the coefficients of models 1 and 2, estimated for each year. For each curve, the significant coefficients (at the 5 percent level) are shown in black.

FIGURE 8.3 **Change in Relative Earnings and Earnings Premium in the Zone Franche from 1995 to 2006: Zone Franche versus Rest of the Economy**

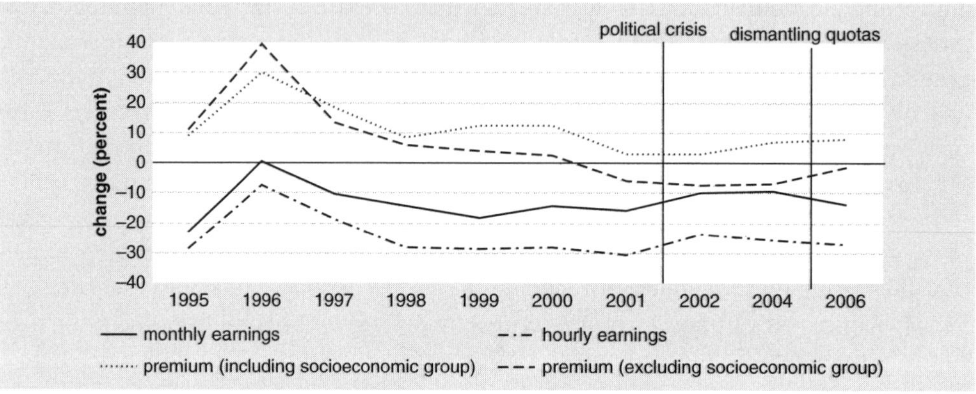

SOURCE: Authors' calculations based on INSTAT/MADIO's 1-2-3 Surveys, phase 1, 1995–2006.

NOTE: Remuneration excludes bonuses. The monthly and hourly wage curves correspond to the ratio of wages in the Zone Franche compared with the other sectors. The premium corresponds to the coefficients of models 1 and 2, estimated for each year. For each curve, the significant coefficients (at the 5 percent level) are shown in black.

particularly with regard to hourly wages, to the detriment of Zone Franche employees. Hourly wages (excluding bonuses) posted a 40 percent difference in 2006, which is twice as much as in 1995 (21 percent; they were actually similar in both sectors in 1996). The hourly premium also fell from significant and positive in the first two years (1995 and 1996) to significant and negative as of 2004. Starting from a positive premium of about 15 percent at the beginning of the period (depending on whether the socioeconomic group is taken into account), a negative premium of approximately the same value is obtained at the end of the period.

Compared with all gainfully employed workers on the labor market (figure 8.3), the analysis also reveals a drop in relative earnings for Zone Franche workers, with an even greater loss of ground for hourly earnings, because the increase in hours worked concerned essentially the Zone Franche. Although it decreased considerably compared with the beginning of the period, the premium was still positive in 2006 for the model excluding socioeconomic group. For the model including socioeconomic group, the premium was no longer significant after 1998 and even became negative after 2001.

This negative trend can be explained to a large extent by the fact that the exceptional activity seen on the domestic market did not benefit Zone Franche companies, which export to highly competitive international markets. Moreover, the rise in the exchange rate from the second half of 2000, followed by the final dismantling of the MFA at the beginning of 2005, reduced the Zone Franche companies' room to maneuver. The premium's downward trend highlights a gradual aligning of wages in the Zone Franche with conditions in the labor market. Despite the upsurge in Zone Franche employment, there was no shortage of salaried labor, which could have put upward pressure on wages.

Why do workers still choose to work in the Zone Franche, even though wages have become lower, all other things equal, than in the rest of the industrial sector—and even though there is no earning premium (including socioeconomic group) any longer compared with the rest of the economy? Answering this question requires analyzing the impact of job rationing on the labor market on sector choices. Because there are very few internal migrations in this country, most workers in the Zone Franche are from Antananarivo (only 20 percent come from another region and 2 percent from a rural area). The main alternatives for this low-skilled, urban, mostly female labor force is between the Zone Franche and the informal sector, which employs surplus labor, and where workers earn even less than in the Zone Franche. No only do workers in the Zone Franche earn more than in the informal sector, but they also benefit from higher labor standards on the whole, as shown in the next section.

Other Labor Standards

Job quality is gauged by more than just money. It is also measured by the nonmonetary elements attached to the job, such as social security coverage, job security, promotion opportunities, and the like. Across all these benefits, Zone Franche companies perform better than other formal industrial companies in the private sector. However, these advantages are progressively being reduced.

BETTER LABOR STANDARDS IN THE ZONE FRANCHE

Table 8.7 shows that three main types of benefits are systematically more common in the Zone Franche than in the rest of the private formal industrial sector: registration with an official social security body (83.5 percent versus 57.4 percent), paid holidays (60.8 percent

TABLE 8.7 **Share of Employees with Job Benefits in the Zone Franche Compared with the Other Sectors, Antananarivo, 2006**
(percent)

Condition	Public sector	Formal private sector	Formal private sector, industrial, non-Zone Franche	Zone Franche	Informal sector	Average
Social security registration	80.7	56.6	57.4	83.5**	2.4	45.9
Company medical service	58.1	42.5	44.7	64.6**	4.7	34.8
Paid holidays	68.1	40.0	40.6	60.8**	2.2	34.5
Pay slip	92.9	76.7	79.1	97.0**	8.4	60.7
Written contract	95.9	76.5	78.1	96.3**	15.3	63.1
Company-paid training	31.4	14.6	15.2	14.7	2.8	14.3
Do not want to change job	79.4	69.3	69.6	72.6	60.0	68.5

SOURCE: Authors' calculations based on INSTAT/ DIAL's 1-2-3 Survey, phase 1, 2006.

NOTE: Logit models in private formal industrial sector, including the following independent variables: gender, years of schooling, experience, tenure, socioeconomic group.

** significant positive coefficient at the 1 percent level.

versus 40.6 percent), and the possibility of consulting a company medical service (64.6 percent versus 44.7 percent). Yet Zone Franche employees are at the greatest advantage when it comes to job security. A higher percentage of them have permanent jobs (98.8 percent versus 96.6 percent) and receive pay slips (97.0 percent versus 79.1 percent). They are also more often covered by a written employment contract (96.3 percent versus 78.1 percent). All of these elements contribute to secure formal working relations. Although there is less in-house promotion of Zone Franche employees, this can be explained by the fact that they have less seniority. Once the differences in jobs and skills have been taken into account, the disparities are no longer significant.

The logit models tested—in which the dependent variable corresponds to a form of cover or protection and the independent variables are the same as for the earnings equations—show that Zone Franche employees enjoy significantly better coverage across all these benefits.[17] In many respects, Zone Franche employees are in as favorable a situation as public sector employees, who are the most highly protected on the labor market.

Overall, Zone Franche companies treat their employees somewhat better than their counterparts in the private formal sector are treated and much better than workers in the informal sector, although, as seen, the wage premium has become negative. Furthermore, as mentioned before, core labor standards are better respected: the percentage of trade union presence is higher and wage gender discrimination is lower (which is confirmed by Glick and Roubaud [2006]).

Doubtless, this favorable treatment of Zone Franche employees, albeit relative, should not be attributed to the companies' philanthropic preferences, given that their main reason for setting up in Madagascar was the low cost of labor. Some characteristics of the EPZs (larger size, foreign-owned firms' "best practices," and so forth) could explain the more favorable conditions. For example, because these companies are sometimes working in a hostile local environment, they are more mindful of the legislation, especially labor standards, and this observance is further stimulated by active trade unions. It is important to belie the common assumption that EPZs undermine working conditions on the national labor market. In Madagascar, it is not the Zone Franche companies that reduce the quality of wage employment, but the poor conditions provided employees on the local labor market that attract foreign companies to the country in the first place. In fact, their presence is likely to benefit the workers by acting as an incentive to other companies to align their labor policies with the usually more advantageous conditions found in the Zone Franche.

In addition to this relative advantage for Zone Franche employees, the zone's companies stepped up their formalization of work relations over the past decade. The proportion of employees benefiting from all work-related benefits (paid holidays, bonuses, medical cover, and the like) has also increased, to the extent that the contractualization of wage relations is now widespread in the Zone Franche, which was far from the case just a few years ago. This fundamental change, which has occurred in record time, is all the more exceptional in that it took several decades for the industrial countries to achieve the same result. The 1980s and 1990s even saw an inverse trend toward increased insecurity in wage relations in most of the emerging countries (see Saavedra [2003] for a study of Latin America). This positive trend for the Malagasy labor force has gradually spread to the formal sector as a whole. The model introduced by the Zone Franche was probably a driving force.

BUT SOCIAL PROGRESS IS BEING REVERSED

The abovementioned advantages of working in the Zone Franche are actually offset by a series of negative factors. Apart from the low wages, the detractions include the workload and work pace, both far higher than elsewhere. Integration into the world market and its demands for competitiveness (costs, delivery times, and quality) force the companies to tighten their labor management, with stricter controls on rates, output, and productivity. The problems caused by steadily increasing working hours, standing at 54 hours in 2006, are all the more acute because the Zone Franche employs large numbers of women who suffer, as elsewhere, from the "double day" phenomenon in that they also have to cope with domestic tasks and bringing up their children (Rambeloma, Rabeson, and Andrianarison 2002).

Moreover, the relative advantages benefiting Zone Franche employees are progressively being reduced for the same reasons explaining the declining trend of relative wages—increased international competition for clothing products. Another factor might contribute to this degradation: the country of origin of investors partly changed after the political crisis, with the share of Asian investors increasing. Because these new investors come from developing countries, their social policies are worse than those of investors from developed countries (which are also subject to pressure on this subject from their customers).

All the main advantages (company medical service, paid holidays, company-paid training) peaked at the beginning of the 2000s—progressively declining since then. Trade union presence has also declined. Similar degradation has also been observed in the rest of the economy, as if after leading social progress, the Zone Franche began contributing to social regression and to the process of informalizing labor under international competitive pressure.

These elements aid the understanding of why employee satisfaction rates in the Zone Franche, albeit high, are no higher than the average (table 8.7).[18] Further proof is in the high staff turnover, calculated by the ratio of the number of employees who left their companies in the year preceding the survey to this same total plus those still employed in the Zone Franche at the time of the survey. Every year, about 1 in 5 Zone Franche employees leaves the job, compared with a little over 1 in 10 in the formal private sector. This rate is far higher than in Mauritius, where it is around only 1 in 20 (Cadot and Nasir 2001).

Conclusion

The Zone Franche was the main driving force behind employment and export growth in Madagascar since the mid-1990s and has made a major contribution to the economic upturn observed since 1995, after a long recession. Contrary to academic wisdom, the Zone Franche was also—until the beginning of the 2000s—the driving force behind the observed improvement in wages and working conditions in the other sectors of the economy. This surprising result is explained by Madagascar being among the least developed countries (where labor standards are very low on average). Most EPZs are located in middle-income countries.

As expected by many economic studies (see especially Nordas [2004]; Cling, Razafindrakoto, and Roubaud [2005]), the final dismantling of MFA customs quotas on January 1, 2005, benefited mainly Asian countries, especially China, and has had a negative impact on most other developing countries, including Madagascar. The fact that the United States and the European Union quickly reinstated some quotas (up to the end of 2007 for the former, and to the end of 2008 for the latter) only gave Madagascar some provisional breathing space.

Since 2005, Zone Franche exports have stagnated and employment has slightly decreased. As a result of both increased international competition (international prices for clothing products fell deeply following the end of quotas) and the behavior of new investors, real wages have decreased in the Zone Franche and labor standards have deteriorated:

- The econometric estimates on individual data show that the remuneration paid by the Zone Franche companies has become significantly lower, other things being equal, than that paid by industrial firms in the formal private sector. Nonetheless, Zone Franche companies still pay their employees more on average than they would receive in the informal sector, which is the main alternative for the low-skilled female labor force.

- The same negative trend is observed for other labor standards, including nonwage benefits, which used to be much higher (except for working hours) than in the formal private sector: not only are the working hours increasingly longer but most relative advantages (company medical service, paid holidays, and so on) are being reduced in the Zone Franche as well as in the rest of the economy.

The accomplishments of the Zone Franche are, therefore, under threat. The Zone Franche's success had added fuel to the idea that using EPZs to develop a productive manufacturing base and promote employment was a positive development path for African countries. This chapter shows that this strategy is no longer sustainable, as a result of the end of the MFA. Yet, no alternative growth model has been designed.

Notes

1. The only econometric studies based on individual establishment data (Lipsey and Sjöholm 2003) and matched data (Martins 2004) concern remuneration from all foreign firms (rather than just EPZs) compared with that paid by domestic firms. These studies posit that foreign firms pay more, other things being equal, but that this premium falls substantially when the manpower's heterogeneity and the firms' individual characteristics are taken into account.

2. For example, the World Bank working paper on EPZs in Africa by Watson (2001) does not even mention the Zone Franche. A British government white paper published in 2004 even states that "[excepting Mauritius] other African countries such as Zimbabwe, Senegal, Madagascar and Cameroon have failed to benefit substantially from EPZs" (HM Treasury and DTI 2004, 30).

3. This chapter draws on Cling, Razafindrakoto, and Roubaud (2005), which covers the period 1995–2001. The analyses made in the previous paper have been completely updated. They take into account recent developments such as the end of apparel quotas and the results of some econometric estimates based on more recent data (four additional years). The latter are largely different and bring substantially new conclusions.

4. Gibbon (2003) holds that ownership in the Zone Franche was mainly Mauritian. However, his observation is not backed up by quantitative data.

5. The answers given by Zone Franche company heads interviewed for the 1998 industrial survey show that 66 percent of Zone Franche companies, accounting for 87 percent of exports, would not have been created had it not been for the special scheme (Razafindrakoto and Roubaud 2002).

6. National customs data are very erratic and not reliable as a measure of the value of Malagasy exports (Cling, Razafindrakoto, and Roubaud 2005). Therefore, we use instead an indirect estimate based on imports from Madagascar (the "mirror-data" method), as most studies on African foreign trade do. Malagasy total goods exports are measured through total world imports from Madagascar. Because the United States and the European Union are its main markets, we use U.S. and EU apparel import data as mirror-data for Zone Franche exports. The mirror-data do not explicitly identify exports from the Zone Franche. Given that nearly all apparel exports come from the Zone Franche and that most of its firms specialize in clothing, it can be assumed that total apparel exports are roughly equivalent to total Zone Franche exports.

7. The four core labor standards are elimination of all forms of forced or compulsory labor, effective abolition of child labor, equality of opportunity and treatment, and freedom of association and right to collective bargaining.

8. Although suggested in ITUC (2008), no specific source was cited and no confirming evidence has been found.

9. Enterprise surveys confirm this finding. Average gross remuneration for employees in the Zone Franche is about one-third lower than that for employees working in the formal industrial sector as a whole (MADIO 1999). Even if only permanent workers are taken into account, the vast majority of the Zone Franche companies are less generous, with differences of 15 percent to 20 percent depending on the year.

10. The proportion of women fell significantly compared with 1995, when they accounted for nearly 84 percent of labor. This trend has been observed in many countries. Nonetheless, Glick and Roubaud (2004) consider that this is not due to a shift toward male-oriented skills as in export-processing manufacturing in other countries. Zone Franche workers' mean years of schooling actually fell from 1995 to 2001.

11. The basic wage is just one element of remuneration, albeit the largest. The growing competition faced by Zone Franche companies has prompted them to favor more individualized wage policies and productivity incentives, by offering productivity bonuses and profit-sharing schemes. The different variable components of remuneration are far from negligible—they represent 11 percent to 22 percent of basic wages depending on the year. These variable components are not found exclusively in the Zone Franche, however. All types of companies offer them, with the notable exception of the informal sector. The public sector (administration and public companies) is extremely generous in this respect. Ultimately, the estimates (not presented here) regarding the basic wage alone are very similar to those based on total earnings.

12. We also tested for nonlinearities on the return on education and professional experience by including years of schooling and professional experience squared in the independent variables. However, the coefficients were found to be not significant.

13. Using the consumer price index for the capital as deflator (base 100 in 1995).

14. An improvement in skills, that is, a significant increase in the average number of years of schooling, is observed from 1995 to 2001. But the significant coefficient of the year dummies shows that other factors (especially the improvement in macroeconomic conditions) also contributed to the sharp increase in real wages. The level of the t-statistics suggests a significant positive trend over time. This can be formally tested for all models by introducing a time trend

in place of the time dummies. The results confirm the existence of a systematic and significant positive time trend (at the 1 percent level in all cases), varying from 6 percent to 7.5 percent depending on the different specifications.

15. Note that, contrary to wages, earned income for nonwage groups includes returns on both human and physical capital. Although not directly estimated in the equation, the return on physical capital is partly captured by the socioeconomic group (employer versus self-employed worker).

16. The estimated models are similar to those presented here, but have not been included. They cover the entire labor market, broken down into five institutional sectors (public administration, public enterprises, formal private sector excluding the Zone Franche, Zone Franche, and informal sector). The results are available from the authors on request.

17. The results of these models are not included here, but are available from the authors on request.

18. This relatively high satisfaction rate may seem to contradict the low average job seniority levels presented in table 8.2. But the satisfaction index as defined here only concerns employees who have kept their jobs. It is overestimated in that it does not take into account employees who have left their jobs. Conversely, the low average levels of job seniority are not just the result of higher turnover in the Zone Franche, but also of the fact that this special scheme for these companies was created fairly recently and their very strong recruitment and hiring campaigns automatically reduce average employee seniority.

References and Other Resources

Banque centrale de Madagascar. 2002. *Rapport annuel 2001*. Antananarivo, Madagascar: Banque centrale de Madagascar.

Cadot, O., and J. Nasir. 2001. "Incentives and Obstacles to Growth: Lessons from Manufacturing Case Studies in Madagascar." Regional Program on Enterprise Development, Discussion Paper No. 117, World Bank, Washington, DC.

Cling, J.-P., M. Razafindrakoto, and F. Roubaud. 2005. "Export Processing Zones in Madagascar: A Success Story under Threat?" *World Development* 33 (5): 785–803.

Desrosieres A., and L. Thevenot. 2002. *Les Catégories socio-professionnelles*. Paris : Editions La Découverte.

Gibbon, P. 2003. "The African Growth and Opportunity Act and the Global Commodity Chain for Clothing." *World Development* 31 (11): 1809–27.

Glick, P. J., and F. Roubaud. 2006. "Export Processing Zone Expansion in an African Country: What Are the Labour Market and Gender Impacts?" *Journal of African Economies* 15 (4): 722–56.

HM Treasury and Department of Trade and Industry. 2004. "Trade and the Global Economy: The Role of International Trade in Productivity, Economic Reform and Growth." Joint Report, HM Treasury and DTI, London.

ICFTU. 2003. "Export Processing Zones: Symbols of Exploitation and a Development Dead-End." International Confederation of Free Trade Unions, Brussels.

ILO (International Labour Organization). 2003. "Employment and Social Policy in Respect of Export Processing Zones (EPZs)." GB.286/ESP/3, International Labour Office, Governing Body, Committee on Employment and Social Policy, Geneva.

ITUC (International Trade Union Confederation). 2008. "Internationally Recognised Core Labour Standards in Madagascar." Report for the WTO General Council Review of the Trade Policies of Madagascar, Geneva, April 2–4.

Jayanthakumaran, K. 2003. "Benefit-Cost Appraisals of Export Processing Zones: A Survey of the Literature." *Development Policy Review* 21 (1): 51–65.

Kusago, T., and Z. Tzannatos. 1998. "Export Processing Zones: A Review in Need of Update." Social Protection Discussion Paper No. 9802, World Bank Washington, DC.

Lipsey, R. E., and F. Sjöholm. 2003. "Foreign Direct Investment, Education and Wages in Indonesian Manufacturing." *Journal of Development Economics* 73 (1): 415–22.

Madani, D. 1999. "A Review of the Role and Impact of Export Processing Zones." Working Paper No. 2238, World Bank, Washington, DC.

MADIO (Madagascar-DIAL-Instat-Orstom). 1999. *Le secteur industriel formel à Madagascar ; Caractéristiques, Performances, Perspectives, enquête annuelle dans l'industrie, Exercice 1997, Premiers résultats.* Publications INSTAT / MADIO. Antananarivo, Madagascar : Institut National de la Statistique.

Martins, P. S. 2004. "Do Foreign Firms Really Pay Higher Wages? Evidence from Different Estimators." IZA Discussion Paper No. 1388, Institute for the Study of Labor (IZA), Bonn.

Mattoo, A., D. Roy, and A. Subramanian. 2003. "The Africa Growth and Opportunity Act and Its Rules of Origin: Generosity Undermined?" *World Economy* 26 (6): 829–51.

Nicita, A., and S. Razzaz. 2003. "Who Benefits and How Much? How Gender Affects Welfare Impacts of a Booming Textile Industry." Policy Research Working Paper No. 3029, World Bank, Washington, DC.

Nordas, H. K. 2004. "The Global Textile and Clothing Industry Post the Agreement on Textiles and Clothing." Discussion Paper No 5, World Trade Organization, Geneva.

Rakotomanana, F., E. Ramilison, and F. Roubaud. 2003. "The Creation of an Annual Employment Survey in Madagascar: An Example for Sub-Saharan Africa." *Inter-Stat* 27: 35–58.

Rambeloma, T., V. Rabeson, and F. Andrianarison. 2002. *Impact de la libéralisation sur l'emploi à Madagascar. Analyse genre : cas des zones franches.* Unpublished, Third World Network – Africa, Réformes Economique et Analyse Genre en Afrique (REAGA), Antananarivo, Madagascar.

Razafindrakoto, M., and F. Roubaud. 1997. Les entreprises franches à Madagascar : économie d'enclave ou promesse d'une nouvelle prospérité ? *Economie de Madagascar*, 2, BCM/INSTAT, Madagascar, 217–48.

———. 2000. La dynamique du marché du travail dans l'agglomération d'Antananarivo entre 1995 et 1999 : la croissance économique profite-t-elle aux ménages ? *Economie de Madagascar*, 4, BCM/INSTAT, Madagascar, 103–37.

———. 2002. Les entreprises franches à Madagascar : Atouts et contraintes d'une insertion mondiale réussie. *Afrique contemporaine*, *202-203* (avril-septembre), 147–63.

———. 2003. "Two Original Poverty Monitoring Tools: The 1-2-3 Surveys and the Rural Observatories." In *New International Poverty Reduction Strategies*, ed. J.-P. Cling, M. Razafindrakoto, and F. Roubaud, 313–39. London, New York: Routledge.

Romero, A. 1995. "Labour Standards and EPZ: Situation and Pressures for Change." *Development Policy Review* 13: 247–76.

Saavedra, J. 2003. "Labor Markets during the 1990s." In *After the Washington Consensus: Restarting Growth and Reform in Latin America*, ed. P. P. Kuczynski and J. Williamson, 213–64. Washington, DC: Institute of International Economics.

Singa Boyenge, J.-P. 2007. "ILO Database on Export Processing Zones (Revised)." Working Paper No. 251, International Labour Office, Geneva.

UNCTAD. 2002. *The Least Developed Countries Report 2002: Escaping the Poverty Trap.* Geneva: United Nations Commission for Trade and Development (UNCTAD).

U.S. Bureau of International Labor Affairs. 2002. "The Department of Labor's 2001 Findings of the Worst Forms of Child Labor (Trade and Development Act of 2000)." Bureau of International Labor Affairs, U.S. Department of Labor, Washington, DC. http://www.dol.gov/ILAB/media/reports/iclp/TDA2001/index.htm

U.S. Department of State. 2006. "Country Reports on Human Rights Practices." Bureau of Democracy, Human Rights, and Labor, Under Secretary for Democracy and Global Affairs, U.S. Department of State, Washington, DC. http://www.state.gov/g/drl/rls/hrrpt/2005/61578.htm.

Watson, P. 2001. "Export Processing Zones: Has Africa Missed the Boat? Not Yet!" Working Paper No. 17, Africa Region, World Bank, Washington, DC.

Index

Boxes, figures, notes, and tables are indicated by *b, f, n*, and *t*, respectively.

9104